PENGUIN BOOKS

TWENTY CHICKENS FOR A SADDLE

Born in 1981, Robyn Scott began her formal education at the age of fourteen, when she started boarding school in Zimbabwe. Moving to New Zealand for her undergraduate degree, she studied bioinformatics at the University of Auckland. In 2004, she was awarded a Gates Scholarship to Cambridge University, where she received an M.Phil. in bioscience enterprise, focusing on the pricing of medicines in developing countries. Robyn lives in London, but visits and works regularly in southern Africa.

To access Penguin Readers Guides online, visit our Web sites at www.penguin.com or www.vpbookclub.com.

TWENTY CHICKENS
FOR A SADDLE

The Story of an

African Childhood

ROBYN SCOTT

Penguin Books

PENGUIN BOOKS

Published by the Penguin Group

Penguin Group (USA) Inc., 375 Hudson Street, New York, New York 10014, U.S.A.
Penguin Group (Canada), 90 Eglinton Avenue East, Suite 700, Toronto,
Ontario, Canada M4P 2Y3 (a division of Pearson Penguin Canada Inc.)
Penguin Books Ltd, 80 Strand, London WC2R 0RL, England
Penguin Ireland, 25 St Stephen's Green, Dublin 2, Ireland (a division of Penguin Books Ltd)
Penguin Group (Australia), 250 Camberwell Road, Camberwell,
Victoria 3124, Australia (a division of Pearson Australia Group Pty Ltd)
Penguin Books India Pvt Ltd, 11 Community Centre,
Panchsheel Park, New Delhi – 110 017, India
Penguin Group (NZ), 67 Apollo Drive, Rosedale, North Shore 0632,
New Zealand (a division of Pearson New Zealand Ltd)
Penguin Books (South Africa) (Pty) Ltd., 24 Sturdee Avenue,
Rosebank, Johannesburg 2196, South Africa

Penguin Books Ltd, Registered Offices:
80 Strand, London WC2R 0RL, England

First published in the United States of America by The Penguin Press,
a member of Penguin Group (USA) Inc. 2008
Published in Penguin Books 2009

1 3 5 7 9 10 8 6 4 2

Photograph credits: Chapter 18: Margaret Bourke-White. By permission of Getty Images. Chapter
256: Peter Sievers. Chapter 26: John Parr. All other photographs from author's family collection.

THE LIBRARY OF CONGRESS HAS CATALOGED THE HARDCOVER EDITION AS FOLLOWS:
Scott, Robyn.
Twenty chickens for a saddle : the story of an African childhood / Robyn Scott.
p.   cm.
ISBN 978-1-59420-159-2 (hc.)
ISBN 978-0-14-311509-0 (pbk.)
1. Scott, Robyn—Childhood and youth.   2. Botswana—Biography.   I. Title.
CT1988.S38A3   2008
968.83'02092—dc22   2007035827

Printed in the United States of America

Map of Botswana and interior illustrations © Lulu Scott
Designed by Claire Naylon Vaccaro

For Linda, Keith, Lulu, and Damien

CONTENTS

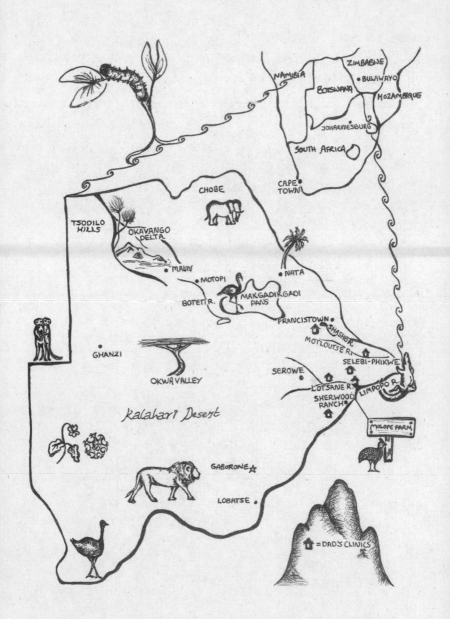

GRANDPA'S VISITORS

Grandpa's Cessna retires

Above the bush, the pink and orange streaked sky had faded to gray. Inside, it was almost dark, and Grandpa, in his chair beneath the room's only window, caught the last of the light. He sat completely still, smiling at our confusion.

His whisper had silenced the conversation. "Look who's joining us for drinks," he had said. But nothing had moved. The door remained closed, the cat curled peacefully on the sofa. No new sounds interrupted the soft ring of chirps, rustles, and faraway hunting barks.

We waited for an explanation. He gave none. His gaze alternated between us and the ceiling; his body remained still. One hand clutched a small glass, full with an equal mixture of red wine and grape juice; the other lay on the armrest, long fingers digging into the worn velvet covers.

Then a flicker near the ceiling, and a shadowy creature plunged out of the gloom.

Just above his head, close enough to brush wisps of thin white hair, it stopped—a giant brown moth, suspended with an unsteady flutter. The moth, joined moments later by a second, began a jolting orbit of his head.

Grandpa gave a satisfied grunt. He lifted his glass and took a small sip. The moths, ignoring him, continued to circle, and just as carefully, he lowered the glass again. He sat motionless, his lips taut and flattened. He hadn't swallowed, and as his eyes followed the moths, a drop of liquid grew at each corner of his mouth, pausing just before it was full enough to slide down his jaw.

Suddenly, a dark butterfly shadow eclipsed his cheek: one of the moths, wings flat against his face, long proboscis reaching for a drop. The second moth descended on the opposite cheek. The first flapped away. It was magical and ridiculous: the ghostly, clumsy creatures taking off and settling again; Grandpa, until then so fiercely intimidating, looking like a gentle, badly painted clown.

He smiled at those dowdy moths as if they were beloved pets; and only when they left, when the last traces of daylight had vanished and a paraffin lamp spluttered to life in the corner of the room, did he return his attention to his audience.

"Nice trick, Ivor," said Dad, as the moths joined clouds of insects that appeared out of nowhere to dive-bomb the lamp. "But what these kids really want to see are snakes."

"Whaddaya say?" Grandpa leaned forward and cupped his hand behind his ear. His voice was high-pitched and sounded strange coming from such a tall, imposing man. Squeezed between Mum and the cat on the sofa, Damien and I stifled a laugh. Lulu didn't manage, giggled, and buried her head in Mum's lap.

Dad repeated himself.

"Hard to please, eh?" Grandpa fixed his gaze on each of us, half amused, half accusing. He turned back to Dad.

"Keith," said Grandpa, pointing to a frayed brown armchair in the corner of the room. "Show the kids what's under that chair."

Dad raised an eyebrow and smiled, but didn't inquire further. He stood up and walked slowly toward the chair. "Come on, chaps," he said, grabbing the armrest, "not suddenly scared are you?"

We all shook our heads. None of us moved. I didn't trust myself to speak. Desperate as I was to see snakes, after all Dad's stories about Grandpa Ivor's wild, laugh-in-the-face-of-danger life, the prospect of whatever lay beneath that chair in this strange house was suddenly terrifying.

I turned to Granny Betty, who sat quietly at the end of the long sofa, stroking the cat with a bony hand. An amused smile flickered across her face, but she remained silent.

"Go on," said Mum, smiling encouragingly, "Dad and Grandpa Ivor know what they're doing. This is what you've been waiting for."

Grandpa glared at us. "Stand behind your father if you're scared," he bellowed.

At least as scared of Grandpa's disapproval, Lulu, Damien, and I reluctantly slid off the sofa and squatted behind Dad, who, with his legs as far back as possible, leaned forward and began to pivot the chair slowly sideways.

Holding our breath, poised to flee, we peered under the rising base.

A black creature, a little smaller than my hand, crouched statue-like on the concrete floor. At one end were pincers, evil-looking but tiny compared with the fat, hairy tail, sharply pointed at the tip, which curled up and forward over the wide body. Perfect, regular seams joined shiny black segments of the tail, body, and pincers, making it seem more like an exquisitely made machine than a real animal.

Dad whistled. "Black hairy thick-tailed scorpion," he said,

emphasizing each word. "If you can't see a snake on your first day, this is as good as it gets."

"Could easily kill one of you chaps," added Grandpa.

But the scorpion didn't seem to be in the mood for killing anyone. It took off with ungraceful speed, scuttling toward the wall, where it disappeared under a bookcase. Dad offered to try and catch it, but Grandpa said there were so many in the house already that Dad should just "leave the little bugger where he is."

B otswana is more than two-thirds desert. Selebi—Grandpa's home and our destination on that first, bewildering day just before Christmas in 1987—is in the other third, which gets just enough rain to miss out on the glamorous distinction of desert, and much too little to settle the ubiquitous red dust or support any but the hardiest of plants. Except for a few months of the year, that is, when the occasional storm cloud bursts and fat raindrops puff dust into the air and pummel sheets of water that flood the baked ground. In a good rainy season, the dry riverbeds that thread their way east to the Limpopo River might flow. Often they don't. For nine months of the year, it is hot; for the rest, it is dry.

There is no time of year when it is not hot or dry.

A hundred and fifty kilometers from Selebi, the borders of Botswana, South Africa, and Zimbabwe meet at the country's easternmost tip. Here the Limpopo peels away from Botswana and heads toward the Indian Ocean. Botswana is securely landlocked. At any point in the country you are at least four hundred kilometers from the sea. But making up for the absence of sea and lakes, spilling hundreds of kilometers across the dry sands in the north, lies the world's largest inland delta.

The bush surrounding the exquisite Okavango Delta, the "jewel of the Kalahari," teems with all of Africa's biggest and most impressive wildlife.

The bush around Selebi teems with cows, goats, and donkeys. There are few fences, and the animals wander mostly unimpeded across the flat land. They are frequently killed on the roads, hit by local cars or huge trucks passing through on their long journeys between southern and central Africa. The land is overgrazed, and any lions, elephants, and rhinos that weren't hunted down left long ago in search of places with more food and fewer people. Only the small, dangerous animals, like snakes and scorpions, which don't mind living alongside humans, are left. For by Botswana standards—a country the size of France with fewer than two million people—the region is populous. Cattle posts of five to twenty huts are sprinkled across the bush, and there are several bigger villages, the largest of which have electricity and running water.

Selebi, which appears on maps as Selebi-Phikwe, consists of just three old houses and several concrete slabs that were once houses. A relic from the early years of the nearby copper and nickel mine, Selebi is the ghost part of town. By the late 1980s, when my parents abruptly decided to return to Botswana— ending a peripatetic decade that had spanned South Africa, England, and New Zealand, and produced three children—Grandpa Ivor and Granny Betty had long been Selebi's sole residents.

Phikwe, which lies ten kilometers away, is the real town; home, when we arrived, to around 40,000 people, most who directly or indirectly derived their living from the mine. Among them were Grandpa Terry and Granny Joan, Mum's parents, who like most Phikwe residents visited the old town only in passing, traveling to or from the little bush airport that, together with the nearby mineshaft and Grandpa Ivor's house, comprised the only still used part of Selebi.

The airport had a tall glass control tower, two faded orange windsocks, and a small customs and immigration building. It was here that my brother, sister, and I first set foot in Botswana, unloaded onto the baking tarmac with the eight frozen turkeys that Grandpa Ivor had packed under the seats when he collected us in Johannesburg.

I was nearly seven, Damien was five, and Lulu was three.

The air on the runway smacked us like a hot wave.

Snakes, lions, and every other fantasy vanished. Heat overwhelmed me as I stood, stunned, in the fierce, dry, completely still air. It was unfairly, unbelievably hot, heat like nothing I had ever felt before. Normal thought, in this temperature and blinding light, was suddenly impossible. Mesmerized, I watched shimmering waves float above the dark tar. Beyond the runway fence posts, the flat green scrub seemed frozen behind the wobbling veil of heat. The almost white sky was empty; nothing stirred in the bushes; a few black cows stood motionless, sleeping beside the fence.

Heat was the only thing moving.

Mum and Dad seemed unperturbed, smiling and chatting as they hauled bags out the plane. Lulu, Damien, and I stood, bewildered, sheltering in the shadow of the wing, quietly waiting for instructions. Eventually, with all our suitcases retrieved, we left Grandpa Ivor fiddling with the switches in the cockpit, and Mum and Dad herded us toward the small building beside the control tower.

Inside, it was breathlessly stuffy and not much cooler. A small fan whirred ineffectively from a stand on the concrete floor in the corner of the room. After an unexplained wait—there was no one else in the queue—a uniformed customs officer instructed Mum and Dad to open all our suitcases on a scratched wooden desk. With a suspicious scowl, he began slowly rummaging through layer after layer of clothes, books, and toys. He looked disappointed each time he reached the bottom of a bag.

"Why's he taking so long?" I whined. "What's he looking for?"

"Nothing." Mum squeezed my shoulder.

"I'm so hot."

"Shhh, Robbie," hissed Dad.

"Why are you smiling like that?" As soon as the officer had approached us, Mum and Dad's excited-to-be-back smiles had been replaced by fixed, unconvincing grins.

Both ignored me and continued to grin wildly at the slow, grumpy officer.

Then suddenly the officer was grinning too. "*Dumela*, Mr. Scott," he said, as Grandpa Ivor, carrying a bulging sack, strode toward the desk.

As they exchanged greetings in quick, soft Setswana, a puddle spread across the floor beneath the sack of defrosting turkeys. The officer didn't seem to notice. Still smiling, he turned to Dad. "*Ee!* The Madala's son," he said warmly. "Welcome to Botswana."

Ignoring the dripping sack and the unchecked suitcases, he stamped our forms and waved us on. Minutes later, we were outside, uncomfortably installed in the tiny, battered pickup truck that Grandpa called his *bakkie*. Mum and Lulu sat in the front; Dad, Damien, and I in the back, wedged among the bags and seven turkeys. Grandpa kept the last one out. "Christmas spirit," he said, striding back toward the building, the dripping bird clutched under his arm. He disappeared inside, emerging, empty-handed, almost immediately.

And one turkey less, we set off to our new home.

Grandpa's house was the last and only stop on an overgrown kilometer-long track that wound through a seemingly endless expanse of small gray thornbushes, short, brilliant green mopane trees, and the occasional graceful knob-thorn tree reaching high above its neighbors. Around the house, all but a few of the tallest trees had been cleared, and the little building stood low and dilapidated on the bare red dirt. With nothing to separate the house and the dirt—no flowerbeds, or paving, or gravel—the dust had crept up the walls and formed a foot-high orange band on the whitewashed bricks.

From a distance, it was hard to see where the house became dirt.

Everything in the house was falling apart; sofas fraying, bedspreads peppered with holes, kitchen counters chipped. The walls were whitewashed, but layers of dust had settled on the ledges where the bricks hadn't been properly aligned. Daylight streamed through every window, but, enclosed by the dusty walls and dark concrete floors, every bright room was nonetheless strangely gloomy.

Dust cloaked and dulled everything: the painting of a sad-looking black lady breastfeeding a baby, a medal hanging on a ribbon, a large black-and-white aerial map. Beneath these—the only interruptions to the otherwise bare lounge walls—an ostrich egg, a china bell with the faces of Prince Charles and Lady Diana, and a tarnished golf trophy decorated the tops of crowded bookshelves. Where they had been shifted slightly, their old positions were precisely remembered by darker, cleaner circles on the wood.

In Grandpa's tiny, overflowing study, maps and yellowing hand-drawn charts covered the walls almost entirely. Piles of tattered flight log books, some reaching higher than me, leaned precariously against tall gray filing cabinets. Much-fingered books and magazines jostled for space in every corner. In the center of the room stood a desk with a pale green typewriter, half covered in a sea of papers, scribbled notes, diagrams, and envelopes.

Opposite the intriguing chaos of this room, across a dimly lit corridor, was Granny Betty's study: tidy by comparison, thick with the smell of cigarettes and air freshener, home to a breathtakingly large and unlikely collection. Hundreds of jigsaw-puzzle boxes—big and small, enough to fill the grandest of toyshops—were stacked around the room: atop a dark wardrobe, under a dresser, in an open cupboard. I tried to count them and lost track. The room must have held more than a lifetime's work.

Low tables pushed against the walls displayed three almost finished pictures. Gleaming with bright poppies, country cottages, and sunsets, these made colorful, incongruous interruptions to the somber furnishings. The puzzles varied in the size and shape of their pieces, but each, caught in its state of incompleteness, was curiously similar. In every vast picture, the gaping holes shared the same blue edges, the same loose blue pieces scattered within them.

"I get so tired of skies." Granny Betty sighed, frowning at one of the blue-rimmed gaps.

Granny Betty, Grandpa Ivor's second wife and Dad's stepmother, sighed as if she were tired of life. Frail, softly spoken, hobbling, she was everything that Grandpa Ivor was not. Even her smile was sad. Only when she laughed, and her face was transformed by shining blue eyes and a wide, white false-teeth grin, did she really look happy.

After showing us the rooms in the center of the house, Granny led us out the back door, passing through a long kitchen, where rubber pipes ran out of an ancient stove, through an oversize hole in the wall, and joined two tall gas cylinders that stood sentry under the window. Outside, a few paces beyond the kitchen door, a rusty Deepfreeze sat alone in the middle of the dirt. Its lid was thick with grit, dry leaves, and bird droppings, and a spiky bush had crept halfway up one side.

Supporting herself against the lid, Granny explained that years ago a spitting cobra had slithered into the maze of pipes at the back of the freezer. When, after several hours, the snake had shown no signs of wanting to come out, Grandpa had dragged the Deepfreeze outside. He had never got around to taking it back indoors.

Grandpa, unabashed, just laughed, "We're hoping it'll work by solar power!" he announced, patting the Deepfreeze and dislodging a small cloud of dust.

Granny and Grandpa slept in a converted veranda at the front of the house, the strangest bedroom I had ever seen. At one end of the long narrow room stood Granny and Grandpa's sagging double bed; at the other, a warped Ping-Pong table, piled high with a jumble of pipes, wood, rolls of plastic, old radios, and unrecognizable machines. Beneath the table, several dusty engines squatted on the concrete floor, crammed tightly beside each other and an assortment of smaller unmemorable objects tossed in among them.

At this, the Ping-Pong table side of the room, casting the chaos in a strange soft light, faded green shade cloth stretched from a three-foot-high wall to just below the eaves. Clearly visible through these gauzy windows, just outside the front of the house, stood a haphazardly packed shed the size of a single garage. In the center of the shed, surrounded by more engines and more junk, rested a battered old airplane fuselage. The wings of the airplane had been removed. Suspended by fraying loops of rope, they now hung inside, from the bedroom roof—one above the Ping-Pong table, the other above Granny and Grandpa's bed.

To reach the lounge from the driveway, you passed through this oddest of rooms: table on the left, bed on the right, wings above—meeting at their tips in the middle of the roof. Sometimes, when the door banged closed, the ropes creaked gently.

On that first day in Botswana, nearly everything about the house was surprising. But it was the passage through the front and back doors that would preserve its wonder. Even years later, it would be impossible to walk beneath the old Aeronca wings or pass beside the lonely Deepfreeze without the fleeting sensation that everything wasn't quite right; that, as with Granny's jigsaws, the last pieces were missing or misplaced.

Nearby, where the bare dirt ran into thorny bush, a second airplane—winged but even more damaged than the first—lay beneath a scraggly thorn tree, disintegrating into the scrub and dust. The red-and-white wreck was the Piper Colt, a part of family legend that, like the Aeronca, I'd felt I had known long before the day the two airplanes left the realm of stories, appearing as real objects in this strange new world.

Airplanes starred in most of our favorite tales about Grandpa Ivor. And although he'd first flown in the South African Air Force during World War II, the backdrop to these jaw-dropping flying stories was always Botswana, which did not become his home until the early 1960s. After the war, repelled by all associated with a time that had seen the loss of a brother and many of his dearest friends, Grandpa had started a string of unsuccessful businesses, and it was not until his forties, when he left South Africa—and with it Granny Mavis, his first wife, and his three young sons, Henry, Keith, and Jonathan—that flying again became his livelihood.

Based, initially, in a remote bush camp near the Okavango Delta, Grandpa Ivor worked as a commercial pilot, flying the first road builders, the last of the great white hunters, game department officials, mining prospectors, and, for a time, Sir Seretse Khama, Botswana's late, great, beloved first president. With a single plane, a Beechcraft Baron, he established the impressive-sounding Okavango Air Services, one of Botswana's first charter flight businesses. With the Aeronca, he began to teach flying, going on to found the country's first flying school.

The school's students included Grandpa's own sons, who made yearly visits to Botswana during their school and then university holidays. By the time he came to teach Jonathan, his youngest, Grandpa's infamously scant reserves of patience had been severely depleted. He was by then living in Selebi, where he'd moved in the early 1970s, with the start of the mine. He instructed Jonathan in the Piper Colt. The Aeronca after a forced landing due to engine failure—was by then languishing in a farmer's field, where Grandpa had simply abandoned the old plane, surrounded by cattle, on the dirt.

After six hours' flying time, father and son were barely speaking. Jonathan protested angrily at Grandpa's intolerance of mistakes. "Fly it yourself, then," yelled Grandpa. Jonathan did, making several uneventful solo flights. Then one day, as he touched down and taxied in toward the Selebi airport building, a whirling tunnel of dirt and leaves sped across the bush toward the runway. Unsure how to handle a dust devil, Jonathan was caught at the wrong angle and the wrong speed. The plane flipped several times, landing upside down on the grass beside the tar.

Jonathan escaped with a few cuts and scratches. The Colt, a wreck, was left there, as it landed, an unsettling welcome for new visitors to Selebi-Phikwe. After many months, Grandpa finally got round to towing it away, with the intention of repairing the battered fuselage and wings. He never did. The day we arrived in Botswana, the little airplane lay under the thorn tree in a sorrier state than it had been in, all those years ago, when a bruised and bewildered Jonathan had crawled out.

Scattered around the wreck stood another small shed, an empty kraal with a ramp for loading cattle and two lopsided trailers—the same trailers that Grandpa Ivor had lived in, decades earlier, in his first bush camps. A short distance away was one other house: a small, squat building, its walls barely recognizable as once white, its broken windows gaping forlornly. A little farther away, hidden by a clump of trees from the main houses, was an even smaller, equally neglected old building where Grandpa said his staff sometimes stayed.

Encircling the houses, trailers, sheds, and plane was a rickety barbed wire boundary fence. Beyond this, in every direction, was bush, stretching endlessly and almost uniformly until it became sky at some faraway point on the flat horizon, interrupted only by a few distant purple hills.

That was all.

The only reminder that anyone else still even existed was a railway track that ran parallel to the fence behind Grandpa's house. Every few hours, passing close enough to rattle the kitchen windows and suspend all conversation, an old black steam train chugged along the line. If the driver saw us waving, he'd wave back, a loud hoot piercing the din of the passing ore-piled carriages. Then the train would rattle out of sight, the lone man in the caboose shrinking to a blur, and the bush's gentle noises resurfacing.

After sunset, shadowy figures shoveling coal into the flames twisted and straightened across the red glow of the furnace.

That train was to become a beloved part of our Botswana.

The deafening clatter, the black smoke streaming into bright blue sky, the flame-lit passage across the darkness—sounds that would become as comforting as the calls of dawn francolins, dusk owls, and the ever-tinkling cowbells, an occasional dramatic presence that, like the poisonous creatures that slithered, crouched, and scuttled everywhere, would soon be utterly natural and reassuring.

That was later, though. Come nightfall on our first day, the lingering image of the furnace only deepened the sense of wondrous danger, of a surreal place in which the strange and the fierce had collided, oddly, where barely believable reality slid effortlessly into the imaginary.

After dinner, gazing into the lamplight shadows, I tried to follow the conversation. Then I wondered where the scorpion had got to, and whether it was alone, and the voices receded as I conjured deadly creatures beneath every shadow. Soon, I was as far away as Lulu and Damien, who slept on the sofa beside me.

Even a discussion about Dad's uncertain new career, I only just managed to follow.

Dad had never enjoyed being a doctor, and he'd come to Botswana to stop, once and for all, being one.

"What you going to do?" I'd nagged, repeatedly, as we packed up in New Zealand.

"Who knows, Robbie. Farm something, maybe. Start a business. I'll cross that dry riverbed when I come to it...."

Then, I'd been obsessed by the possibilities and uncertainties. Now, they were nothing to what might lie beneath the furniture, let alone beyond. By midnight, when we traipsed outside, under the airplane wings, to see the stars, my head was swirling with a menagerie of perils. Of the conversation, all I remembered was Grandpa: he and his flight, plight, fright stories the only equal match for the absorbing wonders of his world.

"Bloody terrible what happened to old Meyer. Did ya hear about that?"

"Who's Meyer?" asked Dad.

"Ya dunno who Meyer is?" Grandpa raised his palms dramatically. "Ya bloody out of touch, Keith. The famous flying doctor...the man was a living legend.... Maids to ministers, every Motswana loved Meyer."

But just months earlier, as we were packing up our house, and Dad was happily closing his practice in Auckland, Dr. Meyer had died. Botswana had been shaken. "Bloody incredible, Keith. In the papers, on the radio. National mourning for the poor old bugger."

On the day Meyer died, a thick blanket of winter mist had shrouded Tonota village.

"He was crazy to try and land," said Grandpa, shaking his head. "Dunno what got into him."

I'd tried to imagine clouds that could make Grandpa think a landing crazy.

That morning, when Grandpa had collected us in Johannesburg, he'd used orange hay-bale twine to secure the door. Having blithely dismissed questions about the daylight streaming through a gap between the door and the fuselage, he'd climbed into the front and announced calmly that the little plane was overloaded. Just so we didn't worry if we came rather close to the end of the runway before takeoff.

I couldn't imagine such clouds. I could barely imagine there ever being any clouds at all in the brilliant blue sky we'd arrived in that afternoon.

Nor did clouds seem any more possible as we stood outside that night and stared up at the brilliant sky. Nothing lay between us and the vast sparkling dome, and above the bush, the stars, like the sun before them, shone impossibly bold and bright.

2

THE COWSHED AND THE WITCH DOCTOR

Lulu and Damien outside the cowshed

The door to the old house opposite Grandpa's was unlocked. But rust had seized the handle, and the wood, warped snugly against the peeling frame, resisted for several minutes as Dad tried to break in.

We'd been staying with Grandpa for just a few days when Dad sprung the startling news upon us. "Come on, then," he'd said, striding off across the dirt between the houses, "let's go and explore."

Mum said, brightly, "At least you'll still hear the train, Robbie."

I said nothing. Staring at the empty railway track that stretched behind Grandpa's house, I regretted at once having said that I would miss the train when we found our own home. It would take a lot more than the comforting sound of the train to make up for this.

Dad slammed himself shoulder-first against the door, bursting through and sending a *whoosh* of dried leaves and dirt into a small room, marked as a kitchen only by a dead-insect-scattered sink. For a moment, the floors, ceiling, and walls were alive with scurrying movement. Then, almost at once, everything was still again as scores of tiny crocodile-like creatures retreated behind piles of wood stacked against the walls.

"Geckos," said Dad. "Good grub for them, with all the insects in here."

One by one, we followed him inside. There were no cupboards, and holes in the wall where the taps must have once been. Hot afternoon sunlight streamed through a dirty window, and dust particles whirled and jigged across the beams, thousands floating up with each new footprint on the powdery carpet of dust.

The next room was larger, with more wood stacked against each wall. Strung across these piles, huge spiderwebs sagged under the weight of uneaten victims; above them, more carcass-laden webs stretched from a stained ceiling to the tops of filthy walls.

It was otherwise completely, depressingly empty.

A faint hum came from the closed door in the opposite wall. The sound was of flies, in their hundreds, and as we stepped through the doorway, clouds swarmed up around us in the stale air. The floor of the long, dimly lit room before us was covered entirely by mounds of dry cow dung.

"That'll take a bit of work," said Mum, sneezing as we retreated into the lounge. "But it's east-facing, so it'll be lovely in the morning sun."

"Mmm," sighed Dad, faraway. "The first mine geologists used to live here, you know. Before the cows moved in. Had some great parties here when I came up to visit Ivor."

"And we'll have lots more." Mum surveyed the room with a smile. "With a bit of paint and a few nice curtains. I wonder what to do about this floor, though . . ." Her voice trailed off as she gazed down at the dirty concrete.

"Lovely to live out in the bush," said Dad. He wrapped his arm around Mum's waist. "Happy, guys?"

Lulu grinned and nodded. As long as Mum and Dad were happy, Lulu was happy. "That's my girl," said Dad, picking her up so she could see out the window.

"Yip," said Damien, sounding not particularly interested. Even at five, Damien had learned not to bother arguing or worrying about our parents' plans—like this one—that definitely couldn't be changed. Damien saved all his energy to fight for things he might actually get.

I envied him for not caring. I glared at Dad, still not quite believing that this was going to be our home.

"Not up to your standards, Robbie?" asked Dad, winking at Mum.

I wanted to cry: partly with disappointment, mostly with infuriation that Mum and Dad had chosen this, of all places, to live in. And that they were so happy about it.

"You said you wanted to live in the bush," added Dad.

I had, and I did. Just not like this; not in an old cowshed. I hung my head miserably.

"Why can't you build one?" I asked. Dad had built one of our houses in New Zealand. It had been much nicer than this. We even took the house with us when we moved to a new farm—cut in half on the back of two big trucks. Like a snail.

"Too much hassle. I'll be busy with the clinics."

"Cheer up," said Mum. "It'll be such fun to fix up. You won't recognize it once we've finished."

"The only hard part," muttered Dad, "will be living next door to Grandpa Ivor."

Mum walked to the window. "Now imagine what a few flowerbeds will do for this view."

"And a veggie garden and an orchard . . ."

"So much potential, Keith."

Mum and Dad went on like this, interrupting each other,

laughing, planning; turning the cowshed into a splendid house, the bare dust into a beautiful garden.

It was exhausting to listen to. I stopped, and stared through the cracked glass at the dirt and the dry bush behind the fence.

A plastic bag had caught against one of the fence posts, and a scrawny goat on the other side nosed gently through the torn white folds. Finding nothing of interest, it strolled over to a finger-leafed acacia tree, paused for a moment, and then rocked back on its hind legs. Front feet resting daintily against the trunk, it stretched upward, nibbling at a few leaves that hung just below the browse line. All the trees had been stripped to the same even level, and after a few attempts the goat gave up, lying down under a mopane tree, peacefully resigned to its fate.

A few days later, rattling across Selebi's blue skies beside Grandpa Ivor, I was feeling much better about mine. Up here, even the most desolate bits of bush were beautiful. Thick treetops masked the goat line, and around the buildings, magnificent green mopane bush radiated unbroken but for the ribbons of road, railway, and the snaking dirt tracks. The cowshed itself was transformed from this dizzying perspective. Tiny beneath us, surrounded by a red dust skirt, it almost fitted Mum's description of "charming cottage."

"Give it a push, then," said Grandpa. "Whaddaya waiting for?"

I felt for the pedal, and hesitated.

"Come on. Just take it easy and you'll be fine."

I pushed gently, and shuddered with excitement as the horizon swung sideways.

"Steady on," Grandpa bellowed from the seat beside me, "this isn't bloody aerobatics. Press the other one."

I did, more gently this time, and the little Cherokee leveled.

"Marvelous," said Grandpa, his grin reappearing. "You'll make a fine little pilot one day. Off you go, then. Give your brother a turn. Hurry up. Haven't got all day here. I'm a busy man..."

I climbed into the back, tumbling over Damien, and pressed my nose to the window.

Staring out into the great blue, still exhilarated from just a few minutes at the helm, I understood why Dad had suddenly decided to give his job one last chance. Flying to work each day, across the endless skies above this endless land, might transform, it seemed to me, any job imaginable: even one you'd never really enjoyed, never even intended to do in the first place.

Dad was an accidental doctor.

As a teenager, fond of animals, and falling in love with the bush during long, wild holidays in Botswana, he'd dreamed of becoming a flying vet and working in a vast African game park. But liberal, beautiful Cape Town University, where he'd wanted to study, did not offer veterinary medicine. And after a year of compulsory army service, he was more reluctant than ever to spend the next half decade in Pretoria, capital city and heart of the old apartheid regime.

So at twenty, Dad had talked himself into a decision he spent most of the next fifteen years regretting.

For fifteen years, he tried desperately to find comfort in his ill-fitting career. Qualifying as a doctor, he moved immediately to the UK to be near Mum, whom he'd met in Botswana shortly before she started university in England. After just a few months, already tiring of general practice, he began to experiment with then-pioneering alternative therapies, including acupuncture, in which he trained under Dr. Felix Mann, one of the early Western experts in the technique.

Not content simply to meet the established demand in England, when Mum graduated he moved with her to Cape Town, where Dad started the city's first medical acupuncture practice. He gave talks, wrote articles, and battled skepticism, and then, after two years, just when his practice was thriving steadily, Dad decided to move on. He and Mum, now married, moved back to England, where Dad studied homeopathy at the Royal London Homeopathic Hospital.

Once more, however, the novelty of a new direction was not enough. After another two years, Mum and Dad moved to New

Zealand, where Dad inherited the practice of the country's only medical homeopath, who was returning to England. An interest in homeopathy here expanded to an interest in biodynamic farming, a system and philosophy that treats the farm as a holistic unit, incorporating organic cultivation methods, as well as homeopathic principles. During the next five years, in addition to his practice, Dad helped form the Biological Producers Association, the first in New Zealand to certify organic food, and took a prominent role in the debate about the impacts of chemical pesticides on health.

But none of this had been enough. And one day, a few months before, when soggy, gentle, green New Zealand was the only world I knew or expected to know, Dad had returned from his practice in Auckland, eyes gleaming. "I've had enough, Lin," he said. "I'm stopping medicine. And I want to move to Botswana."

Mum, who loved impractical, overnight, career-changing, continent-shifting decisions as much as Dad, said, "When do you want to leave?"

Dad said, "As soon as possible."

Two months later we were on a plane to Botswana, leaving, forever, to live in a place where the sun always shone and the enormous sky was always blue; where there were snakes in the shower, lions outside your tent, and endless infinitely dangerous creatures lurking everywhere—according to Dad, at least, who before our departure had stirred me, Lulu, and Damien, into a frenzy of excitement.

Mum, too, had talked excitedly of Botswana. But for her, the lure of the place lay in her parents, Granny Joan and Grandpa Terry, who were already familiar figures after their two lengthy visits to New Zealand. Dad longed for Botswana itself, for all its warmth and space and for the opportunity to reinvent himself. He never mentioned Grandpa Ivor, a mythic figure in this mythic country, as reason to return.

But then, the day we arrived, Dad heard about the death of Dr. Meyer.

The more he considered the idea, the more it became irresistible—the closest he could ever hope to come to his teenage dream. As a flying bush doctor, he told himself, he might at last enjoy medicine.

So Dad remained a doctor, and suddenly, accidentally, Grandpa Ivor became crucial to the new plan. For as well as retraining Dad as a pilot, until Dad got his license, Grandpa would fly Dad to the distant, inaccessible bush clinics.

And so, contrary to all our intentions, instead of building a new house by a river, or buying one of the modern houses in nearby Phikwe, we did what was, according to Mum and Dad, the obvious thing to do, and moved into the cowshed next door to Grandpa Ivor.

Moving into a cowshed wasn't the first time Mum and Dad had surprised our extended family and friends. Becoming on-and-off vegetarians, ardently taking up alternative medicine, and resolving to homeschool their children—all rooted in what would become lasting family philosophies—were among innumerable decisions that had been met with raised eyebrows.

From the moment we arrived, Lulu, Damien, and I were caught in the crossfire—beginning with my birth, when Dad delivered me at home on a snowy January day in England. To ease the pain of an all-night labor, Dad gave Mum acupuncture. Granny Joan, who'd flown over from Botswana for the birth, was horrified. At first, she bravely watched as her naked daughter staggered around the room, Dad following, flicking needle after needle into Mum's ears, bottom, and the tops of her feet. But when Dad pulled out a cigarette lighter and began warming the ends of the needles, it was too much. Granny Joan left the room and didn't appear again until I did.

Eighteen months later, newly settled in a bare rented house in Auckland, Mum and Dad took turns sitting on the single chair provided by the concerned landlady and placing bets as to whether Damien or the furniture shipped from England would appear first. Damien did, but, undaunted, they went ahead with a home birth, Mum delivering him on a mattress, which was then the only other piece of furniture in the house.

Exactly two years on, by which time we were living in a wooden house that Dad had built on a biodynamic farm, it was the turn of our paternal grandmother to brave the unconventional appearance of her grandchild. Granny Mavis couldn't take it either. She passed the duration of Lulu's birth giving our pet ducklings an extra long daily bath. That was the day of my earliest memory, which was not of my baby sister but of her shiny red placenta, which was put in the washing-up bowl until Dad buried it under a specially planted pohutakowa tree in the garden. For Maori good luck, and fertilizer.

It wasn't often, though, that Mum and Dad managed to surprise each other.

Dad's decision to drink a glass of his own urine every day for a week was one such occasion. But even then, Mum was shocked only that Dad could bring himself to swallow pee, not that the old ayurvedic practice might have medicinal benefits.

The floor of the cowshed was another.

"Brown paper, Lin?" Dad's lips twitched, and he scratched his head. "Are you sure?"

"*Varnished* brown paper," said Mum. "The DIY book says the effect is fantastic. Faux flagstone."

Dad shrugged. "You know best, Lin."

Mum bought every sheet of heavy-duty brown paper in the Phikwe stationers. She deposited the enormous pile and a bucket of wallpaper paste on the concrete floor in the lounge. On her direction, Lulu squatted beside the bucket and stirred the thick colorless paste while Damien and I ripped the huge sheets into the rough shape of stone tiles. Mum examined each piece and, if accepted as sufficiently realistic, pasted it onto the floor, overlapping the last one. Once the "tile" was in place, we all helped smooth it down, squeezing any air bubbles out under the edges.

After four long, glue-covered days of ripping, pasting, and varnishing with four polyurethane layers, Mum at last pronounced the job complete.

"See, I told you, Keith," she said, hands on hips, smiling at the gleaming floors, "it's impossible to tell."

"Impossible." Dad nodded. "All the best flagstones have air bubbles."

But Mum was too pleased to be upset.

"Don't be so critical," she replied, smiling. "Anyway, there're only a couple...and they give character."

When Mum had covered the whole cowshed floor in varnished brown paper and Dad had finished fixing up the bathroom and kitchen, they turned their attention to the veranda. And I became toolbox assistant, fetching bolts and sandpaper and drill bits.

"*Cottage*, Robbie!" Mum frowned down at me from the wobbling stool. "Don't keep calling it a cowshed."

"But it still smells of cow poo," I said, determined not to enjoy any part of the cowshed too obviously.

"Nonsense. Well, hardly. Pass me another nail...two, actually."

I fished in the toolbox and handed her the nails. Mum put one between her teeth, grabbed the flap of shade cloth, and with a loud *thwack* drove the other nail through the cloth and into the wooden upright. Taut green gauze now covered nearly the whole front of the newly painted veranda-cum-dining room.

I walked a few paces backward to properly admire the effect, hopping over the unshaded patches of sun-scorched sand.

Mum swayed precariously. "Hold the jolly thing still, Robbie," she mumbled through her nail. "Looks good, hey?"

"It's okay." I shrugged. I went back to my position.

"Come on, admit you like it."

I said nothing, and turned to watch Grandpa Ivor.

He had just arrived on one of his daily visits to give advice and was leaning against the doorway to the veranda, peering over Dad's shoulder. Only after several minutes of pointed sighing had failed to provoke a reaction did he speak.

"You're wasting your money with that lock."

"Hmm." Dad didn't look up. He was screwing a new door handle into the front door, which led into the kitchen. The key to the old lock had long since been lost.

"The whole place is charmed. No one will touch it."

"What?" I let go of the stool. "How come?"

Grandpa leaned back against the wall, crossed his legs, and squinted down at me.

"Well," he said slowly. "You see that field over there?" He swung his arm toward the tree-cleared section between his house and the boundary fence. Tree stumps, spindly yellow grass, and thornbushes covered most of it. The only thing of interest was a red termite mound, curving graciously above the thorny scrub at the far end.

"Years ago a witch doctor paid me a visit—told me there were special herbs growing there. Asked if he could pick them to make his *muti*." Grandpa drew out the last word and stared at me, widening his eyes until there was more red-veined white than bright blue middles.

"What did you say?"

"Whaddaya think I said?" He sounded staggered by my ignorance. "I said, 'Of course! Take as many as you want! Go wild!'" He lowered his voice. "You don't want to mess with witch doctors."

"What will happen?"

"Anything could happen," Grandpa whispered. "Never underestimate the power of these healers out here in the bush."

Dad rolled his eyes at me.

"Anyway, the old bugger was delighted." In exchange for the herbs, Grandpa explained, the witch doctor had made a charm that would protect the whole place for as long as he lived. "Still comes to pick them…"

I glanced at the field, half expecting to see a little hunched man in skins and feathers, not really sure what to expect. There was nothing but bleak grass and bushes, wobbling behind layers of heat waves that rose off the sand. I shuddered.

"Never locked a door since," continued Grandpa, shading his eyes and peering reverently toward his herbs. "Never had a thing stolen."

"You've never had much worth stealing," said Dad.

"Nonsense, these people will steal anything."

Dad snorted.

"Just wait, Keith," said Grandpa, "till you watch a witch doctor's curse kill a healthy man."

Witch doctors sucked blood. That was the only fact I knew about them. And starting from that basis, cursing people to death didn't seem an entirely implausible leap.

Dad had first learned about the blood sucking at his clinic, when a woman came to see him with a bad cough and an infected coin-sized wound on her chest. Asked about the cause, she had stared silently at the floor, and ignored repetitions of the question. After a few attempts, Dad had given up trying to get an answer, cleaned and dressed the wound, and sent her for an X-ray.

It was called scarification, Dad's nurse, Maria, later informed him, a technique used to cleanse bad blood. With a blunt razor, the witch doctor scrapes away a patch of skin until blood wells up in the wound. Then he turns away from the bleeding patient, grabs a handful of live grubs, worms, or insects, and surreptitiously pops them into his mouth. Returning to his client, he puts his mouth over the bleeding wound and sucks energetically. Finally, in a splendid conclusion to the cleansing operation, he spits the vile mixture of blood and grubs out into a waiting dish for inspection by his client.

Dad said, "That's just quackery. Bloody unhygienic quackery. But nothing more sinister."

"What about curses?"

Mum and Dad both assured us, several times, that Grandpa was exaggerating; that the only power witch doctors possessed was to scare people into believing they had power. But it was hard to forget Grandpa's story.

"You think it might be true?" I asked Damien.

"Dunno. Maybe."

"Let's go and look in the field."

"Okay."

"Can I come?" asked Lulu.

"You're too young."

At the edge of the field, where bare dirt became bush, Damien and I stared at each other.

"You go first."

"You're older."

"Let's get Lu."

We told Lulu she could come along, provided she went first.

Lulu obediently trotted off in front of us, her head only just above the bushes. Thorns tore at our legs. Every few steps we had to stop and pick the round spiky *duwweltjie* thorns out of our feet, shoes forgotten in the thrill of the reconnaissance plans.

"Watch out for snakes, Lu."

"Watch out for witch doctors!"

"Blood suckers!"

Farther on, the bushes grew taller and thicker. We made our way toward the termite mound near the end of the field and climbed up the gently sloping skirt at the bottom. The smooth base was thorn-free, but painfully hot after more than half a day of beating sun. "Ow! Ow!" I hopped from foot to foot, swapping the heat. Every time I felt the concrete-hard walls of a termite mound, I thought about termites spitting. Termite mounds, many taller even than Dad, were built entirely out of termite spit and sand.

"Which do you think are the *muti* herbs?"

I studied the few wilted plants between the clumps of grass and larger bushes. There were several different kinds—all different shades of gray-green and dust-covered, some folded up in the midday heat. None looked like they'd make very effective medicine.

"Maybe he's picked them all."

"Let's look for footprints."

Something rustled, and we all froze.

The two houses looked much farther away than the termite mound had looked from the houses. The drawn-out *gwaah-gwaah-gwaaah* of a go-away bird sounded unfriendly, not talking-bird funny, like it usually did. None of us called "Go away" back.

"There's nothing here. Let's go."

We walked a few paces, and then broke into a run. Out here, surrounded by bush, the huge blue sky loomed above us, bigger than ever, like it might swallow us up. Soon we were running as fast as we could, oblivious to the thorns and the clawing branches.

Damien and I collapsed, panting, beside each other on Grandpa's driveway. We were almost breathing normally by the time Lulu came out of the bushes, looking miserable.

"Why did you leave me?" she spluttered.

"We didn't. There's nothing there anyway."

"So why did you run?"

"It was a race."

"I'm telling Mum."

"Then I'll tell her you didn't wear a hat."

"I'm sure I saw something."

"No you didn't."

But none of us wanted to go back to the field to check.

In the end, we consulted Matthews—the new gardener, and authority on all things to do with Botswana.

Matthews said he was fourteen, but he looked much younger, especially in his work clothes, which were, invariably, a too-small holey T-shirt that said "Coke—Can't beat the feeling," gray suit trousers cut off at the knee, and old, oversize steel-capped boots at the end of long, skinny legs. Matthews had explanations for everything, and generally different ones from Mum and Dad's. He'd left school when he was twelve and lived in a hut in a nearby cattle post. Besides several neighboring huts, the only things at his cattle post were a kraal for the cows and goats, and a tiny general store that sold essentials like cornmeal, paraffin, and Sunlight soap, as well as Simba chips, boiled sweets, and a wide range of fizzy drinks and beer.

The cattle post was a twenty-minute walk away along one of the hundreds of dirt paths that crisscrossed the bush around us, and every morning at eight o'clock Matthews strolled out of the mopane bush to begin work for Mum and Dad, and to become a nonstop source of information for us.

"Did a witch doctor really put a charm on this place?"

"Ah!" Matthews's smile disappeared. He scraped his boot on the sand and stared at his feet. Usually he only looked uncomfortable when Mum or Dad, or other adults, asked him questions.

"Grandpa said a witch doctor comes to pick herbs."

"It's true," he muttered, after a pause.

"How do you know?"

"Everyone knows."

"Do people die from curses?"

"Sometimes. Ah, ah, I don't want to talk about this."

"Have you been to a witch doctor?"

"Ah. *Ga ke itse.*"

End of that conversation.

Ga ke itse: conversational brick wall of Botswana. When you hear "*Ga ke itse*" and see downcast Motswana eyes, you give up asking questions. It means "I don't know." But it's frequently used to mean "I do know, but I don't want to answer any more questions," which happens often when Europeans ask more questions than are welcome.

The too-many-questions threshold is low.

"I'm going to ban that bloody expression," announced Dad, once, in a long-day-at-the-clinic, exasperated voice.

"Don't be ridiculous!" Mum looked appalled. "It's cultural. You can't ban people speaking their own language."

"I can if I'm paying their salaries."

"I'll have nothing to do with it."

"Fine. It's the only way I'll ever get a straight answer."

So Dad ordered his nurses, and Matthews, and Ruth, our maid, not to say "*Ga ke itse*" in his presence.

"It's wonderful," he said, after the end of the first *ga ke itse*–free day. "I just wish I could ban my patients from saying it too."

By the end of the week, though, the ban had been lifted.

"I can't bear the silence."

"Serves you right for being such an autocrat, Keith."

Sometimes we also learned things about Setswana, the local language, just from listening to Batswana people speak English.

Like the word *please*, which was rarely said.

"Robbie," Ruth would order, "call your mummy for me." Or Matthews would say, "Tell the doctor I want to speak to him," or "I want a glass of water."

It was surprising, at first; jarring to ears used to polite English formalities.

"There's no equivalent word for *please*," explained Grandpa.

"No word?"

"Well there is, but it's hardly said. It's implied already. Think about it. What's the point of *please*, really?"

In Botswana, if someone wanted something, it was asked for with no frills. And if you said no, that wasn't rude either, but accepted gracefully, without grudges.

"Sensible, if you ask me," said Grandpa.

We still had to say please, though.

We soon grew tired of speculating about the witch doctor. As Mum pointed out, charms or no charms, if he did still come to pick herbs, he wouldn't want to upset Grandpa Ivor by doing anything unpleasant to us.

Anyway, Matthews made sure there were other things to worry about.

As soon as we'd moved into the cowshed, work began on the garden. Under Mum's direction, Matthews spread the cow dung that had been removed from the back room in a meter-wide band around the house, and together they lugged and lined up football-sized stones to make borders for the new flowerbeds.

Everything went smoothly until Mum planted sticks in the ground to mark where she wanted the geraniums, passionfruit creepers, and a row of pawpaw trees. For the front of the house, there was fast-growing bougainvillea that would climb over the shade-cloth veranda and eventually cover the ugly asbestos roof.

"Okay," said Mum. "Why don't you start digging here and work your way round."

Matthews didn't move.

"What's wrong?"

"Ah!"

"Tell me," said Mum, an irritable edge creeping into her voice.

"*Ga ke itse.*"

"Fine. Well if you don't want to tell me, it can't be that bad."

Matthews picked up his spade. He began to dig, in slow motion, like he was lifting concrete instead of soft dirt and cow dung. He looked miserable.

Mum walked off. "Call me when you've finished."

I waited till she was out of earshot.

"What's wrong, Matthews?"

"This is no good," he said, scowling at the rows of flowers waiting to be planted. "Snakes will come into the house."

"But we have snake barriers." The barriers were foot-high pieces of wood, pushed across the doorways when it was too hot to shut the doors, which was most of the time.

"They are no good," said Matthews, impatiently. "You must not have plants near houses."

All the huts at Matthews's cattle post were surrounded by bare, swept earth. Nearly every time we'd passed by, one or two young girls had been swishing a bundle of thin sticks across the immaculate dirt. Maybe he had a point.

"Anyway, I'm not scared of snakes."

"Ah. You must kill them."

"Dad says you're not allowed to kill snakes."

"Ah! *Tst, tst.*"

3

KISSING SNAKES

Lulu and a python

In summer, which seemed to last more than half the year, falling asleep at night was almost impossible. Nor did it become any easier with practice; a year after we arrived, the second summer's night heat and the tireless mosquitoes were as distracting as they were the first day.

We developed a routine.

After Dad had kissed each of us good night—"Sleep tight, mind the scorpions don't bite"—Mum would lean over for her good-night kiss and then tuck in the mosquito net. With mosquito control, as with food and medicines, Mum and Dad, wherever possible, insisted on natural, nonprocessed, nonsynthetic, chemical-free, additive-free, environmentally friendly alternatives. They refused to use the highly effective but chemical-rich Doom spray, which was a permanent fixture in many Botswana households.

"Pull it tighter, Mum." If any of the soft folds touched skin, the mozzies just bit you through the net.

"Is that okay?"

"Yip. Can you see any inside?"

"All clear. Want to be sprayed?"

"Yip."

Then Mum would reach inside with a spray bottle of water, careful not to let in any mozzies, and pump the handle till the fine droplets dampened hot skin and sheets.

"Thanks. Night."

"Sleep well, darling."

But then, when the lights were off and Mum had disappeared down the corridor, the mozzies would start whining; closer and closer to my ear, until I knew the piercing whirr was too near to be coming from beyond the net.

Almost always, one would have somehow managed to hide inside, escaping Mum's notice. Five minutes of trying to squash the mozzie with a book so I didn't get blood on my hands, and nightie, skin, and sheets would be dry again.

Now it would be far too hot to sleep.

Eventually I'd reach out for the tall glass of water, drink half of it, and dribble the rest down the front of my nightie.

Finally, cool soggy cotton and sleep.

Dad said, "If you drink so much, you'll wake up with TB."

Dad meant "tight bladder." He usually meant tuberculosis only when he was talking about his patients.

It was impossible not to drink, though, when you were sleepless with heat.

"Well, if you have to get up, just don't walk barefoot in the dark. Always turn on the lights."

But when I woke, moonlight filled the room. Outside, the sandy expanse between our house and Grandpa Ivor's was almost glowing, streaked with a few long tree shadows. I could see the nose of the airplane poking out of the shed. Grandpa's house was completely dark. It must have been after eleven, probably already early on Wednesday morning—Dad's worst clinic day.

At four thirty, just as the first francolins began squawking their dawn good-mornings, Dad and Grandpa would be leaving for the airport. From there, they would fly nearly a hundred kilometers to the clinic in Tonota village, where Dad would see more than a hundred patients. If he returned in time for dinner, he'd eat his food in glazed-eyed, exhausted silence.

Mum and Dad's door was across the passage from mine. If I turned on the lights, I'd be certain to wake them.

I slid out under the net, tucked it back in, and tiptoed silently past their door. Even in the windowless passage I could see the floor well enough to be certain it was clear.

Against the wall opposite the loo, a woven washing basket overflowed onto the floor with the day's dirty clothes. I gazed at the basket with half-concentrating, emptying-bladder relief. A T-shirt, a few knickers, and a brown cord had fallen onto the floor—the tie from Mum's dressing gown, maybe a belt. I couldn't decide which.

I stopped weeing, midway, seized up with fright.

The cord had moved. And now I realized it had a head, at the end nearest my toes.

"Mum! Dad!" I yelled, snatching my feet up beside me onto the seat.

A faraway, sleepy grunt. And then, "Keith. Come on. Get up."

"What's wrong?" called Dad, in a muffled, grumpy voice.

"A snake! Come quick."

Footsteps padded down the brown-papered corridor, and the door handle started to turn.

"Wait." I closed my legs together and tried to pull my nightie over my knees.

"Remember not to move," said Dad, from behind the door. "Or you'll frighten it."

"You're going to be fine," added Mum, in a soothing but wobbly voice.

Very slowly, the bathroom door swung open, and Mum and Dad appeared in the doorway.

"Interesting," said Dad, peering down at the snake. His hair was standing up in several directions. He wore only pajama shorts. Mum, who didn't wear anything to bed, stood stark naked beside him. Her skin looked surprisingly white in the moonlight.

"Haven't seen one of these before," said Dad.

He flicked on the light, and the snake began to slither toward the base of the loo.

"Aaah, Dad."

"Relax, Robbie." Dad scratched his chin thoughtfully. "It's small. Definitely not a cobra, so it probably won't rear. Would you mind getting me a broom, Lin?" he added, as if he was asking Mum to pass him the salt.

A minute later, by which time the snake had slithered against the porcelain base of the loo, Mum, now wrapped in a dressing gown, returned with the broom. Lulu and Damien came trailing after her, woken by the din from the kitchen, where our new bull terrier, Smiley, had started howling excitedly and hurling himself against the rickety wooden door.

Damien began to giggle.

"It's not funny." I glared at him from my undignified perch. I felt sick with fear. I wondered if any of the bottles of antivenom that Dad kept in the cheese compartment in the fridge would work for this snake, whatever it was.

Dad held the end of the broom handle and, very slowly, lowered the brush end just behind the snake's arrow-patterned head. Then, with a quick flick of his arm, he slapped the broom down onto the neck. The snake thrashed wildly, but its head was held securely still. Dad swept it into the middle of the room.

"Okay, off you go."

I slid off the seat. "Should I flush?"

"If you widdled."

I pumped the handle a few times, washed my hands under the lukewarm water from the cold tap, and retreated to the passage.

It took several minutes—Dad pinning down the angry, wriggling snake; Mum, sitting on the edge of the bath, flicking through the already well-worn snake book—to identify this latest intruder.

"Night adder. Semipoisonous."

Which meant we couldn't just drop it out the window into the flowerbed, or keep it for a few weeks in the glass vivarium, like we sometimes did with harmless snakes.

Instead, Mum and Dad slipped an empty burlap sack over its head, pushing the body in afterward. Then they put the wriggling sack into a cardboard box. On top of that went a tea tray; on top of that, Palgrave's *Trees of Southern Africa.* Finally, Mum punched air holes in the side of the box with a pair of scissors.

In the morning we'd drive far out into the bush, looking for somewhere with no cows or goats or donkeys, and tip the night adder over the back of the *bakkie.* Till then it would spend the rest of the night on the moonlit dining room table.

"Well done for being so brave and not moving," said Dad, giving my shoulder a squeeze.

I didn't point out that the first thing I'd done when I'd seen the snake, contrary to all Dad's warnings, was to move quickly.

"I wasn't really that scared."

"Well, it was only *semi*poisonous, anyway," said Damien. "Couldn't have killed you."

A nd that was all that mattered, really—especially when there were so many snakes that could.

Mostly, we saw only bits and flashes of snakes; a brown shadow slithering through a leafy branch, the flick of a dark tail disappearing into a clump of grass, even just telltale diagonal whip marks in the sand. Not usually enough to make an identification. But enough to let you assume the worst.

"Definitely a mamba."

"Black Mamba: Neurotoxic venom; front-fanged, so it can sink its fangs into any part of the body, can raise its body two meters tall, i.e., can bite you anywhere." Rules for black mamba bites: Breathing may be

paralyzed in minutes. Give mouth-to-mouth; keeps victim alive indefinitely. Otherwise need antivenom within an hour, or death. *N.B.* If bite to neck, poison will spread too quickly for any hope of survival. Tickets! Game over!

"No, *man.* Too skinny. Maybe a boomslang."

"*Boomslang: Haemotoxic venom: back-fanged, so needs to get its jaws around a finger to get its venom into you.*" Unlikely, but horrible. Venom interferes with blood clotting system; victim may die of internal bleeding. Rules for bites: you have a few hours' grace, but then, tickets. Get in car! Get on plane! Cross borders! Do anything, pay anything, to get antivenom.

"Too dark. Probably a Mozambique."

"*Mozambique Spitting Cobra: Cytotoxic venom, which can cause terrible local tissue damage around a bite. Usually spits in direction of eyes, can cause blindness. Spitting range two meters.*" Rules for spit in eyes: Wash eyes immediately in water. *N.B.*: Legs often spat at first—if you feel unexplained droplets on leg when walking past flowerbed, retreat immediately and put on big sunglasses before investigating further.

These inconclusive sightings occurred most often on our evening walks: every day, six o'clock excursions along one of the sandy roads or paths that spread out like a network of large and little veins from the perimeter fence. With the glowing evening sun in our eyes and the messy patchwork of shadows across the sand, it was almost impossible to tell what any fleeting movement might have been.

Afterward, when we'd all walked far off the path to skirt the suspicious tree or bush—dragging a wriggling, howling Smiley who invariably tried to chase whatever it was—Mum and Dad would try to moderate our speculation.

"Could have been a mole snake. Maybe even just a big lizard…" And then, as a tirade of barks drowned their voices, "For God's sake, Smiley. Shut up! Enough now."

Christened for his toothy grinning jaw, the bizarre dog had entered the family six months after we arrived in Botswana. He replaced our first dog, Fawn, a chronically ill doelike mongrel that I'd insisted on taking home from an animal rescue center—only for her to die a few months later. Fawn had seemed to suffer as much from a broken heart as illness. Smiley suffered from a broken mind, rescued from some grim past by a cousin of Dad's who'd spotted the scarred white bull terrier wandering beside a motorway in Johannesburg.

Dad, who loved bull terriers above all other breeds, offered a home immediately, and Grandpa Ivor collected Smiley when he next flew down to Johannesburg. Smiley climbed onto Granny Betty's lap, where, despite having received three times the normal dose of tranquilizer, he fidgeted the entire flight back to Selebi. A few weeks later, when we left him alone for the first time, we returned to find the whole lounge suite torn to pieces, and Smiley, slobbering over a sea of foam on the brown paper tiles, glaring accusingly through red piggy-eyes.

As we argued about the snake sightings, Smiley would be howling dementedly.

"Listen to Smiley. Must be a mamba."

"Smiley barks at geckos."

"But dogs know about snakes. And Smiley's going crazy."

"Smiley went crazy long ago."

This became increasingly hard to dispute. Nor did Smiley demonstrate much evidence of the acute snake sense—sometimes even including a special bark—developed by so many African dogs. Smiley energetically and indiscriminately chased everything that moved, once chewing right through a fallen knob-thorn trunk in pursuit of a two-inch lizard.

But as the trees and bushes darkened under the blue-black dusk sky, and the owls screeched to each other as they began their nighttime hunt, the bush's unseen inhabitants loomed larger and more definitely poisonous. By the time we saw the dark smudge of trees ahead of us—the knob-thorn cluster around our house—and hurried toward it in the last of the light, the matter was usually resolved in favor of something lethal. And then we would sit down to dinner on the veranda, Smiley contentedly snapping at flying insects, listening to the cries, squeals, and rustles in the

blackness around us, and relishing the chilling satisfaction of a
near miss from the relative safety of our little house.

O nly one of Dad's five clinics, his base clinic in Phikwe,
had a telephone.

His others, Dr. Meyer's old clinics in the faraway villages
of Tonota, Machaneng, Tsetsebjwe, and Lesenepole, were tiny
buildings with no ceiling boards beneath their corrugated iron
roofs, no electricity, and no running water. At these clinics, which
he visited only one day each week, Dad sterilized his instruments
using gas power, and washed his hands in bowls of water filled by
his nurses under outdoor taps.

But with many hour-long queues of patients waiting, even
in the relative luxury of the Phikwe clinic, Dad almost never
stopped working to chat on the telephone.

So when, one sluggish morning in our second summer in
Botswana, he rang from work, we didn't doubt that we were
being summoned for something worthwhile.

"I've got a patient here you guys might like to see."

"Who?"

"You'll have to come along to the clinic."

"Why? Dad—"

But the phone had gone dead.

Mum was, as usual, game for any diversion from the routine
of our school day, which had very little routine in the first place.

Mum had decided to homeschool us partly because we lived
out of town in Selebi, and would one day—if Dad ever found his
longed-for game farm deep in the bush—live even farther away.
But she'd first started teaching us at home in New Zealand,
where we'd lived near several good schools, and the main reason was, and had always been, that Mum's particular version of
homeschooling fitted her "firm educational philosophy." Which
was that learning is most effective when there are no clear dis-
tinctions between work and play. Routine threatened the sacredly
blurred line, so she avoided it as much as possible.

Now she said, "Of course we must go. Hurry up. Put your shoes on."

Phikwe was the only clinic that we could possibly visit in anything less than a day-long expedition. The others, in remote villages hundreds of kilometers of bad dirt roads away, could be reached easily only by airplane. Once we'd flown with Dad to Lesenepole, at the base of the beautiful Tswapong hills, sinking toward a tiny dirt airstrip beside the village. Goats and donkeys wandered across the runway, and Dad circled low over the strip to scatter the animals. A few goats remained, but by the time we looped round a second time, a figure was running beneath us, waving a stick at the stragglers. The elderly man, the self-appointed airplane-guard, met us with a warm "Dumela" as we climbed out onto the dirt. Then he set to work, shooing away scores of small children who clambered onto the plane while Dad loaded his medicine trunk into an old bakkie sent to take him to the clinic and we hurried off to explore the village with Mum.

Normally, Phikwe was the clinic we least associated with great excitement, and we speculated wildly as the bakkie sped off down the driveway, clinking quickly over the cattle grid. From Selebi, Phikwe was a fifteen-minute drive, on a mostly smooth, mostly tar road. For the first part of the drive, the road ran parallel to the railway track; then, after a few kilometers, the track diverged and headed off into the bush toward the orange-and-white-striped smelter tower that plumed sulfurous black smoke in the distance.

The road continued into the residential part of town. To reach Dad's clinic we drove between the baking grounds of the tennis and cricket clubs on one side and the row of mine managers' houses on the other. Behind the hedges of these large tree-shaded homes revolving sprinklers tick-tick-ticked endlessly, fighting their constant battle with the withering sun—preserving, against all odds, absurdly green lawns and the delicate flowers of English gardens.

But these bright clean houses and lush green gardens made only a brief oasis. Not much farther on, in the poorer, "blacker" part of town, dust and heat reasserted themselves.

Here, halfway down a small side street, we stopped outside the dingy Three Sisters liquor store. Adverts for Castle Lager and Chibuku, the horrible smelling sorghum beer, covered its walls. Empty cans and fried chicken wrappers littered the surrounding red dirt. Thin, mangy mongrels nosed through the greasy paper and bones.

Both the liquor store and Dad's clinic, which stood on the opposite side of the road, buzzed with customers. Not unusual for the end of the month: beer and private doctors—in that order— were two considerable drains on the monthly paycheck. In the villages, where much of the wealth that afforded such luxuries lay in cattle, Dr. Meyer's old clinic days had followed the cattle- selling days, when the liquor stores too fared well.

But today, even for a post-payday spending spree, the Phikwe clinic was busy. And more than that: an air of recent excitement seemed to linger among the clusters of people who sat chatting beneath the trees in front of the small white clinic, framed by the vast boulders of the *koppie* that loomed up behind the building.

Inside the waiting room, all of the plastic chairs that lined the walls were occupied, small children and babies consigned to the floor or their mothers' laps. Everyone was black, except for one flustered-looking white woman, who stood in a corner pretend- ing to study posters that advised you to eat more green vegetables and to beware of STDs.

She smiled and rolled her eyes at Mum, giving the conspira- torial, despairing look that whites shared in long, slow Botswana queues. Mum just nodded and said a general, cheery "*Dumela*" to the room.

After a few minutes, Dad's nurse, Maria, emerged from the consulting room to summon the next patient. "*Dumela*, Mrs. Scott," she said, giggling as Lulu rushed forward and enveloped her white skirts in a hug. "Ah, you are a naughty one." She chuck- led, patting Lulu's head.

We followed Maria into the examination room, where Dad greeted us with a secretive grin and beckoned us toward the storeroom.

He dismissed our stream of questions. "Patience, chaps. Patience."

The sharp, minty smell of wintergreen was eye-wateringly strong in the storeroom. On one wall, high shelves held bottles and tubs of medicines, labeled and ready to be given to patients. There were also boxes of rubber gloves, needles and syringes, and a collection of small red and green food-coloring bottles that Mum reluctantly bought for Dad when she did the grocery shopping.

The coloring was added to white liquid medicines before they were given to the patients, who believed colorful medicines worked better than white ones. Using food coloring was one of Dr. Meyer's old practices, which—as a purely aesthetic modification to effective medicines—Dad said was an acceptable concession to local beliefs. And while Mum objected, both in principle and because the use of artificial colorings in medicines so contradicted her and Dad's history with natural medicine, Dad just said, "In this environment, something has got to give."

Dad also bought gold- and silver-colored vitamin pills instead of the white ones usually dispensed by the government clinics. But here he stopped. Some went much further. One notoriously greedy doctor had different-colored stethoscopes, for which he charged patients different fees, starting with black—the cheapest and least effective—and finishing, at the other end of the price and potency range, with silver and finally gold.

In the middle of the room, instead of the usual rows of empty bottles waiting to be filled with medicines, a large cardboard box stood on the sorting table.

Dad lifted two big buckets of tablets off the lid of the box.

"Meet your first python, guys," he said, pulling back the cardboard flaps with a flourish.

The black, brown, and white patterned body curled up inside was the biggest, longest snake I had ever seen. Much bigger than the picture in the *Snakes of Southern Africa* book; too big even to fit comfortably in the bottom of the large box, its fat coils piled on top of each other in several layers.

We all gasped.

The python had been the last of the great snakes to elude us.

The others had all eventually appeared in full view around—or sometimes inside—the house: mambas, cobras, puff adders. Once, a slim green boomslang, quivering in the bougainvillea on the bathroom windowsill. All except for the rock-loving, buck-eating python, not satisfied by plants for cover and mice for dinner.

"Can I touch it?"

"Me too."

"Me first."

"Hang on a sec." Dad lowered his hand toward the snake. Then, very quickly, he grabbed its fist-thick neck, holding the head, with its nonpoisonous but piercing fangs, safely immobile.

The snake shifted irritably as we stroked its thick, cool body. It was hard, seeing and touching the beautiful coils like this, to imagine it strangling goats—or possibly small children—and swallowing them whole.

On one side a fist-size patch of scales had been ripped off, revealing raw red flesh.

"The poor chap was pelted with stones before I got to it," said Dad. "But it's not too deep, and I've put a bit of antiseptic on."

"Why the excitement outside?" asked Mum, gently prodding the edges of the wound.

Dad explained that he'd found the python after noticing a group of people hurling stones at something in the boulders of the *koppie* behind the clinic. He'd rushed up the *koppie*, stopped the stone throwing, and pulled the snake out from between the rocks.

"Kill it, kill it!" the growing crowd chanted, as Dad picked up the struggling python.

"No, no," Dad shouted. "Friend. Friend."

But the shouting only mounted. The Batswana's general indiscriminate loathing of snakes was almost impervious to argument. Dad had tried often before with Matthews and Ruth: explaining that, left alone, snakes generally stay clear of humans, that they hardly ever bite people, and that they no more deserve to die than any other bush animal quietly minding its own business. But even when Ruth asked him to kill a harmless mole snake she'd found in the kitchen, and Dad replied that it could harm no one, Ruth remained unconvinced. "Ah, they are very bad!"

Now, Dad started to speak again but hesitated. He cleared his throat and stared at Mum with an amused smile.

"And?" prompted Mum.

"Well, I held its head up to mine," he said. "To show it really was a friend." He paused again, looking slightly embarrassed. "And I kissed it."

"Where?"

"On the top of its head."

"Goodness gracious, Keith."

"Couldn't resist."

"Show-off!" Mum laughed. "You're worse than Ivor."

For once, Dad didn't seem offended by the comparison.

"Made me a bit of a hero, I think," he grinned.

After the kiss, amid wild cheers and laughter from the crowd, Dad carried the python to safety in the clinic. Midway down the *koppie*, it pooed, the enormous brown pile landing squarely on one sock and shoe.

Python poo turned out to be the most durable and foul-smelling poo in the world, and no amount of scrubbing that evening would banish the stench. Lamenting his bad luck and the loss of his favorite pair of shoes, Dad put them aside for gardening. "At least"—he smiled ruefully—"the kiss should do wonders for business."

A year into his practice, he could now smile about it—now that he no longer actually needed wonders done for business. During the first few months in his new Phikwe clinic, Dad had spent most of his time in blue overalls, sawing wood and erecting splendid cupboards for all the medicines he wasn't dispensing. In his first month, he saw, on his busiest day, five patients, and we soon stopped inquiring about the dispiriting figures.

It was only after about six months of agonizing waiting and intensive interior decorating that word of a new doctor and a new clinic finally got around. Thereafter, however, his numbers rose steadily, and by the time he had to replace his shoes, Dad was seeing enough patients to keep him busy throughout the two and a half days a week he spent at the Phikwe clinic.

When Dad established this clinic, there was only one other private doctor, a gentlemanly Indian man, practicing in Phikwe. Dad's growing practice had, however, little effect on Dr. Chothia's busy clinic: most of Dad's patients were either old patients of Dr. Meyer's, who had previously made the long trek to his village clinics, or those who otherwise relied mainly on government doctors. Despite a free government health service, private doctors are widely believed in Botswana to be more effective, and worth the expense. Add to this the country's relatively high per capita income—relative, that is, to the rest of the continent—and there is no shortage of patients for good private doctors.

On the occasions that one of Dr. Chothia's patients did visit Dad, Dad would ask them why, interested to hear any complaints that might help him hone his own service. He never got further, however, than obstinate repetitions of "Ga ke itse." Worried he was missing out on crucial strategic information, he eventually consulted Maria. It had, she told him, nothing to do with speed of service, medicines dispensed, or bedside manner—for all of which Dr. Chothia had a good reputation. Often, she explained, if one doctor's medicines did not work immediately, patients would simply go straight to another. "And sometimes," she said, "we just prefer white doctors. We don't trust the Indians."

The whites also preferred white doctors. But almost all the whites in Phikwe worked for the mine, the heart and the lifeblood of the town. And the mine families received free treatment from the mine doctors, who were, conveniently, all white too. Of the few whites that did try Dad, most defected to Dr. Chothia, complaining bitterly that Dr. Scott didn't keep an appointment book, working on a first-come-first-served basis. Which meant they had to wait for hours in the waiting room, "with everyone else."

Later, there would be one exception.

Half a decade on, when a greater horror dwarfed the discomfort of the crowded waiting room, whites would begin visiting Dad for HIV tests. The mine doctors did HIV tests too. But they also played golf, and attended dinner and cocktail parties with their wives, who played bridge and tennis. The doctors were senior figures in the mine hierarchy and upstanding, well-connected members of Phikwe mine society. For anyone mixing in similar circles and worried about their HIV status, the prospect of something slipping out over a glass of wine or on a pillow, was unbearable. Even if the result was negative, questions might be raised: about the motivation for the test, about whether that scurrilous rumor might actually be true.

For the moment, though, Dad's Phikwe clinic was essentially black.

Dad's village clinics were also all black. But while his Phikwe patients were often well educated, less keen on traditional healers, and spoke good English, his other patients—drawn from small villages or cattle posts—were, as a rule, the opposite. And while Dad might have been joking about snake kissing increasing his business, doctors' popularity was indeed governed by much more than their effectiveness.

Most important, necessary or not, patients paying for a private doctor expected a comprehensive examination, at least one injection, and a wide range of medicines—preferably brightly colored—to take home. The system Dad inherited from Dr. Meyer, the most successful private doctor in the country, catered for both preferences, while being quick enough to make the relatively low fee per patient profitable.

The consultation price was fifty pula: around a third of the monthly salary of the lowest-paid domestic and farm workers, many of whom were counted among his patients. The fee, which included all medicines, was equal for all patients, and Dad called it socialist medicine, because the hypochondriacs subsidized the really sick patients. As a dispensing doctor, he also provided an additional service in the villages, where the nearest pharmacy often involved a journey of several hours.

A straightforward consultation took Dad just under five minutes, which began when the patient, already naked beneath a blue gown, walked into the examination room.

Over the next five minutes, Dad took a history while giving the patient a full-body examination, which included a rectal examination on almost every man and a vaginal examination on every woman. Then he injected every patient, whatever age, even if it was just a shot of vitamin B12. Finally he sent each away with at least one tub of "rubbing" ointment, several packets of pills, and a bottle of some sort of liquid medicine. All this was in addition to any specific requirements, and every patient, their hands full of medicines, would leave prodded, palpated, and thoroughly satisfied. There was no time or place in this new regime for alternative therapies, and Dad abandoned them all.

However, as Dad had discovered soon after we arrived in Botswana, in the minds of many of his village patients, there was more still to the powers of a private doctor.

Tonota village, half an hour's flight north of Selebi, was from the start Dad's busiest village clinic. At Lesenepole, he spent just a few hours, flying back to his Phikwe clinic for the afternoon. The queue of patients at Tonota, many traveling from the nearby city of Francistown, could take him all day. In the early months, Tonota had been particularly important in supplementing the sluggish Phikwe clinic, which Dad established from scratch, instead of the easier route of taking over an existing practice.

Then one day, suddenly, patient numbers at Tonota mysteriously began to drop.

Bemused but not overly worried, Dad put it down to an unfortunate fluke, a slow month. A few weeks later, he had his explanation. His clinic cleaner informed him that Dr. van der Westhuizen, a private Afrikaans doctor working in the area, had changed his clinic day to coincide with the one day a week that Dad visited Tonota.

"That's not all," said Dad, storming into the house, red with indignation, "the rascal has moved to a building just near mine."

Over the following quiet weeks, when Dad's nurses had time to wander to the local takeaway for a *sadza* and greasy fried

chicken lunch and a gossip, they heard that Dr. van der Westhuizen was spreading rumors that Dr. Scott was a bad doctor.

Dad was stuck. He had no real evidence. Even if he reported
Dr. van der Westhuizen, and the legendarily slow and inefficient Health Department did act on the complaint, it would take
months.

Every week Dad returned, furious, bearing news of some
new slander.

"The rotter has been intercepting people on the way to my
clinic," he fumed, "diverting them to his own. Bloody *skellum*.
Wish there was a way to teach him a lesson."

Mum said, "I'm sure he'll learn his lesson one day. Ratbags
like that usually get their comeuppance."

"I'd prefer him to get it now."

"Well," said Mum cheerfully, "think of it this way, the more
badly he behaves, the sooner he's bound to get it."

In the face of the full force and creativity of Mum's optimism,
argument was fruitless. Dad shrugged and laughed, "You know
best, Lin."

One day, a few months later, Dad arrived to a packed waiting
room at Tonota.

No, Dad was told, the doctor had not left. He'd been deserted,
in disgust.

Dr. van der Westhuizen's clinic was just beside the small dirt
runway. The week before, at the sound of Dad's plane approaching, he had hurried outside. Standing on the dust in front of his
waiting patients, he'd muttered angrily and shaken his fist at the
descending plane.

In the eyes of his audience, he was trying to bring down Dr.
Scott's plane with some kind of curse. Word flew around the
stores, water pumps, and bars of the village, and it was not long
before another much more damaging conclusion was drawn.

Dr. van der Westhuizen had been practicing at the same
time as the great Dr. Meyer. It was already public knowledge

that many doctors had resented Dr. Meyer—the busiest doctor in Botswana, who hadn't even lived in Botswana. Every day, ignoring the border, Dr. Meyer had flown in across the Limpopo from his farm in South Africa. Once some of the local doctors had complained, and Dr. Meyer had been stopped from entering. The public fury was so great, however, that the government had granted him special dispensation to enter Botswana without going through the normal customs and immigration formalities.

Then Dr. Meyer had crashed, and Dr. van der Westhuizen was later seen cursing Dr. Scott. Dr. van der Westhuizen, the reasoning went, must have obviously and unforgivably cursed and killed Dr. Meyer to finally get rid of him.

Dad's clinic became steadily busier. Not long afterward, Dr. van der Westhuizen closed his. Later he left altogether and returned to South Africa.

4

NGAKA AND MMANGAKA

Mum and Dad

Ngaka. "Doctor." Magic word, in Botswana.

Even Mum had a special name. *MmaNgaka*, wife of the doctor—hotline to Dad, which could be inconvenient for Mum.

"*Dumela*, MmaNgaka,"

"*Dumela*, Rra," said Mum, smiling at the thin man standing behind her in the queue. She turned quickly back to face the till and murmured something to the three of us who sat sprawled on the floor, immobilized by boredom and heat.

The line in the stuffy little hardware store was stationary. Four or five people waited in front of us. Behind us, the tail of the queue rounded the end of the nail, screw, and bolt aisle. No one was going anywhere, and a discussion about ailments, should it start, would be inescapable. So Mum made a point of looking busy with her children, of being unusually sympathetic to our whining.

We had "popped in" after the weekly grocery shop in Phikwe for a few odds and ends: sandpaper, paint, glue, drill bits. Now, half an hour later, the already wilted lettuce would be slimy brown on the outside, and the milk would be curdling on the backseat.

At the till, moving as if the hot air was syrup, a brightly clothed, enormously fat Motswana woman prodded buttons on the cash register. Only her mouth was animated, smiling and firing a stream of rapid Setswana at her customers. Other customers chatted among themselves. No one else seemed to mind the wait.

"My kidneys are bad." The man behind Mum pulled a face. "*Botlhoko. Botlhoko.*" He tapped his shirt in the vicinity of his kidneys. "I need to see the doctor."

"Well, I'm sure he'll be able to help you," said Mum, turning round reluctantly. It was the usual problem: almost every Motswana man said there was something wrong with his kidneys. The women complained about their wombs.

"*Ee.*" The man nodded. But after a few moments' deliberation, he continued. "And I am only *half-charged.*" His expression suggested this was a greater problem than his kidneys.

"Half-charged?" said Mum.

"I can only do it once a night."

Problems with "doing it" were a thrilling change from troubled kidneys, wombs, and dirty blood. Damien and I immediately stopped tracing patterns on the dusty shelves.

Mum coughed. "Oh, dear," she said in a strained voice, "well, perhaps the doctor can help you with that too."

"*Ee.*"

The man in front of us turned around and said something in Setswana to the half-charged man. Laughter and rapid conversation followed, joined by several other men. In any language, the sympathetic nods, occasional laughs, and thigh slapping clearly accompanied an exchange of embarrassing stories and shared problems.

But the details we could not follow until the cashier spoke, returning the conversation to English.

She had abandoned the cash register altogether and leaned forward across the counter. Huge breasts spread out in front of her like full sacks of cornmeal—breasts stretched by child after child, but kept full thanks to a rich husband who could afford to fatten his wife with generous amounts of beef.

"You men are all wrong," she announced, in a booming voice that silenced the chatter. "We women like it just once."

She paused, eyeing her audience, letting her point sink in. A few chuckles came from the line, which consisted mostly of men. One or two began to murmur in Setswana.

"And," she continued, silencing everyone once more. "We like it *long* and *slow*." She prolonged the last word, and her breasts shook as she laughed at her own unabashed precision. She turned to Mum and eyed her inquiringly.

All eyes followed.

"We do indeed," said Mum, grinning back at the cashier.

Laughter erupted in the queue. A few people yelled enthusiastic *MmaNgaka*s. Heat seeped across my face. I was embarrassed for Mum, mortified for me. Sex was fine—fascinating—in the abstract, between animals, or involving people you didn't know. Involving parents, it was unbearable.

The cashier winked at Mum, and resumed her till-prodding. A babble of Setswana filled the air again, and the queue ground on. *Long and slow*. Like so much in Botswana.

B efore, in New Zealand, Dad was just a doctor, doing a job, just as all my friends' parents—plumbers, lawyers, farmers—did their jobs.

Here, though, it was different. Much more. An identity that he carried around all the time—one that extended like an umbrella over the whole family. An invitation for strangers to give detailed medical histories; sometimes, a kind of passport to courtesy. With a sticker to prove it: on the windshield, next to the license disk and the green Wildlife Society badge, a round circle that said "Doctor's Car: Member of the South African Medical Association."

A year in Botswana, and the magical effect of the doctor had become as unremarkable as the numerous roadblocks and veterinary posts, where it was most frequently and dramatically displayed.

The roadblocks, often erected on the long, lonely roads between towns, were usually police checks for licenses or brake lights. The veterinary posts—booms across the road manned by veterinary officials in little wooden huts on the verge—were barriers to control the spread of foot-and-mouth disease, which broke out occasionally and threatened Botswana's valuable beef export industry. Stationed wherever the road crossed one of the long veterinary fences that patchworked the country, these checkpoints could result in painful delays: your shoes sterilized—in case you'd stood on cow poo—while officials combed the car for potentially disease-carrying meat and dairy before making you drive through a dip full of disinfectant, in case you'd driven over cow poo.

But even the most surly-looking official, strolling toward us, bearing down, would be disarmed by the sight of the sticker.

"*Dumela*, Doctor," he'd say, fixing his attention on the driver's window after a cursory glance inside.

"*Dumela*, Rra."

"*Le tsoga jang?*"

"*Re tsoga sentle.*"

Then, inevitably, something like:

"*Ee*, Doctor. I'm not well." The officer would look pained, lean on the windowsill. "I need some medicine for my kidneys."

"Hmm." Dad would nod and contort his face into a sympathetic frown. "You'd better come and see me at my clinic."

He might add the dates he visited whichever village happened to be nearest.

Usually, we'd be waved on without being searched for foot-and-mouth-carrying meat or a driver's license, or checked for whatever it was.

With only Mum in the car, the effect was not as immediate, but it still eased the brittle tension that so often hangs, palpable, over uniformed officials in Africa. And Mum would deftly steer the conversation toward the doctor.

Occasionally, Lulu, Damien, and I would be addressed too.

"Ah, I know your father."

Or, "How is Dr. Scott?"

And we would say, proudly, "Very well."

And then we would shut up and grin the roadblock-and-border-post lip-cracking grin, which we'd learned and perfected. The look that pleaded: *I have nothing to hide. You'd be wasting your time if you empty the back. Please let me through as soon as possible. If I have to, I'm prepared to give you a cool drink, the newspaper lying on the backseat...*

Grandpa Ivor needed no identifying sticker on his battered white *bakkie* to glide past officials. He wasn't just a *madala*—a respectful title given to all old men—he was The Madala, known by everyone and exempt from the usual rules.

On the rare occasions that being a *ngaka* didn't improve the atmosphere at roadblocks or government departments, Dad would say, "I'm The Madala's son." And then, at once, scowls would vanish, booms would be lifted, and forms would be stamped. When Dad's application for a work permit had been delayed, then mislaid, and finally lost, Grandpa had phoned the Speaker of Parliament. Days later, the forms had been found.

Grandpa had grown old in Botswana as Botswana had grown up, from what was, when he arrived more than two decades earlier, the inconsequential, undeveloped British Protectorate of Bechuanaland, to what had become, by the time we arrived, one of Africa's most prosperous, democratic nations.

After Bechuanaland became in 1966 independent Botswana, Grandpa became a Botswana citizen, one of the few whites in the country prepared to learn Setswana and give up their other passports. Somehow, Grandpa had got away with learning only a handful of Setswana expressions, which he augmented with a variety of swear words. But he had fully relinquished his South African citizenship.

Grandpa hadn't cared. He was a Motswana, here to stay—respected for his age, liked despite his temper, and forgiven things that seemed unforgivable: anger out of all proportion to the inconvenience, insults far beyond limits that could see non-citizens PI'ed from Botswana.

Being *PI'ed*—made a Prohibited Immigrant and deported from the country—is the punishment occasionally meted out to foreigners who commit crimes and, more rarely, to those who offend Batswana sensibilities with racist remarks or fierce political criticism. The controversial law, often seen to be at odds with Botswana's good democratic record, allows the president, at his discretion and without explanation, to expel noncitizens. Grandpa's wild, sometimes racist, frequently dispensed insults would have made him a prime candidate.

Of course Grandpa couldn't be PI'ed. But we weren't citizens, and could be. And sometimes, in the presence of one of his tirades—at shopkeepers, policemen, customs officials—I worried that this time Grandpa had gone too far, that one of us would have to be PI'ed instead of him.

"Will ya bloody well hurry up!" Wild arm gesticulations would always be used to emphasize his fury. "Do ya think I've got all fucking day to waste?...Could do a better bloody job myself...Useless! Lazy! Ineffective bunch! The whole bloody lot of you."

Then, suddenly, as sympathy for his unlucky victim had been obliterated by concern over one's own diminishing prospects of remaining in Botswana, Grandpa would exhaust his swear words, run out of new insults, and stop.

And the recipient, who had been listening silent and stony faced, would sigh, smile, and say something like, "*Ee*, Mr. Scott, I'm so saw-rry. And how is Mrs. Scott?"

"Betty's doing well, thank you." Grandpa would beam back at him. And then they'd have a relaxed exchange, before saying a warm "*Tsamaya sentle*," and "*Sala sentle*"—Go well, and Stay well—and parting like best friends.

5

SCHOOLS OF THOUGHT

The McCourts

Halfway along Kagiso Street, in the heart of Phikwe's greenest, quietest suburb, stood Granny Joan and Grandpa Terry's large, lawn-surrounded house. Like all the mine manager houses, theirs nestled behind thick hedges and tall trees, and from the road all that was visible was the garage and the maid's small room. Beside the latch on the gate hung a metal sign with the picture of a snarling saber-fanged dog, which was similar to the pictures on almost every other gate of every other house in the suburb, and accompanied by the same Setswana words: *Tshaba Ntswa!* "*Beware Dog!*"

Inside, the house smelled of flowers and floor polish, and the polished wooden furniture reflected your face back at you as you walked past. Tall white wall units gleamed with delicate crystal animals arranged on mirrors, large framed photos of Karen, Linda, and Alison—the three daughters, in order of age—grinning in their graduation gowns, and rows of mounted beautifully colored rocks from Granny and Grandpa's days on the Zambian Copperbelt.

There was not a trace of dust or dirt anywhere, not even on the ankle-deep fluffy white carpets in the lounge or on Granny's poodle, Muff, who bore an uncanny resemblance to the fluffy white carpets, and none whatsoever to the picture on the gate.

What lay behind that gate was for us, coming from the old, dirt-surrounded Selebi houses, an entirely different world to that which we were now accustomed. And however much we visited, as I walked through the lush secluded garden to the polished front door of the large, pristine house, I never failed to feel like a foreigner. And often, as Mum pressed the singsong doorbell and Lulu, Damien, and I carefully wiped our feet on the doormat, I thought of Dad, and of how foreign and nervous he must have felt all those years before, as he stood there for the first time, wiping his feet and wondering what awaited him.

It had been Dad's university holidays, and he was staying with Grandpa Ivor in Selebi. Visiting only once a year, Dad knew few people in Phikwe, and a week before the New Year's Eve dance, he was still without a date. When he learned that Terry McCourt had a pretty single daughter about his age who was also at Cape Town University, he headed at once to Kagiso Street.

The lanky young man who answered the doorbell was about the same age as Dad, which was a surprise for Dad, having been told that Terry McCourt had only daughters.

"I'm Keith Scott," he said. "I was hoping Karen might be in."

"She is," replied the man, extending his hand. "I'm Hennie, her fiancé. Come in."

Too taken aback to decline, Dad followed him inside. He was, of course, too late for Karen. But that evening he met Linda—six years younger than he; then only eighteen—and asked her to the dance instead.

It was 1975, and Mum was spending her second Christmas

holiday in Phikwe. She liked Dad immediately, most of all for his total dislike of convention—which was the thing about Dad that Granny Joan and Grandpa Terry immediately disapproved of most. From the start, they'd been vaguely alarmed by the blood relationship to the famously eccentric Ivor Scott, and Dad did little to allay their fears that he would only entrench their middle daughter's already firm inclination toward unorthodoxy.

At Mum and Dad's wedding three years later, a Catholic priest, who was one of the guests, remarked that theirs was the first wedding he'd ever attended where God hadn't got a mention. Granny Joan and Grandpa Terry were still blushing when Dad himself articulated all their worst fears about what their daughter might be letting herself in for.

"Getting married," said Dad solemnly, as he began his wedding speech, "is a bit like having your passport stamped when entering a foreign country. It neither guarantees that you will have a good time, nor that you will stay out of trouble."

A t least twice a week, when Granny Joan looked after us for the afternoon, I'd consider what life might have been like if Mum had been more like Granny Joan, and if she had chosen, instead of Dad, a husband from among the many conventional, sensible bachelors that Grandpa Terry had wanted for her.

It was not an altogether unattractive prospect.

The first few hours of our afternoon visits were spent playing in the big, bright blue, perfectly clean swimming pool. When we tired of this, Granny would check that we were properly dry and had clean feet before calling us inside for slices of cake or freshly baked chocolate éclairs. Sometimes, she'd measure us for new clothes to replace ours, which had mostly come from the Salvation Army shops in New Zealand, which Mum loved and Granny hated. Or she'd lay out half-finished pinned-together dresses and shirts, reels of different colored ribbons, and tubs of buttons, and ask us to choose which we preferred.

Finally, when Granny had disappeared back into the sewing

room, we'd collapse in full-bellied exhaustion on the fluffy white lounge carpets. Then began the best part of our visits: several blissful hours glued to the videos that Granny recorded for us because we didn't have a TV, which Mum thought ruined one's imagination.

Occasionally in Selebi we played rental videos on the tiny portable video machine that Dad had bought for his clinic to show educational videos, and then brought home when none of his patients bothered watching. But this had a screen that was barely bigger than our *Concise Oxford Dictionary*, and trying to follow the tiny figures was exhausting. Sometimes we also saw programs across the road at Grandpa Ivor's, but his ancient flickering television picked up only two grainy channels.

Watching TV on Granny Joan's large, clear screen was an incomparable experience. By the time Mum returned from her all-afternoon queue at the bank and Grandpa got back from work, we often had not moved, and would usually be engrossed by an ancient copy of *The Sound of Music*, which we watched again and again whenever we ran out of new videos.

At five thirty, Granny's lips now bright with the lipstick she reapplied at quarter past four before Grandpa got back from work, it was time for sundowners. On Grandpa's summons everyone would stop, immediately, whatever they were doing and drift toward the sitting room. Grandpa would then disappear behind the big wooden bar while the rest of us placed our orders from the flowery sofas, which you could sit on, legs flat against, instead of stretched uncomfortably forward in case of scorpions hiding underneath.

Grandpa was the personnel manager on the mine. This meant he knew about and was responsible for the jobs of many of Phikwe's working residents, as the mine, employing 5,000 in a town of 40,000, was by far the largest employer.

Grandpa Terry hardly ever raised his voice and rarely swore except for after a few whiskeys, when he'd sometimes say "Jesus Christ" with a sudden Irish lilt even though he'd grown up in England, and had never actually lived in Ireland. Then Granny

Joan would say, "Really, Terry! That's not for young ears," and Grandpa would reply, "You're absolutely right, dear." And then he'd clear his throat, turn to us, and say, "You didn't hear me say that."

"We already know all the swear words," I once pointed out. But Granny just gave an indulgent, disbelieving smile and said anyway it was no excuse for Grandpa Terry to swear. And before I could provide any examples from Grandpa Ivor's large repertoire, Mum interrupted with one of her lines for steering the conversation back to safe territory.

"Dad, how was work today?"

"Mum, how was your game of bridge yesterday?"

And, as a last resort, "You'll never guess who I bumped into at the bank..." Which Granny and Grandpa would usually guess after a few attempts, because the list of friends and acquaintances you might bump into in Phikwe wasn't that long.

Unsafe conversations were anything to do with Lulu, Damien, and me, which could lead to questions about what we were or weren't learning. Mum was adept at dodging the initial questions, but by the time Grandpa was sipping his third Famous Grouse whiskey and Granny her second brandy and ginger ale, they would have generally exhausted her avoidance tactics.

"So, Lin, how did the kids' lessons go this week?"

"Very well." Mum would smile brightly. She might add a vague comment about "interesting lessons" with "a lot of variety," or mention that something had been "particularly thought-provoking."

White lie number one. We didn't have lessons—at least not the sit-down-at-a-desk-and-work-in-a-book lessons that Granny and Grandpa meant. Mum said lessons could be anything that involved learning, but that there was no need to discuss semantics with Granny and Grandpa.

"What did you teach them in math?"

"How to calculate areas."

Exaggeration number one. "Areas," Mum later explained, referred to when we'd helped her work out how many tiles she needed to buy to cover the shower. "Geometry" was the occasion when Dad, who was studying for his pilot's license, showed us how to calculate angles with a protractor. "Multiplication and division," the most tenuous of all, could simply mean our last baking attempt, when Mum had insisted that we halve the sugar in the cake.

Mostly, as far as Lulu, Damien, and I were aware, we just played, and listened to Mum read to us, which, although she always pretended otherwise to Granny Joan and Grandpa Terry, was the only thing she did with any regularity, for any length of time. She read to us most days, and occasionally all day—from breakfast to dinner, stopping only for cups of *rooibos* tea, to tell Ruth what part of the house to clean, and for lunch, munched between paragraphs. The books were always books that also interested her: Joan Aiken, C. S. Lewis, Ursula K. Le Guin, Peter Dickenson, Lucy Boston, Rudyard Kipling, J. R. R. Tolkien. Books with vast, rich stories that swallowed you into their worlds. Books that left you, when the last page had been turned and the dust, flies, and mind-numbing heat resurfaced in your consciousness, pining for the characters like left-behind friends.

So during Granny and Grandpa's risky inquisitions, Damien and I kept our mouths full with fizzy drinks and salty chips, which were both forbidden at home, and hoped Granny and Grandpa wouldn't start asking us what we'd learned. And before long, though they never seemed entirely satisfied with Mum's answers, another round of drinks would be poured, and the conversation would drift back to Phikwe gossip, Botswana politics, or stories of the old days.

B ecause we were often not sure what we had actually learned, and because it generally bore no resemblance to what adults expected normal children our age to be learning in school, what it was could really only be stumbled upon by accident.

Like the time that Grandpa Ivor and I leaned side by side against the rickety kraal fence, gazing across the empty, weed-

and-desiccated-cow-poo-covered dirt, and speculated about the much-dreamed-of day when I would be looking at my own horse, standing in this kraal.

"Whaddaya going to call it, Robbie?" asked Grandpa.

"Dunno. I haven't decided."

"What about…" He paused dramatically and plucked at a strand of wire. "What about naming it after Alexander the Great's horse? Whaddaya think of that?"

"Nah," I sighed, still gazing dreamily across the weed-covered manure. "Bucephalus is a horrible name."

Grandpa swung around to face me with a piercing blue-eyed stare. "Whaddaya say?"

"I think Bucephalus is horrible, Grandpa."

"How old are ya again?"

"I'm nearly eight," I said, impatiently.

Grandpa shook his head, his expression incredulous. "Well, I'll be damned," he bellowed, clutching and shaking a spindly fence post. "Bloody amazing. Amazing. Marvelous. What else d'ya know about Alexander the Great?"

I told him everything I could remember, which took a few minutes as Mum had recently spent several days doing nothing but reading to us from the huge book on Greek history. And Alexander's story, as exciting as they came, was unforgettable. Astride his gallant horse, Alexander had not only conquered vast civilizations, he was also told, and believed, he was part god—a son of Zeus who, in the form of a snake, had seduced his mother, Olympias, taking advantage of her intriguing desire to sleep with snakes in her bed.

"I'm blown away," said Grandpa, squeezing my shoulder as I concluded my account. "Ya make your old grandpa feel like a bloody ignoramus."

Flukes such as this formed a key component of the arsenal Mum used to defend homeschooling. She collected these stories, generally exaggerated them, and, as soon as possible, relayed them to Granny Joan and Grandpa Terry. On this occasion, however, Grandpa Ivor—on counts of both speed and hyperbole—beat her to it. By the time we next visited the Phikwe grandparents, Grandpa Terry had already heard all about Bucephalus over whiskeys in the golf-club bar, where Grandpa Ivor had been loudly waxing lyrical about his grandchildren's unbelievable mastery of Greek history and mythology.

A shared love of golf and whiskey was the first of just three things that Grandpa Ivor and Grandpa Terry had in common. Even in this respect, they were opposites. Grandpa Ivor was a sporadic drinker—nothing, or so much he could barely stand up—and a sporadic golfer—mostly pretty average, with occasional bouts of genius. Grandpa Terry drank consistently— never nothing, never so much that he'd had to spend the night sobering up under the trees outside—and played consistently good golf, attested to by numerous trophies and a framed "hole-in-one" certificate from a Johnnie Walker Whiskey tournament, which hung on the door of the second loo.

"It's there as a joke," said Grandpa Terry, when I asked why he didn't hang it beside the trophies.

In the draw for the weekly four-ball, Grandpa Terry, like all the other golfers, dreaded finding himself in Grandpa Ivor's group.

Grandpa Ivor was always late, his game utterly unpredict-able. The only thing less reliable was his temper, which could, depending on his mood, be directed at one of his fellow golfers, all of them, his Motswana caddie, golf balls, golf clubs, thorn-bushes, the angle of the sun, or the uneven greens, which were "browns" on the dry Phikwe golf course. A passion for the game was Grandpa Ivor's only concession to the norms of golf.

But off the course, after sunset, sitting beside the golf club bar, the two grandpas often chatted. Both great raconteurs, they enjoyed each other's stories, and no one, whatever they thought of Grandpa Ivor, could fail to find him interesting. The two men also shared nearly two decades of history intertwined with Selebi-Phikwe and its mine, BCL—Bamangwato Concessions Limited, named after Botswana's largest tribe, which owned the land around the town.

. . .

In 1967, a year after independence and the year underground exploration in Selebi began, Grandpa Ivor had moved to nearby Francistown. He was by now married to Granny Betty, a nurse, whom he had met flying a medical emergency to Rand Airport in Johannesburg and who had bravely joined him in his rudimentary bush trailer camp near the Okavango Delta before the move to Francistown.

Business in Francistown was good, and Grandpa's Okavango Air Services was thriving. With Phikwe still to be built, and many of its executives based in Francistown, BCL frequently called upon Grandpa Ivor's services. The mine soon became one of his most important clients, and in 1972, as BCL shifted its employees to Phikwe, Grandpa Ivor and Granny Betty moved too, settling in one of the geologists' houses in Selebi, a convenient drive from the airport.

In 1974, a year after the mine became operational, Grandpa Terry and Granny Joan moved to Phikwe from Zambia, where they'd lived since leaving England in their early twenties.

Employed first as a prosecutor in what was then the Northern Rhodesian police force, Grandpa Terry had later worked on the copper mines, based in the small town of Kalulushi, where all three daughters had been born. In 1964, after Northern Rhodesia became independent Zambia, Grandpa Terry became closely involved in localization programs aimed at bringing Zambians into the skilled workforce. And ten years later, for this experience in particular, he was offered the position of personnel manager at Botswana's new mine in Selebi-Phikwe.

At the time, the highly skilled mine employees were almost all expatriates. But all were on renewable two-year contracts. The intention was always to gradually replace the "expats" with citizens, and Grandpa Terry's responsibilities included producing regular localization updates. BCL also sponsored large numbers of Botswana citizens overseas through business and engineering degrees.

While succeeding in this respect, the mine failed dismally in its main objective. Between the discovery of the deposits and the five-year process of sinking the shafts and building the town and smelter, the price of nickel and copper had fallen steeply, and the mine, from the day it started production, ran at a loss.

Meanwhile, vast, quickly accessible diamond deposits had been discovered several hundred kilometers to the northwest. Selebi-Phikwe was already the poor relation to the small town of Orapa, where the first diamond mine opened in 1971. Ten years later, when the BCL mine was still failing to repay its investors, it would be further overshadowed. In 1982 the world's richest diamond mine—supposedly discovered when termites, seeking water for their mounds, brought to the surface rock fragments associated with diamonds—opened a few hundred kilometers to the southwest in Jwaneng.

But diamond towns were "closed towns." If those who were not mine employees wanted to visit, special permission was required, so they could be checked and traced if they made off with any diamonds. Even children needed permission. The few shops were mine shops, the residents all mine employees. Diamond towns did little to encourage the development of small independent businesses and industries, which Botswana badly needed.

So the Botswana government, a major shareholder in BCL, insisted that the unprofitable mine be kept afloat. A small industrial area grew outside Phikwe, and nearer the residential areas, a range of shops opened, among them Granny Betty's tiny, grandly named boutique, the Fashion Scene. Over the years, Grandpa Ivor also started a series of businesses. But flying was his only successful and lasting venture, and it was in the air that most people in Phikwe came to know and marvel at Ivor Scott.

On one of their first encounters, Grandpa Ivor was scheduled to collect Grandpa Terry from the small southern town of Lobatse. Grandpa Ivor had spent the morning across the border in Johannesburg, while Grandpa Terry delivered BCL papers to the Lobatse High Court. Later in the afternoon, Grandpa Terry was dropped off at the Lobatse International Airport—a deserted tar strip with a single, empty watchman's hut at the end of the runway.

An hour after the scheduled pickup time, there was still no sign of Grandpa Ivor's airplane. To pass the time, Grandpa Terry inspected the small hut. Inside was a telephone, with a number to call if you landed at Lobatse International from outside Botswana. The number was for customs and immigration, which would send its officers out to the quiet airport on an as-needed basis.

The sun neared the horizon. Grandpa Terry began to consider walking back into town. Grandpa Ivor, he reasoned, must have somehow got stuck in Johannesburg.

Grandpa Ivor had got stuck in Johannesburg—literally, after ignoring instructions from air traffic control and taxiing into a ditch at the airport. By the time the plane had been towed out of the ditch, Grandpa Ivor was running several hours late.

About to set off back to Lobatse, Grandpa Terry heard the buzz of the plane. A few minutes later Grandpa Ivor touched down. Remaining in the plane, with the engine running, he beckoned wildly to Grandpa Terry, who stood beside the hut.

Grandpa Terry pointed toward the hut and mimed making a phone call.

Grandpa Ivor shook his head. "No time," yelled Grandpa Ivor, as Grandpa Terry reluctantly clambered into the plane. "It's getting dark. They'll take too bloody long. Hurry up, Terry. Haven't got all bloody day. You wanna get home, don't you?"

Back in the air, Grandpa Ivor radioed air traffic control in the nearby capital of Gaborone. He announced he would clear customs and immigration in Selebi, and provided "current" coordinates far north of their location. They touched down in Selebi just as the last of the light disappeared. "Whaddid I tell you?" said Grandpa Ivor. "If we'd waited for those buggers in Lobatse, we'd have been too late to land."

But Grandpa Ivor, as Grandpa Terry later discovered, had been more motivated by the desire to avoid inconvenience than an after-dark landing. This time Grandpa Terry was part of a group of mine executives attending an afternoon meeting in Johannesburg. The meeting ran late, and the plane took off not long before sunset. An hour and a half later, when they began to circle above the black bush around the Selebi runway, the darkness was absolute.

"What's happening, Ivor?" asked one of the passengers.

"Just looking for the runway," replied Grandpa.

After a worried debate in the back of the plane, someone ventured that Ivor should perhaps fly north across the border to Bulawayo, where there was a beacon and flare path to guide him in. Selebi had no flare path, and its beacon was, as usual, out of order.

"Nonsense," yelled Grandpa. "It's down here somewhere. Give me a minute."

True to his word, after a minute, the plane started to sink into the darkness.

Grandpa Terry said nothing. By now he knew that where something interfered with Grandpa Ivor's plans, he was as much unmoved by the discomfort of others as he was by the law. Like with cigarettes, which he used to chain-smoke, delighted when passengers joined in, ignoring those who objected. "Luckily I gave up the same time as Ivor," Grandpa Terry would chuckle. The day Grandpa Ivor stopped smoking, he hung a large No Smoking sign in the back of his plane and thereafter admonished anyone who tried to light up about the dangers of smoking in an airplane.

But not all Grandpa Ivor's passengers knew him so well. Shakily undoing his seat belt, one of the men stood up and clambered toward the front.

"Please, Ivor. For God's sake. Go to Bulawayo."

"Sit down," ordered Grandpa. "You're a danger to us all."

A few minutes later, the plane touched down on the runway in what the then terrified passengers would afterward say was one of the smoothest landings they had ever experienced. When Grandpa Terry asked how he'd done it, Grandpa Ivor explained that the regulars drinking at the runway club had heard him circling. Grandpa was often late, and everyone knew the drill. Someone had immediately driven his *bakkie* to face the runway, and Grandpa Ivor had used the two bright spots of the headlights to guide him in.

. . .

We, the grandchildren, were Grandpa Ivor and Grandpa Terry's final common interest. But beyond a shared desire for our happiness, about us, as about most things, they felt very differently.

On child raising, Grandpa Ivor had as much regard for protocol and the opinions of others as he did as a pilot. University was the only thing he cared about, having always regretted not going himself when he left the air force after the war.

Grandpa Ivor never questioned that Mum—who wasn't a teacher and thought a syllabus stifled creativity—was just as capable of getting us to university as anyone else.

Grandpa Terry did.

"Blossom. Damien's nearly seven. And he can hardly read. Doesn't that concern you? Even a little?"

"He'll read when he's ready, Dad. I'm not going to force him."

"*You* don't have to, Linny." Grandpa was entreating. "Send them to Kopano—it's a very good school. They have people trained to do these things."

"He shouldn't be forced. By anyone. That's my point."

"What if you're wrong?"

"Trained teachers sometimes get it wrong. Look at all the kids who start school already speaking several languages. You learned French for years at school. Can you speak it?"

Grandpa began to say something, but Mum continued hotly. "Children often learn best in unstructured situations, when they don't know they're learning. Especially if they're having fun. So, please, just give me a chance."

"We want to, Lin, of course—and we will—we're only naturally concerned."

Mum gave a happy defiant smile. "Well, don't be."

And then Granny noticed that Lulu, Damien, and I were watching curiously. She frowned at Grandpa. "Glasses are empty, Terry."

"Sorry, dear. How remiss of me." Grandpa sighed and got to

his feet. "The same again?" he asked unnecessarily, as he headed to the bar. "A dash stronger, perhaps? I certainly need a stiff one."

And once again the sun set on Kagiso Street to clinking ice cubes, resigned laughter, and muted discontent.

Before the doubtful faces of those evenings, I'd never questioned Mum's explanation of homeschooling. She'd deliver it passionately and romantically; as a story, which had always made me feel lucky to be part of something rooted in that intriguing time when your parents were together, before you.

"You know," she'd begin, "my last year at university was an epiphany."

That was the year that she had met David Jenkins, a pioneering researcher into the health benefits of dietary fiber. Eyes sparkling, Mum would tell us how she'd been swept along by his passion for his work; how, for the first time, grades became secondary to knowledge. "He revolutionized my outlook on health, and on education," she would sigh dramatically. "I only realized then that I'd spent most of my education half asleep—learning how to pass exams well, and very little else."

Sparked in university, Mum's fascination with the role of nutrition in health and disease never waned. Nor did she ever forget her awe at the pleasure of becoming really interested in something. "And that transformative year lives on still"—Mum would smile—"in my whole-wheat bread and homeschooling."

How come they're always so upset about it?" I asked, as the car crunched across the gravel and swung out into the dark, quiet road.

"Well, I suppose they're a bit hurt," said Mum. "They made sure I got the best education on offer. And now they think I'm saying, 'Thanks very much, but I have a better way.' "

"But you are."

"Well, I suppose I am, in a way. But I'm really very grateful. Look what I learned in the end," she said, her voice becoming grave. "That if you love what you are doing, the joy of learning stays alive. I want to pass that on to my children." She paused, dreamily. Then she said, "And I suppose they're also a bit worried you'll get left behind."

"Will we?"

"'Course not."

"Sure?"

"Sure, Robbie."

Granny and Grandpa were also worried about the side effects of homeschooling. "What about socializing with other kids, Linny? Are they going to fit in later on?" To which Mum would retort that we played very well with each other, and went to ballet and tennis lessons with other children. "Anyway, I don't want to have this discussion anymore. Stop worrying. They're making lots of nice friends their own age."

So it was sheepishly that Mum told Granny Joan the guest list of Lulu's fifth birthday party: Grandpa Ivor, Granny Betty, Grandpa Terry, Granny Joan, Mum, Dad, Robbie, Damien, Maria (Dad's nurse), Somebody (Dad's other new nurse—"because I don't employ just anybody"), Beauty (Dad's Phikwe clinic cleaner), Matthews, Ruth, Moretsana (Ruth's teenage daughter), and Georgina (Ruth's ancient mother, who was Granny Betty's maid and hardly spoke English).

"No little girls?" asked Granny, weakly. "No one from ballet?"

"That's who Lulu's asked for," said Mum.

"Oh, Lordy," said Granny.

But whatever she thought, Granny Joan was, above all else—and was determined to always be—the perfect grandmother. Alarmed by the guest list or not, she would never spoil a birthday. On the day of Lulu's party she drove out to Selebi bearing the biggest, most beautifully decorated cake any of us had ever seen: a perfect swimming pool, with white chocolate sticks for the fence, thick blue jelly in the middle as the water, and little jelly babies floating on top.

Lulu gaped in delight as Granny set down her masterpiece on the dining room table. "Just in case you didn't have one," said Granny, giving Lulu a hug and a kiss, and casting a suspicious eye over the bowls of nuts, the honeyed popcorn balls, the homemade peanut brittle, the fresh fruit kebabs, and the plates of whole-wheat sandwiches. Her gaze settled on the bizarre creation that stood at the center of the table—the cake that Lulu had made that morning under Mum's supervision.

Mum's supervision had, as always, been minimal—her main contribution being to encourage any creative suggestions about altering the recipe. The cake was, as a result, burned at the top and edges, soggy in the middle, and had collapsed to less than an inch thick on one side. The icing was bright pink, made with beet juice instead of artificial coloring. Most of the loose toppings had rolled off the sloping surface, and by the time it had been carried through to the dining room table, only a few chocolate-coated raisins and marshmallows were left. To compensate, Lulu had inserted a bright stem of pink bougainvillea into the center of the cake and sprinkled a few curly seedpods around the edges.

"That's mine," said Lulu, smiling proudly. "But yours is better."

"Yours is more interesting, darling," said Granny Joan.

With Lulu cooing happily, Granny, looking suddenly worried, turned to Mum. "What time will the guests be arriving?" she asked anxiously, readjusting a displaced jelly baby.

Both grandfathers were playing golf and would come later, but Granny Betty soon hobbled across the road and settled herself beside Granny Joan on one of the bumpy wire chairs beneath the big knob-thorn tree. Then came Matthews, wearing a freshly ironed shirt and tie. He greeted the two grandmothers with a nervous *"Dumela"* and then perched awkwardly on a tree stump a little way back from the circle of chairs, where he silently studied and sipped his glass of Coke, which was allowed for birthdays.

"Isn't it hot?" said Mum, hovering between the three quiet, uncomfortable-looking guests. And then, as several long strands of grass drifted down from the birdsong-filled branches, "Aren't those buffalo weavers messy nest builders.... Offer the food around again, Robbie.... Damien, please get Granny Betty a cushion, and while you're up—"

A sharp cackle of laughter rang across the weaver cheeps and stilted conversation. Everyone turned to stare at the driveway, where Ruth, Moretsana, and Georgina, all in high heels, tottered toward us across the dusty red dirt.

"Good gracious," said Granny Betty.

"I think I'm underdressed," said Granny Joan. "And, Lin, is that your shirt?"

Mum grinned. "Decided it was a bit too extravagant for me."

Mum's gold-buttoned shiny cream shirt was the least extravagant part of Ruth's outfit. The shirt was tucked into a pink pleated polyester skirt, and her shoes were gold, matching the shirt buttons, huge gold-plated earrings, and a chunky gold-plated necklace. Her short, thick black hair was slicked backward and upward with gel, and her nails and lips both painted bright red. Moretsana was a smaller, equally bright, replica of her mother. Georgina was less shiny than the two younger women, but no less dressed up, with a thick multicolored cloth wound around her head, an orange-and-white African patterned dress, and similarly chunky jewelry.

Mum leaped up to pour more drinks, and just as the three smiling ladies had sat down with full glasses of Coke and Fanta, Dad's car clinked over the cattle grid. A minute later, doubling the bright polyester, strong floral perfume, and now animated chatter, Maria, Somebody, and Beauty clambered out and joined the party, waving and crying greetings in Setswana and English. Lulu ran from one to the other, hugging everyone excitedly and introducing them to Granny Joan and Granny Betty, who, despite looking a little overwhelmed, smiled, shook hands, and said, "Dumela."

"Happy Birthday" was disastrous. Half the party did not know the song at all. Appalled, Lulu insisted that they must learn at once, and after a number of botched renditions and much hysterical laughter and thigh slapping, everyone got the hang of the words, Lulu blew out her candles, and we all sat down with big slices of swimming pool—except for Mum and the two grandmothers, who valiantly nibbled chunks of Lulu's burned pink bougainvillea cake.

Finishing her slice as quickly as possible, Lulu jumped up

and announced that now everyone must come and swim with her. Mum said, "I know it's your birthday, but don't you think you're being a little demanding?"

Granny Joan said, "You'll get cramp if you swim on a full stomach."

But Lulu ignored both, grabbed Maria and Beauty by the hand, and led the giggling, feebly protesting pair to the back of the house. Damien and I dashed after them, stripping off to our swimming costumes and racing each other to the tall marula tree, from which Dad had suspended a cable for the zip-line that ran across the big blue plastic pool.

By the time we had each plunged in a few times, the rest of the party had assembled under the trees beside the pool and joined Beauty and Maria in cheering us on.

Shaking their heads at Lulu's entreaties to try out the slide, Ruth, Moretsana, Maria, Somebody, and Beauty nevertheless eventually agreed to get into the water. Matthews, who'd had too many bad experiences when we'd tried to teach him to swim, lurked stubbornly just out of splashing distance. Granny Joan, Granny Betty, and Georgina installed themselves on chairs by the pool. The rest of the women traipsed after Mum into the house, emerging in a bizarre assortment of Mum's swimming costumes, mismatching T-shirts and baggy shorts.

With Lulu, Damien, and I now cheering them on, the ladies gamely clambered one after the other into the waist-deep water. Clutching onto each other and the three of us as their feet hit the algae-slippery bottom, they waded, giggling and shrieking, into the middle, T-shirts and shorts billowing. The splashing intensified, and the laughter soon became hysterical. Egged on by us, they then tried dunking themselves. Each time they resurfaced, they laughed harder than before, shaking their heads furiously to get the water out of their ears.

Suddenly, at the center of the tight group, Maria disappeared beneath the surface.

She did not come up again. Someone yelled. Damien and I tugged at Maria's huge bulk. Nothing happened. We shrieked for Mum.

Mum, barefoot but still in her flowery dress, had been watching. She was already climbing up the ladder into the pool. She dived in, a submerged bullet of soaked cotton heading toward the panicking group. After a few seconds of what looked like underwater wrestling, she shot to the surface, clutching a spluttering Maria. Maria was too stunned to talk, but nodded that she was okay. Slowly, helped by Mum and watched from the side by a wide-eyed Granny Joan, Granny Betty, and Georgina, and a smugly grinning Matthews, the bedraggled guests made their way to dry land.

Mum said, "Never mind, we'll have a nice cup of tea and everything will be fine."

Towels were handed out, and as everyone reappeared in their own clothes, Mum poured cups of strong, milky tea, making no protests at the usual Motswana request for three spoons of sugar. Before long we were all eating more cake outside under the knob-thorn tree. And despite the fact that all the bathers admitted to being unable to swim, the four women who had not nearly drowned laughed mercilessly at Maria and called her a terrible swimmer. Which perturbed Maria not at all. She just laughed too and said Lulu must now teach her to swim properly.

Later Mum said she wasn't sure if it was Granny Joan or Maria who had had the more shocking experience that day.

Both took a while to get over it, bringing up the subjects of the birthday guests and the birthday swim, respectively, for months afterward. The other women also enjoyed reminiscing, and the events of that day were replayed many times by all.

All, that is, except for Beauty, who, to Lulu's dismay, Dad fired not long afterward.

Dad had asked her to sweep outside the Phikwe clinic. Beauty refused, declaring she was an inside cleaner, that she would lose face if she cleaned outside. Dad said he wasn't prepared to hire a different cleaner to work outdoors, and if that was how Beauty felt, she would have to leave.

Indignant, Beauty left.

Some weeks later Dad put an advert in the local paper for an administrative assistant. To Dad's astonishment, among the candidates who arrived at the interview was Beauty, cheerful and smiling as if nothing had ever happened.

After exchanging a few pleasantries about family, Dad expressed amazement that she had the cheek to come again to him, of all people, hoping to get a job for which she was not even qualified.

"*Ga ke itse,*" said Beauty, grinning.

Dad said he was afraid he couldn't possibly consider her for the job.

Beauty shrugged and got up to leave.

Dad said, "What are you going to do?"

Beauty said, "I think I'm going to study to become a doctor."

When Grandpa Terry heard the story over sundowners, he chuckled knowingly. This, he said, was something he dealt with all the time. He was forever getting junior Batswana employees coming to the personnel department and demanding a promotion on the grounds that they could do the job of their boss—who, in most cases, they complained, just sat behind a desk, spoke on the phone, clicked ballpoint pens, and shuffled papers.

Dad said Beauty must have watched him using his stethoscope and giving injections and tablets and understandably thought she could do that too.

Grandpa smiled and said, in his gravest I-have-been-in-Africa-for-a-long-time-and-seen-a-lot-of-things voice, that of course, even if you weren't properly trained, aspiration and self-confidence were always the most important starting points.

Everyone chuckled again. Then Mum grinned wickedly.

"Well, then, Dad," she said, "if I turn out to be a hopeless teacher, rest assured you'll at least have confident little Batswana grandchildren who *think* they can do anything."

6

SCHOOL

Lulu and Chamaeleo

The reason we did, unexpectedly, go to school had much more to do with what we might do to Mum than the other way around.

Mum's health had been a problem for almost as long as I could remember. But her "bad days," the days she stayed in bed and read to us while we brought her cups of tea, had become a normal part of life. Her reassurances of "I'll be fine tomorrow" had always satisfied us. She'd always been fine, or her pain had been mild enough for her to function normally.

The news that she could not cope anymore came as a shock.

Her problem, though always present, had never been our

problem. I felt briefly indignant, and then guilty. Then doubly guilty when I saw how guilty Mum felt, about being the reason we went to school.

"I'll hate school," I announced, truthfully. Then, hoping to reassure Mum that it was only because I shared her philosophy of education, I added, "My joy of learning will be extinguished."

"For God's sake, Robbie," said Mum. "Don't always take everyone so literally."

Damien said, "Well, I'll love school."

Lulu said, "I want to go too."

"You're still too young," said Mum. "Thank God."

Lulu had then just turned five. Nearly four years before, a year after Lulu's birth, Mum had had her tubes tied. "Having three kids is exhausting enough," Mum had explained to me, as she'd packed for the hospital. I'd felt abandoned, and irritated. "If you didn't want three kids," I'd said crossly, "why did you mate with Dad three times then?" At which, even Mum's resilient frankness had briefly deserted her.

The operation had left her with chronic pain, and several months later she was diagnosed with a condition that caused her to produce excessive amounts of internal scar tissue. The surgeon operated again to remove this, and to try and prevent new scar tissue developing. Instead it grew back, much worse than before.

In the years that followed, Mum tried endless alternative treatments. Among the most interesting was a bio magnet, the size of a pack of cards, which Dad brought home from work one evening. "Magnetic healing," explained Mum. "To help align my poles," she added, laughing. While Dad demonstrated how magnets worked, conventionally, and Damien and I magnetized paper clips, Mum sewed a pocket into the front of a pair of knickers. She put them on, inserted the magnet, and set off across the bedroom. After a few paces, the sagging knickers slid to her knees. Mum eventually solved the problem by stitching pockets onto the front of several pairs of Dad's strongly elasticized underpants.

Mum thought the magnet might be helping, but she couldn't be sure. She eventually gave the underpants back to Dad, mainly because of the practical difficulties of having a concealed heavy-duty magnet just above her crotch. She had regularly got stuck to the stove, and on one memorable supermarket trip, with a loud thud, to a shopping cart.

Other approaches had "sort of worked." But nothing had really worked, and the pain continued to worsen in Botswana. Increasingly, Mum's ability to cope with us was what worried Granny and Grandpa most about homeschooling. When Mum reluctantly decided to have a further operation, she finally agreed that Damien and I would be better off, at least for a while, at school.

Kopano was the Phikwe mine primary school: free to all the mine children who could pass an English test—which meant mostly the white children—and open to fee-paying students, who, because of the cost and the English requirements, were mostly white or Indian too. Most black children went to the government schools that were found farther out of town or in the villages—clusters of long brown and white buildings with colorful zigzag patterns painted on the walls, dusty soccer fields, and children who walked to school carrying holey satchels and wearing outgrown, faded uniforms.

Approached through a shady, raked gravel car park, Kopano's neat white and green buildings stood in the middle of residential Phikwe. The dark green of the buildings matched the itchy green-and-white-checked dress I had to wear. Damien wore khaki shorts and a white shirt. Both of us wore floppy khaki hats, which on our first day still smelled of starch from the uniform shop.

I held up my hat to make me taller as I waved good-bye to Dad. I kept waving until my arm ached, till long after Dad's car had disappeared as he sped off round the corner to his clinic. By the time I turned around, I was alone. Damien had vanished among the many small khaki-, white-, and green-clad figures streaming into the buildings. I envied Damien being so delighted about going to school; and I envied Lulu for being young enough to escape.

I felt numb as my polished black shoes crunched slowly and automatically across gravel. What the long white buildings and concrete corridors before me held, I had no idea. I assumed the worst. All Mum's arguments for not sending us to school— wildly exaggerated by uncertainty—swirled perniciously around in my head.

By the time I reached the foreboding door labeled Class 4, I was certain I would, in a matter of days, lose my creativity, have my intellectual curiosity stifled, measure all achievement relative to others, and conform to the narrow expectations of the inflexible, antiquated southern African school system. I would, of course, also be landed with a teacher who would take a personal dislike to me. By the end of the year I would be crushed—a mere shadow of my former eight-year-old self, a hopeless casualty of the school system.

I loved school. A month of bells, assemblies, and weekly tests, and I had changed my mind altogether. I liked my teacher, I liked my classmates—some already friends from ballet and tennis lessons—and I loved the fact that I could get gold stars and colorful "Well Done" stamps if I did my work better than most of the rest of the class. When I won the Class 4 student of the week award, handed out by Mr. French, the headmaster, in front of the whole school, I was delirious with pride.

A few weeks later, I was delirious with fever.

In the run-up to the yearly school spelling marathon, I had been up studying every night, coercing whoever was willing into testing me on the hundreds of words that I stared at until they blurred into black squiggles. A week before the test, I developed acute tonsillitis and lay tossing and turning in bed, furious to be missing important revision time.

Mum, who was starting to feel much better after her operation, sat beside me for hours, stroking my forehead, giving me regular doses of homeopathic belladonna, and mumuring soothing things about there being more important things in life than spelling tests.

No longer, as far as I was concerned. When I failed to receive one of the top three scores in the class, I was devastated. But most of all I was spurred on to do better next time. I would never, I resolved, put another foot wrong. I now had a lot to live up to. I was, after all, granddaughter of Terry McCourt—senior member of the Kopano School Board, friends with Mr. French, and multiple winner of the annual Brain of Phikwe Competition.

"Between the two of you," said Mum, "I despair."

I couldn't be stopped from working, and caring; Damien couldn't be started.

Damien said, "I hate school."

He'd changed his mind as quickly as I had. His lessons, he said, were boring; his teacher was also boring. The only thing he really enjoyed was soccer, and playing marbles in the dusty yard at break time. He refused to study for tests, which he said were stupid. Granny Joan and Grandpa Terry said Damien should follow the example of his sister, who had been making such a good impression on everyone. Damien said, "I hate school."

Grandpa Terry said, "Well, that's not a very good attitude to have."

Damien said sulkily, "But all we do is copy things off the blackboard."

Damien's teacher asked to see Mum. She told her that a few days before, she had been showing the class which shapes could make other shapes. When she explained that straight lines couldn't make circles, Damien, who had not breathed a constructive word for days, interrupted. "You're wrong," he said. "Millions of very, very tiny lines could link to form what we see as a circle."

His teacher said to Mum, "I was amazed by his insight and logic, and am left wondering why he can't apply it more constructively."

"*Wondering*," said Mum indignantly afterward. "I ask you!"

As to why Damien was not constructively applying his logic, Mum could have talked for hours. But there was one problem that, to her, was emblematic of everything else.

Coloring-in.

Which was, for Mum, the nadir of education. Homework was pretty low down too. And when we got coloring-in for homework, Mum was furious.

"Can't they think of anything more creative to give you?" she said, seizing my worksheet from the dining room table. "Can't they trust you to draw your own pictures?"

"Give it back, Mum."

"Okay. Okay." Mum had gone pink. "But I'm not having you get stressed and sick again over bloody coloring-in."

"I won't."

"Don't waste any time on it."

"Promise."

But an hour later I was still coloring, redoing the bad bits, determined to do the best coloring-in in the class.

On the last day of our first term, Mum was waiting for us in the car park. Her cheeks were red, her eyes glistening fiercely. She looked shaky but pleased.

"I've just been to see Mr. French."

"Why?" There was a sinking feeling in my stomach. Parents were usually called to the headmaster only in cases of extremely bad behavior. A terrible, shameful thought occurred to me. "Is Damien going to be expelled?"

"No," said Mum, grinning. "But he probably would have been if I'd left him here any longer."

"What?"

"I went to tell Mr. French that you weren't coming back."

"Now? Already?"

Mum had discussed the possibility of homeschooling us again: at some stage, when she was better. I'd blithely said yes, absorbed in the present, and stupidly—despite all past evidence to the contrary—assuming the decision would take months of planning, consultation, and discussion.

"Why wait?" said Mum. "You said you didn't mind. And by

the way, I've invited Matthews to join our lessons. So there'll be four of you now."

"Cool," said Damien, grinning blissfully.

"What did Mr. French say?" I asked, alarmed by Mum's defiant look.

"He wasn't pleased. I told him I thought Kopano was a good school and that I just wanted to try a different approach. But he's taken it all a bit personally."

"Oh."

"Never mind. He'll get over it."

"What about Granny and Grandpa?"

"They'll get over it too. It'll be a bit embarrassing for Grandpa, I imagine, being on the board of a school rejected by his own daughter. But it'll all blow over soon enough."

"Well, I might miss school."

"You'll still get to see all your new friends on weekends."

"I might miss my teacher."

"Well, if you do," said Mum brightly, "you can always go back."

"What if they won't take me back then?"

"Oh, for goodness sake, Robbie. Stop worrying. Life's too short to worry. It'll be fine. Trust me."

Mum was right. It was fine—as Mum and Dad's big decisions always were.

Now, as always, the past and its possibilities were soon banished by the excitement of what lay ahead: the temptation to dwell and regret no match for the love of change that Mum and Dad both lived and breathed so infectiously into the family.

Occasionally, to begin with, I did miss my teacher, the comforting routine, the prospect of gold stars. But as Mum had promised, I still often saw my school friends—who proved to be Kopano's only attraction that wasn't quickly forgettable as we reimmersed ourselves in the adventures, and discoveries, and all-consuming books of Mum's own, unique, and unpredictable version of school.

Where everyone else was concerned, though, Mum was wrong.

It wasn't fine, and it did not blow over. Mr. French was furious. Despite entreaties from one of his own teachers, he flatly refused to let us continue any of the afternoon sports, or join in the school play. "It's all or nothing," he informed Mum icily.

Mum said, "If that's his attitude, it just reinforces my decision."

Grandpa Terry was devastated, most of all because Damien, who had been doing well at soccer, would not be following in his footsteps of almost being a soccer star.

Misty-eyed, Grandpa would often tell us how as a young man, before he had left England, he'd played in trials for the West Bromwich Albion team. "Which was quite something in those days," he would say proudly. Later he'd played for the then Northern Rhodesian team. "But I was just too old by then to really make it big."

His hopes of a soccer-mad son dashed, when Damien was born a generation late, Grandpa had been delighted.

Now he said, "Damien, won't you miss soccer at Kopano?"

Damien said, "Maybe a bit."

Grandpa said, "You've got real talent. Perhaps if you stayed at school and played more soccer, you'd start to like it more."

"No," said Damien. "Anyway, I want to be a ninja, not a soccer player." Whirling his silver nunchaku stars, he stared defiantly at Grandpa through the slits in his ninja hood. Then he jumped up, dashed outside, and scrambled up a jacaranda tree on Granny's beautifully manicured lawn.

Now that we had left school, Damien removed his ninja suit only to go to bed. It was frayed, and the black had faded to gray from all the washes. Mum said she saw no reason why Damien shouldn't wear a ninja suit as much as he liked, and that it was an important outlet for his potentially disruptive energy. The outlet had most recently involved Damien vanishing during a shopping visit to the Phikwe mall. We found him, in a tree on a crowded pavement, thronged by a wildly cheering audience. He was hanging from a branch with one hand, spinning a nunchaku in the

other, and kicking at imaginary foes. Most of the onlookers were
Batswana, and Damien, an instinctive crowd pleaser, was yelling
in his thickest Setswana accent, which, ever since he had tried
it out on Ruth—who complimented him on his Setswana—he'd
believed was as good as the language itself.

Now, swinging from the tree on the lawn, thrilled by his
recent enthusiastic reception in the mall, Damien practiced
his kicks and his accent. *"Eh-he,"* he bellowed, "I am a ninja.
Dumela."

"I give up," Grandpa sighed. "I know when I'm defeated."

"Well, I don't," said Granny, fiercely. "If my only grandson
is going to be a homeschooled ninja with an African accent, he
must at least look respectable." And with that she strode out to
the jacaranda, ordered Damien down, and marched him off to
her sewing room to measure him up for a new ninja suit.

7

SUNBEAMS AND CHAMELEONS

The Sunbeams rowing team

So, suddenly, school was all over: the tests, the bells, the timetables. The coloring-in. Mum gave the uniforms away. Non-Kopano afternoon activities became, once more, major social events, and most afternoons, Mum would drive us into Phikwe for tennis lessons, ballet lessons, modern dancing, art classes, swimming club.

And Sunbeams—the weekly, guilty-smug taste of school, run in the gloomy Kopano hall where I now felt like a naughty intruder, even though Sunbeams had nothing to do with Kopano. "You're ridiculous, Rob," said Damien, who went to Cubs, run outside the hall, out of sight of the girls.

On the first day of Sunbeams, the four or five newcomers,

walking stiffly in our crisp yellow uniforms, were herded to the back of the hall by Mother Sun, an upright, stern-looking woman, whose hair was pulled tightly into a prim bun.

About twenty older girls, arranged in four groups in the four corners of the room, stared at us as if we were mosquitoes to be swatted at the first opportunity. Our plain yellow dresses seemed pitifully bare compared with theirs, which were adorned with scores of colorful badges.

"The Clouds, the Moonbeams, the Stars, and the Raindrops," said Mother Sun, pointing to each group in turn.

She called out our surnames, assigning us alphabetically to the groups in the order she had announced them. Scott was last, so I ended up in the Clouds and was handed a little felt cloud badge to be stitched onto my dress.

Mother Sun proceeded to announce various rules of politeness, niceness, and cheerfulness, to which Sunbeams were expected to conform.

"Now, before you go to your groups, does anyone have any questions?"

No one said anything.

"No one has anything to ask?"

The older girls glared across the huge hall. Mother Sun glared from above us. The girls beside me clutched their felt badges and looked at their feet, resolutely silent.

I took a deep breath. "Why are Sunbeams called Sunbeams and not Brownies?" In all the stories I had ever read, girls who weren't old enough to go to Girl Guides went to Brownies.

"That's the name in England," said Mother Sun. "This is Botswana. We have a different name here."

Gleeful smiles around the room beat down on me. I tried to ignore them and steady my voice.

"But the Cubs here are still called Cubs."

"That's a bit different." Mother Sunbeam gave me a despairing look.

"Why?"

"It just is. Now, I think that's enough questions for the moment. We'll be here all day."

"But—"

"Run along to your groups."

I gaped helplessly, but no one was listening anymore. So I trudged off to the Clouds, angry at such unjust disgrace.

Later, I asked Mum about it.

"Some people think it's offensive to black people."

"But they're not called *blackies*."

"Well, offensive to dark-skinned people, then."

"Why's it offensive, though?"

Mum sighed. "If you're sensitive about your skin color, it might be."

"Why?"

"I've just explained why, Robbie."

Mum said Sunbeams was a politically correct name—and that this made the Sunbeams boat even more of a terrible irony.

The seven Sunbeams were the youngest entrants in the Anything That Floats boat race at Shashe Dam. The muddy shores of the vast, thorn-scrub-lined dam were packed with people milling around strange, colorful contraptions that floated on old tractor-tire tubes, plastic barrels, and wired-together wood frames. Some had tents on top, some sails, some flags. Many looked dangerously lopsided as they bobbed among the reeds. A few teams on the less lopsided boats chatted in huddled groups, pointed toward buoys far out in the flat brown waters, and eyed the other serious-looking teams. Most people strolled up and down the rows of boats, laughing and drinking Castle Lager, even though it was only ten in the morning. Dad said this was hardly surprising, as most of the entrants were from Francistown, the closest town to the dam. Since the abandonment of many of the nearby mines—once at the center of southern Africa's first gold rush—Francistown's main claim to fame had been having one of the highest per capita alcohol consumption rates in the world.

A few people took pictures as they examined the boats. Everyone with a camera took a picture of the Sunbeams' boat.

It was ingenious—made out of the roof of an old Volkswagen van, with bench seats neatly welded inside. We had spent days decorating the shiny metal with Sunbeam yellow and wore outfits to match: brilliant yellow T-shirts, bright white shorts, and head-bands of gold tinsel. Each of us also wore nine real carrots strung around our necks, competing in fancy dress as seven nine-carrot-gold sunbeams.

Seeing myself in the mirror that morning, I had been momen-tarily transfixed by my own reflection. Now, however, on the banks of the dam, standing beside my friend Samantha Tomas, I felt considerably less resplendent. Samantha, whom I'd met in Class 4 at Kopano, was coal black, and on her the white-yellow-gold-carrot combination was a different level of dazzling. But for six of us being white, our team would have been perfect.

Our boat *was* perfect, though. It didn't leak and sat absolutely level in the water. It had been made by professionals—Phikwe Industrial Metal Pressings—who were our sponsors. On the sides of the boat, we'd painted Sunbeams Love PIMP in thick, out-lined capitals, with a heart shape for "love." Mum was captain, having been unanimously voted responsible-adult-in-the-boat. When she had protested that a few years of university rowing was hardly a qualification to captain a Volkswagen roof full of eight-year-olds, none of the other Sunbeam parents had been able—or inclined—to try to better this.

As the race began amid yells and cheers, and the other boats swarmed in front of us, it seemed that Mum had been right to worry. At least half were faster than us—and the harder we pad-dled, the more our paddles collided, and the more we drenched ourselves with warm, muddy water. It was a disastrous start. And by the time our paddling slipped into rhythm with Mum's calls, and we accelerated slightly, the leaders were far ahead. "Never mind. It's just a fun race," shouted Mum, smiling at us. "It's not about winning. Let's just enjoy ourselves. Let's finish with dig-nity." So we paddled gloomily on, abandoning our great hopes, reconciling ourselves to a slow, dignified finish.

But then, just after the halfway buoy, something amazing happened. Chaos unfolded in front of us: neck-and-neck boats collided; angry teams gesticulated wildly at each other and veered off course; several boats in the lead lost poles, barrels, flags, and oarsmen—some were collected, some left bobbing and splashing in the middle of the dam.

All at once, we were near the front. "We can win this," yelled Mum, looking surprised. "Paddle harder." She jumped up as our boat's nose edged ahead of the second-to-lead boat. "Come on," she bellowed, glancing at the lead boat. "Paddle, for goodness sake!" Sweat poured down all of our faces. "We can do this." My arms went numb keeping up the furious pace. On the approaching banks, people started to cheer us. *"Go Sunbeams! Go PIMP! Go!"* It was heady stuff.

Soon even the ten muscled, shirtless men in the lead boat were glancing back nervously at the Sunbeams. As we neared the reeds at the finish line, our nose had drawn halfway along the side of their boat. A few more meters, and we might have won. As it was, we came second, but nonetheless got the most applause.

And so the Anything That Floats complete outsiders—seven eight-year-old Sunbeams and an old Oxford rower sponsored by PIMP—made our own bit of Francistown history. Not quite as glamorous as topping a world alcohol consumption table, but in a small Botswana town where nothing much happens, enough to have us talked about for months.

But extracurricular activities like Sunbeams, however triumphant, were not enough to allay the concerns of Granny Joan and Grandpa Terry, who implored Mum to add some structure to our homeschooling.

"We must have a schoolroom," Mum announced, soon after we had left Kopano. "Even if we don't use it much. We must make things look as normal as possible."

There was no spare space for a schoolroom, so it went into Lulu's bedroom, the long room without any ceiling boards at the back of the house. Lulu's bed was pushed into the corner, her clothes consigned to pullout drawers beneath it. The rest of the room was lined with a long chest of drawers packed with paints, brushes, glue, scissors, paper, and pencils; wicker baskets full of Lego, Monopoly, Scrabble, and chess boxes; and several comfortable chairs. A small wooden table was finally squeezed into the middle of the room.

Mum drilled brackets into the walls to support shelves for our hundreds of storybooks and the smaller collection of home-schooling books, on science, math, history, geography, poetry, mythology, and arts and crafts. Around these she hung a brightly colored map of the world, a southern hemisphere star chart, and a Snakes of Southern Africa poster.

This still left big stretches of bare wall to be covered. And as Mum said that decorating the schoolroom counted as school, the three of us prolonged the process as much as possible. The foundations for the wall hangings were large pieces of white cardboard from the Phikwe stationery shop, but we insisted that the adornments should come from the bush, justifying day-long expeditions in the name of schoolwork.

Some of our finds could be glued directly onto the cardboard. Like the long, fluffy-headed grasses. Or the seedpods—spiky grenades, flat monster snow-pealike pods, and finger-length twists that curled up in crispy, cracking spirals as they spilled their seeds. Others, not yet dry, had to be pressed first between the pages of the huge, heavy dictionaries or Dad's medical books. Like the purple and yellow lanternlike flowers from the African Christmas tree, the delicate fingerlike "bipinnately compound" (doubly divided) acacia leaves, and the waxy, butterfly-shaped mopane leaves, which, with tiny grass heads for feelers, became green butterflies, fluttering through a forest of bark, grasses, pressed flowers, and real stick stick insects.

The real insect poster was less impressive. In the food-sparse bush, most things that died got eaten immediately, making dead and undamaged insects scarce. With choice thus limited, we soon had a mausoleum of violent insect death: chomped-winged butterflies, torn-legged stick insects, missing-winged crickets, and crushed assassin beetles, some still stuck to the carcasses of their victims. Tough, shiny blowflies, which eventually died of exhaustion after crashing into the windowpanes, were the only things intact.

"Hmph." Grandpa Ivor, on one of his regular inspections, frowned at the dismal collection. "I think we can do better than this."

At his instruction, we followed him across the road and into his bedroom, perching obediently on the bed as he began to haul engine parts and ancient electrical appliances off the table tennis table. Startled geckos and lizards darted farther back into the jumble as Grandpa ransacked their hiding places in quick succession. He had cleared enough to cover almost the entire bedroom floor before he found what he was looking for: a shallow wooden box, about the size of a door cut in half. He slid this out with sudden gentleness.

"Whaddaya think?" he asked, twirling the box so that the glass front faced us.

He smiled as we gasped at the spectacular contents. Impaled on long pins were about twenty exquisitely preserved creatures: black and translucent scorpions, black and orange butterflies, startled-eyed praying mantises, huge stick insects, glossy rhinoceros beetles, and shiny-winged dragonflies. "Older than all of you put together," Grandpa informed us.

The cream backing was stained, and each creature was faded with time and the dust that had seeped even behind the glass. But the setting seemed to make the collection only more impressive, and it was hung in pride of place beside the glossy snake chart.

The collection of live creatures, dotted around the schoolroom in boxes and jars, was growing rapidly too. And once Matthews discovered that we were interested in collecting anything that moved and couldn't kill us, we accumulated them at a rate of about one or two a week.

"*Ko-ko, ko-ko,*" Matthews would call, announcing himself with the singsong Setswana knocking words, as he waited outside the back door. Like Grandpa Ivor, Matthews was a daily visitor to the evolving schoolroom. But he preferred to examine our progress from the doorway, peering inside as he proffered some new creature for our collection.

"Come in, Matthews," Mum would say. "Come join us."

But Matthews didn't seem to be getting any more comfortable with his ambiguous role of gardener-soon-to-be-classmate. If he did venture through the doorway, he would cross the carpet as if he might at any moment step on a *devilkie* thorn and eye Mum with the same pained expression he got when she insisted he call her Linda or Mma Linda, but "*for goodness sake, Matthews, not Madam!*" It was one or the other: Matthews or Mum looking uncomfortable.

Matthews could glance at a tree and spot the twig that was really a stick insect suspended mid-step, or the bright green praying mantis whose triangle head and folded legs were indistinguishable from a fragment of leaf and its stem. He also treated it as a matter of pride that he could produce a superior specimen to anything the three of us discovered.

"Ah, it is just a *leettle* one," he scoffed, when we found our first dung beetle pushing a grape-sized ball larger than itself across the dirt.

A few days later, he led us to the edge of the bush and pointed under a low-hanging mopane branch. A dung ball the size of a small orange was rocking ever so slightly on the sand, apparently of its own accord. Only on peering much closer did I see the handstanding beetle, kicking its enormous egg container with its back feet, pausing after each futile shove. And it was then, for the first time, watching that determined little creature at its impossible task, that I understood how the Egyptians could believe such a small beetle was sacred; that it was the dung beetle that day after day rolled the sun across the sky.

Mystified though Matthews appeared by our desire to study and domesticate every small creature we found, he enjoyed indulging the habit. In exchange, we provided a riveted audience for what was, to us, his equally strange relationship with insects.

Principally, this involved eating them. Which Mum said made Matthews entomophagous.

The flying termites—which hatched after the first rains and flapped relentlessly against lamplit windowpanes—Matthews didn't even bother to kill first. The morning after they emerged, when, on the dirt, thousands of abandoned dew-covered wings formed a sparkling carpet, he scooped the crawling bodies straight into his mouth.

"*Sis!*" we yelled, as he chewed and grinned. When we refused to try the ants he selected for us, Matthews gave a contemptuous laugh. He tossed the squishy bodies to Smiley and Keller, my new Labrador puppy, who were both bounding dementedly after the few still-flying ants. Then he walked off in disgust. Later that day, we asked Grandpa Ivor if he was entomophagous with flying ants. "'Course I'm bloody entomophagous." He grabbed one, squashed it, and popped it into his mouth. "Delicious," he said, grimacing. "Ya're all bloody wimps. Full of protein. Tastes like peanut butter."

The thumb-sized blue, orange, and green mopane worms were another delicacy—sun-dried, after they'd had their intestines squeezed out by the hundreds of women who gathered on the roadsides in mopane worm season. "*Sooo* nice," said Matthews, as he nibbled a desiccated body. "*Too* nice." It was still covered in its little black spikes, but he ate everything except the head, which he spat out with a satisfied sigh. This time, he offered to share only halfheartedly. Hundreds of thousands hatch every year, but mopane worms are big business, and many sackfuls are sent to the cities or exported, making them sometimes scarce even in the areas where they are harvested. When we refused a sample, Matthews quickly returned the little bag of worms to his pocket, all four of us looking relieved.

Our adopted chameleon, however, unearthed a friendship-threatening difference of opinion.

The chameleon, christened Chamaeleo after his Latin name—we also had a rat called Rattus, and a crow called Corvus—began confined to the vivarium, like all the other temporary residents. But in order to keep him fed, we soon had to let him out on the windowsill to catch flies. Once placed there, he would happily remain, turning dark green against the paint as he fixed one suspicious eye on his next fly victim and swiveled the other toward the slightest flicker of movement elsewhere in the room.

Relocating him was the difficult part. As soon as you clasped the loose, paper-thin skin over his rib cage, his head would whip around, tiny jaws grabbing on to one of the offending fingers. After one painful nip, Damien wanted nothing more to do with him. I lasted a little longer, but I lost patience when Chamaeleo developed a fierce loathing for Keller. Smiley, we never let get near enough to Chamaeleo to test the relationship. Wagging her tail, Keller would waddle up to Chamaeleo, only to have an affectionate sniff rewarded by angry hissing and a sharp claw on her soft puppy nose.

I soon joined Damien in demanding Chamaeleo's release and replacement with better-tempered, less-demanding species that had been kicked out of the vivarium when Chamaeleo arrived. Lulu would have none of it, though; the more everyone else got fed up with Chamaeleo, the more besotted she became, giving him free range of her bed and carrying him around on her shoulder, laughing and reprimanding him in her soft voice when he chomped or clawed at her earlobe or fingers. Eventually Lulu won and Chamaeleo was allowed to stay, provided she took over his care exclusively and removed him when Ruth came to clean in the schoolroom. Ruth refused otherwise to put a foot inside, and if she saw Lulu carrying him, she would clap her hands over her eyes and let out an appalled *"Ah-ah,"* removing her hands only when Chamaeleo was safely out of sight.

Matthews was equally disgusted.

"Loo-loo," you must let it go."

"I won't!"

"Chameleons are very bad."

"Chamaeleo's not." Lulu started to get teary.

"He'll bring very bad luck."

"I don't care." Lulu walked off, caressing Chamaeleo and making soothing, cooing sounds between squeals of pain.

"What's wrong with them?" I asked Matthews.

"They are very bad."

"But why?"

"They can change color."

"What's wrong with that?"

"*Ah.*" Matthews looked irritated. "That is very bad." He stalked off, not prepared to deal with such stupid questions.

Once, a wide-eyed, distraught young man burst into Dad's clinic. Speaking in good English, he hurriedly explained that he had been bitten by a chameleon, and begged Dad to remove the poison as quickly as possible.

Dad said nothing as he carefully examined the tiny scratch on the patient's finger. Having learned it was better bedside manner initially not to contradict even the most bizarre claims, Dad spent a few minutes carefully disinfecting the area before getting into any argument about chameleon poison.

Chameleons have acrodont dentition, which means, according to the encyclopedia, that they don't officially have teeth. The tiny sharp ridges that look like teeth are actually part of the jawbone itself. These pseudo teeth can, however, inflict a painful nip on people, and rapidly chomp through grasshoppers and flies. But they have no venom. Nor does the amazing, ominous-looking tongue, which can, in a second, extend to more than twice the length of the chameleon's body.

Dad said, "Don't worry. You'll be fine. There's no poison."

"No, Doctor. You must please take it out."

"Chameleons are absolutely harmless," insisted Dad. "They have no poison in them. I promise you."

The patient stared miserably at his finger.

"Tell me," said Dad, "what is it anyway that makes everyone so scared of chameleons?"

The young man looked up in surprise. "Dr. Scott," he said, "would you trust me if I changed color?"

There was a computer-printed sign on the grimy wall at the Department of Labor. That and a photo of then president Quett Masire—framed in the blue, black, and white Botswana flag colors—were the only things to look at as we perched on the hard wooden benches of the waiting room. The sign said:

So-called White People:

They are red when they are born,
They go yellow when they are sick,
They go brown in the sun,
They go blue in the cold,
They go gray when they die,
And they have the cheek to call US colored!!!

8

MUM'S EXPERIMENT

Mum and her students

The *madala*'s grandchildren, the *ngaka*'s children. That was who Lulu, Damien, and I had become when we arrived in Botswana two years before.

To blacks.

To whites, at least to most of the ones that lived in Phikwe, we were the only white children who didn't go to school. But whereas before we had been fairly anonymous—just the children who did not go to school—now we were infamous: the children who had been to school, then spurned the school that was good enough for everyone else, and now no longer went to school.

Which was, in the eyes of most of the whites in Phikwe, infinitely worse.

· · ·

Across the crowded, bustling mall, Jonny Peterson, a Kopano bully and old classmate of Damien's, caught our eye and glared at us.

Even separated by hundreds of strolling, passing bodies, Jonny and his mother, as whites, were clearly visible as they bore down on us. At Kopano, or at the tennis club, you could easily forget that most of Phikwe consisted of Batswana people. Walking through the mall, you saw the true composition of the town. At some stage, everyone had to go there. Lining the busy, grimy pavements of the small central mall were the bank, post office, co-op grocery store, hardware shop, Sandy's butchery, and for clothes and shoes, PEP Stores and Bata.

The mall was hot, noisy, and dirty, and there were often long queues. Mum went only when she had to, and took us with her only when she really had to, on the days Granny Joan was playing bridge and couldn't look after us. Visiting the mall by herself put Mum in an irritable mood. With us there beside her, begging to go home, she became even grumpier. The only worse mall scenario was bumping into Jonny Peterson and his mother. "Shit," muttered Mum, giving a rare, quickly disguised scowl.

Jonny's mother smiled as she reached us.

"Afternoon," Mum said coldly.

Jonny's mother opened her mouth, but Jonny, surveying Lulu and me, interrupted. "My mum says you're going to turn into maids. And you," he continued, settling his triumphant smile on Damien, "are going to be a garden boy." He paused, staring gleefully at Damien, piggy eyes sinking into his fleshy face. "She also—"

"Nonsense!" His mother gripped his shoulder. "Don't be ridiculous, honey." She laughed and made an apologetic face at Mum. "He says amazing things sometimes."

"Really?" Mum's voice was even colder and very level, her I-don't-give-a-damn-what-anyone-says voice. "Well, we must get going."

"Of course. Ghastly place. Well, nice to bump into you, Linda."

Jonny gave us an evil smile.

"We will not," I hissed at him.

But Mum was already dragging us away, through the curio and pavement food section, dodging the milling bodies and the woven baskets, wooden carvings, dried mopane worms, and roasted corncobs displayed on mats laid across the dirty gray paving slabs.

"Ignore that revolting child," she said, as we wove between cars in the baking parking lot, squinting in the glare of windshields under midday sun. "Wretched bloody woman."

It was hard, though, to ignore anything that made Mum cross enough to swear. Mum said "sherbet" instead of "shit," and "*jolly*," not "*bloody*." So even after we had left school, Jonny succeeded in doing what bullies do best.

Botswana's first white maid. Daughter of the doctor. The shame and the dread.

And even though I'd long since lost any pangs of desire to return to school, for the next few days Jonny's words echoed in my head, and unsettling images of me wearing a colorful cloth *doek* knotted over my hair and swishing a long grass broom floated through my dreams.

At Kagiso Street, in the immediate aftermath of the Kopano departure, the air was thick with unspoken thoughts.

All school-related conversations were conducted in extra-brittle voices.

"So tell me, Blossom, how are the lessons going?"

"Very well, Dad," said Mum, brightly. "You know of course we've got a proper schoolroom now."

"I know," said Grandpa. "Joan says it curiously has a very small table. Where do the lessons actually happen?"

Mum blushed, but recovered quickly. "Oh, often at the dining room table. To vary the surroundings. It's so much cooler and breezier there, with the shade cloth."

Grandpa Terry gave me a suspicious glance. I smiled earnestly.

"And structure, Lin. What about a syllabus?"

"I have a syllabus," said Mum, "of a sort."

Grandpa narrowed his eyes.

Granny said, "And what about regularly socializing with other children?"

"Mumsie, we've discussed this so many times," said Mum. "They do. Twice a week, and every weekend. And besides, they're studying with Matthews now."

"Lin, he's your garden boy."

"Garden*ER*, Mum."

Granny sighed. "Well, you know how we feel about home-schooling."

"And you know how I feel about it."

I said, "What about how we're feeling about it?"

No one said anything. I continued, importantly. "We're actually all very satisfied with homeschooling, at the moment. Hey, Lu? Hey, Didge?"

Lulu and Damien nodded vigorously, Damien's new ninja hood slipping over his eyes.

O nce, the day Matthews first joined us, Mum did try a real, Kopano-like lesson, directing us to sit at the dining room table while she handed out pens and crayons and bustled about in a teacherly way.

"Right!" She smiled awkwardly and sat down at the head of the table. "Well. Welcome, Matthews. It's very nice of you to join us." She spoke nervously even though she had just that morning told Matthews which flowerbeds to water in a perfectly normal voice. "*Dumela*," she added, giving Matthews a full-set-of-teeth grin.

"*Dumela*, Mma," said Matthews. He looked even more uncomfortable than he usually did in the house. He slouched over the piece of paper in front of him and studied his fingernails. We said, "*Dumela*, Mum," smirking at the strange combination.

"Good. Well. Okay." Mum explained that we were each to

write a page about anything that interested us, and, when we'd all finished, we would read them out and discuss our ideas.

I wrote something about horses. Damien drew a motorbike, with him on it, and scribbled a few labels and specifications. Lulu, as always, drew a selection of birds, tortoises, chameleons, and bush trees, and gave them all names. Matthews, head bowed, writing quickly, had covered his first page long before any of us. He continued on the other side. Halfway down, he stopped writing and finished off with a drawing of a fat red cow.

"That's wonderful, Matthews," said Mum, when she had taken a look. "Would you like to read it out?"

Matthews nodded and got to his feet. Smiling nervously, he held his essay in front of him. "The cow is a domestic animal..."

He began haltingly, running his finger along the lines. But as he listed fact after fact about cows, he slipped into a steady rhythm, pausing between paragraphs. Each began "The cow..." and continued on a new theme: what cows ate, what time of year they had babies, how many his family owned. Some of the words were Setswana, and he tried to translate these for us, explaining that there were all kinds of cow words, even words for sick and healthy cows.

When Mum corrected the mistakes in his English, Matthews nodded and made notes on his page. But when she suggested that he try to use longer English descriptions instead of the Setswana words, he said, "Ah, that is too difficult." In English, he insisted, there simply were not the right words to talk properly about cows.

At first, Mum encouraged Matthews to write about other things: his family, his cattle post, what he wanted to do when he was older, which was to own lots of cows. But Matthews could find a cow angle in any topic. At the dinner table, Mum and Dad laughed about his passion. "But far be it from me to discourage such enthusiasm," said Mum. "And it'll be good for the kids to learn about such an integral part of local culture."

So the days Matthews joined us became cow-themed. From the illustrated Greek mythology book, Mum read to us about

Io, lusted after by Zeus, who one day turned her into a beautiful white cow to avoid discovery by his jealous wife, Hera. On
the star chart, she showed us where all the constellations fitted
in relation to Taurus. Once, we spent a whole morning studying the cow entry in the animal encyclopedia and tracing the outlines of cows' four different stomachs, arranged in the ingenious
system that enables them to digest even the tough cellulose in
grasses.

Mum lasted for several weeks before she ran out of new cow
ideas. And by then even Matthews had said everything he had
to say about cattle breeds, cattle diseases, and herbs for treating
sick cattle. He had even taught us how to estimate the value of a
cow, depending on its age and size. A big healthy bull was about
2,000 pula, which meant, Matthews informed us, that just five or
six bulls could buy a reasonable secondhand *bakkie*.

I knew—I was sure—everything there was to know about
cattle.

T hen one day a thin but otherwise healthy-looking cow
collapsed just outside our cattle grid. She lay down and
chewed her cud just like any other cow. But long after her herd
had wandered off into the bush, she was still refusing to get up.

Matthews found Lulu and me crouched beside her, offering
her handfuls of hay.

"Ah, no, you mustn't feed that cow," he admonished.

"She's hungry." The cow's moist, orange-peel-textured lips
pouted as she stretched them out for each new handful. She had
already munched her way through a large slice of a hay bale.

"The cow will die anyway."

"What's wrong with her?"

"*Ga ke itse.*" Matthews shrugged. "But she will die."

"How do you know?"

"Ah, I just know. That is a dying cow."

Lulu sniveled and stroked the cow's neck. She didn't flinch,
blinking long curved lashes, staring at us with gentle, molasses-
colored eyes.

"I don't believe you," I said. "Dad says he can't see anything wrong with her."

"Ah, no."

Lulu and I visited the cow several times each day. She continued to drink and eat whatever we offered her and seemed to appreciate us waving the flies from her eyes.

On one visit we found a young Motswana man, standing a few meters away in the bush, studying our cow.

"Is she yours?" I asked.

"No."

"Whose is she?"

"*Ga ke itse.*"

We began to feed her, and the man burst out laughing. He walked off into the bush, shaking his head.

Mum realized the problem first. "The poor old girl hasn't pooed for two days."

Which meant there was a bale of hay stuck somewhere in between her four stomachs. The next morning she was lying flat on her side. She refused to eat, staring at nothing with glassy eyes. Dad said he would have to put her down.

"No one's killing any cows near my property," yelled Grandpa Ivor. "I'm not having the police around here."

Dad pointed out that the cow was in pain and would definitely die anyway.

"If you kill it, the owner will call the police."

"The owner doesn't know he's got a dying cow."

"'Course he knows."

"Then why the hell hasn't he come and killed it himself?"

"The Batswana hate killing their cows. And he's hoping some softhearted whitey will do it for him so he can claim compensation."

Mum gave the cow a mixture of homeopathic remedies, pressing the dropper into the side of her mouth and squeezing the alcoholic mixture onto her tongue. She didn't swallow.

By midday her breathing was shallow. She no longer bothered to blink away the flies. Already, high above, several vultures circled and watched.

Lulu and I guarded the cow. Every time one of the giant brown birds landed in a nearby tree, we ran after it, yelling and waving sticks, Keller bounding through the bush and barking furiously. But as fast as we chased one bird away, another swooped down to a different tree, peering at us through beady eyes and shrugging and shuffling its cloaklike wings, impatient for the inevitable moment when we'd give up. Keller soon did, and collapsed panting under a shady bush. But Lulu and I continued our hopeless pursuit, screaming and swearing at the relentless birds, pausing only to wipe stinging sweat and dust and tears from our eyes.

We guarded her until after dark, whispering good night and stroking her still face and neck. Grandpa remained unrelenting. "She's almost dead anyway. And they'll be here as soon as she pegs." Teary pleas did nothing to change his mind, and I went to sleep feeling sick with guilt. I dreamed of the cow being eaten alive by vultures and jackals that, in the darkness, didn't realize that she was not yet dead.

When we returned just after dawn, a small crowd of men and women were gathered around the cow. There was not much left of her.

"Think of it as biology," said Mum, as we stared at the shiny jumble of organs piled on the sand. "Don't look at her face." Most of the cow had already been chopped up and packed into plastic bags. "It's better that she doesn't go to waste," added Mum. "Imagine how many people she'll feed."

None of this made it any less horrible, though.

Mum asked the eldest man in the group if he knew what had killed her. He nodded and reached into the bloody pile of insides, lifting up what looked like an enormous piece of snot. It was a plastic shopping bag, covered in runny yellow cow dung. "Nine," he said, chuckling.

When the butchering was finished, the nine plastic bags were virtually all that was left behind.

The cow had died of plastic bags—the plastic bags that littered the bush, clinging to trees and bushes and tempting starving animals: goats, which were clever enough to eat only what was hidden in the bags; cows, which weren't. Mum pronounced the ubiquitous bags "a tragedy for one cow, and a catastrophe for the whole environment."

Matthews' verdict was entirely unsympathetic. "Ah," he said, bursting out laughing, "that was a bloody stupid cow!"

Grandpa Terry said, "I have seen people lose their senses over cows."

Once, in a bad drought year when, daily, new carcasses littered the roads and many of the small cattle-post wells dried up, a senior Motswana mine manager in Phikwe had been unable to bring himself to slaughter any of his cows. He had ended up watching his entire herd of Brahmans starve to death; tens of thousands of pula dwindling to fatless skin and bones, gone to the vultures.

In drought years, which came often—and occasionally, terribly, in succession—the rainfall in eastern Botswana could plunge well below what would qualify the region as a desert. Crops would die, and the sparse grass would give way altogether to baked red dirt. In the villages and cattle posts, where many depended on maize and sorghum harvests, food parcels would be delivered, subsidized by the government. As a result, people in Botswana rarely died from drought. But animals did. And cattle—the love and pride of Batswana people, the lifeblood of the rural economy—starved in their thousands: their owners waiting too long, too hopefully, for the precious *pula* that never came.

Not long after Matthews revolutionized our understanding of cows, Ruth asked if Moretsana, who had just finished school, could join our lessons for a few months.

Mum was delighted. She agreed immediately. Then she panicked.

"Maybe I shouldn't have said yes."

"Why?"

"Well, I'm not a qualified teacher."

"You teach Matthews."

"He's missed lots of school."

"You teach us."

"That's different. You're my own children. I can experiment."

"You went to Oxford."

Whenever I worried about what might happen to me from not having a real teacher, I thought about Mum's university. It reassured me that she had at least studied somewhere famous.

"That's irrelevant, Robbie."

But Mum smiled. Oxford reassured her too. It made her think of the time when she'd had the world at her fingertips and was going to do groundbreaking research into nutrition. Before she had got married. And then got pregnant. By mistake. And had me, then Damien, then Lulu, and had become, before she knew it, a housewife in the middle of nowhere, teaching three small children and the adolescent gardener. "Which I don't regret at all," Mum would add, as she finished reminiscing.

Moretsana was a softly spoken, perpetually smiling girl. She was going to go to teacher-training college, wanted to improve her English, and didn't seem to be at all interested in cows. She had hundreds of tiny, shiny black braids in her hair, which she agreed to try and replicate on me and Lulu. But in our fine, slippery hair, they unraveled after just one night, which left us looking like the woman touching a Van de Graaff generator in the science encyclopedia and Moretsana speechless with giggles.

Her English was already good. Because she was a girl, she had started school at six. Young boys, she told us, were often sent into the bush to look after cows, which meant that, like Matthews, many didn't go to school until they were eight or nine.

Moretsana asked Mum complicated English questions, about prepositions, participles, and other parts of speech of which we'd never heard. For the few months that she was with us, for the first and last time, we learned about grammar from Mum, who believed it was important to experience the beauty of a complete language, through good books, before you broke it up into its separate parts.

But Moretsana wanted to learn about English directly, the

same way she'd learned about it in school, and Mum answered in detail all her questions about sentence construction and verbs, nouns, and the tenses that confused her because they didn't exist in Setswana. Once, to our amazement, Mum even stood up and wrote out several verb declensions on the whiteboard in the schoolroom, which had until then only ever been used for our amusement. On the days Moretsana and Matthews came to join us, Mum also made a rare attempt to draw up a timetable that included a variety of subjects, instead of the usual brief—often briefer than Mum planned—session of the three Rs, followed by a long—always longer than she planned—session of the current enthralling book.

Then Moretsana went away. And with cow-dominated lessons no longer there as an attraction for Matthews, his attendance became much more sporadic.

Soon the words of books, through the voice of Mum, had reasserted themselves as our most important teachers. Or befuddlers, in the case of Lulu, who in the beginning understood little of the books that Damien and I wanted Mum to read. Lulu would nevertheless listen as attentively as Damien and I, confused and wide-eyed, but no less transfixed by the otherworldliness of a room echoing with hundreds of pages' worth of somewhere else. And I understood why, and felt, too, how the world of the book crept off the words on the pages, infused its surroundings, and, as long as the words were still being read, became its own parallel reality, with characters as real as everyone else in the room, and a past and a future that was yours as much as theirs.

If we were in between books, Mum would let us do whatever we felt like, assisting where needed. "I'm not going to spoonfeed you knowledge," she'd frequently remind us. If we wanted to build a radio, grow crystal gardens, make papier-mâché puppets, or paint the walls in our rooms a new color, she'd happily help us. Sometimes she would insist on a few hours of the three Rs. But, then, if we wanted to spend the rest of the day playing in the bush or the trailers or the old airplanes, that was fine too. She'd help us make sandwiches, give us bottles of frozen water, and check we had our hats on. Then she'd tell us to watch out for snakes, wave us good-bye, and disappear to her typewriter to write one of the two books she was always working on.

As far as actually telling us what to learn, Mum's was mostly a do-nothing experiment.

9

SHOCKING EXPERIENCES

Feste

Kobus Venter was the first Afrikaans person I had met. He was also the fattest person I had ever seen. When he walked, which he did very slowly, the soft folds on his legs and arms behaved independently from the rest of his body, quivering for several moments after he stopped moving. A roll of fat at the back of his neck curled over his khaki shirt collar; another bulged at the tops of the khaki socks pulled halfway up his vast calves. Shaking his hand was like gripping an oily oven glove. I retrieved mine as quickly as I could. I wondered if Kobus had arthritis and smelly fungal growths between the folds on his belly like the very fat Batswana ladies that Dad hated having to examine at his clinic. When Dad told these women they needed to lose weight for their arthritis, he explained that their arthritic knees were like the small wheels of a *bakkie* trying to support the weight of a truck that couldn't go anywhere.

Kobus was a jumbo jet on *bakkie* wheels. Lulu, Damien, and I stared in openmouthed, undisguised amazement.

"The kids are so excited about seeing the horses," said Mum. "Aren't you?"

"*Ja,*" said Damien, smirking as he imitated Kobus's thick, throat-grating accent. Mum nudged me, and I nodded obedi-ently. In my surprise, I had almost forgotten I was about to own my first pony, the thing I had wanted more than anything in the world since I was four and had first sat on a placid, solemn-eyed creature in the middle of a lush New Zealand field.

Five years later, in the overgrazed bush on the outskirts of Sefophe village, standing beside Kobus's ramshackle house next to a cattle kraal, my fantasy was getting off to a poor start—even for a fantasy. This heady mix of imagination, Anna Sewell's *Black Beauty*, the British Pony Club manual, and the few horsy films I had watched was something along the following lines: A beauti-ful girl, not unlike Tatum O'Neal from *International Velvet*, would lead me over to a stable deep in sweet-smelling sawdust. With tears in her eyes, she would present me with her champion show-jumping pony (a smaller version of *National Velvet*'s Pie crossed with Black Beauty) and declare she had grown too tall to con-tinue riding the exquisite animal. After careful consideration, she would say, she had decided that I, Robyn Scott, should be the one to take over the reins and go on to even greater glories. The fantasy pony, named Feste after the gentle, majestic horse in Lucy Boston's Green Knowe books, would then whicker with the appropriate mixture of regret and delight, before gently plucking carrots and sugar cubes from my hand.

"The boys are just fetching them," said Kobus. "They'll be here any minute."

Mum and Dad continued to chat to Kobus, and I tried to image what Boerperds looked like. *Boer* was because they were horses bred by the Afrikaners, *perd* was Afrikaans for horse.

"Fantastic animals," Dad had said. "Tough as nails." Boerperds, he explained, had carried the Boers all the way from the Cape to the Transvaal during the Great Trek. They had also fought in the Boer War, outlasting the larger, more delicate British horses. "Perfect for Botswana," said Dad, "the bull terrier of horses. Don't want any of these namby-pamby Thoroughbreds," which of course was exactly what I did want.

But a horse was a horse, and I felt weak with excitement.

A few minutes later we heard distant shouting. This grew louder, and soon I could make out the sound of hooves and branches snapping. Suddenly two brown ponies, followed by a tiny black filly, charged out of the mopane trees. They skidded to a halt on the sand and looked around with wild, panicky eyes. Seconds later, two black boys on mules cantered after them, yelling and wielding long rubber *shamboks*. Circling and waving the *shamboks* above their heads, they chased the frightened ponies into the kraal, where they huddled in a corner, their sides heaving and eyes revolving upward to expose ugly white bits.

Now that they were still, I realized both ponies were actually light gray, but so dirty that their real color was visible only in a few patches. The smaller, less skinny pony, the mother of the little black foal, had a pretty face and a neat ponylike body. The slightly bigger one, the mare's brother, had wild eyes, an ugly Roman nose, and a long sloping back that gave him the air of a hyena. Both had bumpy insect bites across their coats, scratches, lumps on their legs, and cracks running up their hooves. They looked straight out of the chapter in the Pony Club manual on what can go wrong with your horse.

The two boys jumped off the mules and climbed inside the kraal. As soon as they approached, the ponies took off, tossing their heads as they galloped around the pen. After several minutes, however, the boys succeeded in fastening rough rope halters over their heads, and the captives stood still again, quivering slightly. I approached the mare and patted her hot neck. She shook a little but didn't seem to mind until I leaned out to stroke her filly. I hadn't even managed to touch the foal before she lunged at me, teeth bared and ears flattened.

"Been in the bush too long," said Kobus. "Just needs a bit of good discipline."

One of the boys, riding a mule, and Matthews, on foot, were going to lead the ponies to Selebi. From Sefophe, this was about twenty kilometers on dirt tracks through the bush, and they set off immediately, each tugging a pony, with the filly trailing her mother.

On the drive back, everyone talked at once, arguing about their names, what to feed them, and when we might ride them, at which point Mum said thoughtfully, "Keith, do you really think it was wise to get *unbroken* ponies?"

"Best way to do it," replied Dad. "They'll have no bad habits."

"But they're rather more wild than we thought," Mum continued in a gentle voice. "Perhaps we should pay someone to break them in."

"Robbie and I can do it."

"Someone who knows how to ride," Mum persisted.

"I've ridden before. And it'll be the best way for Robbie to learn."

"I want to, Mum," I yelled from the backseat. "I want to. I'll learn quickly."

"Hmm," said Mum, and then fell silent.

Dad estimated that it would take around four hours to walk the horses to Selebi. Six hours later, when the mopane trees were turning gold in the quickly disappearing sun, there was still no sign of them. I fished a few more struggling moths out of the water tub, fluffed up the hay nets again, and then climbed back on the concrete loading ramp beside the kraal to wait. Everyone else, even Keller, had got bored and gone back inside. But I was too worried and excited to leave. I read the Pony Club manual until it grew too dark to see the words, and then swung up and down along the rusty metal poles of the loading crush to stop the mosquitoes settling.

In the silver-gray moonlight, seven hours after the ponies had set off, they came trailing down the driveway.

I ran to meet them, greeting Matthews breathlessly. "What happened? Why were you so long?"

"Ah! These are so naughty," Matthews said in a disgusted voice. The mare jumped sideways as I approached, and he gave a savage tug on her halter.

"You must be gentle, Matthews!"

Matthews scowled and stuck his arm forward. It was streaked with deep blood-covered scratches. I saw then that his legs too were covered in scratches, and one knee had a crust of congealed blood and dust.

"Oh," I said, feeling stupid. I kept quiet as I trailed after him and closed the gate. When the ponies were safely shut in the kraal and munching hay, and the boy who worked for Kobus had disappeared to a nearby cattle post, Matthews came to the house. Dad cleaned and dressed his cuts, while Matthews explained that the ponies had twice tried to run home and dragged him through the bush. Mum made Matthews tea and kept saying, "Oh, goodness, I'm so sorry." She insisted he took the next day off, and when he left she gave him a bag of cornmeal and a handful of chocolates from the not-to-be-touched special-occasions cupboard, which alone seemed worth a few bad scratches.

Afterward, Dad said it was a one-off—"we only have to get them here once, Lin"—and Mum should for goodness sake stop feeling so guilty.

The next morning I woke up at five, grabbed a handful of carrots, and ran out into the hazy blue dawn. The air was still cool from the receding night but already ringing with excited dove coos, weaver cheeps, and francolin shrieks. It was the time of day when the bush paraded its full quota of life in the sweet-sharp air; when the sun, appearing as a soft red tear between the tops of bushes and the sky, looked friendly and gentle. By ten o'clock, most sensible life would be in retreat: the occasional bird cry competing only with cicadas; leaves and tiny bush flowers folding up in the heat. This was the hour when you felt best in Botswana. And this, I thought as I ran across the still chilly sand, was one of the best of those.

The kraal was completely empty. The only sign that horses

had been there at all were a few dewdrop-glistening piles of dung and the sagging empty hay nets. I yelled hopelessly as I ran toward the back fence, where one rickety post had been pushed over and the wires lay flat on the sand. There was no sign of the horses in the bush beyond the fence.

"For God's sake," muttered Dad as I shook him awake and babbled hysterically that the horses were lost and possibly dead somewhere in the bush.

"Come help me look for them."

"No way."

I began to cry. "I'll go by myself then."

"You'll be wasting your time. They're probably already home."

"What?"

"At Kobus's. I'm sure he'll call us later."

"Call him now," I wailed.

"It's too early. Go back to sleep."

"I can't."

"Then go and make us some tea, Robbie," mumbled Mum.

I ran to Lulu's room, told her what had happened, and ordered her to come and help me make tea.

Sitting on the kitchen counter, I listed the calamities that might have befallen the horses. Lulu, eyes wide and brimming with tears, lit the gas beneath the kettle, put *rooibos* tea bags in the teapot, and poured long-life UHT milk into a little jug.

"I'll call him at seven," said Dad, hauling himself into a sitting position. "No more nagging."

Mum and Dad sipped the steaming tea while Lulu and I, teary and miserable with worry, stared out the window. Redhead, the redheaded weaver, was working on his new nest. Every summer Redhead started a nest on the same tree outside Mum and Dad's bedroom window. When the nest was nearly finished, a dowdy female weaver would start making regular inspections, flying in and out and tugging at loose bits of grass while Redhead cheeped and puffed out his red and white breast on a nearby branch. Every year, the female would reject the nest, and Redhead, his enthusiasm undiminished, would begin another.

He built two wonky, loosely woven nests every season, and never succeeded in getting a female to lay her eggs, which Mum said broke her heart and Dad said served him right for poor workmanship and maybe it was a good thing he wasn't passing on his genes.

Usually I felt sorry for Redhead, but today his incessant happy cheeping was just irritating.

"What if one of them has fallen in a hole and broken its leg and has to be put down?"

Lulu gasped, and her eyes refilled with tears.

"Stop worrying," said Dad. "Go have some breakfast."

"I'm not hungry."

"Neither am I."

At six thirty Mum said, "I can't bear this anymore," and staggered out of bed to call Kobus. A few minutes later he rang back to say all three ponies were there and, as far as he could tell, in one piece. Lulu and I bounced up and down on the bed in relief.

"No. We cannot go and get them now."

"Why not?"

"Because Matthews needs to recover. And I need to put up an electric fence."

I ate my breakfast in sulky silence.

"Come on, Robbie," said Mum. "It's actually a good thing."

I stared at her in amazement.

If the horses wanted to run back to a place where they had been so bereft of human attention, reasoned Mum, it would be even easier to get them to love us. "Imagine what a little TLC will do."

I continued to eat wordlessly. Mum didn't just see silver linings around clouds, she saw whole diamond-studded eighteen-carat-gold gilt-edged frames. Which could be infuriating, when you were still deep in the misery of the cloud.

Dad erected a tall electric fence and, several days later, Matthews and the ponies trudged once more down the driveway. This time they stayed. But despite lavish TLC, the two adult ponies continued to

bite and kick us with relish. Cowering at the mere sight of a grooming brush or a hosepipe, they remained covered in a thick coat of
dust. Mum declared that their names were almost comically appropriate and that in retrospect we really should have waited till we discovered their true temperaments and real colors before christening
them. But Feste and Quartz stuck. Only the filly's name became a
little more reasonable, evolving from Black Beauty to just Beauty
when she turned out, on closer inspection, to be dark gray.

"It'll just take time," said Dad. "We'll be riding them in a few
months."

"It's the latent stress of years without TLC," said Mum, "compounded by the stress of the move." This, she decided, required
medicinal intervention, and she prescribed daily sugar cubes
laced with drops of Rescue Remedy. When these produced no
obvious improvement, she brought out the entire set of Bach
flower remedies and made bespoke concoctions: "aggressiveness"
and "overprotectiveness" for Feste; "nervousness" and "fear of
hurt" for Quartz.

"You guys want some too?"

We all said yes. Homeopathy and Bach flower remedies
meant either wonderfully sugary little pills, which were the closest we usually got to sweets, or delicious drops of diluted alcohol.

Mum fished in little white tubs with names like *nux vomica*
and *arnica* and handed us each a selection of sweet white pills
to dissolve on our tongues. Mum and Dad had written a book
on homeopathy, so for these she didn't need to look up what to
prescribe. For the Bach flower remedies, though, she studied a
reference book with descriptions of what character problem each
flower improved. Afterward she listed the flowers she'd chosen
on the label of each bottle, which meant it was easy for us to check
the book to see what we were being treated for.

Lulu's bottle: *Lack of confidence, excessive concern for others, worry.*

Damien's bottle: *Poor concentration, occasional moodiness.*

Robbie's bottle: *Bossiness, intolerance, impatience, irritability,
excessive expectations of self and others, inability to cope with failure,
highly strung, opinionated, overly judgmental, inability to compromise,
desire to control others, inflexibility, stubbornness.*

"Why do I have to have so many?"

"Because more apply to you, Robbie."

"They don't," I snapped.

"*Excessive sensitivity*," muttered Mum, picking up the book.

Dad said, "I'm just sorry there isn't one for 'lacking sense of humor.' "

I scowled at him.

"Stop scowling, Robbie," said Mum. "You'll have lines before you're twelve."

"I'm not scowling."

"You are," said Dad. "You're always scowling. We've established this before."

I started to speak, but shut my mouth crossly. The last time I'd tried to argue that I never scowled, Dad had made me wear a thick sticky plaster between my eyebrows for a day. Every time I knitted my brow, I'd felt the plaster scrunch together.

The memory still shocked me. I un-scowled my face and attempted a giggle. "Anyway, I do have a sense of humor."

Dad raised his eyebrows. "Whatever you say, Robbie."

Dad had a theory that I was the only person in the world to be born entirely without a sense of humor. He said I was lucky I had him and Mum as parents because that would force me to develop one. "You'll have a nervous breakdown living with us if you don't learn to take life less seriously," he'd once informed me. Not sure exactly what a nervous breakdown was, I'd nevertheless spent several weeks convinced I must already be having one. Until Dad said that was a joke too, sort of. "Ha, ha, got you again, Robbie."

Unannounced, Kobus appeared one afternoon, driving a listing, battered Toyota *bakkie*. "Just on my way to Phikwe," he explained. "Thought I'd come check on my horses."

"They're not *his*," I hissed to Mum as we traipsed after Kobus and Dad.

" 'Course they're not. But there's no point getting upset."

But by the time Kobus had lumbered around the feed shed and the pens, firing a steady stream of criticism and advice, Mum and Dad were both tight-lipped and rolling their eyes at each other.

The three ponies stood side by side at the far corner of their enclosure, heads hung, staring longingly through the electric fence—in the direction of Kobus's farm. I bit my lip, wishing desperately they wouldn't choose now, of all moments, to look so homesick.

"*Jirre, man,*" said Kobus, shaking his head. "They don't look so *lekker,* hey?"

They didn't, which made it even worse. I wanted to yell at Kobus and tell him that it was his fault for neglecting them; that normal horses wouldn't be behaving like this. Mum was pink-cheeked and narrow-eyed: she took it as a personal affront that our TLC and her remedies had still failed to produce any great effect.

Kobus leaned forward to take another gleeful look at the ponies.

Dad started to speak but stopped. Kobus had already shifted his tremendous bulk against the fence, hanging his arms over the top wire. For a few seconds he didn't move. Then, suddenly, he gasped and started to vibrate—in slow motion, bouncing backward and forward but remaining firmly against the wires. A few more seconds passed, and he toppled back from the fence, stumbling for several paces and then coming to an abrupt halt. He said nothing and glared at us, his face blotchy red, his expression surprised.

"Goodness," said Mum. "Terribly sorry about that."

For a few moments, Kobus just stared at us in a slightly confused way, saying nothing. Then he took a deep breath and exploded. "Focking fence! Why the bloody hell didn't you say you had a focking electric fence?"

Mum and Dad listened, heads tilted, expressions sympathetic. When he had finished, Dad addressed him in a grave voice. "Shocking experience, isn't it?"

"I'm going," muttered Kobus. He started to walk toward his *bakkie.*

"Nice of you to pop in," Mum called after him. "Sorry again."

But Kobus didn't look back. He never returned.

Dad later declared it was worth putting up the electric fence just to see the expression on Kobus's face.

10

GRANDPA IVOR

Grandpa Ivor and Granny Betty

Grandpa Ivor, who never missed one of our attempts to train the horses, was waiting under the knob-thorn tree beside the kraal. He leaned against a fence post, chewing his matchstick, which stopped him missing cigarettes, and whispering to Feste, who watched him with a bored expression.

Spotting us, she flattened her ears. Red-veined whites replaced soft brown centers as she rolled her eyes to the back of her head. Even the sight of Dad and me walking toward the kraal, saddles on our arms, was enough to induce her disgust. By the time the saddle was on top of her, she was shuddering franti-cally, kicking at the poles of the narrow cattle crush, and emitting regular furious snorts, flaring her nostrils to expose foam-flecked red insides.

Breaking in was not going according to plan. Each day, Feste behaved in a similar manner. Except that she got progressively more, not less, demonstrative of her displeasure: the kicks harder, the snorts louder. None of the horse-training books mentioned this problem. Which meant, argued Dad, that Feste was an exception and, therefore, that we could ignore all the other breaking-in rules. Starting with Rule Number One: *Do not mount until the horse fully accepts the saddle.*

Grandpa leaned over the fence. "It's just bravado," he yelled.

"Shhh, Ivor," said Dad.

Grandpa ignored him. "She's just trying to scare you, Robbie."

She was succeeding. Perched on the top horizontal pole of the crush, I watched the wide, shivering back and saddle below me—flat ears at one end, swishing tail at the other. I started to feel sick.

On his previous attempt—his third—Dad had managed to stay on Feste without being thrown off. But now, as Feste smacked her hoof against the ground and dust rose around me, I regretted, again, insisting I was ready to ride her. However, it was too late to change my mind without looking like a wimp: Mum, Lulu, and Damien had joined Grandpa behind the fence, where all four looked on expectantly.

Dad stood in the front of the crush, gripping the rope attached to Feste's bridle, ready to hold her down or, if she behaved calmly, as he predicted, to lead her out of the crush into the kraal.

"Come on, Robbie," said Dad. "It's not going to get any easier."

"Don't hurry her, Keith," called Mum. "Robbie, you must take as much time as you need."

"If you're too scared, I'll do it," said Dad.

"I'm not! I'm going!" I climbed two poles down, bringing my feet almost level with Feste's back. Very slowly, I extended one shaking, jellylike leg over her back and began to lower myself toward the saddle.

"*Shhh*, girl. *Shhh.*" I stroked her mane as my bottom touched the leather. For a moment nothing happened. Then Feste reversed, with a crash, into the poles behind her. She immediately leaped forward, frightened by the noise, and I slid to the back of the saddle, head and body flung back, legs flying up either side of her neck. I yelled in fright and grabbed a pole beside me, straddling the gap between her and the crush as she paused, quivering.

"Hold on to the *saddle*, not the poles," instructed Dad in a calm voice. "And don't shout. You'll frighten her even more."

I grabbed the pommel, just in time for Feste's second rapid reversal. This time she didn't stop to wonder what was on her back. For the next few interminable minutes, she bounced, kicked, shook, and pawed the ground as I hung on, hunched over, certain that I was destined for premature, nine-year-old death. Crushing and trampling seemed equally strong possibilities. Perhaps both.

"Steady, girl, steady…Ouch…Shit…Hang on, Robbie," I heard Dad's voice beside me and was vaguely aware of Grandpa Ivor shouting. But it was only as Feste's acrobatics eventually subsided, and I realized I was bruised but not about to die, that I properly paid attention to the voices.

"Well done. See—that wasn't so bad," said Dad. Feste, soaked in sweat, had come to a twitching standstill. Dad was covered in fine gray dried-cow-dung dust and had rope burns on his hands. Both of us were coughing on the inhaled grit. I continued to cling, speechlessly, to the pommel.

"Brilliant, Robbie. Brilliant!" yelled Grandpa, clapping his hands. "But you've gotta use your wrists."

"Please stop shouting, Ivor," shouted Dad. "What the hell are you on about anyway?"

"The secret to riding is in the wrists," bellowed Grandpa.

"Since when do you know anything about riding?"

"I know you've gotta use your damn wrists."

"Nonsense."

"You're hardly a bloody expert."

"At least I've actually ridden before."

Feste tossed her head and began to paw the ground. I squealed.

"About ten times," yelled Grandpa. "Hardly counts."

"That's nonsense, and you know it."

Feste kicked viciously at a pole. I bent forward again and screwed my eyes shut.

"For goodness sake, Keith," yelled Mum. "Focus on Robbie."

"*Shhh. Shhh*," said Dad, returning his attention to Feste. "Bloody impossible man," he muttered. "Hop off, Robbie. Enough for today."

Over the following weeks—first as I was led around the kraal, later as I began to steer Feste myself—Grandpa issued a steady stream of advice.

"Lean forward...grip with your knees...straighten your elbows...keep your eyes on the horizon!" he would shout, waving his arms for emphasis as he leaned against the acacia tree beside the kraal. And if things went suddenly wrong, he would always return to his central piece of wisdom. "It's all in the wrists...use your bloody wrists," he'd yell as I scrambled to my feet, dusted myself off, and trudged toward Feste. As soon as she had deposited me—frequently in the direction of a tree or the fence—she would charge to the other side of the kraal. Here she would wait, panting, standing placidly as I remounted and she caught her breath in preparation for her next attempt to throw me off.

Grandpa always spoke with compete assurance, and not once did his instructions agree with Dad's or with any of my books on how to ride. Which, Dad said, was "just bloody typical of Ivor. The less he knows about something, the more he tells you what to do."

This rule, as I'd long ago discovered, also worked the other way round.

A few months after we arrived in Botswana, we'd all joined Dad for his first flying lesson. He hadn't flown for more than ten years. "I'm almost as rusty as the plane," he announced as we walked across the hot tarmac to Grandpa's ancient Cherokee six-seater.

The takeoff, however, went smoothly and as soon as we'd leveled off and the engines had eased, Grandpa picked up his latest copy of *New Scientist* magazine. He didn't look up again, reading silently and chewing his way through several matchsticks.

After half an hour, the airport reappeared far beneath us. The plane continued straight ahead. Only when we were close enough to make out the white stripes on the runway did we start to drop; first gently, then in big, stomach-churning lurches.

I looked around nervously. Lulu began to whimper. Mum's face turned pale as she stroked Lulu's hair. Damien's head hung to his lap. Dad was staring intently at the gauges and switches before him. Only Grandpa seemed unperturbed, still chewing his matchstick and studying the magazine.

The lurches got worse. I shut my eyes. My ears popped.

Another giant lurch, and the little plane's wheels thumped hard against the runway. We immediately bounced back up into the air. Several horrible thuds and bounces followed, then the plane clung to the ground with a soft screeching sound. I opened my eyes again as we skidded to a jolting stop at the far end of the runway. Magazines, papers, and old shopping receipts flew past us toward the front. Everything was quiet, except for the slowing engines and Lulu's sniveling. Mum wiped streaks of vomit off Lulu's face. Dad flicked switches on the control panel.

Then Grandpa sighed, closed his magazine, took the match out of his mouth and the earphones off his head, and turned back to look at us.

"Astronauts have a word for that, chaps," he grinned. "It's called RE-ENTRY."

Shaken though he was by the landing, Dad had been entirely unsurprised by Grandpa's nonchalance. "Typical Ivor," was all he'd said. "You've heard my stories."

We had. But it still took time getting used to the fact that Grandpa really was exactly like his stranger-than-fiction character in Dad's tales—fearlessly and recklessly embracing situations that made normal people quail, and generally expecting others to do likewise.

In 1963, when Grandpa Ivor and Granny Mavis divorced,

and Grandpa left for Botswana, Dad was twelve. Henry was fourteen, Jonathan just ten.

From the moment they arrived in Botswana for their holiday visits, the three young boys were given total, unadulterated freedom. Grandpa Ivor's early trailer camp at Motopi, just east of the base of the Okavango Delta, stood on the bank of the Boteti River, one of the most crocodile-infested rivers in the country. This the brothers would swim across, Grandpa Ivor cheering them on as they raced to the opposite bank and back again. Driving in Grandpa's old brakeless Land Rover—"Why drive anything but wrecks on these bloody roads?"—was probably as treacherous. And almost certainly more so on the regular occasions that the unlicensed boys, who'd often had several drinks themselves, had to drive their inebriated driver back home after fetching supplies in nearby Maun, the dusty town at the gateway to the delta.

Whenever they could, Dad, Henry, and Jonathan accompanied Grandpa Ivor on his flights: conducting game counts of the animals around the delta's vast patchwork of water and islands, or dropping hunters deep in the inaccessible bush and collecting them, days later, with their sad, splendid trophies. And, flying beside him over the years, the boys had experienced firsthand many of the famous petrifying-for-normal-people Grandpa Ivor flying stories—taking off overloaded, landing in the bush when an engine failed, flying a plane with so little fuel that he'd touched down, taxied in, and the next day been unable to restart it. Not one drop was left in the tank.

But like snakes and crocodiles, none of these real dangers scared Grandpa. How much of this was just his character, and how much dated to the numbing years of World War II, no one was certain. When we asked him about it—"How many planes? How many bombs? How many dead?"—Grandpa's face would become blank. "For God's sake," he'd mutter, "I'm an old man. Ya can't expect me to remember these things."

His own sons didn't get a great deal further, and until he became much older and began to share his painful memories, I'd know little more than that he'd been awarded the Distinguished

Flying Cross for "exceptional cool under fire." Asked what precisely he'd got it for, he would just shrug. "Nothing much."

Whether or not the war had inured Grandpa to danger, it had certainly deepened that odd, profoundly suspicious part of him, where his real fears now lay.

"I hate flying on the thirteenth," he would say. "Bad stuff. Ronnie died on the thirteenth. Ya know the story? Terrifying story."

We did, but we were always happy to listen again.

Ronald was Grandpa Ivor's brother. Handsome, talented, and charismatic, he was loved by everyone, and adored by Grandpa. But all through his life, Ronnie carried with him one unshakable black mark: the words of his allegedly psychic grandmother, who'd allegedly proclaimed on first seeing the baby, "Cannon fodder." At the start of World War II, Ronnie, like Grandpa Ivor, enrolled in the South African Air Force—he becoming a fighter pilot, Grandpa a bomber pilot.

Ronnie's registration number was 103711.

"Ya see," Grandpa would say, "adds up to thirteen." Scottie, as he became known in the air force, was shot down near Tripoli on Friday the thirteenth, December 1942. Apparently, that same day, his picture fell off his mother's wall and his pet donkey went missing. A year later, to the day, Grandpa was flying across the same skies in which his brother's plane had gone down. "Blacked out," said Grandpa, "don't remember a thing." For fifteen minutes, he recalled nothing, and all communications directed at his plane went unacknowledged. He recovered to find himself miles away from the spot he last remembered.

"Bloody terrifying," he'd say, shaking his head. "Never forget it. Ronnie got to me, I tell you. Absolutely bloody terrifying."

But dead bodies themselves—provided their spirits weren't troublesome—didn't bother Grandpa Ivor in the slightest.

During his early years in Botswana, as one of the few charter pilots, he'd often been called on to fly corpses back to their families in South Africa and Zimbabwe. "Ya could hear them breathe with the pressure changes," he'd say, reminiscing thoughtfully. "Fascinating."

Nowadays he ran a coffin-making factory in Phikwe, in a small corrugated-iron roofed building at the foot of a *koppie*.

Sometimes, when he went to check on things and wanted company, he'd invite one of us along. On a bad day, when there were problems at the factory and Grandpa ranted at the coffin makers, this could result in a long, boring wait among the varnish and sawdust-smelling coffins. But if things went well, Grandpa might tell hours of stories about the old days, or—if I wanted to talk—provide an audience willing to listen, seriously and without teasing, to anything I said.

"This is a bloody wonderful business, Robbie," said Grandpa, flinging open arms toward the cluttered workshop entrance. "Absolutely bloody wonderful!"

I nodded from my uncomfortable perch on the lid of a dark wood, gold-handled coffin.

"You see, you've got guaranteed demand."

"How come?"

"Ah-ha. Well, think about it." Grandpa was pacing up and down the dirt in front of the tiny factory building. Inside, two bored-looking Batswana men were swatting flies and varnishing a new pine coffin. "People always gotta die."

"I knew that."

"Hang on!" He shouted. "It's not so simple. Ya gotta listen to what I'm telling you. Ya listening?"

"Yip."

"Marvelous. You see, the Batswana will spend anything on funerals," he continued. "What's a thousand pula for a coffin when you've gotta kill three cows just to feed your five hundred guests?"

I nodded again, bewildered by the enormous figure.

Grandpa said that in Botswana, going to funerals was practically a national pastime. Not actually knowing the deceased did not, moreover, prevent people from attending. "It's a perfect market, Robbie! Business is all about time and motion and understanding your market." Hands on hips, he paused and glared down at me. "D'ya understand what I'm saying?"

" 'Course I do," I said, still a bit confused.

"Marvelous." He relaxed, smiled, and began his laps again. "You'll make a great little entrepreneur. Might even have you running my company one day."

"Really?"

But Grandpa wasn't listening anymore. "By then I'll be supplying coffins all over the country—and beyond. Internationally." He gazed into the distance above the corrugated tin roof. "A coffin empire!" He took a deep breath. "Now, how does that sound, eh?"

I felt myself grinning stupidly, tingling with pride.

"It sounds wonderful, Grandpa."

It did. And as we sped back home in the rattling old *bakkie*, hooting wildly at dawdling cars, meandering donkey carts, and dozing goats, everything seemed wonderful. "Land of opportunity," yelled Grandpa, turning to me and hurriedly swerving back onto the road. "If you've got vision, you can do anything here. Democratic! Peaceful! Untapped! Look at all that space."

Far ahead of us, swathed in a haze of heat waves, the black strip of road melted into the flat bush. Far beyond that, at some elusive point, the bush became endless, cloudless blue sky. Only a few black bird flecks and the glowing white sphere of sun gave perspective to the gigantic expanse.

Hot, dry, and unforgiving still. But with fast cool air buffeting sticky skin and the untapped world whizzing past, inimitably wonderful too, I stared until my eyes watered in the brightness and dry air.

That's generous of him," said Dad, when I announced I might one day be running Grandpa's coffin empire. "But concentrate on building your own empire first."

"Huh?"

"Grandpa's a dreamer, Robbie."

"But people are always going to die," I blurted. "It's a perfect market."

"Grandpa's built lots of empires in his head before."

"This is different."

"Maybe," laughed Dad. "But I'll believe it when I see it."

The main problem, maintained Dad, was that Grandpa was like a magnet for *skellums* who took advantage of him.

"Like that bloody Motswagole."

Mr. Motswagole was one of Grandpa's business partners in a general store in a nearby village. When he came round to announce a new disaster that required more money, he was always polite and smiling. He spoke excellent English and wore a suit. He wasn't how I imagined a *skellum*.

"*Ah-ah!* Dear, dear me," he would say, rubbing his palms together and shaking his head. "This is a terrible thing. Terrible. Most unfortunate. So regrettable. But then we mustn't weep over spilt milk."

The news always involved something that had been lost, stolen, or broken, and someone who had let him, Mr. Motswagole, down. Grandpa's response always involved yelling, "You're fucking unbelievable, Motswagole," followed by more shouting.

It was unmissable theater. At Grandpa's first furious bellow, Lulu, Damien, and I would charge toward the dusty parking lot beside Grandpa's house, where Mr. Motswagole, leaning against his *bakkie* and studying his feet with a thoughtful expression, would be waiting in silence as Grandpa yelled.

As soon as Grandpa paused, he too would start shouting.

"*Ah-ah.* It is terrible. There are lots of bad people in this country."

"Bloody disgrace," Grandpa would splutter.

"Everyone trying to make money. *Eish!* No respect."

"Bunch of bloody crooks! Scoundrels, Motswagole, I tell you."

"So it is up to us to succeed despite them. After all, it is the early bird that catches the golden egg."

"Absolutely bloody right."

Sometimes Granny Betty would shuffle outside. Quietly stroking the cat, she'd listen with an expression of growing despair.

"You know, Ivor," Mr. Motswagole would continue, "as I

always say, birds of a feather roost together. We are going to have a great success. We have a great business. We are a great team. You are a grrr-reat man."

"No, no, Motswagole. Just good instincts." Grandpa would pat his partner on the back. "Now come in and have a beer." And Grandpa and Mr. Motswagole would disappear through the front door. And Granny Betty would follow slowly, thin shoulders hunched, head bent and shaking.

Once, in a thrilling twist to the performance, Granny Betty interjected, silencing Grandpa Ivor and Mr. Motswagole, who stared at her in amazement. In her soft, smoking-husky voice, she quietly suggested that Grandpa perhaps shouldn't give Mr. Motswagole another loan.

Mr. Motswagole winced. "*Eish*, Mrs. Scott." He gave a pained look and hung his head.

"*What*, Betty?" Grandpa snapped. "Are ya trying to ruin my business too?"

"Ivor, I'm trying to save your business."

"Then whaddaya suggest I bloody well do?"

"Say *no*." She glared at Mr. Motswagole. "And please don't swear in front of the kids."

"Let down my partner?" Grandpa spluttered. "Out of the bloody question."

Granny pointed out that there was no money left to loan. "I can show you the books."

"'Course there's money. You've made a mistake. Been using that bloody Japanese brain again, have you?"

But Granny had already turned away and was hobbling back inside.

Japanese brain was Grandpa's name for the calculator, which he viewed with contempt. "Use your own head," he yelled, when he caught me using one. "That's what it's there for."

"It's too hard."

"Nonsense." He stared at the elaborate sum, running his hand through his thin, standing-on-end white hair. Then he grabbed a pen and wrote down a four-figure number.

"Check it. Whaddaya waiting for?"

I carefully pressed the buttons and stared at Grandpa in wonder.

"Whaddid I tell you? Piece of cake. Don't be so lazy."

Grandpa's presence extended far beyond his physical appearances.

During late evenings by the fire, when the lights across the road had long been extinguished and the last sticky heat had vanished from the air, he was there too: hero and villain—occasionally both—of endless laugh-till-you-hurt, open-your-mouth-in-amazement tales. Sometimes, when Henry or Jonathan and their families were visiting from South Africa, Grandpa Ivor stories could go on for hours, the sons vying gently for the rapt attention of the grandchildren, who, in turn, competed too: Henry's four, Greg, Ryan, Andrew, and Michael, against Keith's three, against Jonathan's two, Daniel and William—each faction gleeful to discover a familiar Grandpa Ivor story that the others had yet to hear. And bedtime rules would then be for once forgotten as the brothers took turns out-Ivor-storytelling each other, choking on their laughter and the sweet smoke of the mopane wood.

I was not the first to be told off for mental shortcuts. Grandpa had been famously unable to teach his flying school students how to use coordinate-calculating equipment, as, working out everything in his head, he'd long forgotten how to use it himself. It was with this amazing mental computing that he'd become so famous for breaking after-dark landing rules, often calculating in his head the location of the runway by triangulating signals from towns hundreds of kilometers away.

Grandpa Ivor broke rules of decency and duty too, forgetting to tell his sons that he had remarried—a fact they only discovered when, after a two-day journey from South Africa, they arrived at his trailer camp at four in the morning and were greeted by Granny Betty in her pajamas. Granny Betty, who was just as surprised, explained, as she lit a fire in the half a forty-four-gallon drum suspended from a tree beside the caravans. A few minutes after she'd set about frying the boys a large eggs-and-bacon breakfast, Grandpa stuck his head out his trailer door. "You guys could have timed it a bit bloody better," he yelled, before disappearing back inside to bed.

Sometimes when Dad was in a rare sentimental mood, he'd say, "I wish Grandpa had spent more time with me when I was a boy."

Even when he and Granny Mavis were still married, Grandpa had often disappeared on many-day drinking binges, with no word to his wife or sons. He hadn't celebrated Christmas; he rarely remembered birthdays. At first, I'd felt sick with pity for Dad: the idea of him doing the same to us was inconceivable. But a few months after we arrived in Botswana, having witnessed several spectacular tirades, I began to think that Dad was probably quite fortunate to have had only limited exposure to Grandpa.

As a grandfather, however, he was perfect: for as long as you didn't stand to be disappointed by Grandpa Ivor, his mix of the brilliant, impossible, generous, and irresponsible made him only more attractive and fascinating, in life and in stories—told by his sons with a mixture of resentment and adoration.

He was as good a teller as he was a subject, and when he was present, it was always Grandpa Ivor who monopolized the storytelling, mimicking, hysterically, the expressions and voices of the strange characters he had come across over the years in Botswana. On these occasions, after a few attempts to interrupt with their own favorite stories, which were usually about him, Dad, Henry, and Jonathan, smile-creased faces bizarre in the firelight, would give up, throwing back their heads and laughing until they wheezed and wiped their eyes.

Whether Grandpa was present depended on whether he and Dad were speaking. They often didn't, sometimes for days—days when Mum, Lulu, Damien, and I had to deliver messages between them. Dad said Grandpa Ivor was irrational, didn't appreciate Granny Betty, and gave all his money away to crooks. Mum said not speaking to him was irrational and that such destructive bloody-mindedness could only be genetic, after which Dad hardly spoke to Mum for several days either.

Then one day Grandpa Ivor decided to make furniture instead of coffins. "Gonna supply furniture to the nation," he announced. "In this economy, that's the market you gotta be in."

It was the early 1990s, and the economy was booming, still mostly on the back of the immense diamond wealth, which since the discovery of diamonds in the 1970s had helped make Botswana one of the world's fastest-growing economies. Hoping to reduce dependence on one industry and increase employment, the government had introduced the Financial Assistance Program, known as FAP. For five years, tax write-offs and salary and equipment subsidies were lavished upon start-up companies. Foreigner owners were eligible too, and Phikwe was full of South African and Zimbabwean businessmen on the "FAP gravy train." These "FAP *skellums*" established companies, pocketed as much as possible, and complained about the lazy blacks in Botswana. After five years, when companies were meant to be running independently and FAP subsidies dried up, they simply folded the business and returned home.

FAP subsidies had enabled Grandpa to keep his business going, even though, after several years, he still hadn't made any money out of his coffins. After another year he hadn't made any money out of furniture either. He fired his employees, closed the business, and went into petrol stations instead. Dad said only Grandpa Ivor could rip off the government and still manage to not make a profit.

Later, Dad would also say that only Grandpa Ivor could manage to close a coffin business just as everyone started to die.

11

WHISPERS ABOUT LIONS

Village

D ad held up his hand to the light, studying it with the same squinty look Mum got when she examined her chin in the mirror for stray whiskers. He unwrapped another Band-Aid and stuck it over a tiny red scratch, adding to the five or six pink waterproof rings he'd begun putting on after he had finished his bowl of Pronutro.

"Why do you need so many?"

"To cover all the cuts."

"But they're all so small."

Every weekend, Dad worked in the ancient shed, building furniture for the cottage and his clinics and fixing engines and motors. He often cut himself and put Band-Aids on the big, blood-oozing cuts—but never before on the tiny thorn scratches that covered all of our legs, arms, and hands. Dad said, "Don't be such a hypochondriac," when we complained about bigger scratches than these.

"Don't be such a hypochondriac, *man*," I said. Lulu and Damien giggled. I smirked.

"Not guilty, Robbie."

Mum and Dad had talked before about acquired immune deficiency syndrome and the human immunodeficiency virus. But they had never before stood out among all the other exotic-sounding STDs that Dad saw at his clinics: syphilis, gonorrhea, chlamydia, herpes, chancroid, trichomoniasis, genital warts—diseases with fascinatingly gruesome symptoms, curiosities from a different world that hadn't ever threatened to interfere with mine.

I felt my legs going weak as I listened to his explanation for the plasters.

"You might catch it?"

"I won't, as long as I'm careful." Dad explained that the plasters were a precaution for external examinations, in case his hands came into contact with any wounds. For internal examinations he always used gloves.

"What if you miss a scratch?"

"I won't."

"How do you know?"

"Because I'm careful. And the chances are minuscule. The virus dies very quickly on contact with air."

"But *you* could die," I gasped.

"How do you know you haven't got it already?" asked Damien.

"Because I test myself regularly."

"Can I have a test?"

"Me too."

"Oh, for God's sake. None of you have it." Dad pushed his chair back and stood up. "Now I'm going to work. Stop worrying."

Mum showed us a diagram of the progression of HIV infection to AIDS: starting with a mild fever immediately after infection, followed by about five years of no symptoms, after which people start to get increasingly sick, before finally developing AIDS, a range of horrible diseases resulting from the near collapse of the victim's immune system.

Apart from the fact that there was no cure and it killed you, this was the scariest part: that people with HIV walked around for five years—sometimes ten, longer than I had lived—looking healthy and infecting other people.

"So anyone could have it, and we wouldn't know?"

"Yes," said Mum. "But the incidence is still low."

"Do you think Ruth has it? She's had lots of boyfriends." All of Ruth's three children had different fathers, none of whom she'd ever married.

"I'm sure not."

"Can I ask her?"

"No, you certainly can't."

"Why?"

"Because it's none of your business."

I watched the shiny knife blade slide back and forth, millimeters away from Ruth's fingertips. She was preparing the vegetables for supper, slicing hundreds of pieces of carrots, zucchini, leeks, and potatoes for vegetable pie, and lettuce, tomatoes, and celery for salad. I had squeezed in beside her at the tiny kitchen counter and was pretending to search for something in the cupboard, casting surreptitious glances at her fingers. Her dark skin made it harder than I had expected to spot cuts.

"Ah." Ruth looked from my face to her hands with a bemused expression. "What is the matter, Robbie?"

"Nothing." I smiled stupidly. "Nothing." I grabbed a carrot and slunk away, guilty and no more at ease.

Supper, which we ate around the big wooden table on the veranda, was one of the best times of the day. It was the time when Dad told stories about his day at the clinic, and we told him about our days, and he and Mum discussed politics and books and argued furiously about the meanings of words until Lulu, Damien, or I was ordered to fetch the giant *Concise Oxford Dictionary* and proclaim the victor. In the dim light of the gas lamp, with the bush and its smells and noises just a layer of shade cloth away, it was almost as exciting as camping. The only downside was chomping into the occasional stink bug overlooked in the bad light, for we'd all long since given up trying to scrutinize each mouthful.

"Robbie, what on earth are you doing?" Dad put down his knife and fork and stared at me.

"Nothing." I lowered the lettuce leaf I had been holding up to the light.

"Then what was that all about?"

"Nothing...well, what if Ruth cut herself and there's blood on the salad?"

"So?"

"AIDS," I muttered.

Dad coughed and looked at his plate.

"It's not funny!" I couldn't believe he didn't take a matter of life and death more seriously.

"Of course it's not," said Mum. She was also smiling. "But you mustn't worry. It's not going to happen."

"How can you be sure?"

Even if Ruth was carrying HIV, explained Dad—"which I'm sure she isn't"—she would not only have to bleed onto the salad, but one of us would have to immediately eat a bloody vegetable before the virus died. Even then, we'd have to have a sore on the inside of our mouth for the virus to get into our bloodstream.

"It's a weak virus," added Dad. "You can't get it from toilet seats. Or sneezing, like with colds. Sex, sharing hypodermic needles, and blood transfusions are the big risks."

"Oh." I still didn't feel like eating my salad.

"And we should all just thank our lucky stars that mosquitoes don't pass it on."

"How come?"

"When they bite you, they inject saliva, not blood. For mozzies to spread HIV, the virus would have to evolve to be transmitted in the saliva. Like malaria."

"Could it evolve?"

"In theory, I suppose," said Dad.

"It would be an evolutionary advantage to the virus," Mum said thoughtfully. "Would help it spread." She looked at me. "But *highly* unlikely," she added, quickly. "Highly, highly unlikely."

But it *was* possible, and suddenly a whole new terror loomed. I treated every mosquito as a suspect—potentially the first carrier of the one-in-many-millions-chance mutant virus. But it was too exhausting to sustain this fear. In Botswana, if you tried to avoid or swat every mosquito you saw, there was no time left to do anything else.

M um said, "I can't understand why you worry about AIDS and then happily ride that ratbag pony."

For the first ten minutes of our rides into the bush, Feste was cooperative, trotting along placidly as Quartz charged backward and forward across the bush, shying at donkey carts, birds, butterflies, mostly nothing. But then, always at exactly the same unmarked, unremarkable spot on the dirt track, Feste would stop.

"Give her a good kick, Robbie," Dad yelled from the other side of the imaginary line. "Show her who's boss."

I flapped my legs against Feste's now very large middle. Nothing happened. "Argh! Come on."

More kicks. Still nothing.

"I'll get you a stick." Dad steered Quartz toward a mopane tree and leaned over to pull off a thin branch. Hundreds of bright green leaves shimmered and rustled, and Quartz sprung forward and sideways, almost unseating Dad. "Damn it. Hang on, Robbie." Dad slid off Quartz and dragged him back to the tree. This time he succeeded in detaching a thin stick, which he handed to me after stripping off all the leaves except for a clump at the very end.

"Just give her a firm slap."

I flicked the stick against her side. Nothing happened. Again. Nothing. "Ahh, Dad. She won't budge."

"Keep going. Don't be afraid."

"I'm not afraid." I raised the spindly branch high in the air.

"*Come on,* girl!" I bellowed, kicking and simultaneously whacking her bottom with the stick. This time Feste did move, very quickly. But instead of going forward, she reared up into the air, and I slid backward, landing with a thud on my back, choking on the cloud of dust kicked up as Feste spun round and took off home at a gallop.

"You okay?" said Dad, peering down at me.

"I'm fine," I snapped. I started to sit up, and flopped back on the dirt. "Ow."

Quartz was tossing his head and jogging on the spot, yanking at the reins. "Bugger," muttered Dad. "Catch your breath for a moment. I'll have to let him go to help you."

I took off my hat and lay squinting up at the blinding blue sky while Dad knotted his reins on the top of Quartz's neck. As soon as he let go, Quartz vanished in another cloud of dust and thundering hooves.

"Can you walk, or do you want to wait for Mum to come find us?"

" 'Course I can walk."

"Look on the bright side," said Dad, as I hobbled home beside him. "At least they're not running back to Kobus's place anymore."

"I still keep falling off."

"True. But at least we know that strategy definitely doesn't work."

The next strategy was to trick Feste by cantering toward the line so fast that by the time she realized, she would have already crossed it.

She didn't. I did, tumbling over her head as she skidded to a halt at exactly the same place.

We tried every tactic: I rode her, Dad rode her, Mum, who didn't really ride, even rode her. Dad pulled her while I chased from behind, we bribed her with carrots, I steered her far off into the bush to avoid the spot on the road. Once we even brought Beauty, the foal, along. Nothing changed, except that Dad and I got better at hanging on and, when we didn't manage, at rolling as we landed on the sand, which made our frequent falls much less painful.

Then one day, about a month after the trouble began, we approached Feste's line armed with sugar cubes, a long rope to hook behind her bottom, a blindfold, and a whip. I dropped my reins as we neared the line, ready to slide off and begin trying different permutations of the equipment. But Feste just kept on walking, the dainty pitter-patter of her hooves on the dirt unbroken by the slightest hesitation. It was as if nothing had ever happened: the imaginary line had simply vanished from her imagination.

Except on Dad's two busiest clinic days, we rode every morning, often rushing out of the cottage at dawn, stopping only to write a note explaining our route to Mum.

The world we rode through was magnificent: in the low mopane scrub, being a little farther from the ground made a great difference, and even on tiny Feste, I could see for miles over the glowing green-gold early-morning bush.

"Let's go watch the planes," I suggested, as we trotted along a track not far from the airport.

"Okay. But don't blame me if there're shenanigans. They won't like it."

A five-meter-wide band of cleared bush surrounded the runway fence. It was covered with thin, dry grass and spindly shrubs. "Watch out for holes," shouted Dad as he drew ahead of me. We trotted on for a few minutes, squinting into the already fierce sun.

"It's going be a real scorcher today," said Dad.

"A cracker," I yelled back.

Nothing stirred on the runway, and the windsocks hung limp beside their poles. On the far side of the tarmac, a row of small airplanes gleamed in the sun. To the left of them, the glass control tower reflected blinding gold light. Nothing interrupted the huge expanse of blue above us.

"Looks like no flights, I'm afraid," Dad called over his shoulder.

"Ah."

"Probably a good thing with these ratbags." Quartz broke into a canter, and Feste accelerated after him. "Yee-hah." Dad threw one hand into the air and lifted his reins up, cowboy style.

Suddenly, Dad and Quartz parted: Quartz plunging to the left, toward the fence, Dad hurtling toward the bush on the right. I was momentarily aware of the guilty francolin, squawking as it flapped up from its hiding place. Then awful tearing pain, crunching sounds, and all I could see was finger-long white spikes and small hook thorns. I was in the middle of a *haak-'n-steek* bush, the worst thornbush in Botswana. I tried to move and screamed as the hooks dug deeper.

"Dad!" I started to cry. "Help. I'm stuck."

"Be there in a sec, Robbie."

After what seemed like ages, Dad appeared in front of me. "*Jees*," he said. "I think I was the lucky one." His face and arms were scratched, and his shirt was torn. "My thornbush was still green—a bit more forgiving than yours."

Even pulling slowly, Dad couldn't stop the dry, brittle thorn tips breaking off under my skin. When Mum eventually found us—she regularly and efficiently mounted rescue expeditions on mornings when the horses returned home riderless—I had to stand on the back of the *bakkie,* balancing: my hands too raw to grip the bars behind the hood and my bottom too sore to sit down, tears of pain and self-pity wiped gently away by the breeze.

I cried again as Mum peeled off my jodhpurs and knickers, which were stuck with dry blood to my skin. "Right, lie on your tummy," instructed Dad, when I was completely naked. I lay facedown on Mum and Dad's double bed, feeling sore and ridiculous. Armed with a pair of surgical tweezers and a hypodermic needle each, Mum and Dad set about picking hundreds of thorns out of my back and bottom. Lulu and Damien came to watch.

"Shuddup," I moaned as they giggled at me. "Ow. Ow."

"Yes, quiet, you two," said Mum. "It's not funny."

"Yes it is," giggled Damien. "Rob's got a thorny bum. Ha. Ha."

"Well it's not funny for Rob," said Mum. But Mum and Dad were laughing too.

"Riding can be a real pain in the butt, Rob," said Dad.

"What a cheek, Keith."

Damien stood at the opposite end of the huge, shallow pit. He held up a long blue wire. "Rob. Lu. These are the best," he shouted. "But if you see any reds or greens, get them too."

Since we had discovered the mine dump, Damien had already made several trips, and to find good fuses we now had to dig beneath the top layer—a dirty jumble of pipes, twisted metal, and dead leaves, blown inside over the decade since the dump had been abandoned. Sand too had found its way in, and small thorn-bushes fought for space with the rusting metal. But once you dug, there were plenty, and we set off on the path back home with about twenty between us.

"Where you gonna test them, Didge?"

"Dunno. Maybe in the pool."

"Dad'll freak out. You'll burn the plastic lining."

"The bath," Damien suggested.

"Even sillier idea."

"Didge, you really think they'll burn?" asked Lulu.

"I've told you," said Damien, impatiently. "John's dad said they work underwater."

John's dad, Hal, ran the VOA—the Voice of America radio broadcasting station in Phikwe. Mum and Dad thought there was something that didn't make sense about Hal: that he was too well qualified, too well traveled, and knew too much about cer-tain things to be running the Phikwe VOA, even if it was the cen-ter of the VOA for Southern Africa. (The only center Phikwe was of anything.) "A front for the CIA," they had speculated. "And, Damien, don't you dare tell him we said that." Damien hadn't. But ever since then he had believed, without question, everything Hal told him.

For a moment, as the creeping, sparkly point on the fuse reached the water in the horses' bucket and spluttered, it seemed that Hal had been wrong after all. But the sparkle had only dimmed; it kept going, all the way along the submerged wire, brightening suddenly as it climbed out into the air again.

Damien became obsessed with the underwater fuses. He would demonstrate them to anyone who was—or pretended to be—interested: Grandpa Ivor and Granny Betty, Matthews, Ruth, Mr. Motswagole, or Granny Joan, when she came for tea. And when he could no longer persuade anyone to watch again, he just lit fuses by himself. Soon he was returning on many-hour missions to the dump, excavating for fuses several feet beneath the surface.

Mum said, "I do worry about him scrounging around in that pit. Must be riddled with snakes."

"Well, there're snakes everywhere," said Dad, sipping his tea. "He knows to watch out."

Dad had just got back from work, and we were having late-afternoon tea and biscuits in the lounge. Outside the window, Damien was crouched over the horses' water bucket, lighting fuses. Glenn Nevill, one of Damien's friends from Phikwe, stood behind him, peering at the bucket.

Dad began talking about his clinic, and I sucked the end of my tea-soaked buttermilk biscuit, dunking it again and again until the tip became too soggy and had to be bitten off.

A loud crack shook the window.

Glenn was standing in a cloud of dust, looking surprised. Damien was stumbling away from the dust, bent over, hands clutched to his face.

A second later, Mum was standing up, overturned tea seeping across the carpet. "Shit, Keith! Damien." Her voice was hollow. It made me feel sick. Then Mum and Dad were both running through the kitchen door at the same time, banging into each other, calling Damien's name. Lulu and I ran after them, not knowing what else to do.

Damien was eerily silent. He was still clutching his eyes. Blood and dust covered the rest of his face. There was more blood on his arms and legs. Glenn was crying. Lulu and I were crying. Mum said, "God, Keith, his eyes." Mum held Damien. Dad knelt down in front of him.

"Come on, lad," he said. His voice was horribly calm. "Give me your hands." Dad pulled Damien's hands back. His eyes were screwed shut. There was blood on the lids. "Now, come on, lad, open your eyes for me."

Damien let out a small sob. Then slowly, he opened his eyes. The whites and two big green centers were still all there. Mum sat down silently on the dirt.

"Come on, chaps," said Dad. "Let's go and have a cup of tea and get you cleaned up."

Later, when Damien lay on the bed and Dad picked out shrapnel and grit with a hypodermic needle, no one laughed. Afterward, Damien helped himself to as much chocolate as he wanted from the special-occasions cupboard. Mum said Lulu and I could have as much as we liked too. She wasn't really listening when we asked. For a few hours that day she just sat on the sofa in silence, biting her nails and staring out the window with a far-away gaze.

But Mum never dwelled on the negative side of anything for too long. "It could have been so much worse," she was soon reminding us. "Finding out now might have avoided a tragedy in the future. Maybe it'll even put Damien off explosives...."

Glenn, who had been standing a few feet back when the deto-nator cap had gone off, was unscathed. Damien had small pieces of detonator shrapnel between his eyes, above his eyes, in his cheeks, and in his arms and legs. Damien had been leaning over the end of the fuse, where it had been attached to the small deto-nator. He hadn't known what it was, hadn't expected a detonator. It was illegal to put fuses with their detonator caps still attached in the dump. Hal was as shocked as Mum and Dad, and the dump became off-limits to Damien and his visiting friends alike.

I soon forgot to worry about AIDS. With so much else that could hurt us—snakes, wild horses, illegal detonators— that often did hurt us, invisible threats, however deadly, did not persist long on the list of daily concerns.

Stories from Dad's clinic were the only reminders. For it was then still several years before painfully thin bodies, and faces and necks with their unmistakable bulging cancers and skin disfigurations, were to be seen on every crowded Phikwe pavement. But for doctors, AIDS was known to few—talked about by still fewer.

Botswana had reported its first AIDS case in 1985, and by 1989 doctors were beginning to regularly see cases of full-blown AIDS. Yet there were still virtually no government education campaigns, no prevention strategies, and certainly no treatments available at government clinics. It would be several years still before the ubiquitous ABC billboards—"Abstain, Be Faithful, Condomise"—towered beside Botswana's roads and border posts, and more than a decade before the drugs became widely available.

A group of private doctors from the BCL mine asked for a meeting with a government minister. The minister agreed immediately and listened attentively to the worrying observations of the doctors, their concerns about the rising infection rate and the resurgence of TB, and the critical importance of acting immediately to educate people about the disease and condom use.

"Now is the government's chance to avert a catastrophe."

When they had finished, the minister nodded. "Gentlemen, you are right," he said, "I agree with everything you say. But I cannot help you. Nothing will be done. You see," he continued, with a sigh, "in Botswana, we have an old saying: '*When you are in the bush, you don't talk about the lions.*'"

12

THE CLINICS

Dad and Grandpa leave for the clinics

At his busiest clinics, Dad saw more than one hundred patients a day. After payday at the end of the month, the number could reach one hundred and fifty. To get through the long queue of patients before nightfall, Dad worked almost continuously. Sometimes, when he returned home late in the evening, his lunchbox was barely touched—a banana, blackened by the fierce heat of the clinics, oozing across uneaten sandwiches.

If one of Dad's nurses was on leave, or sick, or away at a funeral, he couldn't cope. This didn't often happen. But when it did—when the carefully choreographed five-minute consultation system stood to otherwise fall apart—Mum, as well as Dad, would kiss us good-bye in the unfriendly, four-thirty-in-the-morning darkness, and as we drifted back to sleep they would set off together for the airport. Lulu, Damien, and I would spend the day shuttling between our house and Grandpa Ivor's, where Granny Betty would give us breakfast, lunch, and finally dinner, after which we'd curl up on the sofa, where we'd half watch TV, or half doze. With the other half we'd listen, first for the airplane, and then for the car.

Waiting for Dad, with Mum safely there to reassure us, was bad enough. Waiting for both parents, somewhere out there in the darkness, was almost unbearable. On these agonizing evenings, the later it grew, the more awake we'd become and the harder we'd strain our ears for the unmistakable revving of the car rounding the last bend in the driveway where the huge termite mound bulged out onto the road and the stiff boscia tree branches clawed at the side mirrors.

By the time the sharp clicks of the cattle grid rang through the night, we were off Grandpa's sofa, yelling good night, running out into the darkness, and waving at the bright headlights as they swept across the dirt and blazed against the walls of the unlit cottage.

The lights died as the car stopped, and the cottage disappeared once more into blackness. The doors swung open, and clinic smell—disinfectant, latex-rubber-glove powder, sweaty bodies in 104-degree heat—poured out into the night. I breathed deeply of the sweet-sharp mix, letting it wash over me as I kissed Mum and Dad and followed their outlines inside. I loved that smell—the smell of relief at a safe return; and anticipation of the breathtaking stories Dad might have brought back with him this time.

Still in darkness, a Coleman water cooler, two untouched lunchboxes, and Dad's medicine bag clattered onto the dining room table. Then someone reached the kitchen light switch, and bright electric light flooded the room.

At once, I felt terrible for enjoying the smell.

Dad's eyes were bloodshot, his smile tired and weak. But Dad's after-clinic expression I was used to. Mum's I was not. Her lively face had turned numb, and a day of frowning had creased deep lines between her eyebrows. She caught me staring, and smiled. It was the smile you make when an airplane hits bad turbulence, and someone looks at you, and you smile to pretend everything's fine, when all you really want to do is throw up.

Dad made hundreds of trips a year to his four village clinics. Mum made just a handful. But it was through Mum's stories that I got closest to understanding what working in the villages was really like.

Although Dad gradually made improvements to these clinics—painting, plumbing, replacing warped doors—they remained a hot, hellish world away from the Phikwe clinic that Lulu, Damien and I knew so well.

And of his other clinics, Dad told us just the broad facts and the best stories: the number of patients; the time patients took; the sequence of events in the consultation; and, most of all, the amazing tales about the bewildering and funny things patients did. The grim details of the place, he mentioned only if they made a good story.

Like the extraordinary fate of the loos at his clinic in Tonota.

There were three of them, flush toilets instead of the usual long-drops, side by side, their doors set in a concrete wall in the courtyard. Dad only ever peed, entering and exiting the grimy, stinking cubicles as quickly as possible. Then one day, taking a deep breath and flinging open the door, he stopped—transfixed by the sight of an old man, sitting under a lush fig tree, slowly chewing a roasted mealie. The back wall of the loos had disappeared altogether, swallowed up, one day, into a hole created by the badly built septic tank leach field. After that, Dad was forced to use the even filthier subsiding long-drop toilet. He referred to it as the Leaning Bog of Tonota when he gave us progress updates on its decreasing angle to the ground.

About how he actually felt—having to use the filthy loos, working in the stifling heat, seeing the horribly sick patients—Dad rarely spoke. When Dad wanted to forget something unpleasant, he forgot by never giving words to his thoughts. Mum did the opposite. She purged unpleasant things, talking about the horrors until she had nothing left of them inside her. Which sometimes meant that when they argued, they actually had the bigger argument afterward, about the first argument, going round in circles: Mum saying, "Let's talk about why we fought, Keith," Dad saying, "There's nothing to talk about. It's over. What's the point in talking about something you can't change?"

So it was through Mum's accounts of the clinics that I felt the vicarious exhaustion of working for uninterrupted hours in the airless, fanless consulting and dispensing rooms. It was Mum who told us about the smell of too-long-neglected festering sores; about the women with AIDS, clasping their babies with AIDS, who still managed to smile and laugh; about the babies that peed all over the examination couch; about how she'd hold in her own pee for hours till she wanted to burst before braving the disgusting fly-swathed long-drops.

And it was Mum who said how she wanted to weep when, midafternoon, the cramped, pungent waiting room was still overflowing with hours' worth of patients. She wanted to weep for the patients who'd traveled for hours to see Dad; for herself, for having to be there now; and most of all, for Dad, for having to do this every week. "I don't know how your father does it," she'd mutter for several days afterward. "How he manages to give every patient his full attention, no matter how knackered he is. Let me tell you, Robbie, there are moments in that place it feels like hell on earth."

The hands on the kitchen clock pointed to just before ten, which was a late return, even for a busy clinic. "How many today, Dad?" I asked.

"One twenty or so," sighed Dad. "Lost count."

"Why are you so late, then?"

Dad turned to Mum. "Lin, do you want to shower first?"

"You go," said Mum.

"Mum, why are you so late?" I persisted, as Dad disappeared to the bathroom.

Mum stared silently at the windowpane, drying her hands on a dishtowel. The uncurtained glass seethed with insects. Occasionally, one thudded against the glass and plunged, stunned, back into the darkness.

"Mum!"

Mum started to giggle. At first, it was just a few choked hiccups, then, her shoulders shaking, she laughed in long, loud wheezes. Shocked into silence, Lulu, Damien, and I watched quietly as tears rolled down her cheek.

"Sorry," spluttered Mum, wiping her eyes. "It's terrible of me to laugh...terrible.... It's not funny. It was so awful." She stifled another half laugh, half sob, and walked to the lounge, where she collapsed on a chair. Lying back, she put a hand over her mouth and shut her eyes. When she opened them, a few moments later, any trace of laughter was gone, her face suddenly just tired. "Oh Lordy," she said, "what a day."

That day, Mum and Dad learned that the forty-year-old landlord of Dad's clinic had died.

The cleaner told them when they arrived at the clinic in the sparkling early-morning light. He'd died, suddenly, just a few days before, and as Dad only visited each village once a week, this was the first he'd heard of it.

It was early evening before Dad saw his last patient and Mum dispensed the last batch of pills and ointments. The landlord's home was not far from the clinic building, and Mum and Dad set off on foot along the clear sandy paths winding between the hedges that surrounded many huts in the better part of the village.

Outside the large thatched rondavel, about fifty men sat on low wooden benches, chatting and smoking. Sporadic howls emanated from the doorway to the dimly lit room. The men greeted Mum and Dad with hearty *dumelas*. When Dad explained that they wanted to pay their respects to Mma Maoto, the eldest man smiled and indicated that Dad should take a seat. Then he turned to Mum. "Mma, the women are inside," he announced. "You can go in there," he continued, pointing to the doorway of the cavernous rondavel.

Mum didn't move. "Keith," she hissed, "I don't even know this woman. You've got to come with." Dad just shrugged and squatted down on the nearest bench.

The only one left standing, Mum reluctantly made her way to the entrance. The nearly sealed room still held the worst heat of the day, the air thick with the smell of smoke, soap, sweat, sand, and paraffin. Over twenty women sat in the gloom, on stools or cross-legged on the floor. No one seemed to notice Mum, standing hesitantly in the doorway. Some of the women were weeping softly, others wailing in loud bursts, some just sat quietly.

The most sorrowful howls came from a large woman lying, alone, on a mattress at the back of the hut. Mum picked her way in between the other women and knelt down beside the mattress.

Seeing Mum, the woman's cries subsided, and Mum introduced herself as Linda, Dr. Scott's wife. "I'm so sorry, Mma, about your husband," she said, not sure even that Mma Maoto understood English. "I'm so, so sorry."

The woman stared at her, tears rolling down her cheeks, motionless but for her large, heaving bosom. Then, just as Mum began rising to leave, the widow flung her arms upward around Mum's neck. Mum, unbalanced, tumbled onto the mattress and sunk into a pile of blankets and a tight embrace. When she tried to pull herself up, Mma Maoto, who had started to howl again, grabbed her arm, and Mum collapsed back down beside the distraught woman.

Not knowing what else to do, Mum did what she'd done so many times before with Lulu and me when a beloved pet died, and we lay in bed sleepless with tears. She rolled close beside the shaking body, clasped her arms around it, and pulled Mma Maoto's head to her heart. The young widow clutched Mum back, and for the next ten minutes didn't let go as she sobbed and sobbed, and soaked their shirts in tears.

That night was the first time AIDS became more to me than just a sporadic, selfish fear fomented by imagination and a collection of terrifying facts. I didn't know Mma or Rra Maoto; I didn't even know, at the time, that it was AIDS. But imagining the young, lonely mother of six weeping on the mattress in the dim room, it was impossible not to feel shaken—by sadness at the loss, and horror at whatever grim thing had brought such unfair, unexpected death.

Rra Maoto, tall, plump, and strong, was an unusual case. He regularly visited Dad for what he called his "tune-up and service," which Dad gave him for free. A few weeks before his death, he'd come to the clinic complaining of weakness. He was not nauseous or feverish, he had no sores, and his appetite was still good. Dad told him to go to the hospital for some blood tests. And, just in case, for an HIV test.

The next week he was feeling worse, and he had still not gone for the tests. Dad repeated his instructions. The next week he was dead, from heart failure. The heart failure was a consequence of a type of cardiomyopathy, a rare heart condition sometimes caused by the virus before the infected person progresses to full-blown AIDS.

Dad said at least Rra Maoto was not yet gaunt and wasted, which spared his wife any whispered speculation about why a relatively young man died so suddenly. Mma Maoto, herself, didn't believe the diagnosis. Dad told her to get tested, but she didn't want to know if she was HIV-positive, and never came back to Dad as a patient. By the time she, too, might have been showing symptoms, Dad had another landlord in another clinic, and we never found out what became of her.

Dad went to Rra Maoto's funeral, which was sooner than customary after the death. Because so many people came from so far for funerals, time was usually given to make travel arrangements. But the undertakers, who were just starting to feel the industry boom and had yet to expand their capacity, were booked out solidly on every other possible later date—with the young, thin, and mysteriously, suddenly dead.

In Botswana then, in the early 1990s, death in old age was still an expectation.

There were no famines, no wars. Health care, education, and sanitation had improved dramatically since independence. In the late 1980s the health department, in conjunction with the World Health Organization, had undertaken a blitz on STDs, the big outstanding health issue. Because of the difficulty of monitoring patients in the rural areas, every patient with an STD was routinely given a cocktail of the strongest antibiotics available. It had been a great success. Syphilis, gonorrhea, chancroid—the once-rife diseases that had shocked Dad in the first year of his clinics—virtually disappeared.

In 1990, life expectancy in Botswana was in the mid-sixties, one of the highest in Africa. Over the next fifteen years, it would plunge by around three decades. AIDS—in 1990, already common among his patients—wasn't, however, what Dad generally talked about, and was not, in the early days, what we knew his clinics for. After he'd said it once, there was not much to say: he treated the associated complications as best he could, and then he sent people home to die. With the early AIDS drugs prohibitively expensive, and the government not even talking about the lions, there was little prospect of a solution.

So mostly, when Dad held us riveted with his dinnertime stories, he stuck to the absurd, and to the people who were going to live. Or, occasionally, to those who died happily, in old age, waved farewell by their families as they departed for the realm of the ancestors: an already familiar world, closely and powerfully intertwined with the lives and fortunes of the living.

The *baðimo*, or ancestors, are fundamental to the religious beliefs of most Batswana. Nor is theirs a passive role, and their goodwill must be nurtured assiduously. Losing it can have consequences ranging from a poor rainy season, infertility, or an unhappy life to daily misfortunes: failing an exam, losing a job, catching a cold, the death of a cow. Even to the many Christian Batswana, the *baðimo* often remain important.

If the ancestors are not behind a misfortune, witchcraft may be to blame, perhaps at the behest of an angry or jealous colleague or neighbor. Like the displeasure of the *baðimo*, this is at odds with the Batswana's belief in all-important harmony between people, their ancestors, their environment, and their god, Modimo.

All of which means that when a Western doctor tackles a disease, his patient may be seeing the problem through an altogether different lens and, even if the doctor successfully treats the illness, may resort to traditional healers to deal with the "cause." It also means that if a patient dies—perhaps the greatest mark of failure in the West—the death may be considered entirely beyond the responsibility of the doctor.

And because the dead live on, nearby and forever, if you die when you are old and ready to die, no one protests your relocation to the world of ancestral spirits.

Like the very old, white-haired man who walked into Dad's waiting room, coughing noisily. Despite being frail, he walked unaided, and his leathery face remained in a persistent grin as Dad examined him. Dad diagnosed pneumonia. The man was over ninety, several decades too old for AIDS to be the likely underlying cause. Dad gave him an antibiotic, in addition to the usual four-pronged regime—injection, liquid, tablets, and ointment—and with a nod and a toothless smile of thanks the man shuffled outside again.

Half an hour later, Dad was called to the waiting room. Maria pointed to a corner, where the ancient man was sitting quietly, his head lolling back against the wall. The room was full, and the patients either side of him chatted loudly.

"That old man is dead," said Maria, matter-of-factly. "He was waiting for his lift."

Walking over, Dad checked to see if he was breathing, felt for his pulse, and examined his pupils. He was dead.

"Can we take him somewhere?" Dad asked Maria. "To his family?"

Maria spoke to one of the women sitting beside the dead man. After a rapid conversation in Setswana, she turned back to Dad. "Don't move him," she said. "His son will be here soon."

"All right. Tell me when he comes," said Dad, returning to his current patient and trying not to think about the prospect of confronting the son of a man who had died in his waiting room, after being treated.

The dead man sat on the waiting room chair for another hour.

When the dead man's son finally arrived, he greeted Dad

with a warm handshake and smile. He spoke good English and nodded understandingly as Dad explained that his father was very old and weak and had died painlessly. Then he thanked Dad for his attention to the old man, thanked him again for helping to carry the body outside to the *bakkie,* and waved him good-bye as he trundled away down the dirt road.

Dealing with healthy patients, for a doctor, could often be the hardest of all, and it was one such patient who, three years after Dad started practicing, drove him to break one of his most non-negotiable self-imposed codes of conduct—rules for what he considered the reasonable adaptation of general medicine in rural, traditional settings.

"My patients have won," he announced one evening at dinner. He leaned back in his chair and surveyed four curious faces. "I took a patient's blood today."

Ever since he'd started his clinics, Dad had refused to draw blood except for diagnostic reasons. "I will never encourage that ridiculous belief," he'd said many times before. Even facing defecting patients who complained that Dr. Meyer had taken their blood, Dad had told them they could go elsewhere.

Lulu, Damien, and I gaped at Dad. We gaped not about the blood, but because Dad had changed his mind. When Dad made a decision, he never changed his mind. It was the most frustrating, reassuring, and reliable thing about him.

Mum said, "You said you'd never do that, Keith."

"How come, Dad?"

But Dad was looking at Mum. Mum took another mouthful. She chewed slowly, glaring at her plate. Dad said, "Lin, hear me out at least."

"Fine," said Mum. "I'm just incredibly disappointed."

Dad said, "I made that promise before I understood this place."

"Keith," spluttered Mum, "how the hell can understanding a place ever make you think it's okay to perpetuate such dangerous ignorance?" Her knife and fork clattered to her plate. "Quite frankly, I'm shocked."

Doubly stunned, Lulu, Damien, and I looked at the table. Mum never got disappointed and never shouted as reliably as Dad never changed his mind.

"Will you hear me out, Lin?"

"Whatever you want," said Mum coldly.

Three weeks earlier, an elderly man had visited Dad at his Tonota clinic. He had an infected arm, at the site of an IV that had been left in too long. Dad cleaned and dressed the open part of the infection and prescribed him antibiotics and painkillers. On his instruction, Maria explained to the patient that the pain would go and the infection should clear up in a few days.

The man replied in agitated Setswana.

"He wants you to take dirty blood from his arm."

"You know I don't take blood," said Dad. "Tell him."

"I've told him," said Maria. "He says he has dirty blood."

"Tell him again."

Maria translated and turned back to Dad. "He says he won't get better until you take blood."

"He will get better," said Dad. He gave the man a reassuring smile. "*Tsamaya sentle, rra.*" He turned to Maria. "Now give him his medicines and bring in the next patient."

The following Wednesday, the man came back. The wound looked much better. The man looked worse. He gasped in pain as he told Dad, via Maria, how his arm was in even greater agony.

"He wants you to take blood."

"Tell him that I won't. And if he's not happy with me, he can go back to the hospital."

After another exchange, Maria said, "He says the hospital gave him dirty blood."

Dad looked at the patient's card. His village was Matsitama. "Where's that, Maria?"

"Ah, far away," said Maria. "On the road to Orapa."

Dad stared in amazement at the man who had twice traveled two hundred kilometers to see him. He gave him stronger painkillers. "Tell him this is the best I can do. And tell him he will get better. And tell him if he goes to a private doctor again he'll just be wasting his money."

The man, looking dismayed, left with his new batch of pain-killers. The following Wednesday, he came back. The wound had almost healed; the pain, according to the patient, was even worse.

"He wants you to take out the dirty blood," said Maria. "To stop the pain."

Dad said, "Maria, please tell me what I have to say to convince him that his blood is not the problem."

Maria said, "*Ga ke itse.*"

Dad said, "Get me a needle and a syringe."

He cleaned a patch of skin just beside the site of the infection, slid in the needle, and after slowly withdrawing 10 cc's of blood, held up the syringe for inspection. The old man beamed. "*Keitumetse.* Thank you, Ngaka. *Ee,* that blood, it is too dirty!"

Dad sighed and helped himself to some more salad.

Mum, still sounding cross, said, "It would have got better anyway."

"Yes, it probably would have," said Dad. "But I couldn't bear to see him again. And it's a one-off."

The following Wednesday night, Dad said, "I've changed my mind. I'll take blood from anyone who wants."

When he'd arrived at his clinic early that morning, a young woman had intercepted him on his way into the building. She said hello and in good English apologized for interrupting him. "It's my father," she explained, pointing to a *bakkie* parked under a nearby tree. "He wants to thank you."

They walked together toward the *bakkie,* and stopped outside the passenger door. The old man with the infected arm grinned up at Dad. "*Dumela,* Doctor," he said. He held out his arm. The antibiotics had done their job. The wound was completely healed, and any sign of swelling had gone.

"*Dumela,* Rra," said Dad. "*Le tsoga jang?*"

"*Re tsoga sentle,*" said the man, smiling. He spoke to his daughter in Setswana.

"Dr. Scott," said the woman, "my father says thank you for taking his dirty blood. He has no pain. You have cured him."

And with that she got back in the car and drove her father a hundred kilometers home to their village.

And from then on, Dad took blood from every adult patient who requested it—which was most, including his nurses, who, when pushed, acknowledged that it didn't work, but whenever they got sick, nevertheless wanted blood taken. Dad soon became so well prepared and so fast at taking blood that it added on just about fifteen seconds to his average consultation time, which remained, even with the new "treatment," under five minutes.

In the villages, where most of his patients didn't speak English, the efficiency of Dad's consultation system at first depended heavily on his nurses, who translated the stream of questions, instructions, and diagnoses.

But over the years, and although his ability to construct coherent sentences never significantly progressed, with the endless repetition and gesticulation, Dad gradually developed an impressive repertoire of the nouns and adjectives describing body parts and ailments. And with time, as he adorned his stories with more and more Setswana words, we, too, absorbed some of this strangely limited lexicon.

Popelo—"womb," default organ of blame; women's equivalent to the male obsession with kidneys, *diphilo*. But less inexplicable, for Batswana men often won't marry a woman until she has borne a child. Once Dad hired a well-qualified junior nurse whom he told to wear a previous nurse's old uniforms until her new ones arrived. She came to work the next day in civvies. After several repetitions of *"Ga ke itse,"* she sulkily admitted to Dad that she would not wear the clothes of a woman who had miscarried. Dad threatened to fire her for being ridiculous, but relented after she said she'd rather lose her job than risk her fertility and marriageability with the sullied uniform. With womb and kidney complaints, having identified the actual problem, Dad would present it as auxiliary, in no way entirely displacing the favored troubled organ as the source of at least some of the discomfort and responsibility.

Botlhoko—"pain," frequently used in the context of *diphilo* or *popelo*, as was *leswe*—"dirty"—which could also be applied to *madi*. *Madi* was "blood," the other oft blamed organ, which in addition to being dirty, could, in the case of a fever, be *molelo*, or hot. And if kidneys or wombs weren't raised as the initial complaint, patients would usually claim widespread, unspecific *botlhoko*. Government hospital nurses—and, following suit, Dad's nurses—recorded this as "general bodily pains," abbreviated to GBP, which we all called "General Bidily Ponds," after an exhausted Maria once came up with this catchy alternative. A few years after Dad started practicing, GBP was replaced by GBM. When Dad quizzed Maria, she said, looking surprised, that it was "general bodily malaise." How or why malaise came to replace pain, Dad never found out, but both basically meant *botlhoko*.

At least half of Dad's patients arrived with GBP—and later GBM—on their cards, expecting Dad to figure out the real source of pain, the details of which it was not unusual for patients to withhold deliberately.

And then, of course, there were the nether regions. Like *bonna* for penis, and *marago*, for anus or buttocks.

These were the focus of Dad's concern as he examined the young man lying supine on the examination couch, smiling pleasantly as Dad prodded and squeezed and ran his hands from head to toe. Finishing the external examination, Dad reached for a glove to perform the rectal. He did rectals on almost all male patients, partly because prostate trouble was so common, partly because patients liked exhaustive examinations. In this case, Dad did suspect prostatitis.

The glove box was empty, and Dad sent Maria to fetch a new one. While he waited for her to return, he attempted to explain the procedure in Setswana. His patient looked blank. Dad tried again, adding gesticulations to his repetition of *marago* and *monwana*, which meant "finger." This time the man nodded with comprehension.

Maria returned with the glove box, and Dad put on a glove and then sunk his finger in some lubricant. When he turned back to the examination couch, the patient was lying, as instructed, on his side in the fetal position, but with his own finger thrust up his anus.

"Tell him," said Dad, grinning at Maria, "that he's got the right idea. And ask him if I can have my turn now."

Maria, without a flicker of a smile, relayed the instruction, and the examination proceeded as normal.

Whenever anyone said to me "Are you going to be a doctor like your father?" I cited rectal examinations as the principal reason not to. Next was Dad's advice never to become a doctor, and finally my own intention to become a vet, which would complement my career as a famous show jumper. "I won't mind sticking my finger up horses' bums," I'd add, if I'd managed to keep the conversation going that long.

Dad said that performing rectal examinations was the least of his concerns about being a doctor. Much worse was the repetition, which, in his opinion, was just repetition, whether it was giving rectals, or injections.

Desperate to inject variety into his long days, Dad punned endlessly as he talked to his patients. His patients invariably didn't catch the jokes, but Dad chuckled to himself, repeating the best ones to us when he got home. He tried, however, to restrain himself from joking more directly with the patients, who he'd soon discovered were usually more offended than amused.

But the woman on his couch was somewhere between patient 75 and patient 100. Dad was exhausted, and when he slid the lung X-ray from the brown paper envelope, his instincts got the better of him. Stuck to the back of the X-ray, silhouetted against the center of the right lung, was the desiccated carcass of a huge, squashed wall spider, legs splayed as wide as a teacup.

With a flourish, Dad held the X-ray up to the light. "Mma," he exclaimed, pointing to the spider, "there is your problem."

No interpretation was needed. The woman shrieked and slapped her hand over her mouth. For a few seconds she stared, wide-eyed, at the alarming outline, shaking her head incredulously. Then, recovering from her stunned silence, she spluttered *"Ee!"* several times, before descending into a fit of soft chortles.

Dad smiled back, delighted his joke had been so well received. Peeling the spider off the X-ray, he told Maria to explain to the patient that the only problem with her lung was a bit of emphysema.

But listening to Maria, the woman, whose smile had disappeared, shook her head. She retorted with a barrage of angry Setswana. Ruefully, Maria explained to Dad that his patient insisted the spider be removed from her lung.

Dad told Maria to explain that the spider was a joke. As she did so, with the spider in one hand, the X-ray in the other, he brought them together and parted them several times.

The woman shook her head.

Maria said, "She says you must take it out."

"I can't take the damn thing out," said Dad. "It's not in there."

Maria shrugged. "She says you must take it out, or she won't get better."

The woman watched Dad expectantly, clasping her breast above the offending lung. Dad told her to lie back on the couch and reached for a pair of long forceps. As she stared at the roof and said *aaah* at his instruction, he inserted the forceps into her mouth and wriggled them around at the back of her throat. Withdrawing them to just above her lips, he used his other hand to quickly slip the spider between the tips, and slowly raised it to eye level with the patient.

She smiled appreciatively, and Dad, relieved to see the last of it, dropped the spider in the dustbin.

The woman spoke quickly to Maria.

"She wants to take it home," Maria informed him. "To show her family."

Too tired to argue, Dad knelt down beside the dustbin and fished out the spider, which was handed to the delighted patient in a plastic packet along with her antibiotics, ointments, and tonic.

Dad told us stories like this all the time, and bizarre, medically illogical beliefs had long ago ceased to be shocking. So none of us was particularly surprised when Dad said he'd been visited by a middle-aged man who insisted that "snake in my belly" was the real cause of his main symptom, which was pain while peeing.

Dad prescribed him a course of antibiotics, which, he explained, would quickly sort out the bladder infection.

The man refused to get off the examination couch.

"He wants you to take out the snake," said Maria.

"Tell him there is no snake in his belly," snapped Dad. "It's just an infection. Which will be cured by the antibiotics."

Maria spoke to the patient. "He says there is a snake in his belly." The man, by way of explanation, grimaced and patted his stomach.

"Oh, for goodness sake," said Dad. "Well, if he doesn't believe me, someone else can tell him." Dad duly wrote a letter to the government hospital requesting an ultrasound, and the patient, placated, left without further protest.

"It's the only way to deal with these crazy beliefs," Dad told us, sighing deeply as he relayed the story. "You've got to just play along with all the nonsense."

Several weeks later, the man returned with the results of his ultrasound. The scan revealed a ten-centimeter tapered object in the bladder: a severed snake's tail, according to the hospital surgical record. Only possibly entry point: the penis.

Dad, stunned, asked why and how the man had got the tail in his bladder.

The man said, "*Ga ke itse.*"

"Maria," persisted Dad, "why on earth would someone stick a snake's tail into their bladder?"

"*Ga ke itse.*"

"For goodness sake," said Dad, exasperated, "guess! You must have some idea. Is it something from the witch doctors?"

"No."

"Then why?"

Maria looked at the floor. "To widen his penis inside," she said. "So he can pee better. But he forgot to hold on when he stuck it in there."

The man had a urethral stricture, often caused by scarring following poorly treated STDs. The orthodox treatment is also dilatation, albeit with sterile, nondisappearing instruments.

13

LESSONS

Donkeys on the railway line

Whatever the unfortunate de-tailed snake had been—and this Dad couldn't tell us—it wasn't a puff adder. Even as babies, these fattest of snakes had girths that would have made the most ambitious urethra-stretcher quail.

The fully grown "puffie" that lay thrashing before us on the workbench was, at its vast middle, the circumference and shape of a squashed grapefruit. Moving toward the tail, the body narrowed slightly, but reached finger width only a few centimeters before quickly tapering off altogether. Because of the dramatic wedge shape, the pattern on its bumpy skin changed quickly too, from alternating dark brown and orangey V shapes to what, at the stubby tip, looked more like rough horizontal stripes.

I knew exactly what the tail looked like because I was studying it, intently, following the Vs up and down, counting the white flecks, and trying desperately to ignore the horrible sensation of the contorting muscle in my hand.

"Hold it properly, Robbie," ordered Dad.

"I am."

"Then keep it still. Don't be a wimp."

I gripped harder. "I'm not a wimp."

"That's my girl. Now let's turn it over. Hold it steady so I can cut straight."

Accusations of wimpishness had been less successful in soliciting help from Damien. Disgusted by the metallic flesh smell that clung to the still air, and impervious to taunts, he had retreated to a nearby thorn tree, which he leaned against, neck craned toward the makeshift biology lab. Lulu stood beside Dad and me, her head reaching only just above eye level with the twitching body, her face striped with dust and tears. Occasionally, she stuck her hand out and stroked the writhing body, and then returned to stroking the two dogs that stood at our feet, panting with heat and excitement at the smells. Lulu, the least squeamish of the three of us, was just miserable—as she was always in the presence of any animal death.

The fat, flat, severed head—crocodile eyes frozen in death—watched blankly from the back of the workbench. I felt a wave of guilt and quickly looked away.

With the decapitated neck in his left hand, the scalpel in his right, Dad sliced one shallow line lengthwise—from the throat to the cloaca, snakes' multifunctional pooing, weeing, and mating opening. And, in the case of female puff adders, which hatch baby snakes instead of eggs, the hole from which the babies emerge.

Putting down the scalpel, Dad tugged and yanked the skin away from the body. Beneath the colorful coat appeared slippery white muscle: thousands of thin fibers moving in synchrony, tiny movements mirroring the bigger movements of the undulating body. The muscle, Dad explained, could keep going like this for hours. Whereas, he continued—momentarily pulling a gruesome immobile face and standing rigidly—when humans die they get rigor mortis, turning temporarily completely stiff from total muscle contraction, before becoming floppy again.

Having removed the skin, Dad cut through the belly toward the organs. The most colorful of these were the orangey liver and the round green purse of the gall bladder. This he pierced with the tip of the blade. "Not much bile in here," he said, squeezing out a few drops of greenish liquid. "Oh look here. Somebody's just had dinner."

He seized the long, bulging stomach sac. "Any guesses?" he asked. But before we'd had a chance to answer, he thrust in the blade in and sliced quickly along the sac.

Lulu let out a sob. Nestled in the folds was a whole mouse, bedraggled and bigger but otherwise no different from the baby mice in the cardboard box in the schoolroom.

"One less of the little brutes," said Dad. And then, looking at Lulu's tearful face, he added, "Come on, Lu, that's Africa for you, everything's got to eat. And it's dead now.... Don't waste this opportunity.... Now, what sex do you think it is? If I'm not mistaken, these are testes.... Damien, come over here and take a look at this. This'll really make you squirm."

Damien edged forward, watching reluctantly as Dad dug below the cloaca and exposed two small red penises. They were joined at the base. "Hemipenes," Dad muttered triumphantly as Damien retreated to his tree with a look of disgust.

After we had finally examined everything of interest— gingerly at first, then boldly prodding and palpating—Dad scraped the last of the insides into a bucket and laid the still-wriggling muscle beside the repugnant head at the back of the workbench.

"We can bury it all later," he said, brushing aside Lulu's pleas. "Once we've seen how long the muscle keeps moving." He held up the beautifully patterned sheet of skin. "Now, come on, we can't waste this. Follow me."

Warming to his occasional role as teacher, Dad continued to lecture as we traipsed after him, past the shed and the horses' pens and along the dusty path leading to Grandpa Ivor's old trailer. "Now salt has two functions in preservation. First, it absorbs water, so it helps to dry the skin quickly. Second, it kills most of the bacteria and fungi that cause dead tissue to rot. The technical terms for these properties are hygroscopic and antimicrobial..."

Following Dad into the musty, dimly lit trailer, I could at first only just make out the jumbled piles of wood and pipes. Then he pushed aside a roll of plastic that had fallen across a window, and bright light streamed in, catching thousands of dust particles as they floated across the beams, and illuminating the cluttered room.

"We could pin it on that," he said, pointing to a large, rectangular piece of chipboard in the corner. The wood lay unevenly across the tilting trailer floor, one end resting on a pipe, the other on the old, decaying carpet. "Now, remember, you never know what to expect," Dad continued, still in his lecturing voice. "This is just the sort of warm, dark place that snakes love." He squatted down and grabbed the edge of the wood nearest to him. "Always lift things away from you," he said, looking back at us with a stern expression. "You can never be too careful."

We'd all heard this advice many times before. But Dad was on a roll. "You must never pick up anything this way," he said, still eyeing us as he raised the wood toward himself, "or whatever's underneath will go straight for you."

Something stirred beneath the wood.

Then a soft hiss, and a crash, as the board clattered to the floor.

"Shit," yelled Dad. Leaping back beside us, he paused and wiped his forehead with the back of his hand. "I don't bloody believe it," he said, shakily.

After a few deep breaths, he grabbed a thin metal fence pole and, keeping well back, slipped the end of the pole underneath the wood, easing it upward.

Slowly writhing, and hissing irritably at the repeated disturbance, a coiled puff adder again came into view.

"You see, chaps," said Dad, his voice steadier, his tone once again lecturing, "exactly my point. This is Africa. You never know what to expect."

. . .

The snake muscle writhed determinedly for more than four hours. It was almost sunset before Lulu and I buried it, together with the guts, in the hole Dad had dug for us in the animal cemetery under the knob-thorn tree. Kneeling down, Lulu patted the last of the dirt back in place and erected a small cross of twigs. Then she propped up some of the old, fallen crosses, placed a brilliant pink and green bouquet of bougainvillea and mopane leaves across the freshly dug earth, and whispered a soft apology to the puff adder.

After fewer than three years in Selebi, this oft-used graveyard, which stood in the bush a few meters from the house, had become the resting place of an extraordinary menagerie.

Beneath the dark green canopy was my first dog, Fawn, one of the earliest arrivals. There too lay my beloved pet squirrel Impy, adopted by me when he dropped through the roof onto Damien's bed, only to suffocate six months later as he slept in my hair, curled beside my neck one terrible night. Then there were the baby shrews, baby mice, baby birds; a fatally injured hornbill; a half-eaten dead hare, dropped by a careless hawk. And finally, for no creature was too small for Lulu's grief and attention, lizards, dung beetles, bright butterflies picked off windscreens, and long black *shongololo* millipedes, hundreds of tiny legs retracted, bodies coiled tightly in death.

This burial was, however, unique.

Preceded by several other snakes we'd found squashed on the road, the dismembered body wasn't the first of its kind. But everything else had died either before we'd found it, or despite our best efforts to keep it alive. The unfortunate puff adder Dad had decapitated with an ax that morning, breaking his no-killing-snakes rule, when the huge creature, hissing angrily from between the horse feed barrels, had been impossible to retrieve safely and intact with the pole-and-looped-wire snake catcher.

The second snake, cornered in the trailer, proved easier to lasso. Dad stuffed it in an empty horse feed sack, which we put in the *bakkie* and drove far out into the bush. We lowered the sack to the ground and then pulled it away, tipping out the snake. For a moment, it lay still and surprised, its orange-and-brown skin melting into the sand and leaves. Then quickly—too quickly for such a cumbersome body—the long, fat bump on the sand morphed back into a puff adder, which slithered under a thornbush, there disappearing, altogether, beneath the green fingerlike leaves and sharp gray hooks.

The skin of the first snake we salted, stretched, and pinned on the piece of wood from the trailer, which Dad then placed on the roof of the shed to dry. The head, the only thing remaining, I put on a plate in the back of the fridge, determined to keep it fresh until Saturday, when several of our snake-phobic friends from Kopano were due to come out from to Selebi to spend the night.

After a "great day for homeschooling," Mum was extra cheerful. She protested just briefly, allowing the gruesome head to remain in the fridge on condition I put it in a plastic bag. Dad, who would never spoil a good practical joke, applauded the plan and requested only that I didn't inform Ruth about its whereabouts lest dinner be compromised.

The more normal form of our occasional and unplanned lessons with Dad was this: last-minute ringside seats to some life-and-death—or, if not death, gory—drama, where we never knew what we'd learn, only that it would be interesting.

Like the ostrich, which had slit its throat on barbed wire.

The vet couldn't be reached, so the farmer phoned Dad.

"I'd better get going," said Dad, when he'd explained. "It's not like Clinton to exaggerate. Must be a bad one."

Dad went to fetch his doctor's bag, Mum the sun protection. Lulu, Damien, and I, assuming our invitation, were already waiting in the backseat. Mum said, "I hope you've got your hats."

Clinton and Cecile Rice ran a small ostrich farm on the banks of the Macloutse River near Phikwe. We'd seen their ostriches before, but only from afar, and as Dad sped along the bumpy road to the river, Lulu, Damien, and I speculated excitedly about what the massive bird would look like close up, and how much blood there'd be. Dad, for once, couldn't help—"New territory for me too, chaps."

The Rices' farm, transformed by its river, was a different world from the bush we knew so well. Surrounding the house were wide lawns of thick, lush grass; above it was a canopy of dense knob-thorns, which even on seasonal waters grew to almost double the size of Selebi's trees. There were unfamiliar trees too: gray, rough-trunked leadwoods, wide-canopied mashatus, river bush willows, and monkey thorns, sometimes with monkeys themselves, small gray vervets, springing through the branches. And hundreds of birds: at any moment these trees held more species than we'd see in weeks. Occasionally, most enviably of all, the stirring call of the great fish eagle rang above the gentler birdsong.

For the first few minutes of our visits, I'd usually just gaze and listen, awed by the magical effects of water in this dry country.

But today I thought only of the forthcoming veterinary drama, and, hurrying after Clinton, lawns, trees, and littler birds passed unnoticed.

"Thanks for coming so quickly," he said as we strode to the field. "There she is, poor girl."

I stopped and studied the huge bird, feeling mildly disappointed. She looked entirely healthy: standing firmly in the corner of the field, rich brown feathers gleaming and enormous eyes alert, greedily—and amazingly, for a bird that had "slit her throat"—chomping at alfalfa.

"Doesn't look like she's at death's door," muttered Dad.

"Hang on," said Clinton, continuing along the fence. "Come closer."

Reaching the bird and for the first time seeing the other side of her long pink neck, we cried out in disgust.

Unperturbed, she gave us a mild wide-eyed glance before gulping another mouthful of alfalfa. A moment later the alfalfa dropped onto the dirt, pouring out of the gruesome twenty-centimeter vertical slit down her neck. She took another beakful, with the same hopeless outcome.

Dad prepared a syringe of Valium. Then Clinton and two of

his Batswana farm workers sprung on the ostrich, pushing her to the ground and pinning down her huge wings, which could easily break an arm if it got in the way. The restrained bird nevertheless managed to kick out furiously as Dad plunged the needle in her thigh.

"That should do the trick," said Dad, leaping back.

Released, she at once began eating again. Five minutes later, she was still gobbling alfalfa. She seemed no less alert. Dad approached with his needle and sutures, only to have a two-toed, clawed foot fly out at him. Scrambling back, he refilled his syringe and ordered the three men to restrain her once more.

"That'll definitely work," he announced, after injecting the second batch in another flurry of legs and feathers.

After round three, Dad said, "I'm not sure what to do. This is enough Valium to make a man comatose."

The ostrich blinked beautiful lashes over cartoon-huge eyes, and took another mouthful of alfalfa.

"You'll just have to hold her down," said Dad.

So Clinton and his workers wrestled the struggling bird to the ground. Once she was down, Mum, Lulu, Damien, and I joined them, pressing our hands down firmly to keep her still.

After wiping away the alfalfa and sterilizing the wound, Dad began to stitch: first the gaping gullet, and then the skin, knotting carefully after each loop.

The bird, once pinned down, stared ahead with a vapid gaze. But for a few twitches, she kept still, and Dad began to relax, chatting to us as he worked at the painstaking task.

"Pity I didn't have laughing gas. Would've had her in stitches immediately."

Mum said, "Better than being tied up in knots."

"Real name—nitrous oxide," Dad continued, smiling. "Mild euphoria-inducing anesthetic."

"Normally used in dentistry," said Mum.

"Also as an oxidizer to increase power in rockets."

"Also a greenhouse gas."

"Explosive at high temperatures," said Dad, winking at

Damien. "Blast!" he muttered, as the ostrich suddenly shook her neck and a half-finished knot unraveled.

Dad may have braved stitching a fully grown ostrich, but several months later, when Quartz appeared from the bush with a five-centimeter gash on his bottom, even he blanched. Ever since a botched gelding—which had left Quartz, a "rig," with half his testicles—he'd been petrified of needles. Simple vaccinations, during which he'd smashed poles and jumped over four-foot fences, could take hours.

The Phikwe vet had long since refused to treat him.

Grandpa Ivor, seeing the excited gathering by the horse pens, hurried across. "Whaddaya mean, you're not going to stitch?" he yelled. "Ya gotta close the bloody thing. What kind of doctor are you?"

"I'm about to close it," said Dad. "Hold your horses, Ivor."

"This is not a bloody joke."

Dad ignored Grandpa and turned to me. "Hang up a hay net, Robbie. And get him some treats."

By the time Dad returned with swabs and antiseptic, Quartz had eaten several pieces of Rescue Remedy–laced bread and was munching happily through a bunch of carrots. He hardly flinched as Dad cleaned the dust and bits of bark from the broken branch that must have sliced the flesh.

What he planned, Dad wouldn't tell us either, and we watched expectantly as he dried the raw edges. He gave the wound a final dab, produced a small tube of Super Glue from his pocket, removed the cap, and quickly squeezed the glue along one edge before pressing the wound closed.

For about a minute, Dad held the edges together. Then he let go, and patted Quartz on his flank.

Quartz shifted, the skin moving across his hindquarters. But the glue held fast.

It was one of the most impressive procedures I'd ever seen. Even Grandpa, who regularly argued with Dad about detailed medical concepts, was quite overcome. "You've blown me away," he said. "Always loved that stuff—used it on many an airplane in my time—but I never knew you could do that."

"Useful in emergencies," said Dad, enjoying our awe. "But I'm not the first to use it. There's even a special medical version."

"Useful!" said Grandpa. "Not useful. Bloody amazing. Betty!" he bellowed across the road. "Ya gotta come see this. Keith's working miracles."

M um said, "Our mission today is to identify that jolly tree."

Only on medical knowledge was Mum happy to be upstaged by Dad. On everything else, they conducted ongoing battles of intellectual one-upmanship. And just as we worked our way haphazardly through the dictionary following their dinnertime arguments about semantics and etymology, much of our most obscure knowledge arose from similar contests.

Trees invoked some of their greatest competitive ferocity. On evening walks, the first to spot a new species would be triumphant for hours. A correct identification too, and we could expect at least a day of gentle gloating.

The ten-foot sapling beside Grandpa Ivor's airplane shed, with its nondescript leaves and failure to produce any flowers or seedpods to help identification, had thwarted them for ages. To resolve the identity of this tree was the ultimate coup.

With Dad safely away at work, we followed Mum across the road and sat down beneath it, carrying, between us, all four of our tree books.

"Why don't each of you take a book," said Mum. "Remember: leaves—type, arrangement, and color. And for the bark—color, texture, and pattern."

Mum retrieved a magnifying glass from her pocket and began studying the leaves. She sniffed in frustration. Mum liked to say to people, "One of the reasons I've homeschooled my children is so they won't be exposed to that horribly competitive classroom environment."

"Blast," said Mum after several minutes, dropping the magnifying glass. "No idea. Blast! Blast! Perhaps it's not indigenous after all."

None of us had made any headway with the books, and Mum picked up the biggest, Palgrave's, and began leafing through it crossly.

Damien at once held the discarded magnifying glass over a dried leaf, and he'd generated a healthy flame by the time Grandpa Ivor came out to investigate.

"Whaddaya up to, Linda?" And then, seeing the tree books, "Teaching the kids more Latin? Thought they were already fluent," he said, grinning.

Mum and Dad prided themselves on knowing and using the botanical names for trees. And some of our favorite bush trees we grew to love as much for these wonderful musical words as for their appearance: *Boscia albitrunca, Commiphora mollis,* and the most lyrical of all, *Rhigozum brevispinosum.*

Lulu, who also obsessively drew pictures of trees, was far better than Damien and me at remembering the names. By six, she could recite at least twenty. At the golf club, Grandpa Ivor told everyone his little granddaughter was an ancient languages genius.

Now he said, "I've told ya before. That tree's a marula."

Mum smiled and didn't bother to argue. Lulu said quietly, "Grandpa, it's not a *Sclerocarya birrea.* The leaves are completely different."

"Nonsense," said Grandpa. "Whaddaya know, anyway, Little Lulu? Just 'cause you can speak Latin doesn't mean you know what you're talking about."

There was a marula tree in the horses' paddock, behind the cowshed.

The tall mottled-gray trunk was too smooth to climb to shake the branches. So we had to wait, frustrated, as the plum-sized green fruit became perfectly soft and yellow, and plummeted to the ground of their own accord.

They were delicious. Sweet, and tangy—infinitely nicer than

the tiny *Grewia* berries and astringent wild plums, which we ate simply because they came from the bush. After a few days, we couldn't keep up with the marula fruit fall, and the hundreds of round balls fermented till you could smell the sweet alcohol several meters from the tree. Then we always hoped that baboons might appear and get drunk on the fruit, like the wonderful scene in the film *Animals Are Beautiful People*. But other than us, only the horses ate them, and got colic, not drunk.

During marula season, we'd adapt the Space Game to allow for crucial marula refueling stops during our intergalactic travels.

The cowshed was the mother space station; the vast bush around us the universe, for infinitely varied exploration. But beyond these essentials, and a variety of space-travel-related props, the name was slightly misleading. Invented soon after our arrival—and though it would evolve to last in name for five years—really the Space Game was an umbrella description for endless hours of unadulterated playing and adventuring.

Central to the technological elements of the game—masterminded by Damien—was the hi-fi in the lounge, with which we synced our homemade portable computers. These were oblongs of cardboard, onto which we'd carefully drawn all the normal buttons, plus *beam, nuke, teleport, takeoff, speed of sound, speed of light*, before laminating them with precisely applied thick strips of Sellotape. At the start of each day's mission, we synced, and then set off to one of our satellite stations. Blurring technological eras, these included the shed, the wrecked Piper Colt, the collapsing lizard-filled trailers, and the ruins by the abandoned skull-and-bone-littered old abattoir, near the mine dump. The roof of the cowshed was a favorite too, and a vantage point from which we could follow the movements of Matthews, an obliging enemy, who'd hurl friendly abuse when we soaked him with homemade origami water bombs.

Not a month went by without the addition of some new accessory to the game. Often this simply involved a more sophisticated version of the cardboard computers, and Damien reliably devised several new satisfyingly powerful functions for every rerelease: *fission, fusion, force field.*

There were material breakthroughs too.

Like the time Damien convinced a friend to trade his broken walkie-talkies for a key ring that beeped when you whistled. Damien at once disassembled and fixed the walkie-talkies, and the Space Game entered a glorious new era of mobile communications.

Or when Damien was given a motorized go-cart for his eighth birthday and built a tiny trailer for it, at once quadrupling our reach in the universe. Now the three of us would zoom far along the bush tracks, Lulu and I bouncing on the back, spitting out dust spun up by the wheels.

Often we'd drive to the cattle posts, overtaking donkey carts on the way, stopping to buy prohibited boiled sweets, which we considered, by virtue of the long journey, almost as authentically from the bush as the *Grewia* berries. We also frequented the airport, where we'd watch the planes landing, waving at the pilots and critiquing their skills. And sometimes, when the baobab pods were falling, we'd drive to the end of the dirt road, where the forbidden-to-the-go-cart tar began, and park under the marula tree hung with Mum's homemade sign. This read "Scotts" in big slanted letters, and "No through road" in small ones, separated by her painting of a wily-looking yellow-billed hornbill.

Leaving the go-cart under the marula, we'd walk across the railway line and across the main road, stopping at the base of one of the biggest baobabs for miles, which towered here on the roadside like a sentinel to the turnoff for the airport and the Selebi houses.

We all longed for a baobab in our garden. The most splendid of Africa's trees, it had once, according to local legend, grown only in the gardens of paradise, until the day the gods tired of the poor baobab, tore it out of the ground, and hurled it from the heavens to the earth, where it landed upside down and continued to grow, roots in the air, reaching skyward.

But these great trees, with some of the biggest girths in the world, took hundreds of years to grow, so we had to settle for a neighborhood baobab. We knew intimately the valleys and folds on the smooth, swollen gray trunk, which tapered and split into

bulbous branches that seemed absurdly big for their sparse clusters of leaves. Beneath it, sitting in the shade of the enormous
trunk, we'd crack the woody pods and suck the tart white flesh
around the seeds until our mouths ached. When we could eat no
more, and provided we weren't already overloaded with spoils
from our travels, we'd stuff our backpacks full with as many of
the furry green fruit as we could carry, heading home armed with
delicious snacks that would last us days.

The small backpacks were a crucial part of our journeys.

When we departed, they'd be half full with water, sandwiches, apples, the portable computers, a few thebe coins, and
the walkie-talkies. On our return, they'd often be brimming with
new additions, including snakeskins, colorful feathers, huge seedpods, tortoise shells, porcupine quills, sun-bleached bones, useful bits of metal, wire snares that we tore from bushes, beautiful
pieces of gnarled wood for the wall unit, and almost always, dead
or alive, a few of the innumerable wonderful insects of the bush.

Sometimes on the way home, we'd leave some of the one-thebe
coins on the railway line, to be flattened into pin-thin shiny disks
by the train—another great, unspecific force in our high-tech,
nature-rich, fantasy-reality universe. These, we'd collect during
our next lesson. Which is really what the Space Game was: just
a name for our most important class of all, in the art of endless,
boundless discovery and imagination.

14

LIVING ON THE FRINGE

Granny Betty's calf

I'm warning you, Keith," said Grandpa Ivor. "Ya shouldn't mess with these people."

Dad laughed, shading his eyes and smiling as he surveyed the half-cleared field. Standing there now, Dad looked so much like Grandpa had looked when I'd watched him nearly three years earlier, staring at this field and talking about witch doctors: the sun-shielding salute, the large, unmistakably Scott jaw, the expression filled with the same dreamy expectation of seeing more than now lay before him.

Except that, imposed on the bleak field, Dad was seeing a dense expanse of waxy green leaves and bright yellow jojoba flowers where Grandpa had been seeing spells and a witch doctor—whose existence, given that he'd stayed resolutely invisible, I'd long since begun to doubt.

But now turning to Grandpa, and seeing his foreboding expression, I felt a quiver of uncertainty, and relief that Dad had left the termite-mound end untouched, potential *muti* weeds radiating out around the ant fortress.

"There's still lots left, Grandpa."

"I'm sure the old chap will forgive me," said Dad. "He can even pick some of my jojoba if he wants. It's wonderful stuff. He'll probably be delighted."

Grandpa just shrugged. "Don't say I didn't warn you," he muttered, stalking off.

Dad had become so excited when he first read about jojoba oil that he and Mum, leaving us with Granny Joan for three days, had made an exploratory weekend trip down to South Africa to investigate a recently started plantation. They returned, even more enthusiastic, with bags of seeds. Dad immediately hired extra labor to clear the ground. And the following weekend Lulu, Damien, and I spent the day out in the field, helping Dad and Matthews plant.

"Marvelous stuff," said Dad, showing us how deep to sink the wrinkled brown seeds in the dirt. "Native to the Mojave desert. It'll thrive in this place. Will be just like the pictures soon."

Which was hard to believe, looking at the clear red dirt. But Dad's enthusiasm was contagious, and I believed, implicitly, that he could make happen anything he wanted.

Mum, tapping away at her typewriter, was excited for another reason. While we were planting, she was already planning the new "Jojoba Farming" pages in her book.

Like the homeopathy book she and Dad had written, most of Mum's book projects—ranging from a few paragraphs to several chapters—were guides to specific natural medicine subjects. Recently, however, she'd spent hours perched at the Olivetti, working on a real-life account of the triumphs and tribulations of alternative medicine and an alternative lifestyle.

"I've got so much great material," Mum would say distractedly as she banged furiously at the keyboard. "Complementary medicine, nutritional medicine, bush medicine, medicine bushes, biodynamic farming, home births, homeschooling...Crazy to let it go to waste. Someone's surely got to be interested in this. Do you want to hear some?"

And before we'd had a chance to respond either way, Mum would be reading out loud, pausing only to interrupt herself with her own amendments. By the time she'd finished the story in question, she'd have generally forgotten she had asked for our opinion, and would return immediately to her keyboard.

We, the children, occasionally featured, and we'd smugly tell our friends in Phikwe that we would one day be characters in a real book. As to the nature of our appearances, which generally involved us being plied with homeopathic elixirs for projectile vomiting or chronic diarrhea, we remained vague.

The book was called *Living on the Fringe*—the fringe, according to Mum, being the boundaries of what was acceptable in conventional society. Mum and Dad, said Mum, were firmly on it, as, she added, were Ivor and Betty, in a different sort of way.

The jojoba project, she explained, was another classic strand in the fringe.

First, no farmer had yet attempted to grow jojoba in Botswana. Which alone made it irresistible to Dad. Second, the oil had potentially environmentally friendly uses, including as a biodegradable lubricant and a biodiesel fuel. Third, it could be used as a natural alternative to synthetic substances in cosmetics.

Fourth—this sometime feature of the fringe Mum didn't mention, but soon it became apparent—everyone else *wasn't* doing it for a good reason. With a bit more reading and a few more calculations, Dad realized that with the current price he could get for jojoba oil, which was low because of the cheaper, less environmentally friendly synthetic alternatives, he would actually lose money on the crop.

Just a few months after planting, having obsessed daily about the sprouting seedlings, Dad announced he would not be growing jojoba after all. As always, he immediately dispensed with regret and reinvented failure. "Now I can focus properly on getting a real farm," he declared happily. "Our own land."

Dad stopped watering the jojoba. Mum said, "At least keep this lot going."

Dad said, "What's the point? Can't really do anything with them."

"I feel so bad just letting them die."

"If we keep them going, they'll just die when they're older."

"But come on, Keith," said Mum, exasperated. "Aren't you at least interested to see how well they grow here? You've invested so much time in them already."

"So"—Dad shrugged—"now I'm investing it in other things."

Mum sighed, but moments later regained her cheerfulness. "I suppose it's actually really a good thing. If it means we get our farm sooner. Plus, you know, thinking about it now, it also makes for an even better chapter in the book. The more things don't go according to plan, the better the story."

Mum's optimism bordered on pathological. She regularly joked that she wanted her epitaph to be "Making wrong things right"—words that six-year-old Lulu, with my help, had written on a homemade birthday card for Mum, as one of the things she loved most about her mother.

Mum said Dad's epitaph could be "Making things happen, and moving on swiftly."

Dad said, "You can put whatever you like. When I'm gone, I'm gone. Feed me to the lions for all I care."

Mum laughed. "See."

"You don't need to discuss this yet," I protested. "You're not going to die yet."

"You never know," said Dad. "Any of us could kick the bucket, any day."

"Dad!"

Mum said, "That's why the only thing that matters is that you end each day with all things resolved. That you never let the sun set on a sad or angry heart."

Which wasn't difficult, when you gazed across the golden bush at the great red globe at once expanding and disappearing as the glowing horizon sliced it little by little to sleep. Then, as the sky grew alight with pinks and reds and everything in between, the scale and drama of the beauty seemed to reach deep inside, extinguishing all but the greatest frustrations and sorrows.

"Smell that, chaps," said Dad, scuffing his *veldskoen* against the sandy track. "Nothing in the world like the smell of a dirt road in Africa."

The cloud of dust, deep red in the rich light, hung still above the sand, glowing. Dad's face glowed too: with the sun, and with pleasure as he inhaled loudly and gazed toward the light.

Once, on an evening walk, frustrated that I didn't smell it too, I'd crouched down and stuck my nose right inside the dust cloud. "Just smells like dust," I'd coughed, sneezing out a thousand tiny particles.

"When you leave Africa, Robbie—then you'll understand about the dust."

"There's dust everywhere else."

"Not like this."

"Anyway, I'll never leave."

Even if I couldn't smell the difference in the dust, as I watched the spectacular changing light—the polite thanks to the continent for tolerating the heat, sweat, and discomfort of the day—I was certain there wasn't anywhere else I'd rather be.

"I'm sure you'll leave," Dad said. "But you'll keep coming back. Can't shake it off," he added, sighing with contentment.

But Dad wanted his own dust. The more his once exciting clinics became routine, the more he sought solace in the prospect of his ultimate project: having his own land, in Africa, where other people's cows could be kept out and the pillaged bush rehabilitated; where you picked up a littered plastic bag one day and none was there to replace it the next. And most of the time, except for sunsets, when no one could feel anything but perfectly content, Dad wasn't.

After our walks, we'd often sit outside in the last light, swatting mosquitoes and counting the first stars, or watching the huge yellow hunter's moon, masking the stars, rise slowly above the trees. And often, then, as the stars became countless or the moon drifted up above the scrub, Dad would talk about how he'd one day take us to a farm deep in the bush proper, in real Africa: where the moon would shine up above lush bushveld grazed by big antelope, stalked by big cats, with a full, tall-tree-lined river full of crocodiles.

The dream was good enough, and Dad certain enough, to keep us all optimistic—even though, after several years, and although he now had enough money, Dad's ongoing farm search had failed to produce any land that met his requirements: on a river, accessible by road, well positioned for his clinics. And, the most difficult of all, *our* land.

Which, for all the money in the world, most of Botswana could never be.

Around 80 percent of the country is tribal trust land, an ownership system that helps keep Botswana free of the land disputes that trouble so many parts of previously colonized Africa. On unallocated tribal trust land—like the bush around Selebi—anyone can wander freely and graze their animals. It is no-man's-land, any-man's-land, every-man's-land, depending on your perspective. No one can own the land, but by applying through the Land Board you could be granted, for free, a ninety-nine-year lease on a patch of dirt to call your own.

Dad wanted it to *be* our own. But freehold farms were far and few between. And so, for the moment, our African sun would continue to rise and set over big dreams, and a small, wilting field of abandoned jojoba seedlings.

What did I tell you, Keith? Told you your plants wouldn't grow.

And if Dad was growing restless, Lulu, Damien, and I hadn't yet come close to exhausting the amusements offered by the no-man's-bush around us, the two small houses, and their four profoundly fringy adult occupants.

At seven o'clock, the sun already streaming through the windows, I slid out from my sheets and crept through the house into the schoolroom. Lulu was awake in bed, watching the dogs who wrestled on top of the covers, breaking one of Dad's firmest edicts.

She joined me beside the vivarium and fished out the second of the two slender, sleepy brown house snakes. After tucking our pajama shirts securely into our shorts, we each slipped a cool, silky body through the neck of our tops.

Lulu let out a squeal of laughter as the snake squirmed against her belly.

"Shhh, man," I hissed.

"Sorry," Lulu hissed back, smiling and blowing out her cheeks.

Damien, head under his pillow, was fast asleep in the next room. It took several shakes before he clambered out of bed and followed us sleepily to the front door. Careful not to disturb Mum and Dad's nonnegotiable Sunday lie-in, we eased the swing door shut behind us and set off barefoot across the dirt, watching out for thorns and trying to spot snake tracks and jackal prints—laid during the night across yesterday's chaotic mix of car tracks, footprints, horse hooves, and dog paws.

Outside Grandpa's front door, we paused, holding Keller and Smiley by their scruffs to stop them scratching at the gray mesh spring door. A volley of extraordinarily loud and irregular snores confirmed we were in luck. Quietly opening the door, we stopped again for a moment beside the Ping-Pong table. Clutching the dogs, trying not to laugh, we took careful note of must-be-avoided bulges beneath the thin brown bedcover. The sleeping cat and each of Granny Betty's fragile limbs located, we silently mouthed a count of three and sprang, yelling good mornings, onto the end of the bed.

Grandpa hauled himself into a sitting position. "What the bloody hell is this?" he bellowed. Granny Betty blinked and gave us a sleepy smile. Her soft "Good morning" was drowned by the deafening tirade from beside her. "No bloody manners. On Sunday bloody morning. Unbelievable! What the hell do you think you're doing?"

"Waking you up, Grandpa."

"You're in Africa! Have you not learned any respect for your elders?"

"It's seven o'clock, Grandpa. *Late* for Africa."

Lulu and I helped the dogs up onto the bed, and they sprang toward Granny and Grandpa's faces, howling with excitement.

"Fucking circus in here," yelled Grandpa, fending off Keller as she stuck a slobbery, dead-animal-smelling jowl in his face.

"Please, Ivor," murmured Granny. "Come here, darling," she cooed at Keller, holding out a bony hand that Keller immediately coated in slobber.

"Bloody dogs," said Grandpa. "Shouldn't be on the bed. Off! Off! All of you. Children too!"

None of us moved. "Granny let the calf on the bed."

"Not while we were bloody in it," yelled Grandpa, flinging his hands in the air. "And you know Betty and animals. Besotted! Can't do anything about it. Hey, Betty?"

Granny Betty smiled, distantly, transported by the memory of her now grown and gone brown-and-white pet calf that had once made regular visits into the house and onto the bed.

"Ya live in the middle of the bush," spluttered Grandpa, "and still you get no bloody peace. Not even from your own bloody grandchildren."

The tradition of Sunday breakfast with Grandpa Ivor and Granny Betty had begun as soon as we moved into the cowshed. Every week, for nearly three years, we'd provoked a similar, satisfying outburst, which always ended in the same way.

"Suppose you want some grub? Betty! How about some breakfast for these little scavengers?"

"Just what I was thinking," murmured Granny. "If you're hungry?" She grinned mischievously. "Okay. Okay," she said, beginning the slow process of easing herself out from the covers. "I heard you. No need to shout."

Grandpa arranged a pillow between his head and the bumpily plastered wall. "Come on," he snapped, easing himself back against it. "Give your Granny Betty a hand...and open those curtains. Do a bit of bloody work for your breakfast."

By the time Granny had rotated herself into a sitting position on the edge of the bed, we'd brought her a glass of water for her pills, checked her old pink slippers for scorpions, and fetched her turquoise quilted dressing gown from the hook on the door to the lounge.

"Thank you," murmured Granny. "Very kind of you. Bit rusty in the morning. Pills will kick in soon."

"Grape juice fasts, Betty!" said Grandpa. "That's what you need. Not bloody painkillers. Give up smoking and eat more fruit. Look at me. Nearly seventy. Never felt better."

"Now," said Granny, slowly tying the gown around her billowing floral nightie. "Fried, or scrambled?"

Having taken our orders, she shuffled off in the direction of the kitchen. "No, no, I can manage," she said. She stooped down to pat a drooling dog. "Besides, these guys will keep me company. You three look after your Grandpa."

"No peace," muttered Grandpa. "Well, suppose there's enough room here for you all. Hurry up, then. Whaddaya waiting for?"

The morning air was still just cool enough for the thin covers to be inviting, and we slipped quickly into the trough of the sagging bed. As pre-agreed, Lulu and I slid in on either side of Grandpa, snuggling beside him and taking care not to lie on top of the snakes.

"So," said Grandpa, as we settled in between the bulging springs and gazed up at the spiderwebs on the airplane wing, "what trouble have you lot been causing this week? Read anything? Had any brainwaves? Discovered anything? Invented anything?" He eyed us accusingly. "Never too young to start inventing. Never too old either."

Big or small, significant or not, Grandpa met every tale of revelation and creation with the same bright-eyed, delighted attention. It was impossible not to want to talk to him, and as the sound of clanging pots and the smell of frying bacon drifted through the house, we excitedly recounted our week's adventures; soon transfixed by our own stories, elevated in his presence to great raconteurs. Grandpa, as always, had something to say about everything, and each of our stories drifted inevitably into a lecture by him on his own ideas for how things could next time be done better, bigger, and more spectacularly.

Careful not to draw his attention, I looked at Lulu. Very

slowly, the covers pulled up to our necks, we untucked our shirts and each fished out a silky snake. Energetic from the warmth, the slim muscled body writhed in my hand as I slipped it, headfirst, into the sleeve of Grandpa's big cotton nightshirt.

Midsentence, Grandpa paused. He narrowed his eyes for a second, and then continued, voice and expression unchanged.

Lulu, Damien, and I waited, chatting as nonchalantly as we could manage.

Nothing.

Damien gave Grandpa a progress update on the mud brick hut he was building in the bush; Lulu and I talked about the horses.

Grandpa nodded and commented as attentively as usual. After a few minutes, he said, "So I heard a rumor you found some snakes."

"Maybe."

"Now," he continued, frowning up at the wing, "I wonder what they are.... Nonpoisonous, I hope. Can't be a rare species if you've got two...mole snakes perhaps...No, too small for mole snakes. Don't tell me. Ah, I know. Of course." He paused dramatically, rolling his eyes to the top of his head. "Brown house snakes!"

We gaped.

"Ya think you can scare me?" he yelled, fumbling under his shirt and retrieving a bewildered snake in each hand. "Ya should know better by now. Ya want scary. I'll give ya scary! Did I ever tell ya the story about Ronnie? Now that's what I call scary!"

Back at the cowshed, Dad said, "Good joke, chaps. Brace yourselves."

A few months before, Dad would have snuck across the road to discuss retaliation strategy. He'd inherited and amplified Grandpa's particular sense of humor—teasing relentlessly, searching for puns in every conversation, and prizing, above all, a good practical joke. Through humor they'd always got on best.

But now, after the fight, there was only silence.

It wasn't even a worthy thing to fight about. Mr. Motswagole, despite having his own *bakkie*, regularly borrowed Grandpa's *bakkie*, leaving Grandpa stranded. On one such occasion, Grandpa came across the road and asked to borrow our *bakkie*. Dad refused, saying he needed it for after-hours call-outs. Grandpa yelled that Dad was being selfish; Dad shouted at Grandpa for letting Mr. Motswagole take advantage of him and—in turn— of us; Grandpa yelled that Dad didn't know what he was talking about; Dad shouted that Grandpa was being unreasonable; Grandpa yelled that the same applied to Dad, and the two men parted furiously in the middle of the red dirt between the two houses.

A day of not speaking became a week, and a week became two. Suddenly they were really *not speaking*, and the longer the silence lasted—and the sillier the fight began to seem—the harder it became for either of the two deeply proud and stubborn men to take the first step out across the growing void.

So they didn't.

Mostly, bizarrely, life carried on almost as normal. The occasional family dinners—regularly suspended during Grandpa and Dad's small fights—stopped altogether. But Dad still visited Granny, when Grandpa was out. And Grandpa came over when Dad was at his clinics. They passed each other in the driveway without flinching, nodded, and walked on silently. They spoke of each other normally. They both, unbelievably, seemed normal.

When I didn't speak to Dad for a few hours, the energy and agony of not speaking defined my every second. But it was as if Dad and Grandpa had both just left their relationship behind them, on the dirt between the two houses, where the pain of not having one couldn't affect them.

Dad said, "I do miss *MacGyver*."

Before, every Friday night, just after dark, all five of us had crossed the road and squeezed together on the lounge sofa to watch the gripping TV show with Grandpa and Granny. Now it was just Mum, Lulu, Damien, and I.

When MacGyver pulled off a particularly ingenious escape,

Grandpa would say, "Your father would love that one. Don't forget to tell him."

His encouragement was unnecessary. Damien, who idolized the brilliant daredevil, repeated the episodes verbatim, and where possible generally re-created MacGyver's tricks for Dad.

Damien thrived on audiences. If everyone else had tired of listening to him, he'd sit down under Ruth's ironing board with his gigantic Technic Lego set. As he worked, he'd explain his creations and the principles of hydraulics. From time to time, Ruth would say, "*Eh-he*," or "*Ee*, Damien, you are so clever," and Damien, talking about pressure and pistons, slipping into a Setswana accent when he remembered, could happily sit there for hours.

In the presence of friends his own age from Phikwe, Damien became almost demented with excitement.

Never had he been worse than on the Friday night when John, Hal's son, and Peter, an old friend from Kopano, were staying and we all went across the road to watch *MacGyver*. By the end of the episode, the three boys were in a fever of bravado— scuffling with each other and bragging loudly about their plans to sleep outside and fearlessly brave the danger-filled night.

As the credits rolled, barely pausing to say good night to Granny and Grandpa, they rushed out the door, excited war cries ringing across the bush.

I said good night soon afterward and left Lulu and her friend Nicky Ball singing along to Grandpa, who, with little persuasion, had got out his harmonica and launched into a squeaky rendition of "Puff the Magic Dragon."

A few meters from our front door, as I picked my way carefully across the patchy, shadow-streaked sand, smothered laughter erupted from a dense clump of bushes.

"I know you're there, stupid. Don't try and scare me."

More guffaws and then, "Where're Lulu and Nicky?"

"Dunno. Why should I tell you anyway?" I yelled behind me. "Stop being so childish."

Mum had stayed behind with Dad. They were sitting together on the sofa, heads bent over their books.

"How was it?" asked Dad.

"Good one."

"What did he do?"

I began to relay the plot. Mum stared at Dad, frowning and occasionally muttering things like she couldn't believe two grown men had let it come to this.

A high scream rang through the night. Another followed, and then cackling, yelling, more screaming—now angry—and excited dog barks.

Lulu and Nicky burst through the door, white-faced and tearful. A moment later, bellowing war cries, the three boys sprinted past the lounge window toward Damien's mud hut in the bush behind the house.

Dad leaped up from the sofa. "Right. Time those little ratbags got a taste of their own medicine." He disappeared to his bedroom. A minute later, the safe clanged shut, and he emerged, clasping his shotgun.

Mum quickly got up to phone Granny Betty, to tell her not to worry if she heard shots. Dad said, "Follow me. And keep quiet."

As we passed through the schoolroom, Dad flicked off the light, and the back of the house sunk into darkness.

Outside, standing on the doorstep between the flowerbeds, we were at once invisible in the shadow of the house. "Wait here," whispered Dad. "Hold on to the dogs."

Gun in hand, Dad left the shadows and crept out across the moonlit dirt. He'd gone only a few paces before he dived behind a tree as a disgruntled nightjar flapped noisily up above the scrub. But the bush ahead of him remained still and dark, and after a moment's pause, Dad continued on, zigzagging from tree to tree toward the dark blob of the hut, which lay about fifty meters from the house.

For the last few months, Damien had spent long stretches of every day building and admiring the growing hut. Mum, who decided the construction project was a useful contribution to life skills, left him unhindered and suspended most of her scant demands for normal schoolwork. If Damien was alone, Lulu and I were encouraged to come inside and inspect, but on weekends when Peter and John joined Damien, we were strictly prohibited.

Then, under Matthews's direction, the three boys would spend hours mixing dirt, cow dung, ash, and water into the thick red paste that was used to build most of Botswana's huts. Rapidly drying in the sun, this leaden mixture formed rock-solid walls, which had, as of a few weeks ago, finally reached roof height and been topped off with a shaggy, ominously sagging thatched roof.

The hut had no windows, and the open doorway faced away from the house. From our vantage point at the back door, the only signs of occupation were the distant flicker of flashlight through the gap beneath the roof, and the occasional snatch of laughter, muffled by the thick walls. But for these, and the persistent hum of the bush, everything was quiet.

Beside me, I could hear Lulu and Nicky breathing, the dogs panting, the cluck of a roosting bird, a suspicious rustle in the flowerbed.

Then deafening gunshots tore through the night.

Three yelling figures sprinted away from the hut, dodging trees and crashing through bushes. As more gunshots exploded behind them, one of the boys dropped to the ground and began leopard-crawling.

Seconds later, John and Damien shot past us toward the brightly illuminated front of the house. "It's the BDF," yelled John, as they disappeared around the corner.

Peter, still leopard-crawling, reached us at the back door. Leaping to his feet, he seized the handle and pushed past us. "Run," he yelled, oblivious to our strangled giggles. "Run for your life."

A few minutes later, still shaken but desperate to escape our postmortem, the three boys crept back out to the hut. Then and thereafter, apart from denying having being scared, they resisted all attempts to discuss the episode.

When I asked John why he'd thought it was the BDF, short for the Botswana Defense Force, he just shrugged.

"If you thought it was the BDF, why were you scared?"

"I wasn't scared."

Dad said it was probably because of his parents. "Classic Americans—posted to the most peaceful country in Africa and still expect a military coup at any moment."

Mum, Lulu, and I all agreed it was by far Dad's best practical joke to date. Dad said, "You must tell Ivor, he'd love it." We did, running across the road early the next morning.

"Whaddoes ya father think he's up to anyway," Grandpa muttered, "disturbing the bloody peace."

Granny Betty winked at us. "Grandpa didn't even hear the shots," she whispered. "He's just jealous he wasn't there."

"What, Betty!" snapped Grandpa.

"Nothing, Ivor."

"It was the best joke ever, Grandpa."

"Well, go on then," he said. "Tell your Granny Betty all about it. I'm sure she's interested."

And so, keeping our voices loud enough for Grandpa to hear, we described the events of the night to Granny Betty. Grandpa stared out the window and began, first to smile, then to snort with laughter. By the time we got to the bit where John screamed "BDF!" his shoulders were shaking, tears on his cheeks glinting in the sunlight flooding through the window.

A fter the first few months—in a silence that would last more than a year—Dad and Grandpa not speaking began to seem entirely natural. But the less bothered we became by the standoff, the more worried was Mum.

"You do know this is not healthy," she'd say. "It's between the two of them. And I can't change their minds. But I thoroughly disapprove."

"But Grandpa's impossible."

"Maybe," said Mum. But, she argued gently, even if one is in the right, withholding forgiveness takes much more energy than giving it. "Your father's great strength is also a weakness." Once Dad made a decision, said Mum, almost nothing could change his mind. And it was this energy and resolve and ability not to care what the world thought of him that took us from house to house and country to country, that kept us dangling on the fringes of life.

I said, "I like that."

Mum said, "I do too. When I met your father, it was magnetic;

he was so different. I couldn't not be with him. Would've gone to the South Pole with him, if that's where he'd wanted to go." Mum paused, eyes drifting out of focus at the romantic notion. "But," she said, "it doesn't change the simple fact that life's too short to stay angry, and you can't solve problems simply by cutting them out of your life."

But to Lulu, Damien, and me, Dad's life and even Grandpa's life seemed infinite. As long as we could see both, that it couldn't be in the same room didn't seem to matter. To us it was just another in a long line of eccentricities.

And although we always enjoyed listening to Mum's soothing philosophizing, where she was most effective was not in giving urgency to the bizarre fractures in the lives of our seemingly so resilient human family, but in reconciling our lives to the loss of lives of the beloved, endlessly varied creatures living around us in perpetual, demonstrable peril.

L ulu, who shared her bedroom with the snakes, checked on them as soon as she awoke with the first light of morning. She shook me awake, in tears. "The baby's gone."

"How did it get out?" I asked, padding after her across the brown paper flagstones. "Have you looked for it?"

We'd found the tiny brown house snake just a few days earlier. It was exquisite: the length and width of a pencil, the texture of polished thick-grained wood. It was also, we hoped, a different sex to the two big snakes, who'd shown no sign of procreating.

Lulu sniveled. "I think it's been eaten."

"By what?"

"Look."

She stopped in front of the twig-and-leaf-filled glass vivarium and pointed inside. The bigger of the two snakes was, unmistakably, bigger.

Both in tears, we ran to Mum and Dad's room.

"The baby snake's been eaten."

Mum groaned and rolled over.

"Mum! We killed it. The big snake ate it. We should've fed it more."

"Lordy," said Mum, rubbing her eyes. "Oh dear. Come on, hop into bed." We crawled under the sheets, lying side by side in the dent left by Dad. Dad's side of the bed always smelled of Timotei herbal shampoo; Mum's of the tangy tea tree oil that she dabbed onto her face before she went to bed. Mum maintained that the pungent tea tree oil was why the mouse that had chewed off a patch of Dad's hair during the night had left her alone. Dad said it was because he washed his hair more frequently.

Mum waited till our sobs subsided.

"You mustn't blame yourselves," she said, gently. "You couldn't have known they were capable of cannibalism. Tragedies happen when you have pets." She continued to talk, at first groggily, but quickly slipping into her gentle, everything-will-be-all-right voice. "It was such a tiny snake. It probably wouldn't have survived in the wild anyway." She pointed out the window, where the first morning sun glinted through the bougainvillea creepers. "Imagine how many things out there want to eat it."

"But we should have fed them more."

"Yes, perhaps," she said. "But just think—you'll never make the same mistake."

"I'll never have another brown house snake," I sniffed. "We'll have to let them go."

Mum went on, talking about life and death and forgiveness, drawing lessons from the innumerable, previous casualties, most recently the baby shrews that we'd fed hot milk and Pronutro every three hours, all through the night, and which had died after a week, and the tiny weaver babies, blown out of their nest, that, despite regular feeding and endless homeopathic mixtures, had lived for just two days.

Fueled by a steaming cup of *rooibos* tea, and with Damien joining us, Mum soon extended the remit of her talk.

Treat every problem as an opportunity to learn...

Every loss of life, as a reminder to savor life...

Live every day as if it were your last...

Only Mum could turn the death of a juvenile brown house snake into an exhilarating philosophical lecture. Her words sent shivers down my spine, and slowly the guilt and sadness dissipated. She finally rounded off the epic discussion over breakfast with a recital of Rudyard Kipling's *If*.

> *If you can fill the unforgiving minute*
> *With sixty seconds' worth of distance run—*
> *Yours is the Earth and everything that's in it ...*

"Now," she said, snapping us back to the rapidly warming morning and the unpleasant impending decision. "What are you going to do about these snakes?"

Feeding the snakes—horrible from the beginning—had, with every gruesome gecko meal, only got harder. Deposited into the vivarium, the two unfortunate geckos would at once sense trouble. Even if the snakes were out of sight among the mopane leaves or tucked behind a rock, the doomed pair would instantly freeze as we dropped them onto the sandy floor. After a second's pause, they'd dash frantically up the glass walls, often clambering right to the top before their tiny sucker pads gave way and they slid helplessly back down.

After at least five minutes of feigned disinterest, one of the snakes would slither, casually, to a better striking position. Looping the tip of its tail around a slim branch, it would wait patiently here for a panicking gecko to scamper within reach.

The strike, always accurate, was so quick that the gecko seemed to start thrashing before the snake had even moved. Mostly, the snake would have struck side on, near the gecko head. With its prey pinned down, the snake would then edge its jaws toward the gecko's nose and wildly revolving conical eyes. Positioned, at last, for consumption proper, it would now engulf the nose, and proceed, in small, leisurely chomps, toward the tail.

The unfed snake would have meanwhile done little more than swivel a curious eye in the direction of the uneaten gecko. Only once the first gecko had been reduced to a disappearing tail between distended jaws would snake two begin to slither into action. The second gecko was always a much easier catch. By now exhausted, it would mostly just crouch pathetically—paralyzed but for a heaving belly, rising and falling beneath loosely fitting skin—panting and waiting, hopelessly, to be eaten.

Biting my lip as I watched, I'd wait for Lulu's inevitable protest.

"Let's get him out, Rob."

Then making, as always, a token effort to be pragmatic, "We can't, Lu. The other snake'll starve."

"But we can't let him die. Look at him. He's so scared, Rob. Please."

"No."

"Please."

I always gave in.

"Okay, just this time though."

Starving snakes, it turned out, looked no different than well-fed snakes, and it had been easy enough for Lulu and me to convince ourselves that we were doing no great harm.

No longer though, with the poor baby snake being digested as we spoke.

Reluctantly, we agreed that we'd have to let our beloved pets go. We retrieved the two cool creatures for a final cuddle, marveling at their beautiful dark eyes, their smooth, slightly embossed skin, the wonderful sensation as their slim muscled bodies flexed against our hands.

Even Damien, who wasn't normally interested in the snakes, held one and slowly poured it from hand to hand. He stared up at the ceiling where the usual four or five geckos lurked. "Why don't you just feed them gecko tails?" he asked.

When a gecko was frightened, the tail would sometimes detach, continuing to wriggle for several minutes.

"We'll never catch enough."

"What if you shot them down?"

"What?"

"The geckos."

"We don't want to kill them. That's the whole point."

"Not kill them." Damien's eyes gleamed. "Just stun them."

The snakes were returned to the vivarium; the morning was devoted to the construction of a stun gun. The design pursued, to begin with, involved a basic catapult. Bullets were launched using a heavy-duty rubber band, hooked onto a nail at the front end of a foot-long piece of wood, which was drawn back along the length of the wood. Ammunition tested included marbles (much too heavy and certainly lethal to geckos), ball bearings (still too heavy and possibly lethal), dried *Grewia* berries (too light and difficult to shoot straight); and peanuts (same problem).

After several hours, we'd chipped holes in the wall plaster and fired hundreds of berries that hadn't even made it to the wall, vanishing beneath bookshelves and sofas. The design that eventually triumphed, in which the rubber band was both the propulsion and the bullet, was even simpler. Stretched slowly and parallel with the wood, the band, when released, would *thwack* the wall accurately: powerful enough to detach a gecko, soft enough to do so without injury.

The first gecko Damien hit plummeted toward the sofa. It landed upside down, stubby legs still, but soft white belly expanding and contracting. I grabbed it and dangled it from its tail, just above the floor. After a few seconds, it started to wriggle, and with a few gentle shakes, it ejected its tail, dropped to the floor, and dashed back toward the wall.

Like a small fish on a riverbank, the detached tail flapped backward and forward on the vivarium floor. Grains of sand stuck to the raw, auto-severed end. The unfed snake gulped down the wriggling morsel, sand and all, in less than a minute. It consumed a second with similar enthusiasm before happily settling back in a loosely knotted embrace with its still-bloated companion.

The problem was solved. The snakes would stay; we could feed them with moral impunity. Almost. Lulu was still worried about traumatizing the geckos. We consulted Mum, who'd retreated to her typewriter.

"Mmm." Mum didn't look up.

"Mum, does it hurt them to lose tails?"

"I'm sure not."

"See, Lu."

"It looks sore," whined Lulu.

"I'm sure it's just fright," said Mum, distractedly. "Give them some Rescue Remedy."

By dusk, when we crossed the road to Granny and Grandpa's, we had the system perfected. Damien would shoot down the gecko, I'd grab it by the tail, and in the few seconds before it came to, Lulu would ease its jaw slightly open, insert the end of the glass dropper, and eject a single alcoholic drop of Rescue Remedy.

Grandpa watched, eyes gleaming. He clapped loudly as the stumpy-tailed gecko scampered back up to the ceiling. "I'll be damned. How's that for ingenuity, Betty? Whaddid I tell you? These kids are geniuses." He grinned and tapped his head. "Chip off the old block."

"Indeed," said Granny.

"Homeopathic geckos," continued Grandpa. "Almost vegetarian snakes! And the first gecko tail farm in the world. A sustainable resource. It's all bloody marvelous!" He shook his head incredulously. "And that reminds me. Haven't fed my moths. Who wants to help?"

We all nodded. Grandpa was convinced the moths preferred their fruit juice laced with alcohol—as too did we. He fetched us each a glass, and for the next half an hour, as the delighted moths fluttered from mouth to mouth, we sat in the growing darkness, heads tilted back, dribbling fruit juice and wine onto our T-shirts and getting slowly and softly intoxicated.

Y ou guys are not normal," Melaney Nevill enjoyed reminding me.

Melaney was my best friend from Phikwe and a regular visitor to the Selebi cottage, which she called "The Shack."

Her occasional ridicule was, however, well worth the benefits of having a friend who really knew what life was like in Selebi; who understood what I was up against, when I left the cocoon of madness and tried desperately to blend in. Because living on the fringe was great, provided everyone around you was on it too. Otherwise it could be agony.

Melaney lived in a spacious modern house in Phikwe. Her dad, Geoff, worked on the mine, played golf and squash, and at least once a year took the whole family up to Chobe Game Reserve on a fishing holiday. Her younger brother Glenn, who, despite almost blowing himself up with Damien, was not unnaturally obsessed with explosives, played cricket and fished with his dad. Her mother, Lyn, worked for PIMP, which, thanks to her, sponsored the horse shows in addition to random events like the Sunbeams' boat race. Lyn permed her hair, wore makeup and perfume, and never bought clothes at PEP Stores in the Phikwe Mall, where Botswana pop music blared out of the loudspeakers and you could find two-pula T-shirts in big bargain bins. Instead, Lyn took Melaney on shopping trips to Francistown, where there was a big clean Woolworths, where most of the expatriates in Phikwe shopped.

In Lyn's car, even the drive to Francistown was an entirely new, more pleasant experience. The car, which smelled of Lyn's perfume, was cooled by an astoundingly quiet and effective air conditioner. And instead of the serious rousing opera I was used to, we were surrounded by the lighthearted sounds of Jive Bunny, Fleetwood Mac, and a variety of other bands, whose names I was generally too embarrassed to inquire about. From such a comfortable vantage point, even the dry scrub whizzing past us seemed less harsh and bleak.

The only exception to the generally superior experience was the veterinary post. And feeling miffed about the kind of everyday pleasures I was missing, I took some comfort in the fact that, without the doctor's sticker, the two veterinary men insisted on searching the whole car. Eventually, Lyn gave them each a cold Coke and we zoomed on, pulling up shortly afterward at one of the many rest areas with the standard small concrete table, two concrete benches, and a trash can beneath a tree.

Melaney and I made our way behind a large syringa tree to wee, looking out for snakes and taking care to avoid all the other toilet points marked with little bunches of white tissues.

When we emerged, Lyn had scraped the table and seats free of dead leaves and pip-filled baboon poo, and laid out cans of Coke and Fanta and packets of bright red Simba chips and Hula Hoops. With strains of Michael Jackson pouring from the open window, we sat sipping Coke and talking about the upcoming horse show, discussing which events we should enter and who might win and how we might win.

Sucking a salty dissolving chip, I considered what we'd be doing if we were instead having a loo break on a journey with Mum.

The drinks would be pure fruit juice; the food, cottage cheese and lettuce whole-wheat bread sandwiches, followed by dried fruit and nuts. The music would be off, so we could appreciate the sounds of the bush. Melaney and I would probably have fetched the food from the car, because Mum would have got distracted, striding around the clearing and picking up plastic bags.

"How can people do this?" she'd mutter, tossing a new handful into the trash can. "With a bin right here? It's disgraceful..."

Then at some stage—generally midsentence, and with barely a second's pause—tone, subject, and expression would all change as Mum whipped out her lens of optimism. Finding beauty in a cluster of trees, an aloe plant, a butterfly, She would suddenly be marveling at the wonders of nature, oblivious to the rubbish that, moments before, had pained her so much.

If we'd stopped beside one of her beloved *koppies*, Mum could become lost indefinitely in her raptures. "...Now look at that amazing rock-climbing fig...*Ficus abutifolia*...exquisite... absolutely exquisite...and the color of those rocks in this light... so beautiful....Robbie, Mel, come stand over here so you can appreciate it properly..."

If you didn't daily witness such rapid changes, they could be disconcerting.

Melaney would stare, amazed, as Mum—plastic bags in one hand, shading her eyes with the other—froze mid step and stared reverently up at the *koppie*. I would then have to point to the tree in question, its magnificent roots dripping over the large balancing boulders like icing on a Christmas cake.

Having marveled at the tree, at how its flaking powdery bark gleamed silver in the sunlight, Mum would probably move on to eulogizing the vast rocks, and then, quite possibly, shift gear suddenly again, seizing the opportunity for a quick geology lesson.

In the highly unlikely event that Mum did bring up the subject of the horse show, she would tell us how pointless it was to obsess about winning, and how we should expend our energy on more important things. Anyway, if you win, everyone else must lose. Any attempt to argue that winning was fun would be met by another lecture, sometime during which Mum would make the point that she hoped her children would grow up to not be too competitive. To which I would retort, defiantly, that I loved competition, and would always be very competitive. And Melaney would giggle as Mum eyed me with her one-day-you-will-know-better look and then quickly changed the subject.

If we were with Mum, going to Francistown, it would probably be to visit the plant nursery. On the journey back, we'd have in store for us an uncomfortable ride, packed in between a prickly selection of citrus trees and indigenous seedlings that Mum and Dad hadn't succeeded in finding in the bush.

Never, with Mum, would we have been going shopping for clothes.

Which was why, standing in the spacious changing room and clutching the pile of fashionable shorts handed to me by Lyn, I was so confused. My experience with changing rooms was nil. Before then, I'd only been to PEP Stores and one of the factory shops in the Phikwe industrial area, which had been built with the help of FAP subsidies. In neither of these had I ever tried on clothes, as Mum, who "hated shopping with a passion," always wanted to leave as quickly as possible. "I'm afraid I'll just never be sartorially minded," Mum would say, if I complained. "Thank goodness we've got Granny Joan making sure our wardrobes stay respectable."

I turned over the plastic disk, examining the hole in the top and the number 5 stenciled into it. The identical number 5 on the other side provided no further clues. I decided the bored-looking Motswana shop assistant must have mistakenly handed it to me with the clothes. I gave it back to her.

"Ah, no," she said, handing it back. She gestured toward the cubicle. "Take it with you."

"What for?" I asked, bewildered.

But before she'd a chance to explain, Melaney, who had been standing silently behind me, erupted in giggles. "You don't know what that's for?" she asked, making no effort to hide a smirk. "God, Mum'll never believe it."

On hearing about my blunder, Lyn did indeed raise her neatly plucked eyebrows higher than usual. I looked at the floor and blushed. Knowing what it was for, I felt even sillier for not working it out.

I was the Bushman in *The Gods Must Be Crazy*, who'd tried to hand back the unfamiliar and troublesome Coke bottle to the man he mistook for a god.

That night, lying in the spare bed in Melaney's bedroom, still smarting from humiliation, I felt increasingly resentful of Mum, Dad, and of the fringe in general. At times like this, I couldn't believe Mum was actually writing a book that would spell out in detail exactly how different our family was. Enough people knew already. It was unkind to her children.

"You asleep, Mel?"

"Almost."

"I wish I had your mum," I said, not sure what such a declaration would achieve.

Silence.

"You asleep?"

"Thinking."

"Tell me."

"Your Mum's pretty wise," said Melaney. "And you get to not go to school. And not have homework. Or exams."

"I like homework and exams."

Mel sighed. "God, you're so weird sometimes." She turned over and stuck her head under her pillow.

I couldn't believe it. Either way, I was damned: weird for not being normal; weird, too, for wanting to be normal. I lay awake, listening to the unfamiliar sounds of the town: a cacophony of dog barks reverberating along the street as someone strolled past;

a furious neighbor yelling at the howling dogs; a car driving past, blasting loud Botswana pop music, engine revving and wheels screeching as it turned the corner and disappeared onto the main road. A frog croaked from someone's fishpond, or swimming pool. From somewhere, far away, came the distant thumping of a late-night party.

I missed the bush, and I felt bad, and then terrible, about wanting to trade in Mum. I wondered if she'd guess my traitorous thoughts, and I resolved to beg Melaney to keep quiet. Sobered by guilt, I knew that the penalties of having my parents did not, probably, in the wider scheme of things, exceed what I liked about them. But penalties there were. And while some—not knowing about changing rooms, painfully wholesome sandwiches, opera on long car journeys—I knew I'd soon forget, others would persist. Old scabs, grotesque in the harsh light of normality, waiting to be picked at.

Like my saddle, which was for me the nadir of my generally pretty outlandish riding equipment. Donated by friends who'd had horses for generations, the deeply scooped seat was, for a start, much too big for me. To accommodate the old-fashioned shape, and to give Feste some padding, Mum had sewn a special foam saddle pad, which she covered in bright blue cotton. "It matches the riding hat," she said reassuringly. Unfortunately, while the blue did indeed match the homemade sun hat—strapped, at Mum's insistence, over my riding helmet—no one ever got beyond the mesmerizing clash with the enormous saddle, which was a kind of vomit-orange color, topped off with a patchwork of dark splits in the leather.

And when I eventually fell asleep, it was tormented by these thoughts of my saddle—every fault magnified by the wild unforgiving imagination of the late-night mind.

15

CHRISTMAS

Carols by candlelight

I need a new saddle."

Mum said, "Do you *need* one? Or do you *want* one?"

"*Need!*"

Dad said, "Yours is a perfectly effective saddle. It's what you do on it that counts."

"Well, I *really want* one, then. What about for Christmas?"

"It's a very big expense."

"For Christmas *and* my birthday?" My ninth of January birthday meant I often got combined presents. Which I usually discouraged, resenting the inevitable discount of one big present versus two quite big ones.

"Even so, Robbie."

"All right," said Dad, "I have a deal for you. If you find a way to make some money and contribute, I will buy you your saddle."

I stared at Dad, momentarily elated, then worried. "How do I earn money?"

"Not with coffins," said Dad. "And certainly not with Ivor. Use your brain. That's what it's there for."

"Mum?"

"Dad's right. The idea is part of the challenge. I'm sure there're plenty of things. Start small. You could grow something in the vegetable garden, bake something, ask Matthews to teach you how to do wood carving..."

"I can't think," I mumbled. "Lyn would never ask Mel to do this."

" 'Course you can think. And we *are* asking you."

"Come on," said Mum. "Give it a few days' thought. Try to think of something people use all the time. Something you could sell in Phikwe. Something that might not be easy to get hold of."

Free-range eggs.

We were in the kitchen when the idea dawned on me. Mum was lamenting disgraceful intensive farming practices.

"Laid by chickens that live packed in tiny wire cages," she muttered, banging an egg against the side of the pan. "They never see the light of day, you know. Stuffed full of antibiotics, because they get sick from the stress. Then slaughtered the moment they slow down..."

By which time I had canceled my order for an omelette.

"What if I sold free-range eggs? You can't buy them in Phikwe."

Mum and Dad endorsed the plan immediately. As long as I ran it like a proper business, they would help me get started. As I munched my way through a bowl of muesli, it was quickly decided that my combined Christmas and tenth birthday present would be twenty chickens, a fully equipped chicken run, and a six-month supply of chicken food.

"Well," said Dad, as we cleared away the dishes, "it's December already. If you want them in time, we'd better get cracking."

One of the conditions of the present was that I would help Dad with the preparation.

I sat with him as he drew up a shopping list. Ten meters of plywood, two tins of creosote, thirty meters of chicken mesh. All of which could be bought at the Phikwe hardware store. The automatic water and grain feeders, he'd have to get in Johannesburg, the next time he went to collect medicines.

I had never imagined that a few chickens would involve quite so much effort and expenditure. I apologized to Dad.

"If you want to run a good business, you've got to do things properly."

"Isn't it a lot of money?"

"Don't worry about the money."

"Then why," I asked, suddenly irritated, "can't you just buy me a saddle for my birthday?"

"Because this is good experience and a good responsibility, Robbie."

"And keeping accounts will be wonderful for your maths," added Mum.

"My maths is fine," I snapped, resenting having my birthday present used to make Mum feel good about homeschooling. "Anyway, I don't care about that."

But I did—as Mum well knew—care about animals dying.

So when she then suggested that instead of getting young chicks, I could save and rehabilitate year-old "end-of-lay" battery chickens destined for slaughter, she had me: the combination of bona fide farmer, businesswoman, and death-row chicken deliverer was irresistible. I embraced it without further question. And over the following weeks, while Lulu and Damien combed the bush for the traditional Scott thorn-tree Christmas tree, I reneged on my annual duties and instead hovered beside Dad at the workbench.

To begin with, I could do little more than hand him nails or hold down the wood while he sawed. But once the cozy, half-oval hutch had been erected, and the twenty spacious nesting boxes installed at the back, I was able to help properly, taking a paint-brush to the raw golden plywood and plastering on thick, tar-smelling creosote to protect it from termites.

It soon became a painting extravaganza. A few meters from the hutch, which we were creosoting on the bare concrete around the shed, Mum helped Lulu and Damien do the Christmas paint-ing. Second only to presents, the search for and spray-painting of the dead, two-meter-tall thorn tree was the most exciting part of Christmas. Watching the transformation of bare spiky brown branches into exquisite gnarls and needles of shining silver was like watching magic. As was the evolution of the tree decorations: beautiful seedpods, which we spray-painted gold, making glint-ing spirals, spiky round baubles, and long golden pendulums—and, in the messy process, getting gold on our clothes, gold on our skin, gold on the dogs, and, this year, even a few gold splotches on the black chicken hutch.

On Christmas Eve morning, we added the final touch to the tree: a string of flashing lights, wound in between the golden seed-pods and incongruous blobs of cotton wool. The cotton wool was there at Lulu's insistence: an attempt to bring to our baking hot Christmas day some essence of the white, snowy Christmases enjoyed by the northern hemisphere children in our favorite books. The overall effect, if bizarre, was beautiful, and we kept the lounge curtains shut throughout the day to properly admire the flashing, eye-wateringly bright creation in the corner of the room.

Late in the afternoon, the Christmas carols guests arrived from Phikwe. Granny Joan and Grandpa Terry came first, fol-lowed shortly afterward by their two best friends, Alan and Ellie Lowther, their daughter, Sarah, and her two sons. The Lowthers also had a son Mum's age, who Granny and Grandpa had once hoped would be their son-in-law. Fifteen years after Dad had sty-mied this plan, they had a new strategy for joining the two fami-lies, and I frequently overheard infuriating comments like, "Don't the grandchildren play so well together?" *Wink, wink.* "Wouldn't it be funny if Robbie or Lulu ended up with Mark or David?"

"I will never end up with anyone," I'd retort haughtily. To which the two sets of grandparents would smile knowingly. "You say that now, but one day you'll be walking down the aisle on your father's arm."

Dad said, "I should be so lucky. No one's ever going to take Robbie off my hands."

"Good," I replied.

"Keith, how can you say that about your own daughter?"

"Objective analysis."

"Oh, nonsense."

As soon as the Christmas tree had been properly appreciated, and before it got dark, I insisted that everyone follow me into the bush to admire my present in progress. Beneath a silver-barked *Commiphora* tree a few meters from the house, the big black hutch stood facing a long, half-finished chicken run. Hands on hips, I explained my brilliant business venture. Which, as I pointed out, had the dual benefit of making happy chickens and happy customers, who would no longer, as they munched their scrambled eggs, have to think about fluorescent-lit cages full of stressed, antibiotic-filled chickens, unable to move, and desperately pecking at each other.

By the look on the visitors' faces, this was not something they had previously considered while eating their scrambled eggs.

Mum smiled proudly.

I said, "I'm taking advance orders. Two pula fifty for half a dozen happy eggs. Only fifty thebe more than cruel eggs."

Mark and David stared at me, mouths open.

Dad smiled. "See what I mean about Robbie?"

Silence.

Broken by the grandmothers, who each hurriedly pledged to buy several dozen eggs, and, for the moment at least, avoided further speculation on who might end up with who.

"Carols by Candlelight" had always been a misleading term for the annual Christmas Eve fireside gathering. And this evening was no different.

There was candlelight—cast by the candles clasped by everyone except Mum, who was holding the guitar. And we did begin with "Silent Night" and "Away in a Manger." But Mum, the musical director, had only a small repertoire of songs she could both play well and liked playing. None of these were carols, and she rapidly moved to a less festive-season program—which, she argued, when anyone protested in favor of tradition, was only in keeping with a spray-painted thorn bush for a Christmas tree.

The non-carols began, as always, with Mum's favorite, "Puff the Magic Dragon." Followed by "Yellow Submarine," "Jamaica Farewell," "Oh My Darling Clementine," "The Gypsy Rover," and "Leaving on a Jet Plane." With every song, often matched one-for-one with rounds of drinks, the singing grew louder. After a break for dinner, by which time the adults had drunk enough to no longer care that we weren't singing carols, Grandpa Terry was suggesting his favorite Irish songs and Mum was improvising wildly—and with variable success—to "Cockles and Mussels" and "When Irish Eyes Are Smiling," which Grandpa sang in a strong Irish accent.

It was not long before midnight when Mum said "Enough." Her fingers were aching; she still had to wrap some of our presents. But as she lowered her guitar into its felt-lined case, Lulu, Damien, and I begged her to sing our adaptation of "English Country Garden." Mum, who could never resist an opportunity to show off a product of homeschooling, smiled. "If you insist," she said, plucking at the strings, and humming the tune to herself. "Just once, though."

It turned out to be several times. We'd rewritten the old song on a musically focused day and Mum, as usual, had encouraged us to be as creative as possible. The result was that we'd stuck in all our favorite bush trees and birds, with little regard to how they sounded. So it took several renditions before everyone else learned the words, and sang with enough gusto to fudge their way through the bits that didn't quite work.

When they eventually did, though, it was a rousing, splendid finale to the night, and the words rang far across the quiet bush, serenading all around us:

How many wild birds fly to and fro
In a Big Botswana Garden?

We'll tell you now of some that we know
And those we miss you'll surely pardon
Cuckooshrike, barbet and owl
Hammerkop and oriole
Babbler, lark, thrush and guinea fowl
There is joy in the spring
When the birds begin to sing
In a Big Botswana Garden!

How many kinds of wild trees grow
In a Big Botswana Garden?
We'll tell you now of some that we know
And those we miss you'll surely pardon
Mopane, leadwood, and guarri
Marula and fever tree
Baobab, knob-thorn and large molope
Aloe, spekboom, ficus,
Mashatu and sjambok pod
In a Big Botswana Garden!

"Such a lovely evening," said Mum, as we helped clear away the glasses around the fire. "Such a pity Ivor wasn't with us on his harmonica," she added, looking meaningfully at Dad.

Dad said, "Ivor doesn't care about Christmas. Hardly ever gave us presents."

"That of course," said Mum, "is not the point."

Dad shrugged. "He can come here if he wants."

Mum said that would be a bit awkward, seeing that Dad wasn't talking to him. And Dad said it was Ivor who wouldn't talk to him. At which Mum shook her head, stuck out her chin, and began humming "Silent Night" as she swung the flashlight around the glowing embers of the nearly dead fire.

Grandpa Ivor may not have given us or Dad presents. But every Christmas, he loaded up his *bakkie* with several sacks full of little plastic present bags. The bags were prepared by the Phikwe Lions Club, the local branch of the worldwide volunteer service organization that supports a wide range of charitable causes. Each bag was tied with a ribbon and contained a selection of things like Lux soap, boiled sweets, shampoo, Vaseline, a can of beef, Simba chips, and a face cloth.

And every Christmas morning, Lulu, Damien, and I went along with him and Granny Betty to give the bags to patients at the government hospital in Phikwe. We didn't like going, and, at nine o'clock, it was reluctantly that we changed out of our pajamas and abandoned our stocking spoils to cross the road to Grandpa's.

"Come on, guys," said Mum. "It's a lovely thing to do. You'll make their day. And you'll appreciate your own presents more."

Dad said, "Damien, make sure Robbie doesn't try to sell eggs to the patients."

"I would never," I spluttered.

"Bet you would," said Damien.

"Come on, Robbie." Dad smiled. "How about you developing a sense of humor for my Christmas present? Nearly ten years of waiting. But I remain hopeful."

Mum said, "For goodness sake. Will you three hurry up. Grandpa's waiting."

I felt depressed just at the thought of the long, full wards, which would, as always, be brightly decorated for Christmas. Strung above the rows and rows of bodies in beds, the strands of red and green tinsel somehow only made things worse. Generally, the best thing about visits was that they meant the morning passed quickly, making the wait for our afternoon Christmas-present-opening session less agonizing.

There were nice parts. Like when a patient's eyes lit up and they grinned and gripped my hand and thanked me for coming. But sometimes they wanted to keep on talking and holding. And when I tried to pull away, they wouldn't let go. And then, when I looked into the eyes of the smiling old man or sick young woman willing me to stay, I felt hopeless, and scared and repulsed by the thought that if I looked too long, I'd start knowing what they were feeling, and I'd quickly pull away and hurry to join Lulu or Damien at another bed.

I hated the smell, too. In it were all the same smells of Dad's clinic—disinfectant, sweat, and gloves. But mixed with these—which I liked—were the lived-in smells: soggy uneaten food, recently used bedpans, bedclothes overdue for a wash. Dad said that Botswana's hospitals were some of the best and cleanest in Africa, but in the harsh light of the bare bulbs, even the clean floors and walls were nonetheless horrible. Horrible too—horrible for the guilt—was the reaction to the presents: a delighted laugh as someone sniffed his bar of soap; a shaking smiling head as a frail old woman carefully arranged the tiny gifts one by one on the bare bedside table.

With every bag I gave out, I felt worse.

To Grandpa Ivor and Granny Betty, as we progressed down the ward, the reverse seemed to happen. With each new patient, Grandpa joked and laughed more enthusiastically than with the last. And Granny Betty looked happier than she did any other day of the year, chatting and smiling with rare animation. As a nurse, she could ask detailed medical questions, which all the patients loved, and give advice about any problem. She also joked with the arthritic old men and women, showing them her gnarled finger joints and patting her dodgy hip and saying they'd be walking much better than her when they were able to leave their beds.

Even when we'd given out the last bag, Granny and Grandpa wanted to linger, chatting to the nurses and revisiting some of the beds. I couldn't wait to leave. The hospital made me feel worse, not better, about my own presents. I liked problems that you could really solve, completely. And the thought of all the sick, poor people—no different but for a chat and a few cheap gifts—somehow ruined the pleasure of giving. I banished the memory the moment we walked back out into the dust and sunlight. And that afternoon at Granny Joan's and Grandpa Terry's, eating a Christmas feast, opening presents and playing in the pool until the sun went down, I succeeded, almost completely, in not giving the hospital another thought.

Twenty abused chickens were just the kind of neat, soluble problem I did like.

I didn't want to see all the other abused chickens I wasn't rescuing, though. And on the Friday after my birthday—which fell on a clinic day—I waited in the car as Mum and Dad disappeared into the long gray sheds of the battery chicken farm. Closing the window to block out the mournful clucking noise, I turned toward the bush and studied a fat, crested barbet hopping beneath a tree as it searched for insects.

On the way home, I crouched in the back of the car and examined the scrawny brown-and-white hens, huddled together in the crate. Most had big patches of feathers missing; all had been debeaked so they couldn't peck each other to death. They looked exhausted.

Exactly what I had wanted. And as they clucked dejectedly, I clucked comfortingly back, enjoying the satisfying thought of their imminent free-range ecstasy.

But of happiness, let alone ecstasy, there was no sign at all.

When I lifted them out of the crate and gently placed them in the run, the chickens didn't even move. For a few moments, all twenty just crouched there, petrified. Then, squawking and flapping, they ran from the sunlight, charging en masse through the small door into the dark hutch.

I couldn't believe it. The run was ten meters long, shaded by lush summer trees, with patches of green grass, shrubs, and thick soft soil. Two bright red water feeders and shiny tin grain feeders sparkled in the dappled sunlight where they hung from the chicken mesh, hawk-and-eagle-proof roof.

Ten minutes later, not one chicken had moved from the pathetic huddle in the corner of the hot dark hutch.

I had voluntary battery chickens.

Mum had already put Rescue Remedy in the water dispenser, but until the chickens actually ventured outside and drank some, she could offer only optimism. "Don't worry, Robbie. They're in shock. It'll take time."

"Don't be so impatient," said Dad. "Leave them in peace for a bit."

Mum said, "Why don't you come inside and we can finish off your birthday cake?"

"I'm staying here."

"All right. Well, can I bring you anything?"

"My accounts book."

I left the chicken run and perched outside on a fallen log, peering through the mesh. Mum and Lulu came back with the book, my new calculator, pens, pencils, paints, and two glasses of icy fruit juice. "Have fun, then," said Mum. "Call if you need anything."

Lulu sat next to me on the log with her sketchbook. "I'm going to paint your chickens."

"You can hardly see them," I said, still feeling miserable.

But Lulu could paint anything, beautifully and creatively, in front of her or not. As I fingered the neatly squared pages of my thick new accounts book, she sketched the food dispenser, encircled by the outlines of animated hens. I began to do projections—grain consumption, egg production, sales revenue, months till saddle, days till saddle. Lulu, meanwhile, took out her paints and did her own optimistic projections, giving color and a good deal of extra fat and feathers to the chickens, which, for good measure, had deposited ostrich-sized eggs all over the run.

In the top right-hand corner of the sheet, she painted a small saddle. In the top left she wrote, "Happy Birthday Rob! The Chiken Queen!"

Even Damien, who did not, like Lulu, have a natural affinity for my chickens just because they were animals, was being nice. So far, as promised, there had been no explosions in the nearby shed, which was the site of Damien and Matthews's long-running project to build a match gun. The gun design involved a match-powder cartridge, made out of the tube that holds a spoke to a bicycle wheel. Mounted on a wooden gun cutout, the powder was exploded by a pin—a decapitated nail—and, in theory, propelled a bullet, made from a second decapitated nail. Matthews, who claimed to have once made a functioning match gun, was adamant this design could succeed. If ever anyone questioned him, he returned to his central piece of evidence. "I shot a chicken. Dead! One time!" he'd say, grinning proudly.

But with not a single nail bullet successfully fired, I'd long since lost faith in this claim and was much more worried about the explosions further traumatizing my hens.

I did, however, remain suspicious about Matthews's general callousness toward chickens, and when he strolled over to inspect the hens, I followed him into the run. "Don't you dare ever try to shoot them," I said, as he squatted down and peered into the hutch.

Matthews turned round and gave a scornful laugh. "These chickens are no good. No meat. I only shoot chickens you can cook."

"They're lovely chickens," I said, indignantly. "They'll get fat soon."

Matthews grinned. "I'll shoot them later then."

"Matthews!" gasped Lulu. I yelled, "Go away!" And Matthews ran laughing back to the shed.

More than an hour later, with all the chickens still huddled in their hutch, Mum and Dad came down the path from the house, carrying the garden table and chairs. They arranged these outside the run and then fetched plates, cups, a teapot, and my remaining birthday cake, draped in a dishcloth to chase away the flies that always hovered in the vicinity of the horse pens.

"If you won't come to us," said Mum, "we'll come to you."

To my annoyance, Mum then insisted that I invite Matthews, saying that no one should ever feel left out on birthdays. I said he'd threatened to shoot my chickens and I didn't, at present, care if he felt left out.

Mum said of course he had been joking.

Dad said that if I was nice about it and invited Matthews, he'd probably be less inclined to try to shoot my chickens when they got fat. I gave in, and both boys joined us. When everyone was assembled, Mum fetched from the kitchen the steaming enamel-plated kettle, streaked with black burn marks from all the times Lulu, Damien, and I had boiled it on open fires.

As we sipped tea and ate cake, Dad explained how I'd be able to tell exactly when a chicken laid an egg by the distinctive, strained egg-laying sound. "Like this," he said, emitting a few strangled squawks.

The chickens clucked nervously inside the hutch.

"Shhh, Dad!"

"Sorry, Robbie."

Dad stopped squawking, and the clucks died down. Mum poured more tea and we discussed venues for selling the eggs. Saturday mornings at the Phikwe library, it was decided, would be ideal. Mum said she was sure Granny Joan could arrange to make space for me on the table, where donated cakes were sold to raise money for the library.

Then, midway through our second cup of tea—by which time I was deeply absorbed in planning my free-range egg empire— Lulu put her finger on her lips and pointed toward the hutch.

One of the chickens had stuck her head out.

For a few moments she just peered around cautiously. Then, very slowly, her head bobbing backward and forward like a cartoon chicken, she edged her way about a meter out into the run. She stopped, and gave the tea party and the dogs at our feet a suspicious glance. When no one moved, though, she relaxed and gingerly scratched at the soft dirt. A small cloud of dust rose at her feet. She scratched again, harder this time. Dust billowed around her.

And then there was no turning back. She dug in, alternating feet, clawing wildly at the ground, and moments later almost disappearing in an explosion of red dust.

Another chicken came out and quickly joined in the dust bath. Five minutes later, the last hen had left the hutch and a thick cloud of dust swirled above the run as my twenty chickens scratched at the soil and fluffed their feathers as if a dust bath was something they'd done every day of their lives. They had, of course, never even stood on soil, let alone had the space in which to really scratch. But just as our pet rabbits' newborn babies had sucked immediately at their mother's teats, all twenty of these scrawny one-year-old chickens still knew exactly what to do.

Mum put her hand on her heart. "Makes me want to weep," she said, "for all the millions of battery chickens that will never enjoy a dust bath."

I didn't want to weep. But I felt a shiver of pleasure unlike anything I'd felt before. And as I watched the chickens, I could feel my face being stretched by an enormous, uncontrollable grin.

Dad raised his teacup toward the chickens.

"Cheers," he said.

16

THE WHOLE FAMILY'S HALF OF AN ISLAND

Seloma's wedding

Lulu, Damien, and I rushed to the door at once.

The firm knock and simultaneous clear call of *"Ko-ko"* were unmistakable; a confident synthesis of arrival etiquettes that could belong only to Seloma Tiro.

"Hi, Slo," we yelled, bursting out into the dappled sunlight under the bougainvillea.

Seloma grinned warmly. Lulu extended her arms and clutched him in a delighted hug, which he returned, quickly concealing a flicker of surprise at her affection. The seamless cultural blend was there too in his greeting. Unlike so many Batswana adults who virtually ignored children, Seloma greeted each of us in turn, but in the Botswana way, with a *dumela* for each, accompanied by the slow, friendly up-down-up clasp of the Botswana handshake.

Mum he gave a Botswana handshake too, but followed by a kiss and a hug; Dad, a handshake and a friendly pat on the back.

"So nice to see you, Slo," said Dad. "Sit down. What would you like to drink? It's been ages."

Seloma eased himself onto the sofa and sighed. "Too long," he said, smiling and gracefully crossing his legs. "Much too long."

"A beer? Wine?"

"Something soft, please. I've got to drive back to Maun."

Mum said, "You must stay the night, Slo."

"Please stay," said Lulu.

"Thank you, Linda. But I must get home. Neo is expecting me. But thank you."

He turned to Lulu. "My little Kelly is expecting me too," he said gently. "She's even younger than you. I must get back for her. You understand."

Lulu nodded.

"Now tell me, Lulu," he continued. "How are you? You've grown taller. Are you still rescuing insects from the swimming pool every night?"

"Of course." Lulu looked indignant. "I'll always." She began to tell Seloma about the brown house snakes. And I told him about my chickens, and Damien talked about his mud hut. All the while, Seloma listened intently, nodding slowly, and slowly sipping his fruit juice; moving, always, with his particular version of the bewilderingly unhurried ease of the Batswana.

To watch him was fascinating. In cashiers, builders, government officials, the slowness seemed mostly a deliberate ploy to frustrate a normal pace of life; in women leisurely raising their arms as they hitched by the roadside, or old men smoking beside their huts and watching their cows, a laid-back torpor from too many years in the heat. But in Seloma, with his precise, softly spoken English and assured gaze—never averted to the floor when a question was asked—slow was different. In him, it was proud, almost stately. And entirely appropriate, worn like a well-fitting suit.

Dad often teased him about his mix of Motswana and European habits.

"You're to blame." Seloma would smile. "It's your family's fault."

The family was what he'd come about today. Seloma and his longtime girlfriend Neo had decided to get married. "I've just been to see Ivor and Betty," he explained. "I wanted to give them and you and Linda lots of warning to be sure you could come. I couldn't have it without you. Will you come?"

Dad, who wasn't keen on weddings and particularly not the famously long Botswana weddings, stood up and shook Seloma's hand. "Of course, Slo," he said. "You know none of us would miss it for the world."

Wherever she'd lived, Granny Betty had always quickly become known for her soft heart. People and animals alike, she never turned anyone away, whatever the inconvenience to herself. And when, nearly two decades before, she'd been approached by a friend who told her of a clever Motswana boy, in urgent need of assistance with his secondary school fees and costs, she had agreed at once to help. Later, after meeting the diligent, brilliant young Seloma, Granny had offered to fund his whole education—paying school fees, and buying uniforms and textbooks. She also gave him a job in her shop so he could earn pocket money—although Seloma, as she would later discover, had given every thebe straight to his family.

Grandpa, who now considered Seloma his protégé, had, from the start, endorsed the plan. Over the following years, however, after the fall of each embryonic business empire, it was always Granny Betty who'd made sure there was enough money from the Fashion Scene boutique to support Seloma.

But Seloma, for his part, looked on from a culture that has the family transcending the individual. He'd always felt grateful and indebted to both Granny and Grandpa, and, by extension, to Dad and his brothers. He considered the whole Scott clan to be part of his family, and the invitation to his wedding was something that neither Dad nor Grandpa would have dreamed of declining.

Which did not mean, however, as they set off for Francis-town in separate cars, that either had any intention of talking to the other. Mutual avoidance at a huge Botswana marriage cere-mony was nothing in comparison to the feat of more than a year's silence, living opposite each other, next to no one else and nothing else, in the middle of nowhere.

The wedding was as big and diluting as Dad and Grandpa could have hoped.

The church was packed, and because, as usual, Dad was exactly on time and Grandpa extremely late, father and son were safely separated in the pews. It wasn't, moreover, going to be dif-ficult for them to keep an eye on each other and to remain at a safe distance: the two Scott couples were dazzlingly obvious as the only white guests.

At the reception, a jazz band played in front of the grace-ful thatched buildings of the Marang Hotel, and hundreds of flamboyantly dressed, loudly chatting guests thronged the tree-shaded lawns that swept down to the Tati River.

Everything began smoothly. The two men hovered at oppo-site ends of the lawn. Mum and Granny Betty, emissaries of peace, each made a cordial visit to the other couple. After half an hour, Dad and Grandpa had endured not so much as an awkward encounter at the drinks table. The ladies breathed easier: Seloma was well aware of the fight between the two men, and knowing the characters of both, he, of all people, would be sure to keep them well apart at dinner.

He did not. To Mum and Granny Betty's horror, he announced, beaming, that he had seated father and son beside each other, at the top table. With his own parents no longer alive, Seloma had appointed the two white couples his honorary family: internal feuds forced to come second to the honor bestowed.

At this point, as Mum recounted the events of the day, I felt terror just listening. The image of the two titans of resolve and unflinching inflexibility, squaring up for an encounter at a wedding, was horrific. I knew no two people in the world who cared less for decorum, less for what the world and everyone in it thought of them.

Mum said, "I felt sick too."

"What did you do?"

"What could I do? I went to Seloma's table."

"*Aaah.*"

But a year of fighting ended in a moment.

Forced together, Dad and Grandpa both spoke at the same time. And once they started, they couldn't stop. In a stroke, Seloma had removed that great who-will-go-first barrier to reconciliation, and the pride of both remained intact. Soon all four were chatting easily and exchanging aghast smiles during the gift-opening process, in which the giver's name was announced, then the gift unwrapped and, depending on its worthiness, cheered by the merciless crowd.

Several months later—when it was Dad's turn to help Seloma with his own "Grandpa Ivor problem"—Dad and Grandpa were still, miraculously, talking.

The familiar knock and *ko-ko* were the same. But this time, when we met Seloma in our doorway, he smiled only weakly. He looked ill with worry.

"Keith," he said, "you've got to help me reason with your father."

Dad said, flatly, "There is no way to reason with Ivor."

Seloma, a teacher by training, was the headmaster of a school in Maun. He was also a smart businessman. A year earlier he had bought the rights to some prime land in the small town of Nata, which lay at the juncture of the main road to Maun—a crucial transport gateway to the increasingly busy Okavango Delta.

The road between Nata and Maun was sandy, narrow, and deeply rutted. If you were unlucky enough to become stuck behind a truck, overtaking could be almost impossible, as fine dust clouds billowed over the windshield and severely reduced visibility. People still tried, and there were regular head-on collisions. It was the same road that, in the 1960s, Grandpa Ivor had played a crucial role in building, flying in employees of the company replacing what was then just a sandy track with a wider, built-up dirt road, opening up the delta to road traffic.

Thirty years on, though, the road was long overdue for another upgrade. It was now one of the only main roads in Botswana yet to be tarred, and at last there were plans in place to change this. Seloma had foreseen a huge increase in traffic, with Nata the obvious refueling and refreshment stop. He'd needed capital to develop a petrol station, shop, and takeaway, and had approached Grandpa Ivor to go into business with him. Grandpa had procrastinated for months. Eventually, Dad had suggested that Seloma go into business with him instead. But Seloma had been adamant that he couldn't renege on his offer; however difficult Ivor was, he owed him loyalty. Dad had dismissed, outright, the idea of going into business jointly with Seloma and Ivor. And that was the end of that discussion—and the end of another short-lived opportunity for Dad to get out of medicine.

Grandpa eventually put up some money, and a small shop and takeaway were built. But before they would install fuel tanks and pumps, the petrol company then demanded evidence of business activity. For this Seloma needed electricity, and the notoriously relaxed Botswana Power Corporation was six months behind schedule.

Grandpa said not to worry. He would take the huge generator that was gathering dust outside his ex-coffin almost-defunct furniture factory and install it in Nata. For months, he repeated the promise. And did nothing. Seloma repeatedly offered to fetch it. Grandpa said he didn't trust Seloma not to damage it. "He's a baby in the world of business," he ranted. "Just left school. Doesn't know what he's doing." Compounding matters, Grandpa then became just as unreasonably stubborn about providing the money to buy initial stock for the shop.

Seloma was stuck and desperate. And now, when Dad declared reason impossible, he asked for a loan.

Dad said, "Not if you don't have power for the fridges."

Thus, Dad's first condition of a loan was that Seloma must take the generator when Ivor wasn't around. "It's not stealing," said Dad, seeing Seloma's look of horror. "It's for his own bloody business."

The second condition was that Seloma must never tell Grandpa that Dad put him up to the idea. "If he found out, we'd never speak again. Not even my child's wedding would fix that one."

Seloma said he couldn't possibly go against the wishes of an elder.

Dad said, "Don't be such a Motswana about this, Slo."

They argued, in circles, for ages. Seloma maintained it was wrong. Dad reminded Seloma that Seloma himself had sometimes criticized the unchallenged rule of the elders. As a teacher, he'd often said that the reluctance of Batswana students to challenge teachers could be counterproductive for learning.

Seloma sighed. "This is different."

Eventually Dad said, "I'm not going to argue anymore. It's your choice."

Seloma went away and thought about it. Then he asked Dad to help him pick a suitable time and date for the heist.

All day, we waited.

Grandpa returned from his factory, more hysterical than I'd ever seen him. "I've been betrayed...treated him like a son...and he's crossed me...after all Betty and I have done for him....Bloody disgrace....Breaks my heart..."

Grandpa ranted for days. Everyone lay low. Dad refused to comment.

Dad gave Seloma regular bulletins on Grandpa's state of mind. And for several weeks, until the worst of the rage subsided, Seloma remained silent. By this time he had some cheering turnover figures, which helped to thaw Grandpa into a state of grudging acceptance, if not warmth.

The Northgate filling station, shop, and takeaway thrived. For the first time ever, said Dad, Grandpa had a good business, with a good business partner.

Seloma was deeply grateful to Dad, but he also continued to feel bad about taking the generator. One day, not long after, he phoned unexpectedly.

"I've found an island, Keith," he said. "I would like to get it for our whole family."

The island, near Maun, was tribal land, and Seloma was arranging a ninety-nine-year lease for the family.

When he'd completed the lease negotiations, an expedition was planned. A few weeks later, Jonathan, his wife, Christine, and our two young cousins Daniel and William arrived in Selebi, exhausted after a six-hour journey from Johannesburg.

Dad said, "Count me out. I do enough traveling for my clinics."

After nearly four years of flying, the roads to many of Dad's clinics had been improved—some tarred, some resurfaced with gravel. With the car journey easier, he had just sold his airplane—which was difficult to maintain—and was now driving more than 800 kilometers a week.

Grandpa Ivor said, "I've seen it. Wonderful place. Beautiful! Great for tourism. Going to build a tourist camp, I reckon. Leave a legacy for the whole family."

When we pleaded with Grandpa to come, he said, "I'm a busy man. I'm running a growing business. Northgate first. Next Southgate! Westgate! Eastgate! I'm taking petrol all over the country. Don't have time for this gallivanting."

When we pleaded with Dad to come, Dad said, "I'm too knackered."

Mum said, "Come on, Keith, you can't always be so antisocial."

"I'm not being antisocial," said Dad, grinning. "I have to stay and keep Grandpa company."

Half grimacing, half smiling, Mum shook her head in despair.

So an hour before dawn the next morning, squeezed into Jonathan's four-by-four—missing only the two men that the island was intended for most—we set off northwest.

On the way up we sang, "We'll be coming round the island when we come, we'll be coming round the island when we come...."

Until Jonathan said, "I can't concentrate on the bloody road." Which was straight and flat, but full of cows and donkeys. Then we played the license-plate game instead, each picking a number and seeing whose came up most often.

After four long hours, broken only by a wee and drink break in Francistown, we pulled up at the now busy Northgate petrol station, and collected, from Seloma, a map showing how to find the island. We drove on quickly, determined to get to the island and back to Nata for dinner. The landscape sliding past became increasingly dry and dusty, the only excitement provided by several fresh, steaming piles of elephant dung in the middle of the tar, which was striped with the occasional tracks of *bakkies* and donkey carts that had driven on their rims in the road-melting midday heat. There was no sign of the elephants, which Jonathan tried to compensate for by telling us how once, in the days when there were only dirt roads in Botswana, they'd had to wait for two hours on this same road for vast migrating herds of wildebeest and zebra to pass.

After a couple of hundred kilometers on the new tar road, we passed Motopi, where the road runs beside the Boteti River, and where Grandpa Ivor had had his old camp.

An hour later we were in Maun. Here we headed deep into the bush, winding our way along sandy roads in the direction of the famous sparkling islands of the delta. As he drove, Jonathan gave a potted history of the area, over which Grandpa Ivor had so often flown in the old days. It was then, in the 1960s, inaccessible and virtually uninhabited: tsetse flies, which kill cattle and cause "sleeping sickness" in humans, had kept herders and cattle out of the fertile, pristine delta area. But the government had since waged a successful war against the fly, and there were now numerous cattle posts—several of which we stopped at when Mum, who was trying to follow Seloma's map, got us thoroughly lost.

While Mum pored over the map with the men who came over to help her, Lulu, Damien, and I peered at the small buildings and mud and thatch huts, trying to be the first to glimpse a novel interior furnishing to add to our list of favorites. Furniture was one of the first and most visible ways in which people in the villages and cattle posts spent their money, and through the windows or doors of the humble buildings it was not unusual to see rooms crammed with plush red Dralon lounge suites, extravagant wooden ward-robes with elaborate gold handles, and enormous beds covered in shiny polyester quilted bedspreads.

Found across the country, such incongruous wealth is mostly derived from cattle, the heart of the rural economy. In Botswana, you can own and sell up to three hundred head of cattle—collectively worth several hundred thousand pula—before being liable for income tax. Most families in villages and cattle posts own at least a few cattle, which are often used to pay the bride price, or *bogadi*. A few villagers own thousands. But generally, apart from quirks like a love of lavish furnishings, cattle wealth is not flaunted, but kept—sometimes too late in drought years—in the cattle bank.

Slowly, however, habits and values were changing, a fact lamented by Seloma.

A man with a thousand cows, he'd once told us, traditionally had the same food on his table as a man with one cow. "But now things are different," he sighed. We were questioning him about the shiny new vehicles often seen parked on the dust beside small huts in the villages. Seloma shook his head. "That is just igno-rance," he said sadly. "People with money these days don't know that the savings account should come first. And then the house. And then the flashy car." Often the extravagant cars belonged to people who'd made money in the towns, returning to visit their home cattle posts, wanting status and to demonstrate success. Se-loma said, "It is terrible to see."

But Lulu, Damien, and I relished seeing the flashy cars parked in villages. And as we drove slowly toward the island, looking out for new specimens, we described our favorite sightings to Daniel and William—the all-time winner being a large silver Mercedes gleaming on the dirt in front of a tiny hut and a subsiding long-drop loo, next to an unhitched donkey cart. Here, though, the deep sandy roads prohibited most cars, and by the time we eventually found the island, we'd seen nothing more exciting than a few old *bakkies* with high bars on the open back, just wide enough to fit a cow.

Jonathan stopped under a small tree in the middle of a flat, grassy plain.

There was no water in sight—and no animals, except for a few of the ubiquitous goats, nibbling at bushes. Mum pointed to a five-hundred-meter-long strip of land, which was covered in large trees and surrounded by a dry sandy stream. "That must be the island," she said excitedly. She swung her arm to the left. "And that side must be our half."

We didn't even have a whole of a dry island—an island that wasn't actually in the Okavango Delta, Mum reminded me as we walked toward it. "The outskirts," she said, comfortingly. "Seloma says that later, in June, when the floodwaters arrive from Angola, it becomes a real island. But then we'd only be able to get to it by boat. So we're actually lucky to be here when it's dry."

We ran through the sandy grassland and clambered up the bank of the island.

On it, the island seemed more like an island, and I began to feel better. The trees were beautiful: tall and thick-canopied, some beside the bank bending slightly toward the absent water. The dense, dry island brush crackled under our feet as we explored, tearing our clothes on thornbushes, clambering over huge fallen tree trunks, and jumping as startled unseen creatures rustled though the undergrowth.

Every few minutes, Mum, Jonathan, or Christine hissed, "*Shhh.*" Then everyone stopped, as the three adults whipped out their binoculars, peering at yet another new bird in the trees or undergrowth and passing the "bins" around for everyone to have a look, before announcing that the exploration could proceed.

After exploring the whole island, and deciding that our side was definitely the better side with the better trees, we followed the sandy stream, which led after a few minutes into another stream. This one had water: not much water—a deep narrow channel no wider than a person—but water still.

Ecstatic, we stripped and slid in, the water coming to our shoulders as we sat on the sandy bed and floated in the gentle current, all seven of us spread out in a line. Here, from the tiny, refreshing stream, the tall trees and the birds fluttering between their branches, the bath-width channel somehow offered enough promise to make up for all the missing water. The world from it was grandly and starkly beautiful. I wondered, absently, if Grandpa Ivor could explain this to tourists.

Four hours later, well after dark, we reached Nata. After dinner with Seloma and Neo, eaten outside under a thick canopy of trees alive with leaping bush babies, we slept in little thatched cottages at Nata Lodge.

In the morning, before leaving for Selebi, we drove into the Makgadikgadi Salt Pans. These enormous pans were utterly flat, with vast expanses of shimmering gray water stretching to the bright horizon. Around the water was dry, gray, bare, flat land. And standing there on the pans, I felt smaller and more awed by the size of the world than ever before. The parked four-by-four looked like a toy car that might just suddenly vanish in the vastness. The figures walking around it, slipping on swimming costumes, hopping as bare feet touched hot late-morning sand, looked like tiny cartoon people.

The salt pans are the largest in the world, about the size of Portugal, and are dry for much of the year. But for several months after the rainy season they become great, shallow lakes, teeming with algae—ideal feeding and breeding places for thousands of flamingos and hundreds of pelicans, which flapped and paddled aside as we waded and splashed far out into the water.

Fifty meters from the edge, we could still stand, and handstand, feeling the sun and dry air on our waving legs. Mostly, we just floated, though: on our backs, cushioned by the salty buoyant water, staring up at the huge sky. Which was all there was to see—that and the occasional large pink flamingo flapping leisurely across the bright blue. It was perfect; in such an empty place, anything more would have seemed too much.

That evening, around a fire outside the cowshed, we had a final family dinner before the Jonathan Scotts went home.

Grandpa Ivor, as always, was the center of attention, telling stories and, tonight, talking excitedly about the island. "Marvelous, marvelous place," he said, repeatedly. "You've seen it. Must be developed... tourists will flock to it... it'll make us a fortune. I feel it. And I've got good instincts about these things.... Thank God for that Seloma. The man's a bloody gem. Bit inexperienced, bit naive about business, but a real gem. Always knew he'd turn out well. I always had a feeling about it. Hey, Betty?"

Granny Betty nodded and smiled, momentarily raising her eyebrows.

Dad said, "Come on, Ivor. We all know you'll never develop it."

"'Course I will," snorted Grandpa. "Who are you to say what I'll bloody do?"

Jonathan said, "You can develop it, Keith."

"I'm not spending any money on any tribal land," said Dad. "If someone powerful likes your improvements, you could be kicked off. Paid for your investments, but with no real recourse to complain. You can do it, Jot."

"I agree it's a risk," said Jonathan. "Anyway, I'm busy enough having the Aeronca fixed up—"

"I told you," interrupted Grandpa, "I'm gonna bloody do it. Leave a legacy for the whole family. Do ya think I'm just going to let a fortune languish under my nose?"

Early next morning, before Jonathan left, he inspected the damage on the old airplane.

The Aeronca, having stood untouched for several years in the field near Francistown, had one day been attacked by an angry bull, which tore some of the fabric-covered fuselage. Afterward, the farmer announced he was going to trash the plane if Ivor did not come and get it. Still Grandpa had done nothing. But Jonathan, who'd recently wrecked the Piper Colt and was feeling guilty, had organized a rescue mission during his university holidays. He, Dad, and several pilots working for Grandpa's charter business had dismantled the battered aircraft and driven it to Selebi on a truck, where they'd put the body in the shed and hung the wings in Grandpa's bedroom.

More than a decade later, Jonathan had discovered that this Aeronca was one of just a few in the world, and a valuable collectors' item. When he'd told Grandpa the good news, Grandpa had exploded indignantly. "Of course it's bloody valuable. Priceless, probably. I could have told you that. Why do you think I've had it in my own bedroom all these years?" he'd yelled. "So I can keep an eye on the bloody thing!"

Jonathan had offered to organize and pay for the Aeronca's restoration. And now, as he stood on a chair in the bedroom and peered at the wings, Grandpa watched suspiciously.

"You just make sure you look after it," he muttered. "Can't have just anyone messing with this. It's got to be done properly. Gotta be real professionals."

"Of course he'll look after it, Ivor," said Dad, who was inspecting the other wing. "That's the whole point."

Grandpa threw his hands in the air. "Whaddaya mean, of course he'll look after it? Look what he did to the last one." He flung an arm in the direction of the wrecked Piper Colt lying beneath the thorn tree. "And this is an heirloom you're dealing with. A treasure!"

He paused for breath. Neither Dad nor Jonathan said anything. Everyone else waited, riveted. Grandpa had turned bright red.

"Anyway, Keith, whaddaya know about value? Look at that beautiful island. Best opportunity you'll ever get. Veritable tourist gold mine. And ya just wanna throw it away."

Up on his chair, Jonathan snorted. Dad started to laugh.

"You boys have gotta learn some bloody responsibility," bellowed Grandpa. "Here I am, trying to preserve something for the whole family. And you just wanna throw it away. Seloma wouldn't do that. Now there's someone who knows about families and responsibility."

Dad and Jonathan were by now laughing helplessly.

"And my own children," continued Grandpa, "think it's some kind of joke. Have I taught you nothing?"

17

PRIZES FOR THE GIFTED

Phikwe Riding Club

The purple rosette pinned to Feste's bridle was not quite the unambiguous triumph it should have been. On the one hand, a rosette was a rosette. And after more than a year since I'd begun competing, this was just the second gold-embossed, superpleated Phikwe Riding Club ribbon Feste had to her name.

I had, moreover, an admiring crowd—the only aspect of equestrian success I coveted even more than rosettes. Behind the arena fence, sitting on foldout chairs or perched on cooler boxes, watched at least forty people, sipping Cokes and beers.

My eye-catching performance had even attracted a few white-clad observers who'd strolled over from the cricket field adjacent to the riding club.

Everyone was smiling.

Above the chatter, a hollow bark echoed between the tall *koppies* behind the arena. Baboons, somewhere high up among the balancing rocks and paper bark trees. I wondered if they were watching too, laughing at the weird humans below. With a special cackle for me: the weirdest of them all.

Mum stood up and leaned against the fence. "Well done, Robbie."

I grimaced back.

Mum and Dad beamed proudly. To them, I mused irritably, the purple ribbon probably warranted more vicarious pleasure than a normal prize. Given a choice between straightforward success and failure reinvented as triumph over adversity, Mum and Dad would choose the latter every time.

Jill Davies, the competition's judge, pinned a red rosette on the winning gray pony at the front of the line. Brian Fox patted his pony's perfectly clean neck and grinned broadly as Jill shook his hand. Brian always won.

I glanced wistfully at the three ponies beside me, smug with their red, blue, and yellow rosettes. Even yellow, a modest third place, would have at this moment filled me with unqualified joy. Even green, for that matter, had there been enough riders to award a fourth place, which there generally weren't at the tiny Phikwe Riding Club shows.

Anything but purple, the special prize: the stark public reminder that the two trajectories of my plan to transform Feste into a prizewinning show jumper and the plan's execution would never meet; the big signpost warning me that dream and reality were destined to be forever and irredeemably parallel.

Jill returned to the dusty white judges' box and picked up the microphone. "A round of applause for all our riders," she bellowed, "and a special cheer for Robyn Scott—inaugural winner of the Super Glue prize."

The Super Glue prize had been Jill's idea, instigated specially for me after I had, in a feat of what seemed Herculean proportions, managed to cling onto Feste for an entire round of jumps, weathering a vicious and varied cocktail of bucking and rearing between each fence.

Dad let out an ear-splitting whistle.

A few adults raised their beer cans.

I realized, as the triumphant *William Tell* Overture crackled though the speakers and we set off one by one on the victory lap, that Feste and I had got the biggest cheer—bigger even than the winning horse and rider.

That was something at least, I thought, as we charged off in a cloud of dust.

I grinned, despite myself. With Rossini's rousing bars serenading our victory gallop, it was hard to feel too sorry for myself. By now almost eleven, I'd been competing in horse shows for nearly two years, and things had come a long way. In particular, I at least now looked respectable. My eccentric riding attire replaced gradually, my goal of normality had recently been fully attained with the purchase of my beautiful, longed-for new saddle.

We'd made a special trip to Johannesburg to buy it, spending the weekend with the Jonathan Scotts and, on Saturday morning, driving out to the plush, leather-scented Western Shoppe, my favorite shop in the world. It had been thrilling: choosing the saddle, watching Dad pay for it—with some of my own egg money—and carrying the light leather work of art on my arm to the car. However, and although I would never admit this to Mum and Dad, that thrill was nothing to seeing the first chicken dust bath, to collecting the first egg, to selling the first dozen, standing beside Granny Joan at the Phikwe library on Saturday morning. And now, as we slowed and trotted out of the arena, and I glanced down admiringly at my gleaming pommel, I immediately thought of my twenty chickens, as I inevitably found myself doing, when I looked at the saddle.

Improvements in Feste's behavior had been less dramatic. And, all things considered, the purple rosette was quite good going. For if the Super Glue prize was an unlikely award, it was nothing to its memorable predecessor, won nearly two years earlier at my first show.

Jill Davies dropped Feste's tail and scowled.

"If I am not mistaken, Robyn, your pony has twenty ticks between her legs."

Her tone was one of disgust, her voice loud enough for all the other riders lined up beside me to hear. Maybe even loud enough to reach the ears of mothers standing behind the arena fence, mirroring the lineup of children, watching eagerly and relishing any black mark against the opposition of their respective offspring.

Twenty ticks was a jackpot—even if I clearly wasn't in the running for a prize.

I sunk into my hideous orange saddle.

"The fattest I've ever seen," continued Jill, holding up a raisin-sized specimen for my inspection. She dropped it onto the dusty ground, mashing it with her shoe. "Incredible."

"I took off lots already," I said.

But with a final disparaging look, Jill had already moved onto the next pony—a sparkling bay ridden by a glamorous grinning girl, whose neat hairnet shook as she giggled at Jill's praise for her pony's infuriatingly well-plaited mane. I looked down at the bulbous plaits on Feste's neck and blinked back tears.

The memory of this day was still painfully fresh.

In the weeks before the show, delirious with excitement and naive self-confidence, encouraged by ever-enthusiastic Mum and Dad, I had entered every event for which I was eligible. Even then, drunk on optimism, I'd known that Best Turned-Out Pony was a bit of a gamble. Of all the classes, this one attracted the most entrants—about ten—and every other child had grooms to make sure their ponies were spotlessly clean and perfectly presented. In its favor, though, Best Turned-Out Pony only required walking into and out of the arena, which made it the one event in which there was a good chance I wouldn't fall off.

I entered—a decision I regretted the moment I rode out of the bush from Selebi into the frenzied activity of the Phikwe Riding Club stables.

Everywhere, people hurried—between the stables, the cars,

the tack room, carrying grooming boxes, sugar cubes, saddles, and bridles. Everywhere, there was noise. Mothers yelled at their children; children yelled at their mothers; mothers and children both yelled at their black grooms. The grooms, in turn, who couldn't yell back, yelled at the ponies, which stamped and whickered crossly as they were scrubbed, tugged, brushed, and polished.

The tension was palpable. And contagious. I felt sick.

Mum and Dad, after declaring they knew nothing about turning out ponies anyway and could be better employed helping to set up jumps, were nowhere to be seen. Their jolly-well-do-it-yourself approach to life—the sell-eggs-to-buy-a-saddle-philosophy—did not end with the acquisition of material assets. If I wanted to enter Best Turned-Out Pony, I must, they argued, at the very least do the turning-out myself.

Cruelly unfair as it now seemed, with no other option I dragged Feste into a pen and began. Stage one did not go well. I'd never plaited a mane before, and despite countless, increasingly desperate attempts, my plaits persistently ended up as wildly irregular tufts that bore no resemblance to the small neat knobs in the pictures.

My only guidance came from six-year-old Lulu. Perched on the side of the pen, placating Feste with handfuls of hay, she critiqued each plait and offered irritatingly confident advice based on an experiential void matched only by my own.

Occasionally, one of the other mothers or children walked past and stared through the bars of the pen in amazement.

After two hours in the baking sun, there was no obvious difference in the plaits. A few of the other mothers began stopping and offering help or advice, a sure sign that I no longer posed a threat. Too proud to acknowledge defeat, I always politely declined.

Then, with the event rapidly approaching, Lulu said, "I think your plaits are getting worse."

I shoved the packet of plaiting elastics in her hand. "You fix them then," I snapped.

"Okay," said Lulu. She began undoing the bunches.

"Don't undo them."

"You told me to fix them," she said, her voice quavering. "Stop freaking out, Rob."

"I'm not freaking out," I yelled.

I moved on to Feste's white socks, which, due to Feste's loathing of running water, I'd been unable to wash. Here, at least, I had a skill-independent solution. I knew, from watching Lyn Nevill, that the secret behind Melaney's pony's bright white gleam was Reckitts Blue. If you dissolved one of the blue cubes in a bucket of water, the light blue liquid dried leaving coats a brilliant white, similar to its effect on sheets.

I mixed up a bucket and sloshed the mixture over each of Feste's legs, feeling relieved to be making progress.

Then, waiting for her legs to dry, I cautiously inserted my hand under her tail and began plucking off the ticks that clung around her bottom. Reluctant to crush them, I dropped them one by one onto the ground. The dirt at my feet was soon dotted with a large selection of both major tick varieties: the swollen soft-skinned gray ones (which sucked the most blood) and the flatter, tougher black ones (which tore out chunks of their victim's skin when you pulled them off).

The ticks began a slow trek in search of blood, radiating out from my feet.

Lulu jumped down from the bars of the pen, abandoning the plaits.

"What are you doing?"

"If you just leave them there," she said, "someone else will squash them." Kneeling down, she began dropping the escaping ticks into an empty feed bucket.

"Please hurry up, then," I squealed desperately.

The ticks collected, Lulu trotted off into the mopane trees outside the stables to release them. I continued to ferret between Feste's legs. But by the time Lulu had done a second round, Feste's tick community had barely halved. And those I'd already removed had collectively taken with them a lot of flesh. Feste's bottom and teats were bleeding. With each new tick that I removed, she became angrier, lashing out when I felt for another.

The Best Turned-Out Pony class was now less than half an hour away.

I had to get changed. I abandoned the tick removal and ordered Lulu back to the plaits. At this point, I remembered the white socks, which I now saw to my dismay were just as brown as before. Dizzy with panic, I charged to the hosepipe and refilled the bucket. In the hot midmorning sun, there was still just enough time for her legs to dry again. I grabbed two blue cubes, stirred them hurriedly into the water, and sloshed the new batch onto a now furious and prancing Feste.

Then I quickly put on her bridle and saddle, helped Lulu roll up the last of the disastrous plaits, and ran to our car, where I crouched in the back, pulling on a pair of white jodhpurs, my newly polished black boots, a bright white shirt, and my new homemade velvet helmet cover. This made me feel calmer. I, at least, looked more or less presentable. I tied a silver horse brooch around my collar and examined it in the rearview mirror to check it was straight. I smiled at my reflection and dashed back to the pens.

"Oh God, Lu, look."

Lulu, still absorbed in the plaits, looked down and giggled.

"What are you going to do, Rob?"

Feste's legs were definitely light blue.

Wet, I thought feverishly, had to be better than blue.

I grabbed the bucket and ran once more to the hosepipe. Plunging a big green bar of Sunlight soap into the water, I lathered it up, spraying soapy water all over my outfit. Back at the pen I sloshed the third bucket at Feste's legs. Then Lulu and I, each armed with a sponge, crouched in the mud at her feet and rubbed furiously at her legs, dodging well-aimed kicks.

Time was up. I dragged Feste out of the pen, clambered onto the old orange saddle, and kicked her toward the arena, praying that by the time we were inspected, her legs would be dry white. Or at least dry brown.

Fifteen minutes later, recovering from Jill's shaming tick census, I wondered again what color they'd dried. I was too embarrassed to ask Melaney, who sat beside me on her pony, gleaming from head to hoof. That Jill hadn't mentioned it, I decided was an encouraging sign. Until I considered that Jill, who occasionally sported a small purple-blue streak in her hair. For a moment, I wondered whether she perhaps just admired my style.

Gloomily resigned to failure, I watched as Jill and Floss van Leeuwen, the other visiting Zimbabwean judge, made their way from pony to pony—picking up a shiny hoof, running a white cloth over a flank, frowning at a pair of less than perfectly parallel plaits. If Jill frowned enough, Floss scribbled something on her clipboard, at which the child on top would look crestfallen and glare at his or her mother when the judges moved on.

Lulu gave me an encouraging smile. I tried not to look at Feste's plaits, definitely worse for Lulu's efforts, and managed a grin.

Jill and Floss reached the end of the line and strolled off to the corner of the arena. Whispering to each other, peering at the clipboard, and glancing at the lineup, they huddled there for several minutes. Then at last they fetched the rosette box and walked over to face the line of ponies.

First place was no surprise. It was, as Lyn Nevill told me it would be, awarded to the child who had at her disposal Kopano, the best groom in Phikwe. Mother, child, and groom grinned modestly. Nor was second place, which went to a gleaming black pony that had come all the way from Francistown. Everyone cheered again.

For third, however, the race was tighter: there were three eligible pristine ponies. It was anyone's guess, and a hush fell over the crowd.

"And after a very difficult choice," said Jill, "Floss and I have decided that our third prize today goes to..." She paused, cleared her throat, and grinned. "Goes to Feste, ridden by Robyn Scott."

Silence. Then several unconvincing claps. All around, disbelieving faces.

Jill shook my hand. "Well done," she bellowed. Again loud enough for everyone else in the line to hear, she continued, "I'm giving you this because I suspect you are the only child who has turned out her own pony. Am I correct? Did you do this yourself?"

I nodded, dumbly, wondering if I should give Lulu credit too. I didn't.

"So," said Jill, "you deserve it. Even," she added, leaning forward and lowering her voice, "if your pony does have twenty ticks." She paused. "Twenty-one, in fact. If you count the one I've just spotted in her ear." She scowled at me and sighed. "Nevertheless, I suppose I'll still give it to you."

"Sorry," I muttered.

I hoped she took my guilty look for shame, rather than the guilt it was, over a prize won on false pretenses. Had Jill peered more carefully into the depths between Feste's legs, she would have been truly appalled.

Twenty ticks was only the welcoming committee.

Years before I started competing, Jill and her sidekick, Floss, had been driving down from Zimbabwe to judge the regular Phikwe horse shows. The highlight of these events, the judges were feared, respected, and revered—not least of all for the whiff of international glamour that swept into the Phikwe Riding Club with the formidable duo's arrival.

This, the glamour, came in the most unlikely guise. Any uninformed visitor—particularly one unaware of the difficulty of obtaining new vehicles in Zimbabwe—would be flabbergasted by the ancient blue Datsun that provoked such excitement and trepidation as it shuddered to a stop in the stable yard, enveloped in a cloud of dust and black exhaust fumes. To everyone else, though, the shabby little car only augmented the mystique, making the skill and experience of its casually dressed occupants—already unparalled in Phikwe—all the more impressive.

Bulawayo, where Jill and Floss both had large stables, lay just an hour across the Ramokwebana border post to the north of Francistown. But in the riding world, it was light-years away. Bulawayo horse shows attracted hundreds of entrants, some who traveled all the way down from Harare. Phikwe horse shows rarely had more than thirty horse-and-rider teams in total. A visitor from nearby Francistown was exciting. A visitor from Gaborone was cause for celebration.

In Phikwe, ten in a class was considered an excellent turnout.

Which did not mean, as Jill joked one day, that Phikwe's self-confidence or competitive spirit suffered.

It was the end of a three-day show, and we were at the cricket club pavilion, waiting for prize-giving. The trestle table, groaning under the weight of enormous gleaming trophies, was undoubtedly a splendid sight. Without any evidence, I felt quietly confident that these trophies would hold their own anywhere in the world.

Mum grinned conspiratorially at Jill.

In private, Mum and Dad laughed about the opulent rosettes, massive trophies, and expensive sponsored prizes from South Africa. "Small-town syndrome, Robbie. You shouldn't get sucked in." This, they explained, was the phenomenon in small communities whereby the less important the event, the more seriously it's taken, and the bigger the prize. Which was, according to Mum and Dad, rife in Phikwe—at ten-person tennis championships, sponsored swims for eight-year-olds, Kopano spelling quizzes. "And by the way, Robbie, that's not to be repeated."

I had no intention of ever repeating it.

The bigger the trophy, as far as I was concerned, the better. Two little magpies, Melaney and I sat down on the closest bench to the table of silver cups. We picked the opposite end from Brian Fox, who we resented for having the best pony in the stables, winning almost everything, and, when he didn't win, occasionally throwing a tantrum or bursting into tears. And now we had another reason to resent and envy him: Brian was a "gifted child." He'd just been tested. The verdict, "Gifted," was announced in hushed tones around the stable yard—as if it at once sanctified him and exonerated him from any bad behavior.

Staring at the trophies, Melaney and I chatted excitedly as people strolled across the cricket field for prize-giving. Everyone arrived spruced up for this, the grand finale—changing into a fresh pair of jodhpurs and a clean shirt, giving their boots a quick polish, rubbing the fluff and dust off black riding jackets, which altogether lent considerable gravitas to the ceremony. Once fully assembled, the crowd was as impressive and gleaming as the trophies.

If this was small-town syndrome, I was happy to be part of it.

And at this show, for the first time, trophies were not wholly unattainable. Not on Feste, who after the Super Glue prize I continued to ride most of all out of pride. My hopes of mainstream success rested on my new pony, Winnie the Pooh.

Winnie was a beautiful cream dun, with a black mane and tail. He was perfect—but for one problem, which kept me safely on the fringes of the horsey community and ensured the continuing empathy of Jill. Winnie was anorexic. Or at least he looked anorexic, thanks to recent intestinal damage caused by a worm infestation that still impaired his ability to digest. He ate and ate and ate, but his skin, like canvas on tent poles, remained stretched tightly over fatless bones.

The vet had, however, pronounced him fit to be ridden. And when he went on sale, his pitiful appearance had only increased his appeal. Mum, moreover, had seen an opportunity for a triumph of natural medicine—in colonic health, no less, one of her favorite areas. She had set about at once dosing him with a variety of herbal cocktails to enhance bowel flora. To no avail, though, and she'd eventually given up, now even indulging Winnie's peculiar fondness for Coke—which he drank straight from the can, the only family member for whom she would buy junk food.

Winnie, despite his appearance, thrived, and during this show I'd actually won several caffeine-fueled red rosettes—enough to put me in the running for the top child rider trophy.

Transfixed by the trophy, I only half paid attention to the individual event prizes handed out by Jill: saddle oil, a riding crop, and, in the adult classes, a night for two at the Marang Hotel. Even Dad won a prize: some stirrup rubbers, for a round of show jumping on Quartz. It was ironic, I thought, given that Dad's long thin legs dangling either side of pony-sized Quartz knocked over the jumps as often as Quartz's own legs. Dad didn't need publicly to express his amusement at the small-town syndrome. Galloping around the arena, kicking on his undersize mount with his ugly *veldskoen* farmer shoes, Dad himself was a living, embarrassing testament to how unseriously he took it all.

"And the trophy goes to . . ."

Dad gave me a sympathetic shrug. I looked at the floor to hide my disappointment. Oh, how I wished I could wear *veldskoens*. And not care.

"It's not fair."

"In what way, Robbie?" asked Mum. "Brian won the prize, fairly. Have some more salad."

That fact I couldn't argue with. But where Brian Fox was concerned, I did not see things rationally. I hadn't, ever since our brief academic skirmish at Kopano, where Brian had generally beaten me. Competitive show jumping had only made things worse. I chomped morosely at my salad.

"For goodness sake," said Dad. "Lighten up. It was a great show. Don't be such a bad loser."

"First show you haven't fallen off," added Mum, brightly. "Mademoiselle Super Glue."

"Do you think I'm gifted?"

Dad said, "Not if you inherited my gray matter."

Mum smiled sadly. "Oh, Robbie."

"Can I get tested?"

"IQ tests," said Mum, sighing, "measure just a fraction of intelligence. They epitomize one of the great failings of the school system."

"I still want to be tested."

"Well, that's really not necessary."

"Why?"

"Well," she said, gazing at me calmly. "I can tell you right now that you are gifted."

"Really?"

"As is everyone at this table," she continued, and my heart sank. "All human beings, in fact. We all have our special strengths.

Everyone's gifted. And you, Robbie," she concluded with a sage smile, "are no exception."

Dad winked at me. "Bet you wish you'd never asked."

Paint dust whirled around our newly acquired second-hand horsebox.

I had to shout to be heard above the din of the grinder.

"No way," yelled Dad.

He pushed the whirring steel brush back against the wall. The noise increased, and more dust flew into the air.

"Please!"

Abruptly, the noise died. "For God's sake," said Dad. He put down the two-foot grinder, and the brush spun to a halt. "Stop nagging. I'm not letting an eleven-year-old use an angle grinder."

"I want to help," I pleaded. "I'm really strong. It's not fair. You make me do everything myself. Then when I really want to, you don't let me."

Dad looked amused. "All right. You can try it." He tapped the metal storage box in the front of the trailer. "Only on this."

Delighted, I clutched the heavy grinder and lifted it over the box. I felt a thrill of power and excitement as the grinder began to vibrate in my hands. If I couldn't be gifted, or have the best-turned-out pony, I was happy knowing that I at least had the most dangerous pony, and that I was doing to my horsebox what no other child at the Phikwe Riding Club would have done to theirs.

Dad showed me how to guide the brush across the surface, leaving satisfyingly shiny metal where old paint had been. "Good," he said. "Now just make sure you stay in the middle." He watched me as carefully I sanded the center of the metal square shiny. Dust collected on the surface. Dad said, "I'm just going to get a brush to sweep it off. Keep away from the edges, or you'll lose control."

He disappeared down the ramp. I quickly steered the grinder to the peeling paint on the edges of the box. If I could stay on Feste, I could handle an angle grinder. The paint dust whirled up. The edges began to shine.

I guided it toward the corner.

Suddenly the grinder spun around the corner, lurching heavily forward and down. I pulled it back, and it fell against my chest, seizing the fabric of my sweater.

It was winter, and I was wearing my favorite penguin sweater. I briefly wondered if the penguin in the middle, where the brush twisted viciously, would be destroyed. But it was so quick. And then, trying to pull the brush away, I lost my breath and fell sideways. I heard a strange noise as the grinder twisted the material up to my neck, and jammed. And then I thought of nothing.

Dad heard it too. He found me, unconscious, with the grinder slowly tightening the knot at my throat.

The penguin was shredded, and black with oil.

That's what I noticed first, as I blinked awake.

Dad's voice said, "Shit, I'm so sorry, Robbie."

Mum and Dad were peering over me, their faces white.

I said, "Did you see I sanded the edges? I tried to do the corners, but—"

"Robbie," interrupted Mum, her voice quavering, "*shhh*. We don't care about the sanding. Goodness. You very nearly killed yourself."

"Did I? Really?"

"Afraid so," said Dad shakily. "Why on earth are you smiling?"

I said, "I can't wait to tell everyone at the riding club." And feeling suddenly much better, I clambered to my feet and shook the dust off my destroyed penguin sweater. I didn't mind. A close escape from Death by Angle Grinder—something even Brian Fox couldn't match—was definitely worth a favorite sweater.

"How close was I to game over? A few seconds?" I suggested hopefully.

"God, Robbie," said Dad, "for goodness sake. Don't say things like that. I've just nearly been responsible for your death."

"Well, if you're feeling so bad," I said crossly, "just tell me how close I was to dying."

18

THE GOOD KARMA
OF KHAMA

Ruth and Seretse Khama

When I did eventually beat Brian Fox, it was a dismal anticlimax.

It was in the championship round, at the Gaborone show. I was riding Winnie, who excelled himself. I came second, Brian third. But here in the big capital city, outside of the small pond of Phikwe rivalries, the success was not nearly so satisfying as I'd hoped—less satisfying even than almost dying from an angle grinder. The long-sought triumph was untriumphant, our petty conflicts silly amid the large, colorful, and exciting event.

A four-hour drive south from Selebi, Gaborone too was exciting. Not in the same way as Johannesburg, with its sky-scrapers and big concrete highways—Gaborone, which felt more like a large town than a capital city, was a sprawling, dusty place, flanked by gently sloping bush-covered hills, and the more dramatic Kgale Hill. But it was buzzing and colorful—in people, and in place. In Gaborone's restaurants, there were always noisy tables of whites and blacks dining together, and often tables for two, where mixed couples chatted and laughed—both of which were unusual in Phikwe, where even though whites and blacks lived happily alongside each other, they rarely socialized or married.

The Gaborone horse shows were no different. Apart from their size—sometimes attracting more than a hundred riders— the most striking thing about these events was the black riders and spectators.

Riding in Phikwe was a white sport: there were no Batswana in the events, rarely in the crowd. In Gaborone there was a big group of black riders, drawn mainly from the mounted divisions of the Botswana Defense Force. The BDF riders show-jumped in their camouflage jackets, black jodhpurs, and black army boots, making for an eye-catching sight. Generally short on finesse, they were nonetheless often effective. But successful or not, they always rode to enviably enthusiastic applause, largely from the black contingent in the crowd. Even the disqualified BDF riders would leave the arena waving to their supporters, as they were loudly clapped and cheered.

The only white rider I ever saw receive a comparable reception from the BDF groupies was Amanda Fox, Brian's sister. Amanda was as white as any other white. And at first, as her pretty dark bay pony trotted into the arena, the crowd was as distracted and disinterested as ever. Until, that is, the previous rider finished his round, and the loudspeaker crackled.

"Next to go, Amanda Fox. On Dark Lady."

At the announcement, there was a momentary hush from the stands. But then—instead of the usual resurgence of chatter—as the racially emotive name of the beautiful bay pony was digested, there was a whoop from the Batswana in the crowd, followed by deafening clapping, and Amanda jumped her whole round to thunderous applause.

The loudest cheer at a Gaborone show, however, was not during any event, nor was it for a horse or rider. From blacks and whites alike, the warmest reception I ever witnessed went to the guest of honor, an elegant, gray-haired white woman who arrived with a small black entourage to present the prizes under the blue-and-white-striped marquee.

Lady Khama.

She was the first Lady anything I'd ever seen. Watching her hand out prizes and shake hands, wearing a plain white dress and a simple blue peaked cap, she exceeded my every expectation of grace, gentleness, and stateliness. By the time I rose to get my prize and walked toward her, I was trembling with nerves. Up untill then, the closest I'd come to a Botswana celebrity was Grandpa Ivor.

But, standing in front of Lady Khama, I felt immediately at ease. Her handshake was just firm enough; her gaze was sharp but at the same time warm and reassuring. I wanted, as she shook my hand, to keep holding on. I walked reluctantly back to the chairs, more elated by that handshake than by any prize I had ever won.

Ruth Khama was one of Botswana's most loved citizens. With good reason: had I been aware then, at my brief encounter, of what I later learned, I would have been even more awestruck.

I'd known that Ruth was the widow of the great Sir Seretse Khama, Botswana's first president. But that was just historical fact. And it was only during the long drive back from Gaborone, when Mum and Dad explained the details of the Khamas' lives, that I was first captivated by the tale.

It was, in every way, a perfect story.

Beginning with the convention-defying true romance, which blossomed in 1940s postwar England, when the young Ruth Williams met and fell in love with Seretse Khama, then a student at Oxford. Seretse had everything going for him—clever, handsome, charming, the son and heir of the most powerful chief in a vast land—but one giant mark against him. When Ruth's father discovered she intended to marry a black man, he disowned her—a bad start that turned out to be only the beginning of their troubles, which spanned several decades in the thrilling David-and-Goliath part two of the story.

Defying disapproval, Ruth and Seretse married in 1948 and returned to what was then still Bechuanaland, a British protectorate. Here, however, they found themselves up against far more powerful forces than furious parents.

On the one side was Seretse's tribe and influential relatives, many of whom initially condemned the marriage. Seretse, undaunted, lobbied tirelessly. But as he began to win acceptance for Ruth, progress in this respect was dwarfed by the powerful opposition of the British government. The British were put under pressure by the South African government—then implementing apartheid to formalize racial segregation—to prevent a multiracial celebrity couple living on their doorstep. The British needed South Africa's gold and uranium, and in 1950 the colonial government exiled Seretse and Ruth back to England. Six years later they were finally allowed to return, but only after Seretse agreed to renounce his chieftainship of the Bamangwato, the largest of Botswana's more than twenty tribes.

Which was the beginning of part three, the happy ending. Not long after their return, Seretse formed the Botswana Democratic Party, the BDP. In 1966 the British government, under increasing international pressure, granted Bechuanaland independence. Botswana was established, and Seretse Khama was democratically elected in a landslide victory. Queen Elizabeth II awarded him a knighthood the same year, and he became Sir Seretse Khama, Botswana's first president and head of one of Africa's poorest nations.

Not for long, though.

Between his first victory and the end of his presidency in 1980, Seretse presided over a subplot of rapid transformation. This was underpinned by a perfect recipe of wise stewardship—in the form of Seretse's careful fiscal policies, investment in education and development, and racial tolerance—and fueled by sheer good luck, in the form of the diamond mine that, just a few years after independence, it turned out the country was sitting on. And on the back of this immense, wisely spent wealth, Botswana became, under Sir Seretse, one of Africa's most peaceful and prosperous nations.

Y ou must interview both grandpas."
The encounter with Lady Khama had precipitated a week of Khama and Botswana-centric homeschooling.

Beneath this umbrella section of Mum's amorphous, invent-as-you-go-along syllabus had fallen the usual odd mix of subjects. To begin with, she read to us from *A Marriage of Inconvenience*, the new account of Ruth and Seretse's story. Later, we pored over chapters about gemstone mining from the huge set of science encyclopedias, which precipitated the creation of another one of our beloved crystal gardens.

Moving to the Botswana history books, Mum started with the BDF, a theme certain to enthrall even Damien, the hardest of us to keep interested.

Formed in the late 1970s—Ian Khama, Seretse's son, was appointed as deputy commander—the BDF's main purpose had been to defend Botswana against aggression from the neighboring white-ruled regimes in Rhodesia, Namibia, and, particularly, South Africa. Two years before we arrived, the South African army did raid Gaborone, searching for ANC "terrorists" and killing several people.

Also on standby to deal with the problems of civil war in Angola, the BDF had nothing similar to contend with at home. Which took Mum to Botswana's tribal makeup. This is often thought to underpin the country's peaceful history, for while there are more than twenty tribes in Botswana, eight of them, representing the vast majority of the population and including the three largest tribes, are of Tswana origin. But even between the Tswana and the other tribes, some of Zimbabwean lineage, relations are generally good, the most strained being with the Basarwa, or Bushmen. But this has never provoked anything close to war.

Mum, her curiosity trumping her judgment of what would

interest us, began to read more about the "fascinating" detailed tribal breakdown, and was soon reading silently to herself as we ran off to ask Matthews what tribe he was from.

The next day, remembering what she'd originally intended, Mum took us on a special trip to Phikwe to interview Grandpa Terry, who had met Seretse Khama on several occasions.

"Remarkable man," said Grandpa, sounding emotional. "Quite remarkable."

The encounter that Grandpa remembered most vividly was in the 1970s, when Khama visited Phikwe during a campaign for reelection.

Grandpa, as a senior representative of the mine, sat on the podium with the president as he addressed the crowd. He was impressed by Seretse's quick mind and thoughtful policies, but what struck him most was the contrast with similar rallies he had witnessed in postindependence Zambia. There, he told us, President Kenneth Kaunda had lectured to crowds that had remained, throughout, uncritically adoring.

Seretse, too, had firm ideas, which he conveyed during his speech. But afterward, a microphone was handed around his almost entirely Batswana audience and the president was publicly interrogated, which he seemed to relish, inviting some of the loudest hecklers to join him on the platform.

Had he traveled down to Phikwe on government money?

No, said Seretse, calmly. He had used party funds, as per the laws relating to campaigning. He referred the questioner to someone else should he want verification.

Had the president used his position to allocate land to his friends and family?

Presenting a compelling set of facts, and without a hint of indignation, the president addressed this too, and the speaker sat down satisfied.

The questions went on and on until everyone had spoken.

Afterward, when Grandpa was talking to Seretse, he mentioned how struck he'd been by the rigorous questioning that followed the rally.

Seretse Khama smiled. "People here, Mr. McCourt, like to talk. If you don't let them talk, you have problems. I know this, and I let them talk."

Grandpa eyed us gravely. "And that, in my opinion, is what makes this country different to everywhere else in Africa." He went on in a lecturing voice. Mum watched, smiling slyly as Grandpa veered off topic, clearly enjoying himself in his unwitting recruitment to homeschooling.

Botswana became, at independence, Africa's first lasting multiparty democracy.

But long before then, before it even became a British protectorate, the Batswana had been living under their own democracy-like—albeit male-dominated—system.

At the heart of this was the *kgotla*, a large stick-fenced semicircle found in every village. The *kgotla* was and remains both a meeting place and a discussion forum, presided over by the chief. At meetings, everyone has the opportunity to express his or her views, and issues are debated exhaustively, until everyone is satisfied. Often the satisfaction lies as much in the debate as in the conclusion.

The *kgotla* was also traditionally a court, where punishments were meted out and executed. Even after Botswana had established a court-based judicial system, suspects for less serious crimes were given the choice of trial by a magistrate or at the *kgotla*.

"Which brings me to one of my other favorite stories," said Grandpa.

Cilla Wilson was a good friend of Granny Joan's and Grandpa Terry's. She was also the ballet teacher in Phikwe, so both Lulu and I knew her from our early brief forays into the ballet world. We were consequently also familiar with the splendid black stereo system that Grandpa explained had once been stolen from Cilla's ballet hall.

The thief was caught shortly afterward. He chose to be tried at the *kgotla*, and Cilla, as the plaintiff, was requested to attend.

Reluctantly, she drove out to the thief's village near Phikwe on the day of the trial. While the punishment for the crime was debated, Cilla hovered as far from the action as possible. The sentence was ten lashes, to be dispensed at once. Cilla made a dash for her car, only to be stopped and told that, as the aggrieved person, she must also witness the punishment.

The gentle sparrowlike lady watched, appalled, as the thief's shirt was removed and his back given ten searing lashes.

The moment the last one had been delivered, Cilla fled toward her car, slid inside, and started the engine.

About to speed away, she was stopped by a tap on the window. Flabbergasted, she wound down the window. It was the whipped thief. "Mma, can I have a lift back to Phikwe?" he asked.

And she gave him one.

"Anyway," said Grandpa Terry, as he concluded his thoughts on Botswana and the Khamas, "as I always say, the most important thing of all was that the man practiced what he preached. None of this swanning around in Mercedes cavalcades. Seretse drove around Gaborone in an old secondhand Valiant. Says it all."

It didn't stop at land transport. In the early days of his presidency, when Seretse Khama needed to fly, he called on Grandpa Ivor and his battered Beechcraft Baron—the Valiant of the airways, as far as presidential humility and frugality went.

"Do you have Seretse stories?" we asked Grandpa Ivor.

Grandpa looked aghast.

"Do I have Seretse stories? 'Course I bloody do. Flew the guy. Bloody great man he was. Everyone adored him."

Grandpa Ivor's most memorable Seretse Khama story began with Grandpa getting very drunk one night at the Tati Hotel in Francistown.

Near midnight, inebriated, he sat up in shock.

He was flying the president at nine o'clock in the morning. Normally he would have spent the night outside under the stars and the knob-thorn trees, sleeping off the whiskey. But this he couldn't miss, and he staggered outside to his ancient Land Rover.

"Never saw roadblocks in those days," said Grandpa, "so I wasn't worried. Especially on a Friday night. All the cops were getting blotto too."

So it was with a mixture of surprise and alarm that, a hundred meters from the hotel, Grandpa pumped his capricious brakes and jolted to a stop in front of a roadblock.

"*Dumela*," he slurred at the policeman, trying not to exhale.

"*Dumela, rra*," said the officer. "We are checking lights."

Momentarily relieved, Grandpa then cursed as the second officer disappeared behind the car and ordered him to press the brake. A few seconds later, the officer returned, scowling.

"Your right brake light is not working. We have to impound your vehicle."

Grandpa stared at us. "Now, I couldn't bloody well have that happening, could I? So I told it to the chap straight that I was flying the president in the morning. Asked if he wanted to be responsible for the great President Khama missing his flight."

The senior officer looked torn. After a moment's thought, he said, "Let me check it again," and disappeared behind the car.

Grandpa massaged the brakes once more.

"Knew the light wouldn't work," he said. "Hadn't worked for years."

The officer reappeared. "Your right light is now working," he announced, giving the other officer an accusing look. "Go. Go." He waved Grandpa on. And the Land Rover chugged away, before his bewildered colleague had a chance to protest.

Grandpa smiled at us. "All in a good cause. Anyway, old Seretse liked a good tipple himself."

Sir Seretse Khama, who died in office in 1980, left a strong economy and a country that was, by the standards of others on the continent, well educated and relatively corruption-free. Vice President Quett Masire—elected president on Seretse's death—kept Botswana on an even keel: its economy continuing to grow, its record for democracy remaining good. Sir Quett Masire retired in 1999, and Festus Mogae was elected president.

Lady K, as she became affectionately known, died in 2002. She was buried in Serowe alongside Seretse, the Bamangwato tribal heads making a rare exception by burying a woman beside a chief.

Ruth and Seretse left behind them four children who, as the country's royal family—and in the case of their eldest son, its vice president—remain flesh-and-blood reminders of what is perhaps their parents' greatest legacy: a country where, in large part thanks to them, the significance of race generally ends with the fact that blacks and whites and "coloreds" have different skins.

And while occasionally the government does PI expatriates for racist behavior or comments, mostly, when color is discussed, the discussion is free from the loaded sensitivities felt north and south of Botswana's borders. In some of the small expatriate-dominated mining towns like Phikwe, race is felt more strongly. But even there it is rarely a significant source of tension. For the most part—in the rural areas, where there are few whites anyway, and in the bigger cities—Botswana is color-blind.

There are exceptions, of course. And perhaps none more obvious than the Tuli Block, a narrow strip of freehold farms on the Limpopo River, where southeastern Botswana is bordered by one of the most racially divided regions of South Africa.

In every other respect, however, the Tuli Block was perfect.

Perfect, at least, for Dad, who in 1992 found and quickly bought two thousand acres of beautiful, undeveloped bushveld. With the Limpopo River on one boundary, the farm was also bisected by the Lotsane River and had almost eight kilometers of exquisite riverfront. It lay nearly two hundred kilometers from Selebi, the last forty on a badly corrugated dirt road. But Dad, who set about selling his Selebi practice, was able now to rely solely on his busy village clinics, for which the Tuli Block was no worse situated than Selebi.

Perfectly placed, in the middle of nowhere.

19

FIDDIAN GREEN

Leaving the cowshed

The Lotsane River was nearly dry—a giant sandpit but for a few pools of sparkling brown water. Around each pool, the dark mud skirts were pitted with deep hoof-and-paw-print graffiti. Occasionally the still surfaces plopped, as giant whiskered catfish rose, gulped, and sank leisurely back down again.

Lulu and I suggested catching the fish and moving them to bigger pools in the nearby Limpopo.

Dad laughed. "They can look after themselves." Later, he explained, when the sun and the animals sucked dry the last of the pools, the enormous fish would simply bury themselves in the sand and wait for the rains. He beckoned us to an almost dry pool. "Watch the mud carefully."

After a few seconds, something twitched beneath the goo.

"There!" Dad said. "That's one getting comfortable. They're not very nice to eat. Taste muddy."

"Good," said Lulu.

Around the mud, the dry sand was hot enough to burn our feet. The afternoon sun glinted enticingly on the water.

Dad said, "I'm sure we can swim. Much too shallow for crocs."

"Sure?"

"Well, maybe just a small one. No, *man*, just kidding. Beat you in."

The cool, silt-soft water was even better than it looked. We swam and splashed, waded in and out, floated on our backs, and sank beneath the surface until our lungs felt like bursting. "Ha, ha. Thought I'd been eaten by a croc, didn't you?"

Afterward we ate popcorn cooked in a pot on the fire. Then, as the sun began to drop, we set up tents under the tall sweet thorn trees on the riverbank.

It was a few months after we'd bought the farm, and we were camping with our friends, the Blairs—spending our first night on our new land, pitching our tents just a few hundred meters from our planned house site, which was then untouched scrubby bush.

We'd camped before with the Blairs, and I watched, expectantly, as they began to unpack. Long after Mum and Dad had erected their little tent, Ian Blair was still carrying luggage from the car to his and Veronica's enormous boudoir. Veronica wasn't keen on camping, and if she camped, she camped only in style—thick floral duvets, pillows, boxes of tissues, numerous outfits.

Dad said to Ian, "By the time you've unloaded everything, Lin and I will have more room in ours."

Ian shrugged and sighed. "Got to please the ladies."

Veronica said, "Don't complain, Ian. You like your feather pillow too."

Mum and Dad smiled and turned back to the bird book.

Mum was writing a species-sighting list on the back of a packet of biscuits. "There's another one... extraordinary... can't believe this place... birdwatchers' paradise..."

In Selebi, having rapidly identified the major birds, Mum and Dad's bird debates had mostly related to LBJs, short for "Little Brown Jobs," the numerous nondescript sparrowlike birds that are almost impossible to identify:

"Dark gray breast, with brown flecks."

"No, medium to light gray breast. With dark brown flecks."

"Light brown wings with white flecks."

"Another bloody LBJ."

But in the Tuli Block, with its mix of river and bush vegetation, there were more than 350 species, the second-highest density in southern Africa. Mum and Dad pointed and chatted and peered through binoculars, breathless with excitement.

Bright yellow weavers clamored from riverside thorn trees bedecked with their neat straw nests; slim gray herons stood statue-like on rocks, peering at the pools down long elegant necks; brilliant beady-eyed malachite kingfishers perched on dead branches jutting out over the water and eyeing the smooth surface. A majestic fish eagle sat in the top branches of a tall dead knob-thorn tree, its proud, mournful cry ringing far out across the bush and deep inside its listeners, making us shiver with pleasure.

And then there were the guinea fowl, everywhere, their soft spotted feathers littering the riverbank. Their vast numbers were not coincidental. Many years ago, an old Motswana woman had lived here on the banks of the Lotsane. She'd fed and nurtured the guinea fowl population, which had continued to thrive long after she'd died. That was how the farm got its Setswana name, Mmadikgaka: "Mother of the Guinea Fowl."

But Madigaka was too much of a mouthful. So we were looking for a new name for our new farm—a fact I still couldn't quite believe, playing in this campsite on our little piece of paradise. For a while, the name was going to be Koro Farm, after our beloved hornbills—until Dad had told his nurses, who'd burst out laughing and then explained that *koro* also describes a condition in which a man believes he's been bewitched to make his penis grow inward, like the curving beak of a hornbill. And since then, every other name had been vetoed by at least one of us.

As the sun neared the treetops, everyone except Veronica once more stripped to their costumes. Veronica watched her daughters, frowning. "Ian, are you sure it's okay to swim in that water?"

"I'm sure," said Ian. "It's only a small pool. And Keith's an old bush hand."

"It's fine," said Dad reassuringly. "Do you think I'd let my own kids swim if I thought there were any risks?"

Veronica looked unconvinced. Jennifer, Kristeen, and Lorraine Blair all rode horses, and Veronica had watched many of my most spectacular ejections from a bucking, rearing Feste. But she said nothing, and we ran back into the pools, swimming and wallowing until our skin wrinkled.

The revs of an engine drowned the splashing. A *bakkie* appeared over the rise and shuddered to a stop on the bank. The driver, a rotund Motswana man, climbed out. He waved to us. We all waved back. Then Dad, Mum, and Ian waded out to greet him.

We watched as they shook hands on the bank.

Suddenly, everyone turned to the pool. Dad let out a piercing whistle. "Time to get out, chaps," he said. "Come on, don't dawdle."

The man's name was Mr. Phethu. He owned the neighboring farm. Dad said calmly, "Mr. Phethu's just been telling us that a big crocodile lives in that pool."

"The biggest in the Tuli Block," said Mr. Phethu. "You are very brave to swim."

Everyone turned silently to the still-rippling water. Goose bumps spread across my body. My legs felt weak.

When I looked away from the water, Mr. Phethu was peering curiously at the campsite, where the sashes of the Blairs' grand tent were pinned open. You could see the floral duvet. He looked amused.

Damien said, "How big?"

"Three meters. Maybe bigger." Mr. Phethu sighed. "It has eaten two of my cows."

I shivered. Veronica and Mum looked at each other, faces horrified.

Dad simply raised his eyebrows. "Why were your cows on my farm?"

"Ah, well." Mr. Phethu looked quickly at the ground. "Sometimes they run away."

"Indeed," said Dad. "Well, nice to meet you. We look forward to seeing the crocodile. I hope he doesn't get the chance to eat any more of *your* cows."

Later, gazing safely from the bank, we did see him, for the first of many times. He was unforgettable, and unmistakable. Not only was he a giant, he was exceptionally green for a crocodile. He looked like he was covered in algae.

That night, as we ate dinner around the fire, we heard a distant sawing sound.

"What's that?"

"Just a leopard," said Dad. "They're shy. Don't worry."

"Oh, yeah, Keith." Ian grinned. "Anyone for a top-up?" he asked, reaching for the bottle of Rémy Martin cognac, which was his camping equivalent of feather duvets.

"What if there're lions though, Dad? What if they drag us from our tents?"

"I've told you," said Dad. "There are no lions in this part of the Tuli Block."

"Heard that one before."

"Well, fight them off with your feather pillow," said Dad. Then he lit one of his once-in-a-blue-moon cigars and sipped his Rémy, grinning sheepishly in the firelight.

After that camping trip, we christened the farm Molope, in honor of the thick-canopied tree with beautiful bright red flowers that was found throughout the land, and particularly along the rivers. Its common name is the weeping boer-bean, as the flowers drip copious amounts of sweet, sticky nectar. *Molope* is its Setswana name.

But we really chose it for its Latin name, *Schotia brachypetala*.

In late 1993, six years after arriving in Botswana, we began packing up the cowshed.

Earlier that year, Grandpa Terry had retired, and he and Granny Joan were now living in Cape Town. But if moving to Molope Farm would bring us slightly closer to them, from Grandpa Ivor and Granny Betty—six years across the road—it would take us seemingly a world away.

"You'll see me all the time," said Grandpa Ivor. "Won't be able to keep me away. I'm a busy man. But I love the bush."

Mum said, "It's only two hours away from Phikwe. I'll be visiting often. Dad might be able to not see other people. But God knows, I can't."

Dad said, "We're going to be living in the most beautiful place in the world. In a huge house. Our friends will come to us."

He was right: long before we'd even started packing, friends from Phikwe began scheduling weekend visits to the bush. And, Mum assured us, if all this failed to give us enough time for socializing, Dad could drop us off in Phikwe, which he'd be passing through every Wednesday, traveling to and from his Tonota clinic.

All in all, it seemed that we could have our reduced-sugar, fiber-rich, colorant-free cake and eat it.

The greatest pang I felt was for the brown paper floors. The well-trodden parts, though often repaired by Mum, had by now lost much of their effect: worn, duller, and in a few places curling up, definitely paper. But as the furniture was carried outside and loaded onto a truck, part of the floor appeared in all its former glory. Beneath the sofas and wall-units, the faux flagstone gleamed like the day we'd laid it, character-giving air bubbles and all.

Matthews had long since left to find work in Phikwe. But Ruth and Maria were coming with us, as were all our animals—except, of course, for Redhead, the redheaded weaver. On our final morning in Selebi, we all climbed onto Mum and Dad's bed to watch him for the last time, diligently weaving his new nest. The year before, after five solid years of failure, Redhead's wife had finally accepted one of his nests. Recalling this watershed, Mum sighed and said, "Thank goodness. Now I can leave in peace."

Then we climbed out of the bed and stripped the sheets. Dad dismantled the frame and loaded it onto the four-ton Dyna truck parked in the driveway. He had borrowed the truck, but only for a few days, which meant we had to move everything in just two trips. This was the second one. By the time Dad had tied down the last sofa—upright so we could later sit on it at the farm—it sat atop a four-meter-high load.

With such a precarious cargo, the drive to the Tuli Block, normally two hours, took us nearly four. But nothing fell off, and when we arrived at our farm gate, Lulu, Damien, and I clambered up the sides of the truck and onto the sofa, which we sat on, looking out for game, yelling in excitement, as Dad drove the final mile to our new house.

Redhead, the redheaded weaver, was the first wild creature to be named in Selebi. The first to be named on Molope Farm was the crocodile, which we christened Fiddian Green, after one of Dad's old medical school lecturers.

"A fitting beginning," said Dad, "to real Africa at last."

G oodness, that's rather far away.... Where will you shop? ... Will you have electricity? ... a telephone? ... Don't you need to speak Afrikaans?"

These were the reactions of friends who'd never lived in the Tuli Block. The response of the one person we spoke to who had was, "Beautiful place. Just don't stay too long."

"Sorry?"

"Unless you want to become alcoholics or born-again Christians."

"What?"

"That's what the Tuli Block does to Englishmen."

Dad said, "Lin, which do you pick?"

Mum said, "Aah, well, depends on which spirit moves me."

"Smile, Robbie," said Dad. "We're only joking."

"Anyway," added Mum, smiling, "I bet we're the oddest Englishmen the Tuli Block's ever seen. It's the locals who should probably be worried about us moving in."

"The point is," said Dad, "this is land we actually own. Fantastic land. And for that, I don't give a damn whether I like the neighbors. We won't even have to see them if we don't want."

This was not difficult to believe. You could sometimes drive the length of the Tuli Block dirt road and not pass a single car.

The road ran parallel to the Limpopo, and most of the houses—several of which were no longer lived in—lay deep inside the farms, nearer the river. Through the fences, there was only bush, in dark and pastel greens; so strange, at first, missing the brilliant greens of the mopanes. After six years in Selebi, bush without mopane trees required total recalibration.

The dust, too, was different—still with a warm reddish tinge, but much grayer than the brick-red Selebi dirt. More fertile too. And in most cases less overgrazed, with soft yellow grasses covering much of the ground behind the fences. For here no cattle and goats wandered freely through the bush and onto the verges.

A rare stretch of freehold land, the Tuli Block is a legacy of the British Protectorate, when the area was thought strategically important in keeping out the land-hungry South African Boer farmers, living across the Limpopo.

Initially, the land was ceded to the British South Africa Company, led by Cecil Rhodes, who planned to run his Cape-to-Cairo railway along the Limpopo. But it was soon decided that the tributary rivers, like our Lotsane, would make construction too expensive. The railway was redirected via Francistown and the Tuli Block sold off to English farmers, with the same objective of a buffer against the Boers.

A historical irony, given that by 1993 the area had long been the near-total preserve of Afrikaans farmers, who'd once, just before independence, even threatened to secede from Botswana. They never did, but the separatist feelings, the dislike of Botswana's black government, and the resentment against the English never quite died.

R obyn Scott, of Sherwood Ranch, Botswana (P.O. Box 50).
Our postal address, at least, was English. And my
address, I decided, was well worth a forty-kilometer drive to get
the post.

In addition to the post office, Sherwood Ranch had one general store, a petrol station, a takeout, and a small white building
in which Dad now ran a weekly clinic. Mostly it was just a stop
for people heading straight on to the nearby Martin's Drift border post with South Africa. The postboxes numbered not more
than 50, and very rarely did any cars turn left or right, off onto
the dirt roads and into the bush.

In the middle of Molope Farm, halfway up a gently sloping rise, stood our grand new thatched double-story house. To
one side, the land swept down toward the dark green line of the
nearby Lotsane River. Two kilometers to the other side lay the
Limpopo, the river border, and in the distance you could just see
the blue outlines of faraway hills in South Africa.

All around the house was bush, bursting with song, cries,
and all kinds of antelope, glimpsed through the trees: tiny duiker,
impala, kudu, and fat fluffy waterbuck, peering at us suspiciously.

The house was only half finished. For weeks we slept on
camping mattresses and found our way at night by candlelight.
Dad hadn't yet connected the borehole to the plumbing, so we
showered under a plastic water tank on the back of our old Land
Cruiser, watched by curious, saucer-eyed bush babies that came
out at dusk and ping-ponged between the shadowy branches of
the thorn trees.

Inside, the house smelt of fresh golden thatch, and new plaster on the unpainted walls. "Choose your bedroom color," said
Mum. "Then you can paint it yourself. Nothing more satisfying
than painting. Highly therapeutic."

Immersed, dawn to dusk, in the task of finishing the house,
Mum painted, grouted, and pored over the plans, making last-
minute design alterations.

Supposedly, the house was built according to a package design purchased from *Farmer's Weekly* magazine.

But then Mum had decided to "tweak" the plans. "Keith, don't you think we should have another room here? Easy to do. Just need to raise the wall a few meters.... Damien, wouldn't you like a basin in your bedroom? So easy to run a pipe through the wall from the bathroom.... And what if we move the staircase over here?"

The house now bore almost no resemblance to the original drawings. Cake recipes, school syllabuses, architectural plans—it was always the same. Mum was hardwired not to follow instructions. In keeping with her character, she'd also continued to change plans as the house was being built. Which, Dad said, gave him some sympathy for the longsuffering builders, even if they were a "bloody unreliable bunch."

That was part of the reason we had moved in before the house was finished: after a few misplaced windows and gently leaning walls, Dad had decided he couldn't trust the builders to do the final touches unsupervised. "Can't even use a jolly spirit level," he'd mutter as yet another specially imported wooden door wouldn't fit in its frame. "Unbelievable."

The builders at least were nice, and looked just as content whether they were slowly mixing cement or sitting under a tree and eating their lunch. The builder in charge, who regularly went fishing and left the unskilled laborers to finish off jobs, was a gentle colored man called Festus who had bloodshot eyes and wore a perpetual grin. He had the curious habit of inserting the word *actually* into every sentence.

A month or so after we moved in, when the men had started work building a wall across the Lotsane, Mum planted a flowerbed outside the kitchen window. As the shoots grew, one quickly dwarfed others, its tall, densely leafed stem reaching right to the window.

The mystery of the dodgy door frames was solved.

"Actually cannabis," said Dad. He tapped the kitchen wall and grinned. "Between Actually Festus and Mum, it's a wonder this place is still standing."

Mum raised her eyebrows. "Between Fiddian Green and you, Keith, it's a wonder we're still standing."

"Touché," said Dad, smiling appreciatively at Mum.

The gunshots cracked across the still afternoon bush, echoing for a second.

We were having tea in the lounge, all the windows flung open, watching scores of birds demolish the newly replenished fruit and bread. The bird feeder stood just outside the window, a large piece of beautiful gnarled wood suspended between two thorn trees. At the shots, the members of the more jittery species fluttered up into the branches.

"Scoundrels," said Dad, leaping to his feet. "They're poaching down at the river."

He put down his teacup with a clatter, and the last bold crimson-breasted shrikes and yellow-billed hornbills flapped off to more peaceful perches.

"I've had enough," said Dad. "I'm going after them. Me and my trusty steed gonna give them a bit of a surprise."

"Can we come?"

"Nope. Just needs one of us to frighten them. Plus I need to sneak up quietly to catch them red-handed."

"Is it safe?"

" 'Course it's safe. Just small-time *skellums* taking advantage of empty farms. If you want to be useful, start saddling up while I put on some trousers."

Minutes later, Dad was galloping away toward the river, wiry little Quartz charging up the slope like a battle-horse. "Yee-hah," cried Dad as they skidded around the corner, vanishing into the bushes. And we returned to our tea and biscuits, listening for shots and eagerly anticipating the prospect of the poachers getting their comeuppance.

On our first ever visit to the farm, before we'd bought it, we'd come across a young Motswana boy who offered to sell us two captured Egyptian geese that watched us miserably through their lovely dark-ringed eyes. We bought them and set them free,

Dad warning the bewildered boy not to touch them, that things were going to change soon.

Several months after our arrival, we were still finding snares, occasionally with the pitiful dead body of a duiker or impala, the skin on its leg bulging either side of the wire noose. But as word spread that the farm was now lived in, there were fewer snares laid, the poachers concentrating on the empty farms around us.

For the bigger game, there were armed poachers, and we'd heard shots before on neighboring farms, but mainly near the deserted road, which *skellum* local farmers were known to drive along, shooting kudu and impala on their neighbors' farms and sending their Batswana workers over the fence to haul the carcasses into their *bakkies*. We'd never before heard them so close, down at the river. Not shooting animals at their drinking places was an unwritten rule of fair hunting. And the idea of poachers breaking this rule too made us all ache with outrage.

After about fifteen minutes, during which we'd heard a second shot, we put the kettle on in anticipation of Dad's return. After twenty minutes, there was still no sign of him. We speculated whether he might be attempting a citizen's arrest.

Damien said, "I'll drive down and take Dad his gun. Maybe he needs to defend himself."

Lulu gulped.

I said, "He is taking a long time, Mum."

"For goodness sake," said Mum. "This is Botswana. Not a war zone." The poacher, reasoned Mum, would disappear when he saw Dad. "They're only poaching because they think no one's around. Dad'll be back any minute. Now have some more tea and stop worrying."

Then another distant shot.

Mum said, "I'm sure it's just the poacher finishing off a wounded animal. Dad will find him soon."

Twenty minutes later, the door banged, and Dad walked slowly into the lounge.

"What happened?"

Dad sank into the couch and stared thoughtfully out the window.

"Dad?"

"Keith?"

"The bastard shot at us."

"Is Quartz okay?"

"He's fine," said Dad. "So is your father, if you're interested."

Mum poured fresh tea and handed Dad a cup. "Well, go on, tell us what happened."

Reaching the Limpopo, Dad had slowed Quartz to a walk as he rode quietly into the neighboring farm. He'd heard voices ahead and some way along the riverbank he'd seen footprints and drag marks across a stretch of dry riverbed between our neighbor's farm and the South African riverbank.

"Ratbags," muttered Dad. "They'd been sitting on the South African side, potting at animals drinking from pools on the Botswana side and then hauling the carcasses back across the sand banks."

But then someone had missed and wounded an animal. They'd crossed the river and were tracking it along the bank on the Botswana side. Dad saw a flash of white flesh and khaki in the bushes ahead of him.

"*Voetsek*," he bellowed. "I'll call the police." He kicked Quartz into a trot toward the figure crashing through the undergrowth. "If I ever see you here again, you'll spend the rest of your life in a Botswana jail."

Then the movement stopped. Seconds later, a loud crack echoed along the river.

"Ear-splitting," said Dad. "Literally. Felt the bullet whiz right past my ear."

"Were you scared?"

Dad said, "Well, I decided not to hang around and chat."

"Sherbet," said Mum. "Well, he was probably just trying to frighten you off. And at least he would have got a serious fright himself."

"True," Dad sighed. "And we were warned about being English in the Tuli Block. Just didn't think it'd happen so quickly.

Oh, well," he continued, adopting a reverent tone, "I should be rejoicing. But for the grace of the Good Lord I might not be here."

"Indeed," said Mum. She put down her teacup. "Well, if you're taking that route, I think I'll take the other and hit the bottle. Fancy a stiff drink?"

These shots were much closer.

Four. Maybe five.

I didn't have time to count. All three horses bolted in fright, bucking wildly and veering into the bushes as they tore off down the dirt track.

It took a few hundred meters before we brought them back to a trot. The shots had come from across the Limpopo, but the riverside brush and the dense, immensely tall trees allowed only glimpses of the water and the opposite bank. We could see nothing.

"That's odd," said Dad. "Can't be poachers. And I didn't think Louis John was the type to shoot by the water."

Louis John and Martie Botha owned the South African farm opposite this stretch of the Limpopo. They didn't live on the farm, but loved the bush and visited often. They also ran a professional hunting business, and the hunters were supposed to conform to strict hunting etiquette.

Dad said, "They must have got a ratbag client. Better go take a look."

Following Dad, Lulu and I turned into the bush and nudged the horses up the bank, toward the big dam wall.

Built long before we arrived, this dam held water throughout the dry season, and the trees here were some of the most magnificent on the farm. The crocodiles, like the trees, had thrived on the reliable water: at night, when we shone flashlights across the deep wide expanse of the dam, the beams illuminated scores of pairs of evil red eyes. And while Fiddian Green, who rarely left his favorite pool in the Lotsane, may have been the biggest croc in the neighborhood, there were many more here, in the splendid and sinister

Limpopo, which with its very deep, wide water and very tall old trees made the nearby Lotsane seem like a mere paddling pool.

So, as we rounded the top of the bank, I couldn't believe what I saw. Fifty meters across the river, just above the dam wall, four figures splashed in the deep water—Louis John, Martie, and a young boy and girl, whom we hadn't yet met.

"They're bonkers," I marveled.

Dad cupped his hands around his mouth. "Afternoon," he bellowed.

The figures waved and yelled hello.

Then Louis John clambered up the bank and walked across the narrow dam wall. He stopped just before he reached our bank, reluctant to proceed with a technically illegal border crossing, and grinned warmly. "Nice to see you," he said in his strong Afrikaans accent.

Dad said, "We heard some shots. Thought it might be your hunters, or poachers."

Louis John shook his head. "That was Louis John junior. He was shooting at the water. To frighten the crocs so we can swim."

Lulu and I gaped.

Even Dad looked taken aback. "You really think that works?"

"*Ja*. After the shots, you just mustn't stay in for too long."

"How long is that?"

"*Ag*, a few minutes." He shrugged. "Five, ten. Not too long. Lovely temperature."

"I'll take your word for it," said Dad.

"I can tell you, it's very safe."

Dad laughed. "Anyway, you should all come over for drinks this evening. It would be nice to meet your kids."

Louis John thanked Dad but declined. "The border patrols," he said, ominously. "I don't want my kids to end up in jail."

Dad said, "They hardly ever patrol the river. And I'm sure they wouldn't put you in jail. Anyway, you're only on the wall for a few minutes."

"*Ag*, no, really, Keith," said Louis John. "But you come for drinks with us. You Scotts don't seem scared of these things."

And so we began to find our way in our new home, and to meet, befriend, bemuse, and occasionally befoe, our various neighbors: a cast of characters who together provided a range of wonder and noxiousness far surpassing even that of the Tuli Block's technically wild residents.

20

NEIGHBORS

Swimming across the Lotsane

Jean van Riet said, "It's a pity you missed old Koos van der Merwe. Did you hear about him?"

"No."

Jean chuckled gently. "*Jirre!* He was something."

The late Koos van der Merwe, said Jean, had been lonely, fond of a drink, and would regularly drive out of his farm gate and park his large Chevrolet across a narrow stretch of the Tuli Block dirt road. Installed thus, drinking steadily, he'd refuse to let anyone pass until they had shared a brandy and a chat with him.

"No! Really?"

"*Ja, man. Jirre,* there're some strange *okes* in this place."

Jean—pronounced "Jaan"—stroked his dogs continuously

as he talked, one hand on a tall, sorrowful-looking whippet, the other on a pig-sized, deeply scarred bull terrier. Both stood in front of him, wagging their tails and resting their heads adoringly in his lap.

"Can I offer you all more drinks?" he said in a gentle Afrikaans accent.

After nods of assent, he disappeared into the house, trailed by the dogs.

The house was old and small—an oblong divided into four gloomy rooms, bachelor forlorn. But the view was spectacular, for the little building stood right on the riverbank, overlooking a deep dammed pool in the Limpopo.

Sitting under the dense high canopy of trees, we could hear the snorts and see the humps of a large pod of hippos. To one side of the house stood rows of orange trees, nearly ripe fruit tugging down the branches. Behind us, farther back from the river, were cattle pens, a dusty football pitch, a dirt airstrip, and a large metal hangar for Jean's microlight plane.

Once, he'd taken us all up, one after the other, flying across the farm between our two farms and circling our house before returning along the Limpopo: the treetops whizzing by only feet below the wheels, so low that we could see the outlines of crocodiles suspended just beneath the surface, watching the banks.

Jean emerged from the house carrying the drinks—beers for Mum and Dad and glasses of bright orange Oros concentrate drink for Lulu, Damien, and me. Mum frowned slightly at the Oros and the biltong that Jean offered around. It pained her that he lived on a diet consisting mainly of meat—redeemed only by the occasional serving of homegrown cabbage or an orange.

Mum said, "It's getting late. You must come across and join us for a meal."

Jean smiled. "*Ag*, no, Linda. Thank you. I don't want to trouble you."

Damien said, "Please come, Jean."

"Yes, no, really," said Mum. "Not at all. It would be no imposition. But nor must you feel obliged. I wouldn't be offended if you didn't come."

She paused, looking flustered. Jean frowned. Dad smiled into his beer.

"Jean," said Dad, "do you want to come for supper?"

"Okay, Keith," said Jean. "Thank you."

Mum blushed and laughed. "Oh, dear. Sorry, doing it again."

Mum's conversations with people for whom English was a second language were riveting. The more she struggled to make herself clear, the longer her words, and the more entangled in double negatives. Jean's English was good, and with him Mum was quite modest. Speaking to those less fluent, it was much worse. And the more confusion Mum caused, the harder she tried, plumbing the dustiest depths of her English, and occasionally Latin and French, vocabularies.

Mum's polysyllables had rendered many a Tuli Block local dumbfounded—an effect whose magnitude was exceeded only by the reaction to her cooking.

But later that evening, when she placed a steaming dish of vegetable pie on the table, Jean's face showed no more than a flicker of disappointment before he grinned appreciatively. More than six months after our arrival, and many dinners since the start of our friendship, Jean had learned not to get his hopes up. He applied a liberal sprinkling of salt and began stoically chewing his way though the large mound of broccoli and white sauce.

Lulu, Mum, and I had been full-time vegetarians for the last few years. Damien and Dad were happy to go either way. So apart from the occasional fillet or roast chicken, there was rarely meat on our table.

Jean was an inured survivor of Mum's vegetarian concoctions.

Dion Steyn, a divorced Afrikaans man who lived on a nearby farm, was not. He had tried, soldiering through several meals of vegetable pie, spinach quiche, and lentil hotpot. Then one evening he'd joined us for dinner the day before Mum's fortnightly, cross-border, 150-kilometer shopping trip to Ellisras in South Africa.

The cupboards were bare. Mum made green spinach pasta. The sauce, made using boiled, liquidized spinach from the garden, was green too. With it, she served a green salad. The combination was electrifying.

Even Mum noticed. "Turned out rather greener than I'd expected," she said apologetically.

"Strange, that," said Dad.

Dion smiled weakly. He ate his plate of green pasta topped with green sauce and never again accepted a dinner invitation. He'd come for evening drinks, but as soon as dinner was mentioned, he would quickly decline: "Thank you very much. But I have a beef stew waiting."

With a look of relief, Jean swallowed the last mouthful and put down his fork. He took a large gulp of beer. "Linda, thank you. Again."

"Always a pleasure," said Mum. "Anyway, we owe you a lifetime of meals."

Dad agreed.

"*Ag*, no, *man*," said Jean, blushing. "It's nothing."

From the moment we'd arrived in the Tuli Block, Jean had helped us: fixing pumps, advising on dam building, and lending us tools and machinery. Having arrived only about five years before us, by Tuli Block standards Jean was a newcomer. He also suggested whom we could and couldn't trust—something he had learned mostly by experience—and explained the complex, longstanding web of Tuli Block feuds. Almost everyone had something against everyone else; but come an outsider, and fierce old enemies could rapidly unite to bring him down.

"*Jirre*," he said, "there're some naughty *okes* in this place."

When Dad told Jean he'd chased poachers on horseback, Jean looked appalled. "*Ag*, no, Keith!" That Dad had then been shot at didn't surprise him at all.

We'd all liked Jean at once, and eleven-year-old Damien quickly came to adore him. Jean, who was in his late twenties, had become Damien's new idol and best friend. Most afternoons, when Lulu and I were riding, Damien would hop on his motorbike and make the five-kilometer drive to Jean's farm. There he'd follow Jean around as he inspected his game, cattle, and citrus plantations, or join the football matches Jean played with his Batswana farm workers on the dirt pitch behind his house.

Mum said, "Grandpa Terry gets his footballer grandson wish at last. Just not quite as he expected."

Damien also went hunting impala, although he dared not reveal this to Lulu and me. We only discovered much later, when Jean, forgetting he wasn't supposed to say anything, said, "*Jirre,* Damien's a good shot."

Damien went pale. Lulu and I, tears of betrayal in our eyes, yelled furiously. Jean watched with a look of guilty amazement.

After we'd stopped shouting, Damien said, "I mainly just shoot at tin cans."

Jean nodded. "*Ja,* me too."

L ouis John said, "Have you been swimming yet? The hippos have gone."

We were in South Africa, technically, sitting on the river-bank of Louis John's farm, watching the glinting sheet of water above the dam wall. It was perfectly still, the leaves of trees vis-ible in the silky mirror image.

"No way," said Mum. "Our swimming pool is finished. We'll stick to that, thanks."

Dad said, "It's full of muddy river water at the moment. The kids get scared enough swimming in that. Seem to think a croc might crawl a few kilometers and stop off for a quick dip. Hey, chaps?"

"We saw a hippo standing in our driveway," I said indignantly.

"*Ja,*" said Damien. "He was huge."

Dad said, "He didn't climb in the swimming pool, did he? He was just passing by, moving between rivers."

Louis John smiled. Louis John junior and Riette eyed Lulu, Damien, and me with curious expressions. We looked away foolishly.

Damien said, "Anyway, it's just the girls who're scared of swimming in our pool."

I said, "Rubbish. We were the ones who swum across the Lotsane on the horses. That was fun."

Lulu nodded. "Yeah, that was cool."

Dad started to speak, but paused. Then he said, "Didn't realize you two had enjoyed it so much. We must do it again."

"Okay," I said.

"Okay," said Lulu.

We both smiled weakly, sick with nostalgic and prospective terror, furious to be caught out like this by Dad.

The three horses had danced and pawed excitedly at the damp leafy earth.

They had never swum before, but the moment we'd rounded the top of the Lotsane riverbank—the river suddenly before us, lying between us and home—they'd known exactly what was about to happen.

"Well, I'm going in," said Dad. "Come if you like."

"What about Fiddian?"

"He'd never go for a horse. Got much smaller, easier pickings."

I turned to Lulu, who, white-faced and silent, stared at the murky water. Earlier, at the house, the idea of swimming with the horses had seemed very different. Now, at the water's edge, bareback, barefoot, and barelegged, I felt profoundly stupid for having agreed.

"He did eat two cows, Dad," I said, trying to sound matter-of-fact.

"Yeah, Dad," squeaked Lulu.

"We've been through this," replied Dad impatiently. "They were drinking on the bank. That's when crocs grab things. Just make a big splash. You'll be fine. Anyway, Lulu, you're safe. No sane croc would try and eat Winnie."

"What about me?" I was riding Ashby, the podgy bay show jumper bought for me when Lulu inherited Winnie.

"Bye," said Dad. "Yee-hah," he yelled, kicking Quartz forward and down the steep muddy bank. Quartz plunged in eagerly, disappearing but for his neck.

"Come on, chaps," called Dad, the water lapping just below his waist. "Lovely in here. Thought you weren't scared."

"We're not," I yelled. And before I could think about it, I nudged Ashby's well-padded sides. "Come on, boy. In you go."

And then we were skidding down the bank. And then we were in, swimming. Cold, deep croc-filled water surrounded my legs and lower body. Shuddering, I quickly tucked them up beside me, almost kneeling on Ashby's submerged back. All around was deep muddy water, stretching twenty meters at least to the opposite bank.

Behind me came a cry and then a splash. "See, Dad," shouted Lulu, "we're not scared."

Winnie drew alongside me. "If I see a croc now, Rob," Lulu whispered, "I will die."

"Me too."

Egging the horses on, Lulu and I quickly caught up with Quartz.

"Slow down," said Dad. "You must appreciate the view. Fantastic, isn't it? See, once you're in, it's not at all scary. Hey?"

"No," I croaked.

"Not at all," said Lulu.

We both grinned unconvincingly.

"That's my girls," said Dad.

Louis John junior and Riette were still smiling. Louis John junior was about a year older than me, Riette was Damien's age. They weren't confident speaking English, and we spoke no Afrikaans. But they clearly found us amusing.

Damien said, "Well, I *donnered* a croc."

Grinning confidently, adopting just the slightest of Afrikaans accents, he explained how he'd been paddling in his low plastic canoe when the eyes and warty nostrils had begun to trail him. "*Jirre*, it was big," said Damien. "This far between the eyes and nose." He held his hands nearly two feet apart. "I wasn't scared, though. When its nose got to the back of the canoe, I just turned around and clobbered it with my paddle. Disappeared." Damien grinned. "Think I scared the shit out of it."

Dad gave him a warning look.

Louis John just nodded thoughtfully. "*Ja*, that's how you've got to deal with these small crocs. They're scared of people now. Not like when I was a boy."

He poured more drinks, explaining that before the crocs had been widely hunted, they'd been much bigger, and much braver. Then he told us how as a ten-year-old he used to hunt crocs at night with a gun, floating in half a forty-four-gallon drum on the river, shining a flashlight in search of the little red eyes.

"That was scary," he said.

In this farmed part of the Tuli Block, many of the more exciting and bigger species had been hunted or chased out completely. On Molope Farm, one of the largest resident animals was a lone wildebeest. No one knew how he had come to be here by himself, but we assumed he must have lost his mother as a baby. He had since decided he was a waterbuck and cut a truly weird figure grazing beside his adopted herd of the fluffy antelope—which were odd in their own right, with their absurd white-ringed bottoms, like they'd sat on freshly painted toilet seats.

Zebra, giraffe, and rhino were found only on some of the nearby game-fenced farms, and in the large game areas of the northern Tuli Block. Elephants moved through just a few times a decade, destroying trees and fences. And lions hadn't been seen in this part of the Tuli Block for several years.

But then, only a few months after we moved in, lion spoor appeared, tracking along the river from farm to farm, and eventually to our farm.

"Terrible," said Jean, shaking his head.

We were walking along the Lotsane, Jean helping us follow the occasional spoor through the brush and riverside scrub. It was thrilling, and terrifying. We jumped at every crackle in the bushes—except for Jean, who strolled along, talking mainly about the weather and how much the Tuli Block needed rain.

"Pity," agreed Dad. "Having lions around does make evening walks a little less relaxed."

Jean laughed, "*Ag*, no. Don't worry about that. These lions are scared of people. It's terrible because they're taking cows. Someone up the river lost three the other night."

"Ah."

The tracks drifted away from the river brush and became easier to follow. Then we saw drag marks, leading to the expansive shade of an umbrella thorn. There, beneath the tree, not more than a kilometer from our house, lay the scant remains of an impala. All around in the dirt were paw prints: big lion paws, and the smaller prints of hyenas, which had cleaned the bones, and dragged some a few meters off into the bush.

"A day old," said Jean. "Maybe less."

"One of them is a brute," said Dad, pointing to a saucer-size print.

We returned the next morning with plaster of paris from Dad's clinic and made several splendid casts of the biggest prints, which we later used to lay tracks—and alarm visitors.

A few days later, the lions were spotted several farms down the river. To our considerable relief, they never returned. And they never crossed into South Africa.

At last we had something to rival swimming with crocodiles. "We tracked lions," we told Louis John junior and Riette. "They're scared of people," we then assured them coolly. And for the first time the two tough, bushwise children looked genuinely impressed.

A sked about the Bothas' blast-the-water-before-swimming technique, Jean shook his head. "*Jirre*, they're crazy."

We nodded, shaking our heads too, enjoying for once not being the idiot new arrivals.

Jean said, "They might get bilharzia."

"Huh?"

"You are joking," said Mum.

"*Ag*, no, Linda, I got so sick with bilharzia."

We gazed at him in wonder. Bilharzia is a parasitic disease humans can catch by swimming in stagnant or slow-flowing water. It can be very debilitating, but it's generally curable and rarely lethal—nothing to a crocodile.

Faced with five disbelieving smirks, Jean told us gravely about one now famous occasion when he'd been having drinks with Roy Young, the nearby crocodile farmer. They were sitting outside Roy's house on the banks of the Limpopo, which a few years before had flooded, sweeping all Roy's biggest breeding stock from their fenced concrete pools back into the river.

In the small river pool in front of them, crocodiles floated everywhere. Gazing at the eyes, nostrils, and slowly swishing bodies, Roy had said, "I'll give you a million bucks to swim across."

Jean said, "I told him, 'Do you think I'm crazy? I don't want to get bilharzia ever again.'"

We laughed once more, and Jean looked offended. You hardly ever hear of people being eaten by crocodiles, he explained. Except for that one time, when old Hendrik Swart shot and cut open a croc and found a red shoe inside. "But maybe I'm just different," he conceded. "Lots of other *okes* swim in the river here. Especially after parties." He paused, smiling thoughtfully. Then he said, "Did Leon de Wit ever tell you what he saw on the news?"

"No."

Jean chuckled.

Leon was a friend of Jean's who lived a few farms up the river. Now in his late thirties, Leon was a busy farmer, with a respectable wife who would never permit drunken river pranks. In the evenings, he drank slowly and moderately on his balcony overlooking the river, and afterward, he went back inside to bed.

In the Tuli Block, televisions could pick up South African stations, and Leon, like almost everyone else, watched the nightly SABC news bulletin.

Mystery crocodile sighted in dam.

Leon blinked as he listened to the report on the unexplained sighting of a single large crocodile in a small dam a few hundred kilometers from the capital, Pretoria. There had been no crocs in the area for years. No one could understand how it got there.

After the news, Leon picked up the phone and called one of his old drinking mates. His memory confirmed, he sat back and sighed.

Jirre!

Years ago, he and several others had been drinking beside the Limpopo and had decided it would be fun to go croc hunting. They did, and caught a young crocodile, which they hauled onto the bank. They put it in a sack, tossed it in the back of Leon's *bakkie*, which stood beside the river, and carried on partying.

First thing in the morning Leon departed, as planned, for Pretoria, not noticing the immobile sack when he set off to the border post. No one at the border post noticed either. A few hours later, stopping for a pee on the side of the road, he first saw the sack, now thrashing, the crocodile having warmed up in the morning sun in the back of his *bakkie*. As he could hardly arrive in the capital city with a crocodile, he stopped at the nearest dam, disposed of the disgruntled creature, and forgot all about it, until the now enormous crocodile appeared on South African TV nearly a decade later.

Around the same time that Leon de Wit's croc resurfaced, an English TV crew appeared in the Tuli Block, following another sinister sighting:

Fugitive lord seen in Botswana's Tuli Block. Gambling with the local residents.

For hours, the crew drove up and down the Tuli Block road, finding only abandoned old farmsteads and the homes of Afrikaans farmers. "Have you seen this man?" they asked again and again, displaying a constructed picture of what the elderly lord would probably look like. "You know, the famous English Lord Lucan, who killed his children's nanny."

Each time, shaking heads. No one had heard of the story. No one had seen him. Anyway, the only Englishmen nearby were the new doctor from Selebi-Phikwe—no, much too young—and Roy Young, the crocodile farmer.

Roy Young had, however, lived in the area for years. And

no, he didn't resemble the picture. Nevertheless, desperate for any lead, the frustrated posse set off toward the Youngs' farm, which lay about twenty kilometers to the north of us. En route, their car broke down, and they had to spend a night of terror in the bush, surrounded by unfamiliar barks and cries.

The next day, Charlotte Young, Roy's wife, greeted the exhausted, disheveled team. To looks of dismay, she told the visitors Roy was not in. Too tired now to beat around the bush, they thrust the picture toward her and demanded, "Is this man your husband?"

"No, definitely not," said Charlotte.

And thus, with one old crocodile and one crocodile farmer, ended the Tuli Block's unsung and unfulfilled short-lived claims to fame.

While an escaped croc from the Tuli Block might thrive unnoticed for years, as any of the locals could have told the British TV crew, an escaped English lord wouldn't have stood the slightest chance of going underground in the Tuli Block.

In the Tuli Block, outsiders, especially English outsiders, did not blend in.

Even Jean, an Afrikaner, stood out: his mother tongue, a love of hunting, and an insatiable appetite for meat aside, his background made him almost as conspicuous in the Tuli Block as we were.

It had been Jean's grandfather, too, a man Jean spoke of with misty-eyed affection, who first established the South African family's links with Botswana.

Jean Baptist van Riet had bought the farm just a few years before Grandpa Ivor had left Johannesburg to escape his divorce and to begin a new life in Botswana. For van Reit, Botswana was an escape route too, but a preemptive one only. He had remained at his home in the Free State—one of South Africa's traditionally more conservative provinces—where he became deputy president of the newly formed Liberal Party. If things got too dangerous for him and his family under the apartheid regime, they would use the Botswana farm as a bolt-hole. As it was, though, the Liberal Party disbanded in the late 1960s, when the South African government outlawed mixed-race political parties, and van Riet stayed in South Africa, the Tuli land standing empty until the younger Jean arrived, just a few years before us.

Now in his nineties, the sprightly gentleman still drove up to the Tuli Block with Jean's parents. He loved the bush and strode around the land with his grandson, dispensing advice on farming, which had been his livelihood, and the other outlet for his once notorious politics.

On one of their visits, the four van Riets drove across to our farm, laden with gifts of homemade jam, chutneys, and biscuits from their Free State farm, and we sat outside drinking pots of *rooibos* tea while Mum and Dad plied Jean senior with questions.

Eyes twinkling, the old Jean told us delightedly how the profit-sharing agreement with his black workers had in the 1960s caused fury among local Free State farmers—only to be surpassed when he then built proper houses with running water and installed flush loos for his laborers.

"They called me," he said, shaking his head and chuckling, "the man who even builds *kakhuisies* for his *kaffirs*."

Dad said, "These guys here still wouldn't like it."

Mum sighed. *"Plus ça change, plus c'est la même chose!"*

Our staff did not have flush toilets, as we did in the house. But their long-drop toilets were well built, and Dad had erected a large prefabricated building with an emergency clinic at one end, and the rest divided into bedrooms, a lounge with a television, two bathrooms, and a kitchen. It was not grand. But over the months, when local farmers had come to the clinic, many had been shocked by Dad's explanation that the rest of the building was for his staff. *Jirre!*

In the Tuli Block most black workers lived in ramshackle mud huts and tiny buildings, sharing bedrooms and collecting water from a communal outside tap. Pay was poor too. When we first went to the Tuli Block Farmers' Association meetings—held under the grand thatched gazebo on the lawns of the chairman's house—pointed remarks were made about how newcomers mustn't offer higher wages. Or else all Tuli Block farmers would have to pay the price.

Livelihoods might be ruined!

Which was not to suggest that many of the Tuli Block farmers were poor. Most had hundreds of head of cattle and owned large farms. Like Jean's family, many also owned a farm on the South African side of the river, directly opposite their Tuli Block farm.

In some cases, this was out of very different motives to the van Riets': rumor had it that many a Tuli Block family fortune had been made on the back of the once rife diamond and cattle smuggling route across the Limpopo. By the 1990s, however, the police had become more vigilant, and smuggling was a dying industry. One old smuggler turned this to his advantage. Bragging to a neighbor, he explained that by moving his watermelons across the Limpopo and selling them in South Africa, he'd almost doubled his profits. It would be crazy not to. All one had to do was pick the right time and date—about which he also was happy to advise.

Not at all. We're neighbors, after all.

On the chosen night, the would-be smuggler loaded up his *bakkie* with watermelons and drove down to the Limpopo. Around the river, all was still and quiet, and his workers began ferrying the melons across.

Suddenly there was sweeping flashlight and shouting. Policemen jumped out of the undergrowth and took the farmer off to jail, where he spent the night. Later, the neighbor expressed his utmost shock and sympathy. Terrible, but these things happen to the best of us.

Mostly, however, the web of feuds between old Tuli Block families was spun and reinforced by legitimate business. Like the cabbage wars, which began not long after we arrived, when one successful cabbage farmer started selling all cabbages to a busy vegetable shop in the town of Palapye. Not more than a month had passed before his rival began selling discounted cabbages from his truck, parked directly outside the vegetable shop.

The list went on: in the Tuli Block, it seemed, everyone had something against almost everyone else. Although, at the Farmers' Association meetings, this was sometimes hard to believe. Come a discussion on wages, or some such generally supported cause, and all fights would be put aside. Standing up in the semicircle of chairs, shaking his fist as he spoke, a farmer would be cheered by his bitterest rivals, all united in adversity.

Apart from the occasional impassioned rant, these gatherings were tedious: one khaki-clad farmer after the next complaining—generally in poor English—about exactly the same thing as the speaker before. Wages too high, government assistance too low, roads not maintained...

Mostly, during the discussions, Lulu, Damien, and I read books on the lawns or climbed the huge trees in the beautiful gardens of the chairman's house. Sometimes we spoke a little to the Afrikaans children, including once a boy called Stefaans who seemed nice and liked horses. He was a year older than me. I asked him what he wanted to be.

"I've always wanted to be a vet," I explained.

"I've always wanted to be a butcher," he said cheerfully.

After the meetings, the men stood around the *braai*, drinking beer and turning slabs of steak and coils of thick *boerewors* sausage that dripped sizzling fat onto the coals. The women attended to the other food. Clustered around tables on the lawns of this little oasis in the middle of the bush, the farmers' wives were an amazing spectacle: gleaming with gold jewelry, high-heeled shoes, nail polish, and extravagant outfits more suited to a wedding. Pink and orange featured strongly, often together. Cheeks glowed with bright blusher. Lipstick was frequently reapplied. Many sported implausibly colored hair, permed or blow-dried into a state of shock.

Driving home after our first meeting, Mum said, "The *tannies* must think I'm a terrible wife. Don't dress up for you. Don't feed you."

On the tables, the shiny, coiffed women had laid out white bread rolls, coleslaw drenched in sweet mayonnaise, and bean salads in a thick sugary sauce. Mum's bright mixed salad, dressed with an olive oil and balsamic vinaigrette, had hardly been touched. Dad had finished it when he returned for second helpings, surrounded by women as he ladled food onto his plate. All the Afrikaans women served their husbands, and they'd stared from Mum to Dad with undisguised disapproval.

"But just so you know, Keith," added Mum, "not over my dead body will I ever serve you from a buffet."

"Fine," said Dad, "but you must then accept that you'll never get to see me in khaki shorts three sizes too small."

In the backseat, Lulu, Damien, and I howled in disgust.

"*Jirre*, Keith," said Mum, laughing. "On second thought, it might just be worth serving you for that spectacle."

After several meetings, during which Dad frequently spoke out about mostly unchallenged motions, it became clear that he was the only person really prepared to stand up to the powerful incumbent chairman. A group of disillusioned farmers took Dad aside, pointed this out, and asked him to stand for the position in the next general meeting. Dad said, "No, thanks. I don't want to get involved in your politics."

To us Dad said, "I'm not farming. And for what I want to do with this place, I don't need them." Dad was rehabilitating: for our once-overgrazed farm, he had grand plans to clear away invading thorn scrub, restore savanna grasses, stop soil erosion, and plant more indigenous trees. And for this, the only thing Dad needed was water—the price of which unexpectedly turned out to be not his own involvement in local affairs, but his children's.

21

GOOD NEIGHBORS

The gazebo

Dad leaned back in his chair and eyed us expectantly. "Well?"

Damien said, "Okay. I'll go if you want."

"Me too," said Lulu.

"Great," said Dad. "What about you, Robbie?"

I stared out the window at the bird feeder, not trusting myself to look at Dad. We'd been in the Tuli Block nearly six months. Life on the farm, until now, had been perfect.

"It's illegal," I snapped. I turned to Mum. "Isn't it?"

"Not exactly," said Mum. "I have other reservations, though."

"How come?"

"Well, I think they should ask black children."

"And I agree with Mum," said Dad, "but that's never going to happen in Pikfontein. The point is, we need good neighbors. And this is an easy way to help Fourie."

"Look it's not ideal," said Mum, "but it's a one-off, and it'll be a good cultural experience. Come on," she added, smiling, "you'll probably find you quite enjoy it."

"I know I'll hate it."

"Then it'll be character building," said Dad.

"My character's fine," I snapped.

"Clearly not, Robbie."

I glared at Dad. Dad smiled back at me.

Lulu and Damien looked eagerly from Dad to me. Mum sighed. She was the one who had to broker peace after the regular furious arguments between Dad and me—usually over much smaller things than this.

"I can't believe," I fumed, "that you're going to do this to your own children." I turned to Lulu and Damien. "And I can't believe either that you two are just letting him."

"Chill, Rob," said Damien. "What's the big problem?"

"The principle," I yelled, feeling my face going red. "We're being bartered. By our parents. For water. Doesn't that bother you?"

"Listen, Robbie," interrupted Dad. "I'm not *making* you do anything. I'm *asking* you for a favor. And before you refuse, just remember that in life we all have to do things we don't like."

"You've just said I don't *have* to do this," I spluttered.

"It's only two days. I go to my clinics for three days. Every week."

I tried and failed to think of something to say. With this, Dad had me. I gaped, and he smiled. I jumped up and ran toward the house. "Think about it," he called after me.

But he knew, as well as I did, that I was defeated.

Since leaving Selebi, Dad had compressed his workweek, his days now longer than ever. He'd also inherited more village clinics—the last of Dr. Meyer's old practices, which had, at the time of his death, been taken over by another flying doctor, Dr. Odendaal. Until, in 1992, in a tragic echo of the past, Dr. Odendaal had crashed in bad weather too, killing himself and his pregnant wife. Now in just three days, Dad drove over a thousand kilometers, to six different villages—Tonota, Machaneng, Tsetsebjwe, Bobonong, Sefophe, and Sherwood—to see up to three hundred patients. For three days, we hardly saw him. We all felt terrible about the draining work and, come Thursday, relief that for the next four days Dad would be free to work on the farm, doing the ambitious, costly rehabilitation projects that he so loved, and which—together with his responsibilities to us—kept him chained to his lucrative practices.

It was several months since we'd moved in. The house was finished, and, as I sat on my bed, torn by guilt and fury, I looked out of my window onto the early stages of Dad's gargantuan bush-clearing project, which he'd begun directly in front of the house.

The owner before us had run too many cattle on too little land, and much of the work involved removing the scrubby thorn-bushes that had invaded the overgrazed soils. For this, Dad had hired a number of casual workers, who under his direction were chopping down thousands of bushes, wrenching out the bigger ones with a chain tied to the old Land Cruiser.

It was slow work, and the bush in front of the house had been cleared fewer than fifty meters deep. Dad was not deterred. One day, as he often excitedly reminded us, the new lawn in front of the house would sweep into an open grassy plain, clear but for a few tall trees, returned to the natural savannah state of the land. And there he would build a watering hole, where we'd watch the game drink just meters from our house.

Nor would he stop there: Dad was going to clear and restore all two thousand acres of Molope Farm. Eventually, from the house, we'd see the trees of the Lotsane River, which by then would be even taller and greener, watered by Dad's many planned dams that would raise the water table across the farm and provide a lifeline to the trees and animals in the drier years.

With the Lotsane, all this was straightforward: we owned both banks and could build any dam we liked, wherever we liked. Not so though on the Limpopo. Here you needed the cooperation of your South African neighbor, who by law had equal water rights. And herein lay the present problem.

The site for Dad's new Limpopo dam was opposite Fourie du Plessis's farm.

A few months earlier Fourie had agreed, in principle, to help with the construction of the wall and share the water equally. We'd all been delighted; this dam would trap water in a particularly barren part of the river that was always the first to dry up when the Limpopo stopped flowing. Worried that Fourie would renege on his offer, whenever he'd paddled across, Dad had repeatedly extended offers of help. "Anything I can do to assist you. Just give me a call."

"Is it still okay?" we'd ask anxiously, when Dad returned.

"Fine. Says there's nothing I can do to help."

But then, as it turned out, it wasn't Dad's help that Fourie needed.

The Afrikaans school in Pikfontein, where Fourie's nieces studied, was about to lose a teacher. The South African government funded teachers' salaries based on enrolled student numbers, and the Pikfontein school had fallen just three children short for the upcoming school inspector's visit.

Lulu, Damien, and I didn't speak Afrikaans and we'd never met Fourie's nieces. The prospect of two days in the all-white, all-Afrikaans Pikfontein boarding school was horrible. Compounded by the indignation of being bartered, it was a first-class nightmare.

I was stuck, though. I loved the farm rehabilitation projects, and felt guilty about Dad's clinics.

Somewhat regretting all the times I'd said as much, I marched back outside and glared at Dad. "I'll only go if I can do my own work."

"I'm sure that'll be fine, Robbie."

"And not have to go to lessons."

"That too."

"And not be disturbed."

"Anything for the duchess."

A few days later, Fourie came to the house to discuss strategy. "*Jirre*," he said, sipping a beer, "this is very kind of you all. I don't know what we would have done without your help."

Mum started to say something. Instead she bit her lip and gave a grim smile. The more she'd thought about it, the more disgusted she'd been that the Pikfontein parents were prepared to import English-speaking children from Botswana, when they could easily find in South Africa three black children who actually spoke Afrikaans. But then they, of course, would have to stay once they were enrolled, whereas we could be promptly returned.

I was just generally disgusted. Fourie caught me scowling at him.

"*Ag*, Robyn, you'll enjoy it." He gave me a patronizing smile. "You can play netball with all the other girls. There is a very good netball team."

"My future," I replied coldly, "does not lie in netball."

Fourie stared at me, bewildered.

Mum made a small choking sound and looked away.

Dad said, "Right, then, when do you need these little brutes?"

By the following Monday morning, when Dad prepared to leave for his clinics, I'd calmed down enough to give him a civil kiss good-bye. "Drive carefully, Dad," I said, as I always said. "Watch out for animals on the road."

"Will do. Always do. Now go easy on the poor kids in Pikfontein. And remember, Robbie," he said gravely, "you'll look back on this, and you almost certainly won't laugh."

I smiled defiantly as he drove away. Then I went inside to pack.

At midday, summoned by Mum, we loaded our luggage into the four-by-four.

Each of us took a small bag equipped with clothes and toiletries for two nights. Lulu added her hideous, almost life-sized orangutan soft toy. Damien, who had nothing else, helped me carry outside my large cardboard box, which according to the label once held latex rubber gloves.

The box was for my work, and contained assignments from the correspondence course that Lulu, Damien, and I had been more or less following for about a year. My current module was on the theme of fishing, fisheries, and the environment. In each module, which contained a fortnight's worth of work, the English, geography, science, and math components related to the same general theme. Like fishing, most were broad, practical topics—agriculture, architecture, transport—that you were encouraged to develop creatively.

The flexibility and scope for pursing intellectual or practical fancies was the main reason Mum had chosen the course, which was inconveniently run from New Zealand. Even so, from the start, she'd incorrigibly bent the rules. We were meant to work five days a week, but we often still devoted whole days to reading or other projects. When Damien had wanted to spend a day taking apart his motorbike, Mum had happily obliged, with her usual, "You can always catch up later." During "school time" we built cross-country courses for the horses, paddled on the river, and often just hung around Dad as he oversaw dam building and explained to us basic structural engineering. One school day, in anticipation of the forthcoming winter, we'd helped Dad construct a solar swimming pool heater made out of coiled black plastic pipes between sheets of glass, which looked impressive but turned out to be completely ineffective.

Then, every two weeks, a few days before we were due to post the work, suddenly Mum would become officious. The gaps would be hurriedly finished, the assignments quickly wrapped, and a stressful forty-eight hours would be finally concluded with an exhilarating drive to the Sherwood Ranch Post Office.

If our faraway teachers in New Zealand had wanted to protest, they probably knew it was pointless. With the slow Botswana post, we wouldn't receive the marked modules for another month. And it took us only the duration of the drive back to the farm to relax and return to the almost-any-excuse-not-to-work-will-do school days.

No excuse, of course, could beat actually going to school. And when we finally sped off toward the border post, Lulu and Damien had nothing with them resembling work.

I had more than I could manage in a week, working day and night. In the cardboard box, in addition to two weeks' worth of assignments, paper, pens, and a calculator, was our large electronic Olivetti typewriter, which though I hardly used, I felt would lend gravity to my request to be left alone in the library. Reasoning that everything would be in Afrikaans, I'd also packed the Oxford dictionary and an encyclopedia. For my free time, when I feared being coerced into school activities, I'd searched our bookshelves and thrown in the thickest Dickens and Shake-speare I could find.

I was determined to emerge untouched and unpleased by Pikfontein.

On the two-hour drive there, Lulu and Damien chatted and giggled as they practiced our limited Afrikaans vocabulary:

lekker, "good, great"
voetsek, "go away" (rudely)
kak, "shit, crap"
donner, "to beat up"
morer, "to beat up"
bliksem, "to beat up"

(As a class of words, those relating to beating up are particularly expressive in Afrikaans.)

But even Lulu and Damien fell silent when we drove through the gray pillars of the school and pulled up in front of the long gray concrete buildings. The old blue, white, and orange South African flag hung flaccidly from a pole. A small white sign, rusting in one corner, read PIKFONTEIN SKOOL.

Mum switched off the engine. After a moment's silence, she said, "You've got to admit it's ironic that this should be your first visit to school after Kopano."

None of us said anything.

"Two nights will go in a flash," she added. "And better to start with low expectations. . . . And look at that exquisite jacaranda tree . . . so beautiful. Such a pity it's not indigenous. Now come on, guys. This is such an adventure . . ."

Inside the headmaster's office, we were enrolled officially as students. The headmaster was a small, blandly dressed man with very neatly combed hair. I watched his face for signs of guilt as he added our names below the Schmidts and Schoemans. There were none.

"Thank you so much for helping us, Mrs. Scott," he said. He didn't thank Lulu, Damien, or me. Instead he turned to us and said, "I've explained to the students why you're here. The whole school is expecting you."

He left the office and reappeared with a boy of Damien's age and a girl about my age. "Piet and Deanne will show you your rooms."

Piet and Deanne smiled shyly. They were both barefoot. Out at the car, Piet saw my box and went to summon another boy to carry it. Damien grabbed his bag, and dashed after Piet without another word.

Mum walked with Lulu and me, smiling reassuringly. As we followed her, Deanne described the buildings, which were all the same ugly gray. She spoke in slow, careful English, smiling apologetically when she made a mistake. "You must teach me," she said. And I liked her, despite myself.

"The hall, the church, the science rooms, the English rooms, the library..." Then we entered the corridor of a long building. "This is where you will sleep," she said, turning into the doorway of a gloomy room.

The floor was dark, bare concrete. The room was a four-by-four-meter square. Against each wall was a steel bed with a brightly covered duvet. In the corner stood a tall dresser. There were no pictures.

On one of the beds sat another girl, also about my age.

"This is Annalise," said Deanne. Annalise smiled shyly at us. Lulu and I smiled back, and shook hands. Then we stood awkwardly by our beds, glaring at Mum.

Mum said, guiltily, "Well, nice to have company."

Lulu and I said nothing. Mum swallowed.

Then there was a yell, and we all turned to the single small window.

Through the burglar bars we watched as Damien whizzed past on a bicycle, his front wheel high in the air. A group of boys ran after him, cheering.

Mum laughed. "Well, one less to worry about." Then she said, "I must go or I'll miss the border," and we followed her out to the car, where she kissed and hugged us good-bye. "It'll fly past. And just think of that dam."

Back in the depressing room, Deanne informed us that we had half an hour before dinner. Then, sitting cross-legged on her bed, she explained the school routine to us: lessons in the mornings and afternoons, then sport, then free time in the evenings, followed by dinner in the big hall. Except on Sundays, when the whole school went to morning church and had the afternoon free.

"We get dressed up for *kerk*," she said, hopping off the bed.

From the dresser, she retrieved shiny white high-heeled shoes with bows at the front, and a lacy white dress bedecked with white ribbon bows. She squeezed her bare, tough feet into the shoes and, holding the dress up in front of her shorts and shirt, twirled before us.

"Mine's pink," said Annalise. She joined Deanne by the dresser and displayed a similar outfit, which was entirely bright pink, including the high heels.

Lulu and I stared in amazement at these girly miniatures of the *tannies* at the Tuli Block Farmers' Association meetings. We hadn't worn so much lace and ribbons since our short-lived ballet lessons; we'd never worn high heels.

"They're nice," we said.

The shoes and dresses replaced, we went to the bathrooms to wash our hands and then followed the two girls along several corridors to the big dining hall.

Already seated at long trestle tables were most of the school's several hundred students. Everyone looked up curiously and stopped talking. The cook had made a special vegetarian meal for Lulu and me, and ushered by our roommates—followed by hundreds of eyes—we collected plates of overcooked vegetables and sat down beside the two girls.

When the last of the students had hurried to their seats, the headmaster stood up.

"Tonight," he said, in slow English, "we must all welcome Robyn, Damien, and Lauren Scott, who we are very pleased to have with us." He paused, and gazed around the room. "They are doing a nice thing for us, and we must all be very nice to them." He added a few words in Afrikaans and concluded with an English grace.

"Amen."

"Amen."

Knives and forks clattered on plates, and the meal began.

Lulu and I ate quietly, hoping the stares would stop. We need not have worried: Damien soon made sure that the entire hall was looking at him. Talking loudly between mouthfuls, he spoke in English, but in a thick Afrikaans accent, adorned with occasional Afrikaans words. *Donner! Kak! Lekker! Jirre! Yissus!* Even from two tables away, I could hear most of what he said.

It was his old trick. His methods no more refined, Damien was just as successful a social chameleon here as he'd been as a little boy talking to Batswana in his thick Setswana accent. Every few minutes, the group of boys around him burst out laughing. By dessert, he was inserting *fock—fuck* with an Afrikaans accent— every few sentences. I tried to give him a warning look, but he avoided my eye. After dinner, he disappeared to the boys' dormitories before Lulu or I had a chance to get near him.

Later, as we climbed into bed, Deanne said, "Your brother is nice."

"He's a *windgat*," I said. *Windgat* meant a reckless show-off, which I knew because Dad often described the young Tuli Block men as *windgats*.

Deanne laughed. "*Ja*, but friendly."

Lights went out at nine o'clock. After a few minutes, the two girls were breathing deep, sleeping breaths.

"You okay, Lu?" I whispered.

"Yip."

"Don't snore."

"You don't snore either." She started to giggle.

"*Shhh, man.*"

Lulu's soft giggling was suddenly drowned by a ripping fart sound. Lulu let out a muffled squeal. I bit my sheet, choking back laughter. We lay in strained, wakeful silence; cheeks bursting with held back laughter, faces in our pillows.

After about five minutes, another fart trumpeted through the room.

Someone stirred in one of the two beds.

Seconds later, another fart.

"*Ag, sis, man*, Annalise," said Deanne. "*Shhh!*"

"Sorry," came Annalise's low sleepy voice.

"*Yissus*, Annalise," giggled Deanne.

Annalise started to giggle too, sheepishly.

Lulu and I joined in, and this time, when the giggling finally subsided, we fell asleep too, bellies aching with burned custard pudding and laughter.

After breakfast, Lulu and Damien went off to join the day's lessons for their age groups, which, except for English, were taught in Afrikaans. I dragged my box off to the empty library, where I worked until midday. Over lunch, Damien behaved exactly as before, adding a few newly acquired Afrikaans words. Lulu said she was having fun and introduced her new friend, a little blond girl called Louisa. Louisa hardly spoke any English, but she and Lulu talked happily to each other in their respective languages.

By four o'clock in the afternoon, I'd done more work than I'd ever done in a day before. I was just congratulating myself on a successful escape when Deanne crept inside. "You must come to Religious Education," she whispered. "The *dominee* is making a special English lesson for you."

"I'm still working."

"He told me to call you," said Deanne, looking scared. "Please come."

Reluctantly, I followed her to a smalls packed room. About forty twelve- and thirteen-year-olds were seated on the floor, forming a semicircle at the feet of a swarthy, mustached man. Lulu and Damien were already there and looked relieved when I walked in. I sat down, as far from the front as possible.

"Welcome! Welcome!" said the *dominee*. He explained, in a droning voice, that for our benefit he was going to teach his lesson in English. Not being sure what subject would suit everyone, he'd selected the beginning. "The Garden of Eden," he said, ominously.

The lecture was tedious, mainly about sinfulness, and I only half listened. No one else seemed to be listening either. Whispers swept back and forth across the room, in the opposite direction to the *dominee*'s swiveling gaze.

Some of the boys in the class passed around sheets of paper and examined them admiringly. When one was at last handed to the boy beside me, I leaned over to have a look. It was a large, meticulously drawn shotgun, signed "Damien Scott" in the bottom corner. A few minutes later I glimpsed another one—this time a handgun, also signed by Damien.

Then a girl beside me pressed something into my hand, and when the *dominee* next looked away, I bent down to examine it. It was a folded piece of paper. Inside, in big irregular writing, it read:

> *Dear Robyn,*
> *Hello. My name is Jannie. I only wanted to tell to*
> *you that I think you are very pretty!*
> *I would like to sometime get to no you a bit more.*
> *Love,*
> *Jannie.*

I looked up, blushing and furious. The girl who'd passed me the note pointed surreptitiously to the corner of the room. A big sandy-haired boy looked guiltily at the floor. The boys around him smirked.

I frowned at them and then scowled at Jannie when he raised his head and smiled at me. I looked away and studied the note, plotting my reply and wondering if he wanted to be a butcher—which, since speaking to Stefaans at the Farmers' Association meeting, I suspected every Afrikaans boy in the Northern Transvaal of wanting to be.

The *dominee*'s suddenly inquiring tone interrupted my thoughts. "Now," he said, narrowing his eyes at Lulu, Damien, and me, "it would be very interesting for everyone here if you could tell us about your religious lives in Botswana."

The whole class turned to look at us.

"You live on a farm in Botswana. In the Tuli Block. Is that right?"

We all nodded.

"I am told it's quite far away. Where do you go to church?"

None of us spoke, and the faces grew more curious in the uncomfortable silence. I felt weak. The problem with Jannie paled by comparison to such a question in this hostile environment. In a town where everyone went to *kerk*, we couldn't admit to the *domi-nee*, of all people, that we did not. But lying to a *dominee*—about God—was not an appealing option either.

Lulu and Damien looked hopefully at me. If I didn't speak, they would, which would be disastrous. Lulu would at once tell the simple, unqualified truth. Damien could go either way; possibly the blunt truth, but, in his present please-everyone behavior, possibly a blatantly far-fetched whopper.

"Yes, the Tuli Block is very far away," I blurted out. "Two hundred kilometers from the nearest proper town. Which is Selebi-Phikwe. That's where we used to live. So it's now a long trip to go to church. But there are several churches in Selebi-Phikwe..."

Without a pause I began describing the Catholic church to which Lyn Nevill occasionally dragged Melaney and me. Including as much boring detail as possible, and omitting the details of with whom I'd been to church, I prattled away and had just started to recount part of a previous sermon when the *dominee* interrupted me.

"Thank you very much," he said. "Very interesting. Let's end with a prayer."

I sighed with relief. Lulu and Damien looked impressed.

Afterward, I replied to Jannie's letter, on the same piece of paper so I could also correct his English.

> Dear Jannie,
> I don't particularly want to get to <u>know</u> you more.
> Anyway, I'm leaving tomorrow and never coming back.
> Robyn
> P.S. See correction.

Perhaps it was misleading the *dominee*, but thereafter everything went downhill.

At dinner, Damien was quiet and sat a little away from the other boys. He had a big red mark beside his eye. Afterward, he hung around in the dining hall.

"What happened, Didge?"

"Got beaten up," he said, wincing. "Really *donnered*."

I suddenly regretted my note. "Was it Jannie?"

"No, three other boys."

"Who?"

"Doesn't matter, Rob."

"Why?"

"Just 'cause." He shrugged. "Think I talked too much."

"I'm going to speak to them," I said indignantly. "And report them."

"No, Rob, don't," said Damien. "Please don't. I'll just get beaten up again."

Back in the bedroom, Deanne and Annalise hardly spoke to me. This time it was about Jannie: word had spread that I'd shunned him. That night there was no farting to laugh about.

By breakfast, Damien's eye had turned purple. Only Lulu, chatting happily to Louisa, still seemed cheerful. I spent the morning in the library, feeling too annoyed to work effectively. But after lunch, cheered by the prospect of Mum's imminent arrival, I followed everyone else out to the field to watch the athletics competition.

Lulu was running. Neither Damien nor I had wanted to take part: he too sore, I too angry. Waiting for her race, Lulu chatted to the other runners, all of whom were barefoot. After a few minutes, she removed her shoes too.

Among the runners, by Lulu's side, was Louisa, the two-hundred-meters champion, and as the girls lined up, the audience whistled and called her name.

The pistol fired, and the runners set off. Louisa got more cheers, which became louder as Lulu raced beside her at the front of the pack.

Quickly pulling away from the others, the two girls raced neck and neck. Fifty meters from the finish, cheered only by me and Damien, Lulu accelerated, winning by several meters. There was silence in the stands, grim hostile faces all around us. Even the headmaster looked upset as he presented Lulu with her prize.

For a while, Lulu sat beside the other runners. But when it became clear that no one was going to speak to her, she joined me and Damien, looking miserable.

Mum arrived to find the three of us sitting together on the

stands at the end of the field. "Why haven't you got hats on? Oh, my goodness, Damien, what happened?"

Our good-byes were quick and unfriendly. The headmaster was considerably less warm to Mum. Mum barely spoke at all.

"It was my fault," Damien insisted.

"Nonsense. Nothing justifies that."

"I did tell someone to *voetsek*."

"Idiot," I said.

Damien said, "Thought we were supposed to be protected."

Driving back to the border, we took turns recounting the dramas of the last two days, relishing the unpleasantness, shouting with laughter now that we were free.

Building up slowly to Jannie and the interrogation by the *dominee*, I mentioned Damien's gun pictures.

Mum said, "Why were you drawing guns?"

Damien explained that on the first morning he'd drawn a gun, and the boys had been so impressed that he'd spent the rest of his two days in classes churning them out. "Got *donnered* anyway," he mumbled.

"They were so good, Mum," said Lulu. "Three types."

"Five, actually," said Damien. "Perfect replicas. Even drew the pistol to scale."

"When did you see a pistol?" asked Mum.

"Not sure," muttered Damien. "Sometime."

"Didgy?" said Mum. "Come on."

"At Rassie's place," mumbled Damien.

"And then, Mum," I interrupted, "I got a note..."

"Hang on, Robbie," said Mum. "Damien, tell me about these guns."

A few weeks earlier, Damien had been at Jean's when he'd met Rassie Potgieter, a young farmer who'd paddled downstream from his farm on the South African side of the Limpopo. The conversation soon got around to guns.

"Got a hell of lot of guns," said Rassie.

"How many?" Damien asked.

"*Jirre.* Not sure anymore. A hell of a lot."

After a few drinks, Rassie agreed to show him, and Damien helped him paddle back up the Limpopo.

"There was a whole shed," said Damien. "Full of guns. Ten or twelve at least. Ammo for everything too."

Rassie had pointed out his personal favorites among his collection. "*Lekker,* hey? You want to shoot some?"

"*Ja.*"

For half an hour, Damien and Rassie had tested out guns.

"On what?"

"Trees," said Damien. "And birds. But *I* didn't shoot any of the birds," he added quickly. "And Rassie was drunk, so he kept missing."

"Drunk?" said Mum, her knuckles going white on the steering wheel.

"Well not actually *that* drunk," said Damien hastily. "But definitely drunk enough to miss the birds. I think," he continued after a thoughtful pause, "that he actually only got very drunk after he left me in the shed."

"He left you there?" said Mum. "By yourself?"

"He offered me a brandy," said Damien, "but I told him I wasn't allowed to drink."

"He left an eleven-year-old in a shed full of guns and ammunition?"

"*Ja,*" said Damien. "For ages, that's how come I can remember everything. But then I took a pistol and the R4 fully automatic assault rifle out onto the firing range to practice."

"Cripes," said Mum. "Maybe you'd be safer getting beaten up in Pikfontein."

"How can you say that, Mum?" I spluttered.

But Damien interrupted me. "No it's cool, Rob. Anyway I wouldn't get beaten up again. Next time, I'd definitely *donner* them."

Back at the house, Dad pronounced Damien's bruise "not serious."

Damien looked disappointed. "No scar?"

"Nope."

"I'll be emotionally scarred," I said.

"Nonsense," said Dad. "The only ones who might be are Jannie and Louisa. Spurned and beaten by two English *meisies*. Now come on, Robbie, it's all water under the dam."

Damien was banned from seeing Rassie. But otherwise life returned to normal. Before long Pikfontein came up in conversation only when Dad had run out of more creative ways to tease me.

"I'll send you off to Pikfontein. Marry you off to Jannie."

And I would seethe indignantly while Dad muttered that the whole thing had been worth it just for this. But Dad was relentless enough to tire even me. After a few weeks, I was too bored to protest.

"Well, I'll be damned," mused Dad. "Never thought you'd laugh about this. Told you it'd be character building. A glimmer of hope for your sense of humor yet. After what, only twelve years."

"Thirteen," I corrected him.

It was early 1994. In a few months South Africa would have its first democratic election. And in a small state to the southwest of us, trouble was brewing on Botswana's borders.

Bophuthatswana wasn't even a real state. Situated within South Africa's borders, and created, like all the other Bantustans of the apartheid regime, as a way to further segregate races, this "black state" or homeland had been given nominal independence by the South African government. By the rest of the world, however, it and other Bantustans were seen as puppets of the apartheid regime and not recognized as independent states. And now, in the run-up to the elections, the Bantustans were about to be officially reincorporated back into the new South Africa.

Fearful of being marginalized, Lucas Mangope, Bophuthatswana's longtime head of state, widely considered a stooge of the apartheid government, was resisting strongly. The Bophuthatswana Defense Force opened fire on protesting civil servants and, in a bid to restrict negative media coverage of his clampdown, Mangope closed several television and radio stations. Meanwhile, in a farcical twist, the Afrikaner Weerstandsbeweging, the staunchly right-wing white racist group, stepped in to support Mangope.

At the opposite end of the political spectrum, but equally fearful of marginalization, the AWB saw the clashes as an opportunity to preserve the old ways. It rallied its supporters, and armed AWB members got in their *bakkies* and set off to fight for the old South Africa.

In the Tuli Block, we watched South African news footage of AWB members caught on camera in Bophuthatswana. The AWB opened fire at people on the roadside. The police and, ironically, several lower-ranked soldiers of the Bophuthatswana Defense Force—now in some chaos—returned the fire, and three AWB members were shot and killed.

"Who do they think they are?" Dad fumed as we listened to interviews with the khaki-clad white men holding guns. "Arrogant sods. Why can't they just bloody accept what's happening in South Africa?"

"They must really live in another world," said Mum.

"Probably our part of the world," said Dad.

I said, "They look like the members of the Tuli Block Farmers' Association."

Everyone laughed. Then Mum put a hand over her mouth.

"No, that's unfair," she said. "Listen to us. We must stop talking like this. We're becoming as bigoted as they are. Keith, look what we're doing to our children. This is pure prejudice speaking."

Shocked by the killings of its members, the AWB quickly retreated from its humiliating mission, the news coverage died down, and the process of reincorporation continued successfully.

Several weeks later we heard word on the Tuli Block grapevine that Rassie and his friends had got back safely to their Limpopo farms.

"From?"

"Bophuthatswana."

"What? No! That's terrible."

"*Ja.* Those *okes* were hell of a lucky. *Jirre.* They could have been shot!"

Later, the clash was to be hailed as the end of military resistance to the new democratic South Africa.

22

SCHOOL

Nike and Robbie on the Land Cruiser

Passive resistance, however, remained and in some areas flourished. Months after the elections, in many of the small towns in the old Northern Transvaal—the new "Limpopo Province"—there was still no sign of the Rainbow Nation's rainbow.

In the Spar where we did our fortnightly grocery shopping, the black bag packers still looked just as scared of the white Afrikaans *tannies* at the tills, who still told them off like disobedient children. Some towns even continued to defiantly fly the old flag—as did Pikfontein Skool. And by 1995, the year I went to school proper, the Pikfontein Skool had remained steadfastly all white.

At the Bulawayo Dominican Convent, my new school, only about a third of the students were white. Which, as Mum liked to stress, was one of the reasons she was so pleased that I'd chosen the Convent. "It's all worked out so well," she'd been telling anyone curious about my sudden entry into the formal education system. "Just as I'd always planned."

"Really?" Less tactful friends expressed surprise to learn that Mum had had, all along, a plan for her children to go to school.

"Well, I *planned* that they would be the ones to choose when they wanted to go to school. And now Robbie has. Exactly when she was ready."

"Ah."

"And now we've been lucky enough to get her into the Convent. Which is a wonderful school. And has a much better racial balance than Girls' College."

This was Mum at her optimistic, backward-reasoning best.

A lack of options was, in fact, the main reason I was going to the Convent and not to Girls' College—the other private girls' school in Bulawayo, where several Phikwe friends were studying, and the obvious choice. And the reason I had no options was mainly because the sudden desire to go to school had possessed me at exactly the worst possible time—midway through the second year of high school, well into the syllabus, and long after the places had been filled.

Girls' College, discovering I hadn't been to school, did not even bother to interview me. "Sorry, we're completely full. Perhaps if you'd come a year and a half ago... maybe try again next year..."

The Convent, initially, was no different. I was eventually given an interview only because a friend in the Bulawayo horsey community, who'd given me several riding lessons, put in a good word for me with his mother, who was one of the teachers.

I knew no one at the Convent. All my friends, including Melaney, were at Girls' College, which, unlike the convent, was a proper boarding school. By then, however, I didn't care.

I was ecstatic. Once I had decided to go to school, I couldn't bear to wait another day. I'd suddenly had enough of homeschooling. I was desperate for structure, desperate for tests and exams, and desperate for classmates. I longed for homework.

"Just be yourself," Mum consoled as I fretted in the days before the interview. "Remember that there will be some differences between the syllabuses, and it's not what you know and don't know that matters so much as your whole approach to learning."

Unconvinced by this argument—even without Dad's doubtful smile—I began frantically revising the last year of my correspondence assignments. Until an even worse thought occurred to me, after which I spent the remaining time trying desperately to speed-read the Bible. "I'm never going to do it," I moaned, as Mum assured me all would be well. "The nuns will hate me."

So it was with some relief that I discovered my interviewer, the deputy headmistress, was not a nun. As the interview went on, I continued to relax, for despite the cross and biblical pictures on her office walls, Mrs. Joliffe seemed to be staying clear of the subject of God. Instead she talked a lot about the school, explaining with a soft voice and serious expression how they, at the Convent, prided themselves on being one of the top-performing schools in the country.

"You'd have to work very hard if you were accepted, Robyn."

I said I would. "I can't wait to have exams and homework."

Mrs. Joliffe gave me a quizzical gaze. "Really?"

"Really," I said. And when she still looked unconvinced, I added, "My friends at Girls' College think I'm strange."

"Indeed," said Mrs. Joliffe. "Well, you'd probably get even more homework here."

Then she asked me what achievements I was proudest of.

I said running a very profitable business selling free-range eggs, laid by rescued battery chickens, to buy a saddle.

Mrs. Joliffe's mouth twitched, and she looked down at the papers on her desk. Then she said she thought she'd asked me enough questions. Explaining that I must now do an exam, she handed me a pen and printed sheets of the rough ugly Zimbabwean paper, which was used for everything from immigration forms to shop receipts.

She wished me good luck, then left me in her office, with instructions to begin with the math paper.

Some of the topics I could do easily. With some, I didn't know where to begin.

As the problems I couldn't do stacked up, my stomach began to ache with panic. Suddenly I wished I'd had the chance to show off my limited biblical knowledge after all. I stared miserably at the cross—which provided no inspiration—and then at the *Veritas* school shield, which I would now never call my own.

"It's terrible," I mumbled, when Mrs. Joliffe returned to collect the paper. "Sorry."

"Well, let's not jump to conclusions," she said brightly. "And you've still got your English exam. Good luck, again."

"Thanks." I managed a weak smile as she left the office. I studied the cross again, gathering my thoughts. My only hope now, I decided, lay in a display of great moral fortitude.

It was on this basis that I carefully chose from the list of essay questions.

"Money is the root of all evil." Discuss.

I wrote quickly, outlining every evil of money and materialism I could think of. I explained how true happiness lay in things that could not be bought; how trying to buy happiness and power might beget evil. As all Mum's philosophical lectures and parables and big words came flooding back to me, I became increasingly compelled by my own argument. With every sentence I grew more confident and verbose.

It was only when I remembered to check the clock—and I realized that with minutes remaining, I'd completely forgotten really to discuss anything—that a flutter of panic returned. Of course, I hurriedly wrote, all the aforementioned depended on exactly how money was used.

Approaching footsteps echoed along the corridor, and I scribbled my concluding sentences: That money could, in fact, do great good . . . but only in the hands of the right people and institutions, such as nuns and convents. I considered an exclamation mark, but decided I'd probably been clear enough and put down my pen.

"You look happier," said Mrs. Joliffe, as she bustled around, stacking the papers.

"Well, I think my English exam was a considerable improvement."

"Excellent," she smiled. "I'm sure it's very good."

Afterward, though, away from the cross, in the bright light and noise of the bustling Bulawayo streets, I started to worry. "I was too blatant," I moaned.

"Well," mused Mum, "I suppose it could sound a tad over-done. Especially after you'd just explained how much you loved your egg business."

"I've ruined it."

"No, no." She smiled quickly. "I'm sure not. And actually, thinking about it now, on the positive side, it shows how keen you are. So either way, Robbie, it's probably a good thing."

W hat was made of it, I'd never know. But at the beginning of the next term, Mum was driving me up to Zimbabwe along with all the other Botswana teenagers returning to high school.

Just across the border, the city of Bulawayo was a favorite of Phikwe families, and there were several familiar faces ahead of us as we joined the crawling, many-hundred-long queue on the Zimbabwean side of Plumtree Border Post.

"Fingers crossed," said Mum, sighing. "Remember to smile."

Remembering to smile could be difficult. The agonizingly long wait in the dingy building, unpleasant in itself, was made worse by the near total uncertainty of what might happen when you eventually reached the official—by which time, you were usually grim with frustration and worry.

Wrong stamp, wrong visa, wrong form, wrong permit, wrong insurance.

On an average day, crossing the busy, inefficient Zimbabwean border would take an hour; on a very busy day it could take three. Occasionally, there were stories of people waiting all day in border post queues.

The only comfort came from watching busloads of people join the queue behind us; from knowing it could have been worse. But this lasted just until some unsociable person pushed past to the front. The whites in the queue would then scowl silently at each other. But they did no more, always leaving it to irritated black people to do the protesting.

Just a few hundred meters from Botswana, the atmosphere was as starkly different here as the flags and the forms. On the Botswana side, whites queue-jumped as much as anyone and quickly complained if anyone else did. Here, in front of edgy Zimbabwean border officials, no white dared draw attention.

But Zimbabwe still had the better high schools, and for most white Botswana parents, the hideous border crossings were a tolerable price to pay. Some read magazines. Most just whispered irritably as they checked and rechecked their forms. An incorrectly filled-out form could have you sent straight to the back again. I checked mine twice and then gave it to Mum to check once more.

Then I made faces at a small, smiling baby strapped to its mother's back that drew alongside us in the snake of the queue. The baby giggled and then coughed, its head lolling out the top of the tightly bound cloth. Fresh mucus seeped onto the dry yellow snot around its nostrils. The mother, who clutched a dark green Zimbabwean passport, began to cough too; a deep, wet, racking cough.

I wondered if she had TB.

Which would be ironic, I thought, as I gripped my hard-won new study visa and tried not to inhale too deeply.

I'd often been to Bulawayo for horse shows. I'd even lived in Bulawayo for a few months to improve my riding, bringing my correspondence work with me and boarding with Floss van Leeuwen, who'd taken me to horse shows and given me daily intensive riding lessons at her stables. This time, I would again be staying with Floss, as the Convent didn't have boarding facilities. Even the schools that did, like Girls' College, struggled to meet the demand from foreign students. Many stayed with friends or in private boarding houses, and Melaney Nevill and the Jolly

sisters, two other horsey friends from Phikwe studying at Girls'
College, would be boarding with me at Floss's.

But while before I'd come freely, now that I was officially
studying, paying school fees, I was a health hazard: acceptance
to the Convent, it turned out, was the easiest of the hurdles to getting a study visa. For final approval, I'd even needed an X-ray to
check for TB—which, I speculated as mother and baby coughed
simultaneously, I might well be about to catch in this airless border building.

Before I'd even arrived.

Then the queue and the sick woman shuffled on, two steps
closer to Zimbabwe and school.

Pikfontein Skool may have been an utterly foreign place,
but Pikfontein hadn't felt anything like a foreign town.

Barring the flags and the Afrikaans signs, northern South
Africa basically looked like Botswana. The cars, mostly Toyota
bakkies and shiny new Corollas, were the same, as were many
of the shops—Spar for groceries, PEP Stores for cheap clothes,
Woolworths for expensive ones. Botswana imported most of its
groceries from South Africa, so the shelves were stacked with the
same Koo jams, Simba chips, and Ouma biscuits, and with the
pula pegged a few percent above the rand, even the prices were
similar.

The ugly brown buildings of the Dominican Convent School
and Catholic Cathedral stood in the center of a city that felt,
smelled, and looked profoundly foreign.

Lining Bulawayo's impressively wide streets—wide enough,
Cecil Rhodes had insisted, for a wagon to complete a U-turn—
were shops with fading signs and names never seen farther south:
Meikles department store, TM supermarket, Solomons, all selling
locally made products priced in dollar amounts at least ten times
those in Botswana. In reality, goods were nearly ten times cheaper,
and people from Botswana loved shopping in Zimbabwe because
of the even more favorable exchange rate available on the black
market. This was operated from the pavements by hundreds of

money changers, waiting to take your foreign money in exchange for wads of Zimbabwean dollars, often craftily bulked out with ordinary paper for the unwary.

Outside the streets buzzed with more people, in more of a hurry.

Raggedly dressed curio sellers crowded many of the pavements, and whereas the placid Botswana vendors awaited inquiries, the Zimbabweans sprung out into your path, grinning madly, waving everything from intricate bead necklaces to two-meter wooden giraffes. If you claimed no money, they offered to trade for foreign goods—any foreign goods, as we'd discovered on one holiday in Victoria Falls when an eight-year-old Damien had vanished and reappeared barefoot, bareheaded, and staggering under the weight of a watermelon-size solid wood hippo.

Quoting inflated prices, these relentless salesmen pounced on all foreign cars, which were almost as recognizable by their age and make as by their number plate.

The vast majority of Zimbabwean cars were of a similar era and decrepitude to Jill Davies's old Datsun. Many were ancient Datsuns. Old Peugeots, Citroens, Morrises, and Fords were also common among the extraordinary specimens that rattled, listed, belched, ground, stalled, and generally begged for overdue retirement as they trundled along Bulawayo's streets.

In such company, it was quite something to stand out—a feat that Floss van Leeuwen's shabby Bedford truck nonetheless accomplished with aplomb.

Making full use of the spacious roads, its roar drowning all but the most chronically ill engines, the elephantine cream-colored truck dwarfed everything else. To park comfortably, it needed a good one and a half spaces. This was rare on busy Lobengula Street, which ran past the Convent, and Floss would often just stop the shuddering beast in the road, forcing other cars to drive around as she waited for me to emerge from afternoon lessons.

Back at Floss's stables, spoiled for choice, I'd spend all my spare time riding. I loved it. And, barring one exception, I couldn't believe my luck to live in a place with so many horses.

The exception was when the Bedford arrived at the Convent

piled high with yet another massive load of feed sacks and spiky hay bales.

Which meant the day's groceries would be in the front.

Which meant I had to clamber on top of the bales.

On these afternoons, I'd dash to the truck, scrambling on the back as quickly as possible. Installed thus, perched high on the mountain of hay, pieces of grass poking through my ugly light blue uniform, I'd do my best to avoid the gaze of my new classmates as they streamed out of the buildings. And as the engine roared and the Bedford rattled off in a cloud of smoke, I'd stare steadfastly ahead, reassuring myself that, all things considered, I was blending in quite well.

Later, as my classmates became close friends, I'd learn that the Bedford had paled in comparison to all the other odd things about me—most relating to the way I behaved in lessons. But to begin with, I was much too pleased to be there, and too absorbed by classroom novelties, to consider how different I might appear in nonmaterial respects.

Nor did I have much time to dwell on what everyone else made of me. The daily workload was high for everyone, and I had the extra task of revising past sections of the syllabus. At the end of my first term I'd be writing the same exam as everyone else, based on nearly two years' work I'd mostly missed.

It was a daunting task, and when I did occasionally come across something in which I was ahead of everyone else, I was delighted. Probability was one of these. I soon found I could rapidly answer questions that left everyone else blank-faced. The teacher praised my amazing grasp of the subject, and after lessons I was able to help my new friends with their homework.

"How do you know all this?"

"Roulette."

"Huh?"

"Designing systems to beat the house."

"A gambling system? To bet?"

"Yip. Usually variations of the old Laubouchere cancellation system. But we never used it. The zero gets you every time."

"Who's we?"

"My dad and I."

"Doesn't your mum mind?"

"Nope. She said it was good for my maths. She used to do it too."

"Aren't you too young?

"Are they addicts?"

A few girls laughed, and I suddenly noticed just how shocked everyone looked.

I felt my face going red. "No, no. It's not like that," I said. I hurriedly explained that I'd never actually been in a casino, that working on gambling systems was just one of Dad's hobbies, that he hadn't actually gambled since he'd first played systems in London casinos with Mum when she was still at university. But lately, as he'd become increasingly frustrated with his clinics, he had taken to getting out the small plastic roulette wheel and the sheets of calculations. I told the girls how I'd helped him: sitting in his upstairs study, looking out over the Tuli Block bushveld, spinning the wheel and poring over strings of odds and evens and reds and blacks and cursing the zero and the ceiling, which gets you every time.

Such odd areas of expertise were, however, fairly rare. And in math I had more gaps than any other subject. Despite this, math soon became my favorite lesson. For once I understood how something worked, the answer was all there: a full, perfectly satisfying conclusion to a problem, with no loose ends that couldn't be pursued.

In other subjects, there were suddenly unfamiliar limits. For the first time ever my questions were answered with, "You don't need to know that."

I was shocked. I kept trying. But after a few weeks, my waving hand was often just ignored. I persisted still. And then, about a month after I arrived, I was finally tackled by a teacher.

It was in a geography class, taught by a kind, if fierce, nun called Sister Ludgera. I'd asked her to explain one of the points on the blackboard. She'd replied, answering a different question altogether, and then proceeding straight to the next point.

I raised my arm. "No more questions," she said.

I stretched my arm even higher.

"Robyn," she snapped, "I've just said no more questions."

My desk was at the back of the room. Every girl in the class turned around to stare at me. Some smiled. Some looked scared.

"But you didn't actually answer the question I just asked," I said.

"I believe I did."

"Well, I don't understand your explanation."

Sister Ludgera, red-cheeked, looked at me in amazement. "Robyn," she said coldly, "you're going to have to learn to appreciate that this is a class of more than thirty other students, and I have a responsibility to teach you a syllabus. Just because *you* cannot understand something does not mean you can have it personally explained."

"Sister Ludgera," I replied, trying to steady my voice as I felt my own cheeks burning, "I'm sure no one else in the class understands what you just said." I looked around me. "Who understands?"

No one said anything. Suddenly everyone was looking down at their desks.

"Robyn!" said Sister Ludgera. "I am the teacher. No more questions!"

For the rest of the lesson, resolving never to speak to her again, I stared, amazed and furious, at my desk. The greater shock, however, was still to come, over lunch, in the large junior schoolyard across the road.

"I can't believe it," I fumed, as six of us sat down around one of the shady concrete tables. "She wouldn't even listen to what I was asking."

"Why do you care, though?"

"Because it's so unjust."

"Teachers can be like that. Forget it. No point fighting."

I tried to argue, but was totally outnumbered.

One by one, every girl provided why-not-to-bother-to-fight examples from their school lives. Some pointed to the windows of the classrooms in which a biased, grumpy, or unthinking teacher had inflicted some memorable injustice—a withering remark, a slighted suggestion, an undeserved punishment, a damning comparison. Often it was just once, and often it was petty. But that, and seeing it happen to others, had been enough.

I was stunned, and indignant on behalf of my friends. Having always wondered if I was missing out by not going to school, this, for me, was a small epiphany. I couldn't imagine what it would feel like, not being bothered to fight, in a school, for the principle of understanding.

Deeply relieved that my spirit of protest was intact—and resolved to preserve it—I left that lunch hour fiercely determined not ever to let my teachers get to me.

Mrs. Burrows, one of our English teachers, was among my favorites.

Relevant to the syllabus or not, she loved discussing books, and when she spoke of them, her sorrowful face would light up with a huge grin, which reminded me a bit of Granny Betty. Of all the teachers, she was also the most tolerant of my endless questions and opinions. For this, alone, I liked her.

But Mrs. Burrows gravitated to angst, and in literature-related discussions of the human condition, the family condition, and the female condition, she tended to dwell on the problems considerably more than the joys.

One day she arrived in class carrying a large stereo. In it, she explained, was a tape recording of Celine Dion's "Because You Loved Me," which she was going to play as a sad example of how women could lose their sense of self-worth by caring too much about the opinion of the opposite sex.

She pressed play, and for a few minutes the mournful song filled the room.

"Isn't this amazing?" sighed Mrs. Burrows, as Celine crooned her last impassioned lines.

Several girls nodded understandingly.

The tone set thus, there followed a discussion on female teenage insecurities. In a class of more than thirty fourteen- and fifteen-year-old girls, most of whom had been at the Convent since the age of six, she had no trouble soliciting animated participation. The examples lasted until the bell, and obviously deciding we all had a lot more to say, Mrs. Burrows assigned for home-work an essay in which we could further delve into our demons.

Then she hurried out of the room, leaving on the blackboard one precisely written line: *"What I don't like about myself." Discuss.*

Later, as I studied the irritatingly leading question, I thought of Mum and how she invariably saw the best in everything. Then of Dad, who whenever I lost my fledgling sense of humor, grinned mockingly and sang his favorite Bing Crosby, "Ac-Cent-Tchu-Ate the Positive."

I opened my exercise book and wrote the date and a title.

At the end of the next lesson, as we handed in our books, I told Mrs. Burrows that I personally believed the best way to deal with our problems was to think about all the good things instead. If she wanted to give me zero out of twenty, I'd obviously be upset. However, I explained, zero was nevertheless preferable to writing such a potentially psychologically destructive essay.

"All right, Robyn," she said, looking alarmed. "I'll mark whatever you've written."

"Thank you," I replied, trying not to show my relief. In truth I would have much rather written her essay than get a zero. Tri-umphant that my bravado had paid off, I left quickly.

At the door I turned round to see Mrs. Burrows gazing, bewildered, at my open book. I would get one of the best marks in the class for my essay on "What I like about myself."

What the convent liked about me, I only discovered several months later.

The revelation occurred in the most unlikely setting of a Reli-gious Education lesson, which, with my dismal Bible knowledge, was undoubtedly my worst subject.

When Sister Brunhilda, the German num who taught us RE, announced one of her spot tests, I would feel ill.

Her tests consisted of asking each girl, out loud, a single dif-ferent question. For which she would award either "Zero," "Von half," or "Von."

The questions were of wildly varying difficulty, and whether anyone passed was mostly down to luck. Or, in a few cases, how in favor they were—the only reason I generally scraped through with at least "Von half."

"*Ja*, Hobbin," she said, smiling warmly at me, "Vat can you tell me? Ah, yes. I have it. Vas it twelve or ten apostles?" She raised her hand abruptly to the outraged mutters of "Easy." "*Ja!* be quiet. My little ruffians."

And despite themselves, everyone laughed. Sister Brunhilda tweaked her habit, smoothing her skirt, and gazed around the room with twinkling eyes and a superior grin. It was the same grin she wore on the regular occasions she reminded us how when she was a young woman in Germany, she could have been a model, but she'd instead chosen to be a nun.

"Twelve," I said, uncertainly.

"Very good, Hobbin."

She gave me a lingering, indulgent smile. Then her face grew stern. Shaking her head and wagging her finger, she spun around to face one of my cheekiest friends. "*Ja*, Tiffany McGaw," she said. "Ze real ruffian. Ah, now you can tell me vat vas the name of the father of Joseph. And vat did he do?"

Toward the middle of the first term, Sister Brunhilda arrived in class and announced that the theme of today's lesson would be mothers and fathers. "And ve are all going to talk about our own lovely parents," she said. "*Ja!* Such important people in our lives."

Having picked on several girls, she nodded impatiently as they each described what their parents did. Then, grinning, she turned to me.

"Now, Hobbin," she said, "tell us all about your father. He is a doctor, no?"

"A flying doctor," I corrected her. "But he's sold his plane now."

"*Ja*," she said, casting her beaming gaze around the class. "But he is not just that. He is also a missionary doctor!"

"No, he's not," I corrected her, too surprised to think through my answer. "He charges for consultations."

"Vot?" Sister Brunhilda looked at me, uncomprehending.

"Eighty pula now," I explained. "The same for every patient. Cash only."

She stared at me silently, so I continued.

"He used to do medical aid. But that didn't really work, because patients in Botswana expect immediate results. If one doctor's medicine doesn't work quickly, they go straight off to another one, and keep hopping from one private doctor to the next. So the health insurance companies get sticky about paying out. My father just decided the admin was too much."

But Sister Brunhilda wasn't really listening.

"Hobbin," she said slowly. "Are you saying your father takes money from all ze poor, sick people in the villages?"

Meeting her incredulous gaze, I suddenly thought of my rapid acceptance; my money-is-the-root-of-all-evil entrance essay; my mysteriously favorable treatment in RE.

I felt dizzy with panic. I was going to be expelled for misleading nuns.

"Well, yes, he does charge," I said hastily, "but his patients could go to the free government hospitals. They choose to go to a private doctor. And anyway, many people in the villages have lots of cattle and aren't so poor."

Sister Brunhilda continued to look gently devastated.

"And he offers another service," I added. "He's a dispensing doctor. And there aren't pharmacies in most of the villages where he has clinics. So if he didn't go there, people would have to travel really far to get their medicines."

Sister Brunhilda began to speak but lost her words. The class was absolutely quiet; the silence terrible.

"Also," I spluttered, "the medicines are included in the consultation fee. Which my dad calls socialist medicine because all the hypochondriacs, who are often the wealthier patients, subsidize poor people who only visit when they're really sick." I fixed Sister Brunhilda with an earnest gaze. "And so my father actually *loses* money on the really sick poor people who need lots of medicines."

Sister Brunhilda smiled weakly. "*Ja*, Hobbin. Thank you. I think now ve vill hear from somebody else."

For weeks afterward, when I saw a nun in the corridors I

looked at the floor and skulked quickly past along the walls. When I saw Sister Angela, the headmistress, I fled. But I was not expelled. And by the end of term, when we had one of our final lessons on the theme of religious initiation rituals, Sister Brunhilda was even gracing me with the occasional smile.

"Now every one of you vill have been through zese," she said. "All religions have them. Us Catholics. Other Christians." She paused, and looked around the class. "And Muslims and Hindus too," she added, looking pointedly at the handful of girls in these categories. "I am right. Yes, of course I am right. I know zese things. Has anyone not been baptized? Or done something like baptism in zer religion? No. I thought not. Now…"

Then her smile disappeared. "Ah, vat? Hobbin? No!"

Everyone turned around. I dropped my arm.

Sister Brunhilda let out a startled little cough. She stared at me wide-eyed. Then she said, "Hobbin, are you sure? For certain? Never? No!"

"Definitely," I said. "Or my brother and sister. My mother wanted us to choose what we wanted to be when we were old enough to decide."

"Oh, really?" Sister Brunhilda looked genuinely shocked.

"And I haven't decided yet."

Sister Brunhilda blinked and shook her head. Her face was full of pity. But apparently too overcome to pursue the devastating discovery, she went on with the lesson, during which she made several pointed references to purgatory.

But concerns about purgatory were dwarfed by renewed expulsion panic.

I consulted Tiffany, who'd previously assured me I would not be expelled just for not being a missionary's daughter.

"Well, I've never heard of anyone being expelled for this," she said, uncertainly. "You get expelled for drinking or smoking or getting pregnant."

"So I'll be okay?"

"I suppose." She looked unconvinced. "But I've also never heard of anyone who wasn't baptized getting in here. Maybe you should just quickly get done and tell her it was a mistake."

"I don't want to do that."

Tiffany shrugged. "Bulawayo's so small, she'd probably find out anyway. So dunno what you should do." She smiled at me. "Pray, maybe?"

I did nothing and prepared to gallantly take the worst. Later that week, looking purposeful, Sister Brunhilda cornered me in the gloomy corridor.

"Hello, Sister," I said, swallowing.

Sister Brunhilda gave me a fond smile and patted me on the arm. "Vel. Hobbin," she said sweetly, "I have been thinking about zis baptism. Now I am quite sure zat you are really old enough to decide now." She paused, fixing me with her piercing blue eyes. Then she said, "And I vanted to recommend that you choose to be a Catholic. Ve have so much to offer."

Suddenly my small but crucial power dawned on me. I looked at her earnestly. "I know, Sister," I said.

"And it vould be so easy, Hobbin. You could go for lessons here and be baptized in ze cathedral. It's just across the road, you know." She gestured in the direction of the ugly brown cathedral where the school sometimes went for mass. "Beautiful place. So restful."

"It is, Sister."

"Vel, the sooner the better. Ve could start your lessons straight away. This week?"

"But it's nearly exams," I said, squirming. "You wouldn't want me to fail."

"Ja! No." She looked shocked. "You vould never fail for devoting time to God! Just a few hours a week ... very simple ..."

Sister Brunhilda's eyes sparkled with pleasure. I couldn't help liking her, even when she was trying to be a missionary.

I said, "I need more time to decide. All I really know for certain right now is that I don't want to be a born-again Christian. Or a Jehovah's Witness. Or a member of the Dutch Reformed Church in South Africa, where all our neighbors go. But I definitely wouldn't entirely rule out considering Catholicism. At some stage."

Sister Brunhilda opened her mouth to speak.

"And," I interrupted, "as my mother always says, you should

wait till you're really sure, till you really want something, to decide. Then you appreciate it more. And if I did choose to be a Catholic, you'd want me really to appreciate being one. Wouldn't you?"

"*Ja*, of course. But—"

"You see," I continued, starting to enjoy myself, "that's what happened with school. My mother let us all decide when we wanted to go. And where we wanted to go. And I only decided this year. But that's why I love the Convent so much. It's because I took so long to decide and because I waited till I was completely sure. And choosing your religion, Sister, has to be more important than choosing your school."

"No, of course!"

"So," I said apologetically, "it's obviously going to take me at least a bit longer. But I promise I'll let you know as soon as I do."

For a few moments, Sister Brunhilda eyed me with a mixture of despair and profound frustration. Then she sighed, cocked her head, and smiled. "Vel, Hobbin, I am sure zat ve are all very pleased to have you with us here."

LULU AND DAMIEN

Robbie, Lulu, and Damien in the rapids

Back on the farm for the long Christmas holidays, Mum studied my report with a look of mild disbelief. "Well, I never!" she said thoughtfully. "This is fascinating."

"Good, hey? Told you I worked hard."

Mum frowned. "You know, of course, Robbie, that it doesn't matter where you come in class… only that you do the best you can do…"

I rolled my eyes.

Mum returned to the report. "But, nevertheless, this is still amazing."

"Why are you looking so surprised?"

"Well," said Mum, "to tell you the truth, I had no idea how

you'd fare against your peers. And now don't be offended by this, but I always thought you three were all, well, rather average."

"What?"

Mum smiled gently. "But now I see I must have judged you too harshly.... Not being a trained teacher, I just didn't really know what to expect of children your age.... Fascinating... look at this, Keith."

Dad examined the little white booklet. "Very good," he said. "Personally, I reckon your most impressive achievement is being not a baptized daughter of not a missionary and still getting Sister Brunhilda's seal of approval. *'Hobbin has shown commendable interest and done vel.'* Vel indeed!"

I said, "She's hoping I'll become a Catholic."

Dad said, "Well, if things carry on as they are, I might become a missionary doctor first." He smiled grimly. "Don't get so many of my profitable hypochondriacs these days."

A week later, Damien, who'd decided to go to school just a few months after me, returned to the farm for his Christmas holidays.

We had dinner by candlelight outside, in the new thatched gazebo beside the pool: all five of us together again for the first time in six months, the longest we'd ever all been apart.

Mum was beaming uncontrollably, looking from face to face.

Dad said, "Just when I thought I was getting rid of the little blighters."

"Keith!"

"If you want them closer, Lin, we can always send them to Pikfontein."

Damien mumbled, "I could definitely *donner* them now."

Dad said, "Don't mumble, lad."

"Sorry," grunted Damien.

Mumbling and grunting were both part of Damien's new heightened coolness from school, and for the first few days after his return, we barely understood a word he said.

When Damien had suddenly announced he wanted to go to school, Mum, being Mum, at once said of course. The only thing she cared about was that he didn't go to Zimbabwe, where she felt the old-fashioned, ultra-disciplined all-boys schools would bring out the worst in Damien's "potentially rebellious nature."

Dad's old school in Grahamstown in South Africa she dismissed, too, as being of a similar ilk. Dad, who didn't usually feel so strongly about our education, agreed.

"Look how badly I turned out," he said.

Mum said, "Give me a bit of time, I'll think of something."

Which Mum, as Mum always managed to do, did.

In this case, she thought of it listening to a South African radio program that was featuring a new progressive school in the Franschhoek wine lands in the Cape. The syllabus was flexible and practically oriented, the classes were small, and there were no uniforms.

The moment the program finished, Mum picked up the phone and called the school. A few weeks later Damien was enrolled at Bridge House. Undaunted by the fact that the school had no boarding facilities, and—unlike in Bulawayo—knowing no one in the town, Mum enlisted the help of the headmaster, who sent a circular to the parents, asking if anyone would be prepared to let a boy from Botswana board with them. Three families offered, and we flew to Cape Town to choose Damien's new "parents."

Now back from his first term, Damien said little about it, except for mumbling, "School's *kif*," as he hitched up his new enormous shorts.

He walked a few paces, and the shorts redescended.

"*Sis*, Didge," said Lulu. "We can see your undies."

"So."

I said, "At least he has an incentive to change them now."

Mum said, "Damien's just making up for lost time of not being cool."

Damien's report said things like, "Very bright, but could try harder."

"You should try harder, then," I admonished.

"Why?" he mumbled. "I pass. And I don't want to be a *boffin* like you."

"Don't mumble. And I'm not a *boffin*. And you shouldn't care so much what other people think."

Damien grinned mildly. "I don't, Rob. I just prefer practicing roller hockey."

Lulu said, "You care about looking cool."

Dad said, "Will you three stop ruining the bloody peace."

Every nonclinic evening, as the sun sunk large and golden over the bush, we'd walk or drive down the dusty road to the banks of the Lotsane, where we'd clamber into the boats and paddle up the still water. If the light was right, the water was a perfect mirror: the lush, elegant trees inverted back down, the ripples of the boat in the center creating small waves in the orangey watery sky.

The trees were growing, too. Now, at last, after one false start, they had water all year round. The first dam on the Lotsane, built by Actually Festus, had been quickly and completely washed away. Dad had said philosophically, "Rather the dam than the house." And unperturbed, he'd set about building a bigger and better one. The new dam was splendid—reinforced by solid concrete buttresses, with large gabions to stabilize the banks, the wire cages bulging with massive immovable rocks—holding water that backed up the winding river for nearly a kilometer.

Fiddian Green no longer had to trek to the Limpopo when his pool dried up.

From the dam wall, we'd paddle upstream until we reached the sharp bend in the river, where the bottom of the canoes scraped against barely submerged rocks, and the water ended in a great expanse of flat granite rock that swept up the right bank. Here we'd clamber out onto the warm stone, sipping drinks in the last of the light and studying the water for crocs.

This rocky vantage point was also the planned site of Dad's next dam.

"When it's full," he said, sweeping his hand up the river, "we'll have three kilometers of water. Imagine that, chaps. Imagine the tree growth."

Striding up and down the rocks, talking to no one in particular, Dad explained why the location of the wall was perfect for holding the most water and at the same time preventing eddies gouging out the bank and eating around the wall. He smiled as he spoke and gesticulated, all the deepening marks of strain from his work vanishing here, down by the river, where the tonic of the bush was at its most potent.

The smell of dust and the pungent scent of waterbuck somewhere nearby lingered in the air. In the trees opposite, vervet monkeys chatted nosily, peering down at us, shaking the leaves as they sprang between branches. Far upstream, a lone kudu, legs slightly splayed, drank from a pool in the golden sand soon to be concealed by Dad's new grand dam's waters. Downstream, perched on rocks that poked above the water, brilliant white egrets stared languidly at the surface, where fish plopped and darted, eating and avoiding being eaten. The eyes and snout of a crocodile appeared briefly, and then sank below again.

After months away, it was newly breathtaking: vividly and profoundly beautiful, peaceful but bursting with life, which was ferocious but fragile and delicately but perfectly balanced. Around us here was an entire intense world, fiercely present, where past and future were all but irrelevant.

On Lulu, Damien, and me, as on Dad, the world worked its magic too: smoothing the readjustments needed when best friends and ever-present companions are suddenly not there, and then, suddenly, back again. Day by day, it coaxed us gently back into life and friendship as before: I stopped prattling about loving school, Damien grunted less and adopted his old shorts, and Lulu ceased lamenting that Damien and I had changed.

The farm was a small bubble that dispelled the concerns and hang-ups of the world beyond. And it was the river, its most exquisite epicenter, that catalyzed the final shedding of our new brittle skins.

It was about two weeks after we'd been reunited, and we'd lingered later than usual in the canoes, watching from the water as the first stars appeared. By the time we glided to a stop, the plastic edges of the boats nudging the dam wall, it was almost completely dark.

We began to clamber out onto the wall. Except for Damien, who didn't move.

"I just have to go back and do something."

"What?"

"Nothing." He dug his paddle into the water, swinging his small canoe around.

"It's dark."

"I'll be quick," said Damien. And then the splashing of paddles, and his little red canoe, black in the gloom, disappeared around the bend in the river.

"Watch out for crocs."

"And hippos."

Five minutes later, Damien paddled back out from the darkness. He carried nothing. He refused to explain what he'd gone to do.

It took all four of us hours to coax it out of him.

"There was a drowning moth," he said sheepishly. "I went to rescue it."

Lulu and I grinned, speechless with delight and admiration.

"Was just a moth." Damien blushed. "Was nothing."

About school, Damien and I did agree on one thing. It was boring.

Not all the time; maybe just a few hours a day. Not enough to ruin the good parts. But often it was, without doubt, boring.

And this was a novelty. In a decade of homeschooling, we'd never known boredom, and never noticed its absence, until it became part of daily routine. Only now, back together, and lost once more in perpetually engaging hours, did I first become conscious of the privilege of never being bored.

Some of the time, as ever, we occupied ourselves, with our

own things: riding, tearing apart engines, reading for hours in the gazebo, lost in great books.

But the best hours, as they'd always been, were together.

For under Mum's gentle stewardship, Lulu, Damien, and I had become skilled professionals in the art of being endlessly thrilled. Now, even as teenagers, we quickly remixed the cocktail of imagination and invention that had given us ten years of shared amusement and adventures.

On this intoxicating brew, we'd traveled far and wide and with ceaseless variety.

Even when we'd left the Space Game behind in Selebi, the mix of machines, animals, and bush, albeit in a lower fantasy form, had continued to dominate our days. Arriving in the Tuli Block, we all at once learned to drive the ancient, virtually brakeless Land Cruiser, giving us our greatest group mobility to date. Taking turns at the wheel, Lulu's head barely reaching over the dashboard, we'd hurtle around the farm roads with nominal objectives like looking for poachers or game viewing or checking on the horses. But mainly, as ever, we just enjoyed being out together in the vast, varied bush, talking and arguing and never knowing upon what we might stumble.

Back together on the farm, in the Cruiser, steaming down the Limpopo road, it was comforting to know that nothing had really changed.

"I told you, Rob," yelled Damien. "*Quick* with the clutch when you release."

The Cruiser's broken synchromesh ground horribly.

"I *was* quick," I shouted back, accelerating with a jolt.

Damien sat in the passenger seat, his arm crooked casually on the window. Lulu perched between us. On her lap, she clutched Nike the Jack Russell—Nike because of the kinked tick shape made by her tail—who snapped at insects hurtling through the frame of the glassless windshield.

A hundred meters in front of us, an impala dashed across the road.

Nike howled. "Watch out," screamed Lulu.

I braked savagely, and stalled. "Lulu, *man*. It's miles away."

"Chill, Lu," said Damien. "Chill, Rob,"

Now, watched eagerly by Lulu and Damien, turning the key, coaxing the erratic ignition, I felt the same mild performance panic I used to feel in Selebi turning the key in the 50cc Honda Melody scooter. Damien had unearthed the scooter in Grandpa Ivor's shed, languishing there since the days when he and his pilots used to ride it to the airport. Having taken it to pieces, Damien managed to get it more or less working. But the carburetor was rusted open at full throttle, so we had to drive it with one hand on the key, alternating, terrifyingly, between on and off full throttle.

The Land Cruiser was a less scary, equally temperamental reincarnation of the Melody.

Restarting, I reground the gears.

"Jees, Rob," said Lulu, "even I can double declutch perfectly now."

"I'm out of practice," I snapped. "I can't drive in Bulawayo."

Damien said, "I'm out of practice too. Hasn't affected me."

"Yeah, Rob," said Lulu.

I said, "Anyway, you're the one who nearly drove it into the river."

A few months before, Lulu had started the Land Cruiser, in a panic, on a bank by the Limpopo. Keller had just jumped into the deep water, and Lulu was hoping the sound of the engine would lure her out. Instead, because the brakes didn't work, as soon as she took it out of neutral—forgetting to put stones behind the wheels—the *bakkie* rolled backward, avoiding hitting Mum and plunging into the river only because of a fortuitously placed molope tree.

Lulu said, "I forgot about the brakes."

"Well, I forgot about the clutch."

We bickered amicably until we reached the dam wall. Then we parked the Cruiser and walked to the bank to check for crocs. The Limpopo was now flowing strongly with the late end-of-year rains, and soil-laden water splashed noisily over the two-meter wall, swirling and churning at the base.

We were in luck.

Toward the middle of the wall, on the downstream side, a small croc clung to one of the sloping concrete buttresses. The foot-wide buttress rose against the wall at a 60-degree angle, and the croc faced upward, its mouth gaping into the water that poured over the top. It was the laziest, cleverest fishing imaginable. We watched in admiration as two glinting fish flopped over the wall and into the crocodile's open jaws.

After about ten minutes, the croc slid backward off the wall and disappeared in the orange foam. There was no sign of any others. The midmorning sun, glinting blindingly off the water, was starting to make the air uncomfortably warm and sticky.

"It's too hot. Let's go back."

"Let's hypnotize Lu," suggested Damien as we clambered back up the bank.

"Noo," said Lulu. "You just want to laugh at me."

Damien grinned. "So. Anyway, you like it."

"You can drive back," I offered.

Lulu thought about it for a moment. "Okay."

Mum liked to tell people, "I attribute my kids' ability to amuse themselves, to a large extent, to not having a TV... by the time we eventually got a TV, you know, they were all older. They understood the value of getting out and doing stuff. Trying things themselves. Being creative. Rather than just vegetating in front of that terrible box."

I was thirteen when we'd eventually got a TV.

At the end of the hypnotist's show, it said on the screen: *Do not attempt anything you have seen during this show at home.*

Damien said, "Let's try it."

Our cousin Michael, Henry's son, was visiting from Cape Town.

"*Kif, man,*" he said. He leaped to his feet. "Bet you can't do me."

A few days after he'd arrived, Michael already had a big bandage on his hand. Damien had been showing him how to build a tennis ball cannon out of empty tin cans welded on top of each other. In the thrill of firing the first ball, Michael had forgotten Damien's instructions; setting off the cannon with the apparatus pointing sideways instead of upward, and in the process blowing off part of his thumb.

Selecting Lulu's double bed for the experimental site, we took turns swinging her necklaces in front of each other's eyes, giggling and feigning collapse.

"Your eyes are getting heavier and heavier," we said, imitating the slow, seductive voice of the hypnotist.

"Your eyelids are starting to feel like lead," I said to Lulu. "You are so tired," I repeated, for the fifth time, getting bored. My own eyes wandered to the crimson-breasted shrikes hopping in the branches outside. "You're so tired, Lu. You're feeling very, very relaxed."

Lulu nestled back into her pillow, smiled, and rolled her eyeballs to the top of her head. Then she closed her eyes.

"Ha, ha, Lu. Very funny."

"Lu?"

Grinning beatifically at the ceiling, Lulu didn't stir.

Michael and Damien stopped talking. Michael poked her. "Hey, Lu?"

Nothing. Inspired by a scene from the hypnotist show, I told Lulu that she was now a tiny baby again. She immediately curled up and started making funny half sucking, half gulping noises, almost like she was drowning.

I said, "I'm getting Mum and Dad."

I found them upstairs.

"I think Lu's hypnotized," I panted. "We were watching this hypnotist show and then we tried it out and then she rolled her eyes when I was swinging the necklace... now she thinks she's a baby and she's doing something really weird."

"Really?" said Dad calmly. "Well, let's take a look."

He and Mum came downstairs and examined Lulu, who was still curled up, sucking and gulping. Dad scratched his chin thoughtfully.

"You're right, Robbie," he said. "She's definitely hypnotized. That's exactly how it was when she was feeding, as Mum had so much milk. You all had to gulp more than suck. Very impressive. No one could ever do me, you know."

"She looks so happy," said Mum. "Really takes me back. But I suppose you should wake her up."

Eyes gleaming, Michael and Damien protested. Dad gave them a warning look, and I crouched down beside Lulu.

"You are not a baby anymore," I said, returning to a solemn, though now wavering, voice. "You've had a lovely sleep. But now you're going to wake up again... slowly, very slowly, your eyes are going to open..."

Lulu shifted, uncurled herself, and blinked, her big brown eyes wide with sleepy wonder.

"That was nice," she said. "Can I go again?"

"No," said Mum. "Not yet, at least." She turned to me. "Robbie, come with me."

I followed her up to the study, where she dug around in the large "alternative" section of the bookshelves and retrieved a book on hypnosis. She handed it to me. "When you understand a bit more about it," she said, "then you can have another go."

I finished the book in a day. It was fascinating: what you can do; what you can't; how to build in safeguards; the theory of hypnosis, in which the critical logical left side of the brain is temporarily suspended; and the long and sometimes venerable history of the technique, which, in the nineteenth century, when the early anesthetics first came out, was seen as conventional anesthesia, while the new chemical anesthetics were sometimes viewed with suspicion.

Then I began to practice on Lulu, who eagerly volunteered as a guinea pig. Damien, now that I'd succeeded once, didn't want me to go near him. He also resented me for having managed to put Lulu under, where he had not, and he came to observe the first session with a look of sulky disinterest.

By the end of it, he was grinning. "Bossy and determined," he announced, "that's all it is. That's why you're so good at it, Rob."

Based on the book, I devised a self-imposed code of good hypnotic practice: always briefing Lulu on what I was going to do, always building in a trigger so she would wake up if something upset her. With that in place, we tried out all the hypnotist tricks, and spent hours aching with laughter at the extraordinary effects of selectively numbed consciousness.

"The number seven has gone from your vocabulary. Gone from your mind."

Lulu nodded.

"Seven is utterly gone. Okay."

Another nod.

"Okay. Now count your fingers."

Making two fists, Lulu obediently lifted her fingers. "One, two, three, four, five, six, eight, nine, ten... eleven." She frowned, uncertainly. "Eleven?... No!"

"Count each hand and then add them up."

She counted, and added. "Ten. Weird! That's so weird," she mused, half frowning, half smiling.

The permutations were endless, and Lulu was a willing, if bemused, marionette.

It was sorely tempting to overstep ethical boundaries.

"No, Didge," I said, again and again, as Damien grinned mischievously at his suggestions. "We have to do this properly. This is not a joke," I'd add gravely.

But once, when I went to the loo in the middle of a long session, Damien fetched a piece of biltong—chewy salted strips of dried meat that Dad occasionally made from the kudu or impala he shot, mainly to feed our staff, once every few months.

"Delicious," Damien said to Lulu as she lay on the couch. "You love biltong. Here, have some."

Lulu said, "No. I'm a vegetarian. You know I don't eat biltong. Go away."

Then she sat up suddenly, crying at the memory of such a close encounter with flesh.

When I came back, Damien was white. "I'll never do it again," he was promising a distraught Lulu. "Don't cry. You didn't even eat any anyway. But sorry I tried to make you. I'll never do it again... but I just thought you might like it if you tried it... and it wasn't a cow. A kudu. Shot humanely in the wild, so not so bad..."

D ad said, "Will you three keep it down in the back! We're not far from Pikfontein. I can take you there instead."

Lulu immediately howled with laughter. Shaking uncontrollably, she gently thudded her forehead against the back of Dad's headrest.

Our intended destination was Johannesburg, where Damien was getting a flight back to school for the start of the January term.

"Sorry," I said, as Lulu spluttered into silence.

In the backseat, we were hypnotizing Lulu to pass the time on the five-hour drive. In the front, Mum and Dad had put on a CD of Beethoven's Fifth Piano Concerto, one of their favorites.

A few minutes later, Dad said, "Who wants to give me a shoulder massage?"

Another burst of giggles drowned the beautiful music. Lulu clutched her stomach. "I need to wee again," she spluttered.

Mum turned to the back with a stern face. "Come on, now. This is really enough now."

Lulu met Mum's eyes, her lips trembling. Then her face cracked into an insane grin. She dissolved once more, choking and hiccupping and slapping her thighs. Mum tried not to laugh, contorting her face with the strain. She gave up, wiping her shining eyes and shaking her head helplessly.

I'd earlier whispered to Lulu that Mum and Dad were the two funniest people in the world; that nothing they said could fail to be anything but hysterically amusing.

Dad said, "Not you too now, Lin. About jolly time you kids left home—"

But Lulu cut him short. Peals of high, sweet laughter filled the car. Mum, Damien, and I joined in, fueling Lulu's hysterics.

Dad reached for the volume and turned Beethoven full blast.

But we kept laughing. Then Dad's shoulders shook too. In the rearview mirror I saw a tear run down his cheek, and his helpless wheezes soon joined the din.

Only when Dad pulled up under a tree for a "widdle stop"

did he successfully restore calm. I quickly unhypnotized Lulu, and we dashed into the scratchy bushes, shifting our bottoms uncomfortably and envying Damien and Dad.

Here, we didn't even think to look for snakes. Ready, even as we widdled, to run for the car, we peeked above the grass and watched the passing cars for signs of slowing down.

We'd already passed the first national road sign reading, "WARNING! YOU ARE NOW ENTERING A HIGH-RISK AREA FOR HIJACKING."

This was the higher-adrenaline South African equivalent of crossing the Zimbabwean border post. I felt a similar relief of safe passage as I jumped back in the car and locked the door. Dad said, "Why're you hurrying? No one's ever going to hijack a hearse."

Which was exactly what our new car looked like. It was a double-cab *bakkie*, with extra darkly tinted windows for the bright Botswana sun. To carry his large medicine trunks, Dad had ordered an extra long canopy, to be made and fitted by a company in Johannesburg that normally converted expensive saloon cars into stretch limousines. When we'd arrived to collect our newly modified car, parked in a huge workshop among absurdly long Mercedes, we'd stopped dead in surprise at the effect. "Sherbet, Keith," said Mum, "what an irony. Don't know whether to laugh or cry." Dad said, "Well, at least its resale value will go up."

In Johannesburg, we had a day's shopping before Damien's flight.

Damien agreed solemnly to wear sun protection and take the vitamin pills that Mum bought him. In return, Mum reluctantly agreed to buy him a new pair of even bigger jeans. The moment he put his new jeans on, he grew cooler and gruntier again.

At the airport, Dad said, "They won't let you on the plane like that, lad. Pull up your *broeks*."

Damien shifted his trousers slightly. "Bye."

We said good-bye awkwardly, still not used to good-byes.

Apart from Christmas and Easter, Damien and my holidays didn't overlap, and we wouldn't all be together again for months.

Lulu wept.

"Good luck with roller hockey, Didge," I said. "Work hard."

"Good luck with your business plan, Rob," said Damien. "And please try to chill."

MUM

M~um~

Mum said, "Bernard is never going to forgive me for this one."

It was now more than a year since I'd started school. On the way back up to Bulawayo for the beginning of the new term, Mum and I had stopped in Phikwe at Jean Kiekopf's house. Jean, who was a good friend of Mum's, lay on her back, on the bed, smiling peacefully. Hypnotized.

The curtains were closed to mute the sparkling midmorning sun, but a few beams streamed through the gaps, illuminating the room in restful half-light. Mum and I perched on chairs beside the bed.

"*Shhh*, Mum," I hissed. "Concentrate."

I was impatient to finish quickly so I could do my preschool stationery shopping. I was also stressed by the responsibility of the task before me. I'd done sleeping problems, eating problems, excessive worrying. But I'd never yet, in my occasional role as self-taught semiprofessional hypnotist, ventured this far.

Mum whispered, "It's probably a good thing you're not actually going to be there. It'll be bad enough with me. I don't really think poor Bernard would cope with a fifteen-year-old gate-crashing his op."

Bernard Sobotta was our dentist, and he and his wife, Mali, had become good friends. Before moving to Botswana, Bernard had worked as a dentist in the German navy. He was gentle, and thorough. But largely due to Mum, who grew apoplectic at the suggestion of mercury fillings and dismissed all arguments in their favor, a tense undercurrent had persisted in the Scott family teeth's relationship with Bernard.

Jean Keikopf, who had a general phobia of dental work, was less worried about mercury than she was about the long, gory process of having to have an impacted wisdom tooth cut out of her jaw. "I just cannot bear," she'd said, "the thought of this op... he's going to cut my gum open and saw it out of my jaw, for God's sake."

Bernard had told Jean she could have the operation done under a general anesthetic, but only in Gaborone. "And I hate generals anyway," she'd said. "But now I don't know how I'm going to get through it all." She'd shuddered, paling at the thought. "Even with a local anesthetic."

It was Mum who had the hypnosis idea.

That I wasn't going to be around for the operation didn't deter Mum for a moment. "Robbie, you can put Jean under before you go back to school. Prep her. Build in some strong triggers to help me get her back under. Then I can go in with her for the op... and reinitiate the state once she's in the chair..."

I'd hypnotized Jean a number of times before, and she agreed at once.

Feeling flattered, and curious to experiment, I agreed too.

"But you've got to follow instructions, Mum," I said. "I've done a lot of work on Jean. I don't want you messing it up."

Mum's eyes twinkled. "Of course, Robbie," she said, "absolutely. You're the expert. Will follow your instructions to the letter."

"You must watch her breathing," I now instructed. "Listen carefully."

We bent over Jean, listening to several deep, very slightly rasping breaths.

"See. Should be like this. If it changes, something's going wrong."

Mum nodded.

"That's one of the best indicators.... Rapid eyeball movement under closed eyes can also be a sign of discomfort. Also remember— always keep talking.... I'll tell her that your voice will be extremely soothing."

"Okay."

"Say something now, then."

Mum said, "Jean, you're feeling very relaxed."

I said, "Jean, when you have your operation, Linda's lovely soothing voice will make you extremely relaxed. Just like now."

Mum said, again, "Jean, you're feeling very, very relaxed."

Jean grinned and shivered with pleasure.

I smiled approvingly at Mum and continued. "Always keep your voice very level and rhyth-mi-cal," I said, doing the same. "Before the work starts, give her a strong image to focus on ... bring her back to this every time there's any discomfort..."

I finished with a few minutes of deep, happy relaxation and then told Jean I was going to wake her up, but that as soon as Linda told her to go into a deep relaxing sleep again, she would. I also added, for good measure, that Bernard's dentist chair was a very safe and comfortable place to be, and she was going to be very pleased to sit in it. Then I woke Jean up.

She grinned dreamily at me. "Wow, Robbie," she sighed. "Thank you so much. That was lovely. You could be a professional, you know."

"It was a pleasure," I said importantly, "and I have considered

doing it as a business. But it'd really be too draining. And probably difficult to find enough clients in Bulawayo."

I also suspected that advertising myself as a part-time hypnotist would destroy my tenuous favor with Sister Brunhilda. Managing not being baptized was difficult enough. And
hypnosis would be harder to blame on my family than baptism—
the strategy I'd most recently employed when Sister Brunhilda
had raised the matter.

"*Ja*, Hobbin." She grinned meaningfully. "You have been
thinking, no? Any decisions yet?"

"The problem, Sister," I explained, "is that I'm still quite confused. My family makes it so hard to decide."

Sister Brunhilda narrowed her eyes. "Oh, no, *really*?"

"Well, my mum's parents are Catholics. But they don't go
to church anymore, and my Grandpa Terry says they're 'RCs.'
Retired Catholics. And my dad's dad, my grandpa Ivor, is from
a Christian family, but he never really took it seriously.... And
then he married a Jew, my granny Mavis, who didn't practice as
a Jew. Then they got divorced and she went to India and found
an Indian swami guru. And now, recently, my grandpa Ivor has
also been getting into Eastern religions. And then there's my dad,
who's technically Jewish through his mum, but doesn't really
believe in anything. And my mum is just generally spiritual and
believes in bits of everything. So it's very hard for me."

Sister Brunhilda shook her head silently and, acknowledging
temporary defeat, left it there. But she rallied quickly. At the next
opportunity, she selected me to do the reading in mass, in front
of the whole school. "*Ja*, this is an honor," she reminded me pointedly. "Such a lovely thing to do. Such a good speaker. You liked
it, Hobbin. No?"

I said I did, and then I explained respectfully that I was still
thinking.

Meanwhile, I tried to keep a low profile, which was getting increasingly difficult thanks to my burgeoning stationery
business.

The local Zimbabwean stationery was horrible: the paper was a coarse, ugly brown. The pens and highlighters were badly made, with poor colors that faded and ran across the rough paper. The erasers, sticky tape, and correction fluid were ineffective. The opportunity was obvious: even during my first overwhelming days of school, I'd noticed my classmates enviously eyeing my box of stationery.

My announcement that I was going to start importing stationery produced a flood of orders, which quickly expanded beyond my own class. Before long, as I sat on benches outside with my friends at break times, armed with my accounts book and bag of goods, I was catering to a stream of girls of all ages.

I did a particularly good trade in fluorescent pens and Tipp-Ex, and after a few months the bright colors and shiny white streaks were appearing in exercise books and notice boards across the school. Then teachers started ordering, and I began break-time deliveries to the staff room door.

Conducted as furtively as I could manage, these transactions with the non-nun teachers were deeply tense. A nun could walk round the corner at any time, and, caught with a wad of Zimbabwean dollars, I always felt guilty—like some terrible corrupting intruder. Before I'd arrived, the most commercial student activities at the Convent had been charity cake sales.

L eaving Jean in a peaceful posthypnotic high, Mum and I drove across town to the Phikwe mall. "The teachers are some of my best customers," I explained as I headed to the pen aisle. "Red and pink are best sellers. They use them for marking."

I rummaged through the boxes, handing Mum colorful bunches of pens.

"That's nice," she mused. "So even if you get a disappointing mark, you have the satisfaction of it being written in your own wares.... Now, come on, Robbie, please hurry up..."

Mum was insisting on "just a quick visit to Selebi" before I returned to school. We were already running late, after she had decided to bake her need-a-chainsaw-to-cut-it bread just as we prepared to leave the farm. The car smelled of yeast from a loaf that Mum had brought along with us, cooling in its tin, covered by a dish towel.

"It's important you see Ivor and Betty," she said again as we sped along the familiar road beside the railway line. "They're getting old. And you know how much they love it. Hey, look, there's the good old train..."

We waved to the driver, and Mum hooted energetically as the black monster whooshed past us in the opposite direction.

"So funny to see it again," she continued, "it was so much a part of our lives. Gosh we did have good times here."

"I should have got more pens," I said. "I hate running out of stock."

Mum said, "I'll make sure you get some. I promise. Have I ever let you down?"

"Suppose not."

"Well, then, stop worrying. Look, there's the great old baobab."

Mum had, from the start, been a crucial part of my stationery business: giving me the first stock as a present, bringing supplies on her visits to Bulawayo, and arranging to send emergency orders up with other Phikwe families visiting Bulawayo. All this was typical of Mum. But, sometimes, in an uncharitable mood, I suspected she also still felt guilty about business venture number one.

For more than a year, the twenty rehabilitated hens had thrived. Then they started to stop laying. Every comfort and supplement I could think of was to no avail, and eventually the weary hens dwindled to a couple of eggs each a week.

"You can't run a business like this, Robbie," said Dad. Mum agreed. The chickens, they suggested, could be sold off to people at the local cattle posts, and I could rescue a brand-new batch of twenty battered battery hens.

Thrilled by a repeat of the noble mission, it didn't occur to me to dwell on whether a one-egg-a-week-chicken would be of any use to anyone else. Mum and Dad, who were unusually vague, did the selling, and I was soon absorbed tending to my new bedraggled brood.

I missed the other chickens, but contented myself that one of my favorite hens had gone to Ruth. For a few weeks, whenever we passed Ruth's ramshackle little house on our driveway, I peered fondly at my old hen scratching in the dust. I wondered where she was laying her eggs; if she ever laid them in the house, into which she sometimes wandered.

Then one day, I screamed.

Mum braked violently, and we skidded to a halt—just a few scraggly thornbushes between us and the dirt clearing in front of Ruth's house.

"What on earth, Robbie? . . . Oh, no . . . oh, dear . . . oh, Lordy. . . . Don't look, Lulu."

Outside the hut, beside the fire, Ruth bent over a tree stump that she used as a stool. In one hand she held a raised ax; in the other she held my chicken, head on the block. The ax fell as I jumped out the car.

I yelled.

Ruth dropped the ax. She stood up in surprise, still holding the head in the other hand. She waved cheerfully. "*Dumela*, Robbie!"

I was speechless, though, and frozen where I stood, transfixed by the chicken's body, which had clambered to its feet.

Pausing for a second, she ran toward the bush, as fast as any normal frightened chicken. Then she veered back into the swept clearing. Then she headed to the bush again. Like a macabre cartoon, I almost expected the head to at any moment reappear and settle back on the body.

Then there was a squeal.

Emmanuel, Ruth's six-year-old son, leaped up from the dust where he'd been playing. He hurtled after the chicken but missed as she swerved with uncanny eyeless, brainless sight. Laughing and pulling himself up off the dirt, he charged again and launched himself, rugby style, at the dust. This time, he hit the headless hen. Standing up, he held the struggling body proudly in front of him. Ruth said something to him in Setswana.

"*Dumela*, Robbie," Emmanuel called shyly.

Dealing with the aftermath took all Mum's powers of philosophical spin.

Dad just said, "What did you think happened? It's the most humane way to go."

I reluctantly acknowledged the grim reality. But thereafter, whenever I cuddled one of my hens, the ghastly image loomed in the back of my mind. And when the second twenty chickens stopped laying, I sold them off sadly and closed my business.

"Don't worry," Mum had said, "something else is bound to come along soon. And you've got your saddle. You've done what you set out to do. And you've educated Phikwe about free-range eggs. And you've given forty chickens a very good life. All in all, it couldn't have gone better."

Now, as we bumped past Ruth's old house, I stared at the fateful stool and the little building, which seemed especially forlorn. Nowadays, only Ruth's ancient mother Georgina still lived in the old house. Farther on, outside the cowshed, were the unfamiliar cars belonging to the new family staying there.

In front of Grandpa Ivor's house, a new Toyota Camry stood beside the ancient white *bakkie* that so long ago had carried the five of us and the frozen turkeys home.

"Business is fantastic," said Grandpa. "Of course, I still have to keep an eye on that Seloma, though. Baby in the world of business... I tell him, 'Slo, I've been bloody running businesses for years! I know what I'm doing!' And still he doesn't bloody listen..."

Granny Betty offered us tea, which even Mum was pragmatic enough to decline. After her hip replacement, Granny moved at an almost glacial pace. Tea could take hours, and she insisted on doing it herself, as well as preparing a snack for the animals so they didn't feel left out.

The two dogs and the cat were now obese. It was as if Granny was feeding them instead of herself. She had grown very thin and frailer than ever. She subsisted, Grandpa complained, on a few biscuits, sweets, and scraps of food at dinner.

Granny's eyes sparkled defiantly as Grandpa said, "Betty and her bloody junk food. No wonder she's not well."

Grandpa was thin too. "More grape fasts," he explained. "No booze. No meat. Never felt better."

Mum and Grandpa discussed nutrition, which reminded Mum about the bread. "I knew there was a reason I should bake," she said, rushing out to the car.

When she unveiled the enormous loaf, Granny looked almost ill. But Grandpa clutched the whole-wheat brick with delight. "Wonderful, Linda. So kind of you." He turned to me. "Your mother's a wonderful woman, Robbie."

I nodded. "But you've got to eat it quickly. Or you can't cut it at all."

Mum said, "That's not strictly true."

"Not a problem," bellowed Grandpa, "I'm a health freak now! Got to pass my medical." Grandpa was seventy-five. His medical was for his flying license, which he was determined to retake. "Brain's still sharp as anything," he said, tapping his now totally bald head.

I told Grandpa about my stationery business.

"Bloody marvelous," said Grandpa.

Then I explained I was thinking of importing curios from Zimbabwe and selling them in Botswana, where the crafts were less diverse and more expensive.

"Bloody marvelous idea," said Grandpa again. "I'll sell them up at Nata for you too. Petrol, food, crafts. We can offer it all. No limits in this place."

"My concern," I interrupted, "is the customs people. The Zimbabweans don't look at the stationery 'cause I'm a student. But the Bots side might get suspicious."

Grandpa snorted. "Not a problem. I'll tell you what to do. I used to fly in imports from Bulawayo. Did I ever tell you about that? Beer. For our parties... We had great parties here with all the pilots. Ask your father. I don't drink the wretched stuff now, of course. But we used to get through a lot. Anyway, never had a problem... You know what I mean." He winked. "Just kept the airport guys well stocked. Little generosity never goes amiss."

"I would never," I said indignantly.

"Bloody right," said Grandpa. "Bad stuff. You're absolutely right. Bloody marvelous." He grinned, wildly and infectiously. I grinned back.

"Thanks for your advice," I said, as I kissed him good-bye.

"Not a problem," said Grandpa. "Anytime."

Hurtling back to Phikwe, later than ever, I felt the old conquer-the-world buzz. "I enjoyed it," I said grudgingly. "Thanks for taking me."

Mum said, "I just wish your father would see more of Ivor."

Dad did visit the old houses. But he visited mainly to see Granny Betty. Dad said he couldn't stand listening to Grandpa complaining about the long-suffering Seloma, to whom he now owed most of his income.

Mum said, "But he's your father, Keith. And in many ways an amazing man. Even if he is absolutely impossible."

Dad just shrugged.

Mum was the family keeper, the one who could forgive faults in just about anyone for the sake of harmony. As we spread out across southern Africa, she was the one who straddled all the distances and fought determinedly to keep us connected.

"Write lots," I said, as we hugged good-bye in Bulawayo. "Tell me everything. Especially how Jean's op goes."

"Will do," said Mum. "Always do. Will write as soon as I get home."

"Before you get lost in your book."

"Promise."

Dearest Robbie,

It's 9 p.m. and I have just got back. I am exhausted after the drive home (caught behind three buses on the Zim side of the border), but am keeping to my word and scribbling a quick note before bed. Dad will post tomorrow on the way home from his clinics.

Not much to report here, except that Dad was filling up with petrol at Sherwood and bumped into old Piet Louw, who said he'd heard a "very reliable rumor" that there'd been heavy rains in the Lotsane's catchment area and the river was definitely on its way down. Can't help getting excited, even after all the disappointments—and even coming from PL, who should be disbelieved immediately on the grounds of what he said afterward. He and Dad got chatting about fishing, and Dad remarked that there didn't seem to be as many bream in the river as last year. Piet said, "*Ag*, no, Keith. You mustn't worry. You won't catch any fish this month. Everyone here knows that you only catch fish in months with an 'R' in them."

On that sage note, that's all from me for the moment. Hope your stationery stock has held out for the first few days.

Lots of love,
Mum

Dearest Robbie,
The Lotsane has come down at last—later than needed for the poor old trees, but at least *Oom* Piet can feel smug. Anyway, it's been flowing strongly for several days now and both dam walls are still totally submerged (but showing, as far as we can tell, no signs of collapse). We can hear the thundering river all the way from the house, and have been drifting to sleep to the wonderful sound of falling, rushing water over the dam wall.

The horses are all in fine fettle. My latest strategy for Winnie is to give him presoaked whole mealie kernels, and I'm convinced he's looking not quite so terribly thin as he was. You'll laugh at me, but I'm still sure there's a natural solution to counter his intestinal damage. I let him graze on our lawn, but he always ends up hanging around the kitchen door waiting for some more of my bread—success at last, even if it's a horse that cannot get enough of it. He even prefers it to Coke, so I regard that as a real triumph.

Living on the Fringe is going well and I am absorbed as ever (though, note, still writing to you!). I'm planning to send the MS. to some South African publishers, when I get around to finishing it. The trouble, as usual, is that I am so distracted by other ideas for books—my current favourite being one on the placebo effect, which I've been reading up on. The power of the mind is truly amazing and we should be focusing on safe ways to harness it in medicine.

Talking of that, gosh, I almost forgot. Jean K's op went amazingly. I put her "half" under before we went, and as soon as she saw Bernard's chair she jumped into it and squirmed with pleasure. And then it was so easy to put her under fully. Bernard was remarkably sanguine about the whole bizarre episode—me stroking her hand and telling her she was floating on clouds, walking in forests etc., while he sawed away at her jaw bone. He even admitted he had to stop himself from floating away too at one stage. Jean sends you a big thank-you hug.

The sun is setting and the dogs are getting impatient, so we must head off for a walk.

LOL,

Mumsie.

P.S. Dad and Lulu send their love. Lulu misses you and Damien terribly, as do I, but we are bearing up.

P.P.S. More stationery on its way with Lyn, who's visiting Mel next week.

Dearest R,

Hope your stationery arrived safely.

Big news here is that we saw a leopard down at the Limpopo. The dogs of course chased, but it thankfully quickly disappeared. Then had another tense few moments when Keller jumped in the water pursuing a rabbit-sized cane rat in the reeds. She paddled around for ages, oblivious to our shouts, but emerged intact, with no visible sign of a croc gliding behind her like that last horrific time they all jumped in. I still shudder to think of it. Anyway, you can imagine what a frenzy Lulu was in.

Just a few days later we found two dead kudu locked in battle—their horns were still interlinked, and it broke our hearts to look at them. One had a broken leg, and they must have died a slow lingering death because they couldn't separate. Gosh, nature can be cruel. But on a positive note, the grass is looking amazing in Dad's cleared stretches of bush. According to the grass book, the new varieties coming up are a sign of rapidly recovering grassland. Dad is so chuffed. Rivers still both flowing strongly, and we are having the most exquisite paddles in heavenly waters.

Oh, had to laugh, Robbie. Jean v R came around for dinner and said he hasn't been feeling very well. He's convinced it's the oranges he's been eating. Said he has one a day. Can you believe it? The man lives on a diet of red meat and beer, and when he feels bad he assumes it's the oranges. This place! I gave him a piece of my mind, as you can imagine.

Anyway, on the subject of Jean, he's also been looking quite chuffed recently. Some of his mates decided he'd been a bachelor for too long and put an ad—without his knowledge— in *Landbouweekblad* (the Afrikaans version of *Farmer's Weekly*). This particular ad section (the equivalent of the *Farmer's Weekly* "Hitching Post") is called "Opsitkers." This means "courting candle" and refers to the old Afrikaner tradition of courting, where a candle was lit at the start of the visit, and when it had burned down, the suitor had to leave. Anyway, we didn't see the ad but apparently they said things like fun-loving 30-year-old farmer in the Tuli Block desperate for a wife... comes with thousands of hectares, many head of cattle, oodles of game etc. Jean was initially furious, but couldn't help grinning as he described how he'd been inundated with scented, lipstick-covered envelopes. I do hope he finds someone, he's such a lovely chap. Suspect, however, the female readership of *Landbouweekblad* may not be Jean's cup of tea.

Another bit of news is that Damien is moving to St. George's Grammar in Cape Town, which has a great liberal tradition and a small friendly boarding house. His adopted parents have moved to the UAE, and he also wants to be closer to the action in a big cool city. You know Didge. It's also much closer to Gran and Gramps and Karen, and so, if Damien ever does decide to play soccer, he will have some family to cheer him on. Will let you know how he settles in.

I know you're busy, but please do write soon. I am still working on Dad to write. He claims he's set such a great precedent for himself with his last letter that he needs more time to concoct a work of similar genius. Lulu is painting you a card as I write.

Lots of love,
Mumsie

Dearest Robbie,

I know you're coming home soon, but I thought you might like a few Tuli Block capers to distract you in the midst of your exams.

Visitor-wise, it's been pretty quiet here. But last weekend the Balls came down from Phikwe for Lu's birthday and we were treated to the truly classic spectacle of Rawdon, Sally, and little James—all squashed on Rawdon's ancient motorbike—roaring up the driveway. After 190 kms they were unsurprisingly exhausted and bathed in dust, but cheerful as ever. Luckily Dad had already collected Nicky on the way back from his clinic, or I expect they would have found a way to cram her on too. Always nice to be reminded there's one family in Botswana odder than us!

RE that subject, word has it our nickname in the Tuli Block is *snaakse mense,* which means "strange people." I'm quite flattered, actually. God forbid if we weren't considered strange among this lot. Except for Jean, of course, whom we do like so much. He actually calls the Northern Transvaal Afrikaners *snaakse mense,* as they are so different from the Free State Afrikaners he was brought up with. He says he used to laugh when he visited the Tuli Block as a boy and saw that all the men had combs sticking out above their socks!

Anyway, we had a lovely time with the Balls, plus a little unplanned excitement during an evening paddle on the

Limpopo. Sally, Rawdon, and I took the Indian canoe, plus
the two jackies, and Dad paddled the little single. The kids
stayed behind to decorate the gazebo for the party. All went
well until a huge *legavaan* plunged off a branch overhanging
the water. Then Watson yelped and dived off the boat. Sally
and I both leaned over simultaneously to rescue him and the
boat capsized right in the middle of the river. It was terrifying, and made even worse by the fact that I could barely
swim due to hysterical laughter. I suspect all the noise kept
the crocs at bay.

Today we had great animal excitement of a rather different sort. Ben has not been looking good for several weeks,
trailing in after all the other horses and then standing in his
pen ignoring his food and looking forlorn. We had no idea
why until today when Dad saw him weeing—or not weeing.
He was actually just dribbling very thick pus-filled yellow
urine. Then Dad felt his penis and realized the problem. Several kidney stones had lodged in his urethra. Dad got his
scalpel at once and sliced open the constricted tip of poor
Ben's penis, while Lulu and I stroked his neck. Dad fished
out three substantial stones, and then the most amazing thing
happened. Enormous old Ben let out this tremendous groan,
and began to widdle. He kept going and going—weeing and
groaning in ecstasy for about five minutes (and that's not my
normal hyperbole). His eyes reminded me of Lulu's when
you hypnotize her. Anyway, it was one of the most satisfying
things I've seen in a long time. I wanted to groan too from
vicarious relief. I knew how he felt of course—I had to have
a catheter inserted after my second operation and could have
kissed the nurse who released me from my agony.

Don't work too hard.

Dad and Lu send their love,

Lots of love,

Mum.

P.S. Dad may be an appalling letter writer but he still
thinks of you. Knowing you'd hate missing the penis op, he

put the kidney stones in a jar, especially for you to inspect later. They are in the fridge as I write (labeled just in case Ruth tries to get creative with the vegetable pie) awaiting your imminent return.

P.P.S. Damien delighted as some photographers chose him for a photo shoot. They needed a model for an illustration of how not to look as a student. With his long unkempt hair, which St. George's has been remarkably tolerant about, and scruffy look, he was immediately selected. The funniest part is that it has appeared in an Afrikaans school textbook—cousin Daniel discovered it and is brimming with pride. What a hoot, although Granny was outraged. Anyway, you can form your own opinion when you and everyone else converge on the farm next week. There'll be fourteen of us staying in the house. What fun.

Four of the fourteen were my school friends Sheena Stirling, Michelle Brice, Tiffany McGaw, and her sister, Rachel. "Don't worry about us," Tiffany told her parents as the four set off from Bulawayo. "It's good tar road almost all the way. Anyway, Rob's Dad's a doctor, so if anything happens on the farm we'll be fine."

I was already back at home. Mum had picked me up in Bulawayo several days earlier, and we'd joined, at the farm, Dad, Damien, and Lulu, as well as Mum's sister Alison and our two young cousins Kim and James. They were visiting from New Zealand, where Alison had moved just after we left. Five-year-old James was desperately excited to be in Africa: place of endless adventures, where anything can happen.

The phone rang late in the afternoon, just when the Bulawayo party was expected to arrive. It was Tiffany, calling from Sherwood, where the four girls had been given a lift after crashing their car on the dirt road, just twenty kilometers from the farm. Tiffany, who was driving, had lost control, skidded, swerved, and then swerved even more when Rachel grabbed the wheel, trying to help. The little car had flown right over the fence, smashing into a tree on the other side. Tiffany and Rachel were fine; Sheena had a big gash on her arm, Michelle on her face.

They were sitting at Sherwood, covered in blood, still bleeding, and waiting for help.

"Shit," said Mum, dropping the phone. "Shit. Shit. Shit. I can't believe it. Of all bloody days." For that day only, Dad was away in Johannesburg, collecting medicines and staying with his old friend Colin Miles, a pilot who'd trained with Grandpa Ivor. He'd be driving back the following morning with Colin's daughter Dominique and her boyfriend, who were joining the chaotic party. Mum phoned Dad, who said, "You'll probably have to take them to the hospital. But before you go, try Jean. Hasn't Sonja just arrived to stay with him? Maybe she can go with you."

Sonja van Riet was a softly spoken, five-foot-two heart surgeon. She offered at once to accompany the rescue party to Sherwood, and we collected her at Jean's farm.

Sheena and Michelle both urgently needed stitches. Michelle's gash stretched hideously across her face; her hair was matted with blood. Sonja said, "Michelle should really see a plastic surgeon."

Michelle said, "My parents are going to kill me."

"After they've killed me," said Tiffany.

Mum said cheerfully, "Rubbish. They'll be celebrating that you're safe. Now, where do you suggest we take them, Sonja? Gaborone? Jo'burg?"

Sonja said, quietly, "Well, just to make absolutely sure, you should take Michelle to Phikwe tomorrow for an X-ray. But I can stitch them both up. If they don't mind that I'm a bit out of practice." Then she explained that, in addition to her main work as a heart surgeon, she'd also done some plastic surgery.

Mum said, "What about your equipment?"

But Sonja had brought her extra-fine sutures with her on her visit to the Tuli Block.

So everyone drove back to the farm, where Sonja spent more than three hours stitching up Sheena and Michelle, watched by everyone, including a wide-eyed James, who was still awake when Sonja finally finished at ten o'clock that night. Michelle had seventeen stitches, which would later leave her with only the faintest of scars.

"Done," said Sonja. "I hope that's okay."

Mum said, "Give me a sec, and I'll drive you back home."

"No, Linda," said Sonja. "Please don't worry, I'll walk. If you don't mind lending me a flashlight."

We all stared at her in amazement; the walk to Jean's was five kilometers, through the bush. "For goodness sake, Sonja," said Mum, laughing and hugging her. "You deserve a ride in a limo. I'm just sorry I can only offer a *bakkie*."

Sonja said, "Well, you've had a busy day. I really don't want to trouble you."

Late the next day, when Dad arrived back from Jo'burg, he and Damien towed the battered car back to Sherwood. Everyone else was by then installed by the pool, sipping stiff drinks, which Mum was still prescribing for aftershock, along with the usual Rescue Remedy. She had quickly squashed a plan for one of the Bulawayo parents to drive down and collect the girls early. "Nonsense...now the girls need a good holiday more than ever—they must stay. And there's nothing like a big fright to make life seem even better.... We're going to have a fantastic time."

And we did.

Dearest Robbie and Lulu,

I can't believe the holidays went so quickly. Even harder to believe, Lu, is that you are at school now too—that all my birds have finally flown the nest. The house feels so strange, like it has lost its heart. But enough of that, as I know you're both dying for farm updates, and the last few weeks have been quite newsworthy—for the Tuli Block.

Dad's had a recent run of interesting medical/veterinary dramas. First, a farmer brought around one of his laborers who'd had his penis and testicles basically bitten off by a rather savage *boerboel* dog. Dad, unfortunately, could do nothing for the poor chap and sent him straight off to hospital.

Then the other day, Roy and Charlotte Young came over

with their son, Adam (can't remember if you've ever met him?), who was dripping blood from a big gash on his forehead. He had dived into the Limpopo (for fun!?) and split his head on a rock before any croc could get near him. Dad had a quick look and said, "Now let's all have a cup of tea first." So we had a leisurely cuppa in the gazebo, Adam dabbing his bleeding wound all the while. Then Dad stitched him up.

He is amazingly impressive in emergencies, old Dad. Remember how he did the same thing when Damien split his head open on the side of the pool—made us all have tea first to calm down. Shame, he's really quite low about his clinics these days, the same old story.

Lots of love,

Mumsie.

P.S. Please do both write when you have some time. As you know, I'm always agog to hear your stories. Robbie, Dad and I chuckled for ages over your last letter. Has your petition come to anything? Gosh, I sometimes pity your teachers. Damien's, too, come to think of it. One of his teachers is also, according to Damien, a real problem and has been setting them tests on subjects she hasn't properly covered. When dialogue did nothing, Damien rallied the whole class to boycott the next test. But come the test, after expressing great enthusiasm, everyone else chickened out at the last moment. Not old Didge, though. He sat through the entire test, arms crossed, and didn't write a word. Got zero, of course. So proud of him. The teacher told him that while she respected his stand, she wasn't going to change his mark.

By the way, he's finally established his computer business with a Chinese classmate—registered as Tseng Scott Technologies—after we lent him R10K. He says it's going well (and to tell you as much). He's already got several orders, one from a teacher.

P.P.S. Talking of science, I feel a bit like an impatient scientist with the results of a fifteen-year experiment at last coming in—the complete results, now that Lulu's with you.

Dearest Mum and Dad,

So sorry it has taken me ages to reply, but between school, business, and riding, I'm pretty frantic. Anyway, here goes making up for my slack correspondence.

Firstly, Mum, to answer your question re the petition. In the end I collected more than twenty signatures, which I handed to Sister Angela. I decided that having a whole class of O-level results in severe jeopardy warranted going straight to the headmistress. She was a bit surprised, but really quite nice about it. Although she did look a little affronted when I said my specific request, on behalf of all the girls who'd signed, was to have Mrs. Beale transferred to another class. She said she'd get back to me, and she did thank me for bringing it to her attention.

We didn't get the transfer, unfortunately. But she did get a talking-to, and the lessons have been much better since then. We're paying customers, after all, can't understand why we shouldn't demand good service. Did Damien's lone boycott produce any results? Please tell him my stationery business is going excellently too.

On the subject of boycotts, I had another run-in with a teacher—Mrs. Taylor, this time—about asking too many questions. Got blatantly ignored in one lesson, so I didn't say a word for a whole week. It was really funny, as there were suddenly long awkward silences when Mrs. Taylor asked if anyone had any questions. Eventually she basically asked me to start talking again. I agreed but took the opportunity to make a point. I explained that asking questions was the only way I kept interested, and if I wasn't interested, I'd only be wasting her time as well as my own and might as well not be there. She just nodded. I later heard from another teacher that the comment got passed around the staff room. So hopefully all the other teachers will take note.

All things considered, no surprise, I suppose, that everyone is amazed by Lulu. People keep commenting to me about how "gentle" and "quiet" she is. Anyway, she seems to be fitting in well. She's finding the work all okay and making lots of friends. Doing amazingly in swimming too. "It's all the sprint training with crocs," she jokes. Occasionally hypnotize her and Nicky Ball for homesickness, which they both say helps a lot.

By the way, I wouldn't worry too much about Lulu, even if she is ostensibly much less tough than me. The other day at break time, I walked outside to see her standing in the middle of the pavement, gesturing wildly, ordering every girl in the school, even the prefects, to walk around her. Couldn't believe it, as she's terrified of the prefects, and as you know she never orders anyone around. Also everyone was staring at her, which she normally hates. Only understood when I got closer and saw the long procession of Matabele ants crossing the pavement. "Careful, please don't crush them," Lulu was pleading—glaring fiercely in the face of any protest or ridicule. "There're just poor little ants... please step over or walk around..." Felt so proud of her.

Now, Mum, to the latest results from experimental subject, Daughter 1. Since reading your NLP book in the holidays, I have been trying out some of the memory techniques, in particular this idea that you can activate the visual memory by moving your eyeballs up and to the left. It seems to be helping, and a few weeks ago I was practicing between lessons. The girl next to me asked what on earth I was up to, so I explained the theory. By the time the teacher arrived, practically the whole class was at it—alternately looking at their pages and flicking their eyes up to the left. She was pretty bewildered, as you can imagine, and gave me a strange look when I told her it was neurolinguistic programming and that she should really read about it, given all its applications in teaching.

In the latest on the baptism struggle, Sister Brunhilda is trying the new angle of reminding me that prefect selection is coming up soon. "*Ja*, Hobbin, zis vould be helpful." I told her, affronted, that I wouldn't want to choose a religion for such a shallow reason. So for the moment, at least, I hopefully have the upper hand.

That's about all my news, but before I sign off, I must tell one more story, mainly in a strategic bid to get Dad to write. The other day I was at Tiffany's house, and her sister's boyfriend was visiting. He's a bit of a joker, and likes asking ridiculous questions to tease people. I am aware of this, but I'm mortified to admit that he caught me off guard when he asked me, "So what's the price of eggs, Robyn?" He is clever and several years older than me, and my first thought was delight as, for once, he had asked a question about which I was really well informed.

I told him I wasn't exactly sure what the price was in Zim, but allowing for inflation since I'd closed my business, discounting for non free-range, and adjusting for the exchange rate, I said I'd guess it was x, or whatever I said. Everyone started laughing, and even he was genuinely speechless. I, of course, felt like a fool and tell this story only as a plea to get you to write, Dad. As you can see my sense of humor desperately needs nurturing. You don't want all your hard work to go to waste, do you? Anyway, seeing Mum is getting so much amusement out of our stories, it seems only fair we should hear a little more about her.

Await your reply with bated breath.

Lots of love,

Robbie.

Homeschooling, and its aftermath, was not a one-way experiment. From our side—Dad's, Lulu's, Damien's, and mine—the experiment was: What happens when you (a) interrupt the promising scientific career of an eccentric twenty-three-year-old with seventeen years of looking after and teaching three children, and (b) abruptly end the exposure, leaving the bewildered forty-year-old subject in the bush, in the middle of nowhere, surrounded by people whose language she doesn't speak, and views she doesn't share?

Some of the results we collected during the holidays. But then, when we, the children, were all around, the impact of (b) was somewhat muted. Undoubtedly the best, if biased, results came from Dad, relayed in his sporadic mammoth letters, which always centered around Mum, and for added entertainment, at some point, always slipped from fact into fantasy. Guessing where the switch occurred—by no means easy—was part of the pleasure.

Dear Chaps,

Sorry it's taken me so unbelievably long to get around to writing to you. I've been very busy with the clinics and the usual demands of the farm—fixing pumps, chasing poachers etc. I've also had to keep an eye on Mum, who's been in severe book mode, and unpredictably emerges from her screen, declaring dazedly that she has writer's block. I then have to be ready to go on red alert, knowing she will undoubtedly proceed to create havoc in the house and surroundings. I will briefly put this in context now, and elaborate further in the following paragraphs.

As you know, she's spending almost all of her time on finishing off *Living on the Fringe*. (I suspect she's determined to get some mileage out of the last few harrowing decades.) I also suspect that when she gets writer's block, the title becomes a self-fulfilling prophecy, i.e. she goes forth and surfs the fringe for new material. Anyway, onerous though it is looking after her, I cannot in good conscience neglect your SOS, Robbie. The thought of you losing your sense of humor again fills me with almost more alarm than the very real danger of Mum losing her sanity.

So to begin. Well, you'll be nostalgic to know that the house still smells of carbonized chickpeas (and no doubt still will when you return) from Mum's last attempt to burn it down. If you remember, we were amazed that we could smell the smoke from a kilometer away. It turns out, however, we greatly underestimated the reach of Mum's haute cuisine: all over the Tuli Block, people are now talking about a strange burned legume smell, hitherto unknown in the region. (Except for the few residents who've had the traumatic experience of dining with us.) Anyway, after days of scrubbing even Ruth gave up on the pressure cooker, which Mum at last threw away.

This purge turned out to be prophetic of her approach henceforth: i.e. dispensing with cooking altogether, and radical turfing-out sessions. For days, it seemed, I returned to drawers and cupboards open and various precious items being chucked in the rubbish pile and Mum saying, "I feel so liberated." So it was with some relief that I came home one day and saw Mum bending over into the fridge. You must understand I had been subsisting on a diet of vegetable pie, which as you know is the only dish Ruth can cook, and my least favorite.

Filled with sudden passion at the thought of my wife at last cooking me a meal—Robbie, this is a test for you, you did ask for it—I affectionately clasped Mum's left buttock. Now I know, in book mode, she sometimes reacts unexpectedly, but I was nonetheless taken aback by her howl and sudden ability to speak perfect Setswana. Until Mum stood up, and I saw it was Ruth, wearing one of Mum's long flowery dresses. Ruth looked appalled and rushed out the kitchen as I quickly apologized and tried to explain. Still blushing, I found Mum at the sewing machine. "Oh, yes," she said. "I've decided I really need some new clothes, for my new self, and I didn't want the others to go to waste. They fit Ruth perfectly, don't they?"

Sewing ushered in Phase II of the symptoms: Frenzied creation. Now never one to restrict herself to womanly tasks, Mum soon abandoned the sewing machine and began hauling wheelbarrows full of bricks to the gazebo, where she'd decided to build a built-in gas stove and a surface area for outdoor cooking (which cheered me up). I suggested she wait until Joseph, Shimane, and I had finished the critical work on the burst pipe and could help her. But Mum insisted she couldn't wait, and that a bit of heavy labor never hurt anyone. "I'm only worried about skin cancer," she pronounced, trundling the barrow along with her biggest Washable, Squashable Australian hat and an enormous swimming towel draped over her shoulders.

Turns out the god of skin cancer took revenge, for a few hours later we heard this tremendous howl. Mum then appears looking white (even for her sun-free skin) and explains she'd felt this thing on her arm but couldn't see properly because of her sunglasses and had assumed it was just the massive towel. The towel, however, grew increasingly lifelike, and she eventually looked down to see that a large, brightly colored garter snake (semipoisonous) had crawled out of the wheelbarrow handle and wrapped itself around her arm. Breaking all the keep-still-around-snakes rules, she yelled to high heaven and flung the poor creature halfway across the garden.

The saga did not end here, however. Mum at last saw some sense and commandeered the help of S and J to do the heavy brickwork, she overseeing proceedings and doing the grouting between the laid bricks. Now I have to admit she did a pretty impressive job, but I must warn you about complimenting her too much when you see it. Self-appreciation has already got her into trouble. The other day, she was admiring it in front of Shimane and Joseph—stepping back to see it from every angle, including the pool, which she walked backward into, hat, towel, glasses, and all. The two guys were initially too shocked to indulge in the usual Motswana *schadenfreude*. But when she walked away, the cackles began, and we've been hearing eruptions of laughter ever since from down the road.

Anyway, after finishing with the outdoor stove, Mum was faced with a bit of a quandary for her next project. This was the lounge suite, which she suddenly decided she was tired of. Now she couldn't very well throw this out. Nor could she hope to find suitable upholstery material at the Sherwood Ranch store. I, stupidly, assumed she would get over her sudden urge and simply wait until her next shopping trip.

However, I returned from an afternoon of building the new deck by the Limpopo to find that Mum has dragged the settee and the two chairs out onto the lawn. One chair was already looking suspiciously lighter, and as I approached I saw Mum was wielding a paintbrush. "I had such a brilliant idea," she said. "Fabric paint! I can turn the blue denim into green denim. Look how good it looks." I pointed out that the green chair had very clear paintbrush streaks. But Mum's only reply was to say, "Nonsense, not really. Anyway, they give character." *Plus ça change,* as she would say.

Finally, Mum's latest is to diagnose her writer's block as being due to a lack of enough natural light, despite the huge windows in the study, which she, I might add, designed. She has thus set up office in the lean-to, displacing my tools from the workbench. She maintains that the breeze and the dappled light through the passion fruit creeper offer the perfect surroundings for making the creative juices flow. Here she sits, typing away, connected with an extension lead, listening to South African radio, which she claims is her only connection to the real world and will stop her going completely mad. Well, who am I to complain? Anything that helps. Must go to bed now for an early night. Monday tomorrow.

Hope you're both in good form.

Love,

Dad.

Mum said, indignantly, "Of course I didn't set up office on the workbench."

TALKING ABOUT LIONS

Resting lions

The restaurant in the Harare parliamentary buildings was already almost full when our guide ushered us in. Rich smells of something like beef stew filled the warm air, and the room buzzed with laughter, chatter, and cutlery clinking on plates. Engrossed in their lunches and conversations, most of the smartly dressed diners ignored us. Only a few glanced curiously at the wary procession of uniformed students, each from a different school in a different Zimbabwean province.

The girl beside me, whom I'd talked to on the way to the restaurant, gasped. She pointed surreptitiously to a corner table. "That's a minister," she whispered.

"Of what?"

But at that point the minister looked at us, and my companion muttered something unintelligible as her eyes fell to the floor. Despite my nudges, she remained silent.

Several other government representatives joined us, and we sat down at the table. One of the men said a few words about the history of the essay competition, and about what a pleasure it was to be hosting some of Zimbabwe's fine young thinkers, who would shape the future of this great country. Then he announced that our meals would arrive shortly. "Please eat," he said, gesturing to little bowls scattered across the table.

The bowls were passed around, and everyone except me obediently took a handful. "I'm fine, thank you," I said, passing on the dish of small, shriveled carcasses.

The man who sat opposite me smiled. "You must have some."

"No thanks, I'm fine, really."

The students beside me looked shocked. The speaker looked surprised. "But these are a great delicacy. They are mopane worms. You must try some," he said emphatically.

Now the whole table was watching me. I was the only white person at the table, and one of only two white people in the restaurant: I knew what everyone was thinking.

"I know what they are," I said hurriedly. "And it's not because I don't like mopane worms. I'm a vegetarian. And that's not because I don't like meat. But my rule is that I don't eat anything I'm not prepared to kill myself."

Disbelieving smiles broke out around me. "You wouldn't kill a worm?"

"They're still animals. I only kill mosquitoes. Which you obviously can't eat," I babbled. "I know it sounds strange. But my family's quite unusual. My little sister won't even kill mosquitoes."

The man opposite frowned and took a handful of worms for himself. He said, "I have never heard anything like that," and turned away to speak to the boy beside him.

Appalled by my disastrous start, when he next paused I was ready. "Out of interest," I butted in, "do you import your mopane worms from Botswana? I used to live in Selebi-Phikwe, which is surrounded by mopane bush. The worms were big business there."

"These are from Zimbabwe," he said. "We have mopane trees too," he added in a condescending tone. Then he said, "How long have you been living in Zimbabwe?"

"I don't, really," I replied, blushing. "I'm just at boarding school in Bulawayo. My parents still live in Botswana. I came here," I added pointedly, "because Zimbabwe has much better high schools than Botswana."

And at last he smiled. "Better than everywhere else," he said. "You know we have the highest literacy rate in Africa."

"I know."

Then he told me the Bulawayo Convent was an excellent school, and that President Mugabe's own daughters went to the sister convent school in Harare. He asked me where I went to junior school. I explained that my mother had taught me. I added proudly that my grandfather used to fly President Khama, whom we both agreed was great man. Then we discussed diamonds and cattle in Botswana, and agriculture, which was so important to Zimbabwe.

Absorbed in our wide-ranging conversation, it was only about halfway through lunch that I became aware that none of the other students were talking to the adults. They answered questions, but volunteered nothing. Most of them whispered to each other, or watched me in amazement as I opined confidently. Suddenly realizing how impudent I must seem, I fell silent and resolved to try and ask fewer questions.

I forgot, however, as soon as we began our tour of the parliament buildings.

The tour was part of the prize, and part of the reason I had entered the government-run essay competition, despite its profoundly off-putting title, which asked for a discussion of how various societal imbalances, such as gender, racial, and economic, in areas such as politics, business, and the civil service could be redressed without compromising Zimbabwe's cultural norms, traditions, and heritage.

It was impossible to read the question without feeling bored. No other girl in my class had given it more than a second glance. It was 1998, the first demanding year of the A-level syllabus, and even the teachers hadn't encouraged participation, as they usually did. But I entered essay and poetry competitions as a matter of habit, and I wanted to see parliament.

Not rating my chances very highly, I scribbled some considerably more politically correct opinions than I felt.

"That's rather brave," said my English teacher, when I handed in my entry.

I said, "I'm banking on no one else in Matabeleland bothering to enter."

Evidently, no one did. A few months later, I was announced as the regional winner and invited up to Harare.

Now, as we walked through the gloomy wood-paneled corridors, hung with dusty pictures of the queen and various ministers, I couldn't restrain myself. I caught up with our guide. "Are we likely to see the president?" I asked hopefully.

The closest I'd come to seeing President Mugabe was on the road out to Bulawayo's airport, which led toward Floss's farm. The old Bedford had been traveling in the opposite direction to the cavalcade, but at the first sight of the lead motorbikes, Floss had pulled off onto the verge and stopped. It was rumored, if you didn't, that you'd be shot at. And even in an ancient Bedford, piled with hay and four uniformed schoolgirls, no one was prepared to test the theory. As the scores of shiny vehicles had roared past, of the president, however, I'd seen only darkly tinted windows.

The guide smiled at my inquiry. "Of course not," he said. Then he explained that President Mugabe generally came only twice a year: to open parliament, and then to close parliament.

We followed him into the viewing gallery of a room where a desultory and tedious debate was taking place. It seemed, judging by the nodding heads and wandering gazes beneath us, to be just as boring to the participants. The guide led us out before I had time to establish what was being discussed. And that was it: we made our way through more slightly worn and faded rooms and corridors, and back into the bright daylight of Harare's busy streets.

Later, we were taken by bus to the famous Heroes Acre. Disappointed by parliament, I'd been cheered by the news of this trip, which was billed as an important part of understanding Zimbabwe's history. The journey there was fun, too: by the time we climbed into the late-running bus, the group was starting to relax, and as we wound slowly out of Harare toward the hill where the monument stood, we chatted and laughed about our families, schools, and A-levels. Apart from a few discussions in Shona, everyone spoke in perfect English, and no one mentioned the history we were about to relive.

I knew about it, of course. I'd learned in history classes about the civil war and the long bloody struggle for independence from white rule. And although it was never otherwise discussed among my black and white classmates, for many adult white Zimbabweans, the war lurked just beneath the surface, bubbling up in racist comments.

To me, it was a new kind of racism; for whereas in the Tuli Block and across the Limpopo racism was characterized by arrogance, here it was almost inevitably infused with bitterness. "...Ruining their own country...happens *every* time in Africa, look at Zambia, look at Mozambique...you know I always said it would happen, and look, now it's happened.... Look at the economy, they just can't manage their own money...look at the corruption.... probably would have been better off under Ian Smith after all...damn *munts*..."

I'd heard worse from whites in the Tuli Block—blacks are stupid, dirty, lazy, undeserving. But there, coming from people who poached on each other's farms and only fished in the months containing an R, such statements always seemed more ludicrous than anything else—revolting, but not entirely surprising. Here, the generally milder white racism was much more unsettling. For here the comments came from the parents of friends, or adults at the almost all-white horse shows—people I liked and respected, whose opinions I valued. Quips like, "I don't need a washing machine, I have a muntomatic," would produce peals of laughter. Mum said, "Well, I'm pleased you're disgusted. Though it doesn't surprise me. Zambia was the same. You should thank your lucky stars you've grown up in Botswana and escaped that baggage."

But as we stood atop the Heroes Acre hill, and our guides began to narrate the years of white repression and brutality, the bloodshed, and the brave deeds of the black heroes whose tombs surrounded us, I realized that for now, here at least, I hadn't escaped. As they spoke, voices rising with passion, I crept back against a tall stone wall, not wanting to meet their eyes, or those of the black students who looked suddenly somber and, I imagined, much less friendly.

I felt embarrassed, indignant, and it was there, at seventeen, for the first time in my life, that I felt really white. Not white in the privileged-by-wealth-and-don't-eat-mopane-worms way, but in the generic, heavy, guilty label-of-oppressor way. And for one of the first times in my life, too, I was lost for words.

I wanted to yell that I'd never had anything to do with this horrible past; that I was from Botswana, just next door, where there was hardly any of this. But I was white, and he was talking about whites, and one couldn't argue with that. And gazing across the vast expanse of concrete and stone, up to the pinnacle on the top of the hill, down along the endless flights of steps that disappeared below, I longed, silently, for Botswana.

That's what made AIDS in Botswana all the more impossibly tragic.

For although by the 1990s AIDS was quietly ravaging, and was to continue to ravage, much of the rest of Africa and beyond, it was in Botswana where the virus first really showcased itself in the developing world, catapulting this peaceful, prosperous country into the realm of imminent African catastrophes.

Botswana's position as a transport gateway is thought to have kick-started it. Traveling down to South Africa, trucks from Uganda, the Congo, Zambia, and Zimbabwe passed through populous eastern Botswana. En route, drivers paused for hurried sexual encounters with poor local women. Quick sex, without a condom, earned about thirty pula. With condoms, the money was considerably less. But the women could also earn double the quick-sex fee. With "dry sex," a prized specialty, there is no condom either. Additionally the woman pretreats her vagina with herbs or diluted bleach, which cause inflammation and prevent lubrication. With the resulting internal damage, the spread of the virus is almost certain.

Having arrived and taken root, the virus tore around the country, which has a highly mobile population compared with its neighbors. The high proportion of migrant workers, many traveling from the rural areas to the cities or to South Africa, is believed to have fueled this internal spread, splitting up families and increasing the chances of multiple sexual partners. Whatever the precise apportioning of blame—and this is still disputed—by the mid-1990s, when I went away to school, Botswana had one of the highest rates of HIV infection in the world.

Little more than a decade after its first reported AIDS case, it was estimated that around one-quarter of Botswana's adults were HIV-positive.

Almost every holiday—with each term away, falling more in appreciation and love with our home—I'd return to some new sign or word of a change in gear in gentle Botswana's own, first, terrible war.

In 1996, Dad stopped wearing Band-Aids.

"You forgot your Band-Aids."

"Don't need them anymore."

"What?"

His scratches, he explained, were now always covered. No longer would he touch a patient without gloves. Even for external examinations. "Just getting too damn risky." In addition to the omnipresent gloves, now when Dad injected babies he had a second nurse to hold the child in case it thrashed and caused a needle stick injury. In case this failed, and he or his nurses got a needle stick, he now also carried around a course of the new emergency antiretrovirals—postexposure prophylaxis, or PEP. Taken within hours and for a month, these were more than 95 percent effective in preventing infection.

"So you can at last stop worrying, Robbie," he said, "I'm not going to get it. Worry about everyone else who's got it. For them, there's nothing."

After his clinics, the strain on Dad's face now told of more than just exhaustion and boredom. "If the government doesn't bloody do something," he said bitterly, "a quarter of Botswana is going to die. A quarter!"

I thought about it; about a quarter of the people in the country just not being there. In Phikwe, infamous for Botswana's highest prevalence, it was up to a half. I tried to imagine every second person in the busy Phikwe mall just gone. All lined up in coffins.

I couldn't imagine it, and I quickly gave up. Shocked by the emotional anesthetic of the stupendous figure, I didn't like trying.

But incomprehensible as the impact was, at home, with Dad broadcasting facts and stories from his ringside seat, AIDS was too close and too horribly gripping not to think about. By 1995 close to half of his patients had full-blown AIDS. His practice had become defined by AIDS. Dad discussed AIDS often, from every angle, and in a series of his vignettes, arguments, and often appalling medical details, Lulu, Damien, and I were educated haphazardly in the sometimes absurd, tragic, and terrifying pieces of a disaster unfolding on an unprecedented scale.

Even in a country that doesn't normally talk about lions, by the mid-1990s AIDS had become too great a problem to ignore. "When there are enough lions in the bush," said Dad, "even the ostrich must take its head out of the sand." The government had finally started dramatic HIV awareness and condom distribution campaigns, and within my last few years of school, AIDS and HIV became among the most famous acronyms in the country.

The evidence was plentiful. Thousands of people traveled weekly to hundreds of funerals for the young and suddenly sick. And everywhere, on every street, walked the painfully thin— which in Botswana one didn't choose to be. Once, when I came home, having put on weight after months away from Mum's wholesome lentil stews, Ruth greeted me and caught me by the arm. "Ah," she said. "You are fatter, Robbie." I blushed, indignant, but then saw Ruth's admiring smile. She patted me appreciatively and walked off.

In the context of the inexplicably thin and the youthful dead, however, still AIDS was never mentioned. Everyone knew about AIDS, but no one officially died because of AIDS. Of TB, pneumonia, and cancer—but never AIDS.

"It's not surprising," said Dad. "When there's nothing you can do about it."

Everything was back to front. HIV awareness followed after most of the infections, and now the infections still hadn't been followed with drugs. The dramatic but patchy awareness campaigns, combined with the lack of antiretroviral drugs, had fomented stigma, which fueled comforting superstitions. People were talking about the lions, but getting the lions all wrong.

"You do not," said Dad, again and again, "get it from sex with a woman who's had a miscarriage."

"But the *sangoma* told me," the patients would argue.

"I generally lose," said Dad. "Who wants to face a problem when it's too late to do anything?"

This was the trouble with testing. Or not testing. Which was one of the particular troubles.

"Get Tested!" begged the government campaigns. "Know your status!"

But no one came forward. No one wanted to know his or her status. Dad, however, didn't need to test to see the virus. With more and more people developing full-blown AIDS, the signs were obvious and rife: loss of appetite and weight loss, TB, oral or genital thrush, bad oral or genital herpes, Kaposi's sarcoma, and other more subtle indicators, such as when the hair at the nape of the neck of black people with tightly curled hair would suddenly grow straight and downy.

In his clinics, Dad had put up posters saying "Get Tested!" and bought testing kits. And then he'd thrown almost all of them away, unused and expired.

D oesn't surprise me, Keith. I know all about it. Fuck! It's a disaster for this country."

Charles Sheldon was one of those rare people who managed

to render "fuck" at once inoffensive and highly effective. If he added it to a compliment, the compliment felt all the more sincere. Now, as he shook his head, the word gave heightened gravity to his statement, and enhanced his uncharacteristically somber expression.

Charlie was a property developer in Gaborone and an old friend of Mum and Dad's. He was friends, it seemed, with just about everyone else too. Warm, generous, and legendarily sociable, he was known and liked throughout Gaborone and beyond. He returned the affection to everyone, unstintingly, and would just as readily throw his arm around his maid and say, "You're so fucking cool, babe," as he would around awkwardly affectionate Dad, or his other great friend, the beloved Lady Khama.

Charlie had got drunk and misbehaved at the parties and gatherings of the most important people in the country. He was always forgiven, however, and would be there again next time, behaving just as badly, entertaining, shocking, and charming everyone. He was a kind of younger, more reasonable, more sociable version of Grandpa Ivor.

Now, though, as we sat out in the gazebo after dinner, he was unusually serious and calm. He seemed serious and calm even next to Robyn, his wife, whose level serenity mostly made her husband seem even more manic than he was. Every now and again, Charlie would pay tribute to her by announcing, "Byns is cool, she's a Buddhist." Which always made me glad I wasn't nicknamed from the second half of my name, and then made me wonder if I'd care, if I was a Buddhist.

Charlie, Byns, and their three boys had driven up from Gaborone for the weekend.

After an evening walk and dinner, the four adults were drinking and telling stories. Exhausted from hours in the pool, Damien and the Sheldon boys sprawled on the cushioned bed-benches where we—and a Mozambique spitting cobra—sometimes slept outside. Lulu, curled on the end of the mattress by the pool, stood up sleepily every few minutes, doggedly rescuing tiny flapping insects from the illuminated water.

I sat at the table, wanting to fall asleep but desperate not to miss out on any of the conversation. Which had, as conversations now usually did, eventually made its way to the inevitable discussion. Just as white South Africans always talked about the terrible crime, and white Zimbabweans always talked about the plummeting economy, at Botswana dinner tables white people now talked about AIDS.

"It was all there," sighed Charlie. "The employees would have been able to buy their own houses. I would have made money. Lots of people would have made piles of money. It was good for everyone."

For more than a year, Charlie had been putting together a multimillion-pula deal that would have provided individually owned houses to thousands of employees of one of Botswana's largest institutions, through the provision of interest-free loans. Various building societies had agreed to finance the construction of the houses, and the debt would be repaid by rental income.

Even Charlie, known for pulling off the most politically tricky projects, had been amazed when all the details had been worked out and the agreements were finally in place.

The employees were told about the scheme and invited to sign up. Your own house, for an interest-free loan, they said, waiting for a stampede.

No more than a handful came forward. In a few months, the whole project collapsed.

"No one saw this one coming."

The building society loans were underwritten by a large insurance agency, which required each applicant to take out a life insurance policy. And each policy required a medical examination, which required an HIV test.

No one wanted to take an HIV test.

"I offer an effectively free house," said Charlie, "and I still can't get anyone to take a test. Keith, I don't know how the fuck you're going to get paying customers to let you take one."

In 1996, a year later, Dad still hadn't. So he did on-the-spot diagnoses. If someone had enough of the signs, Dad informed them that they almost certainly had AIDS. Word soon spread, and in just a few weeks, his practice numbers had fallen dramatically.

"I ran out of patience," said Dad, smiling grimly, "and then I ran out of patients."

His nurses said, "You are the only doctor who tells people they have AIDS. People don't like it."

"Tough," said Dad. "I'm a doctor. It's my responsibility."

His nurses just shrugged. Dad continued to diagnose relentlessly, explaining to the patients that partners and children must be told and tested. Little by little his patients came back. But it took months for the numbers to return to normal.

And even then, no one wanted to test, to know for sure. Except for a single patient: a healthy-looking Motswana teacher, who didn't have any of the signs.

"They say you do AIDS tests, Dr. Scott," she said. "I want one."

Surprised by her request, Dad was even more surprised by the result.

He double-checked it and turned to her, smiling. "You are HIV-negative," he said.

"I don't have AIDS?" asked the woman.

"No," said Dad cheerfully, "and you are HIV-negative, so you won't develop it."

"But I have AIDS," she insisted.

"What?" Dad stared at her, bewildered. "No you don't, I promise. Look at your result."

"You are lying," she said, "I have AIDS. The whole of Botswana has AIDS. In this country, we all have AIDS."

Dad fumed about the government.

Not, initially, about the lack of antiretrovirals: until the late 1990s, the medicines were still prohibitively expensive, even for the wealthy Botswana government. But about education and prevention—areas in which the government, in the early years of the epidemic, took too long to do too little.

Even well into the first campaign, there was still no comprehensive approach. One of the neglected problems that most angered Dad was that married couples of public sector employees were still regularly posted to different ends of the country. "They don't do the most obvious things," he'd mutter, after he'd had yet another teacher, nurse, or border official, asking for a medical certificate, stating that the stress of separation was affecting their health, to support their case for a transfer. "Makes so much of the good work go to waste," said Dad. "It's a bloody disgrace."

At home, "Bloody disgrace" was Dad's general verdict about the government's approach to AIDS. "Which it is, overall," he said. "They might be doing something. But it's not enough."

But Dad's angle depended on whom he was speaking to. Standing on the lawns after a Tuli Block Farmers' Association meeting, I once heard him tell a very different tale. The subject was the escalating problem of staff taking off too much time for funerals. It continued the theme discussed in the meeting, of wages being too high.

"Half of my guys have it," someone complained.

"Well, you know what these *people* are like with sex. Anyone. Anytime."

Nodding heads.

"And the government does nothing."

"Typical Africans. Let their own people die."

This time, not everyone nodded. Now some people in the gathering looked uncertain. But there were still many nods and mumbles of assent.

Dad's face had gone blank with anger. The only time I'd seen him angrier was when a white doctor we met said, "AIDS was sent by God to deal with black overpopulation." Then Dad had just walked away without a word. This time he stayed, glaring at the gathering with a look that made me scared on their behalf.

"This government is doing a hell of a lot," he said, coldly and slowly. "A hell of a lot more than many other governments. I should know. And they are dealing with a complex problem rooted in economic, geographical, cultural, and social issues. Any government in the world would struggle to cope."

Dad paused, letting his words sink in. Taken aback, no one spoke. I flushed with pride. Mum raised her eyebrows slightly, her eyes sparkling. Usually she just looked exhausted when Dad climbed on his soapbox.

"This is a disease affected by all kinds of factors," Dad continued to his angry and sheepish audience. "And there are all kinds of beliefs involved. I don't fully understand it yet. And I'm a doctor running what is virtually an AIDS practice. There is ignorance. Of course. But there's ignorance everywhere. It's ignorant just to blame the government or just to blame promiscuity." He eyed the offending speakers. "It's bloody disgraceful," he concluded furiously.

I wanted to clap, but the silence was paralyzing.

Such extremely racist views on the disease were unusual, though. For most whites in Botswana, AIDS was what it was: a complex humanitarian tragedy. Albeit a removed tragedy, generally experienced secondhand—a depressing story about an elderly maid, or a friend's maid, with a dead child, or two dead children, who was now supporting all her grandchildren in a single-roomed house.

"Keith, you must understand," friends would say after recounting some desperate situation, "I do what I can to help Precious and all her grandchildren. But the problem is so enormous. What's behind it? How can it be stopped?"

Dad would give his opinion: the need for comprehensive awareness and prevention programs; the need for drugs; the need to tackle superstitions.

"Like what?"

Getting the virus from having sex with a woman who has had a miscarriage, curing it by having sex with a virgin. "A lot of my patients in the villages don't understand infectious diseases," Dad explained to intrigued white audiences. "They think it's something passed from one person to another, leaving the transmitter HIV-free."

The *sangomas*, or traditional healers, many of whom encouraged this belief, maintained that HIV, like other STDs, had always been around. They also claimed they could diagnose HIV by throwing the bones. This problem was so widespread that the Ministry of Health invited a group of *sangomas* in for an experiment, which was to be reported in the local papers. The healers were given equal samples of HIV-positive and HIV-negative blood and asked to throw the bones. They were correct no more than 50 percent of the time—no better than chance.

Still, this failed to discredit them in the minds of many people. "Surely not?"

"Of course," said Dad, "these are entrenched beliefs. You're often dealing with rural, uneducated people who still believe that ancestors play a part in daily life. And who pay witch doctors to curse their enemies."

Occasionally, Dad's explanations would affront "PC" whites. "Surely all this stuff is just a white Western viewpoint... an uninformed stereotype of complex African cultural beliefs... an easy assumption of backwardness?"

Dad hated political correctness almost as much as he hated the "AIDS has been sent by God" argument. Mum said, "Political correctness is antithetical to your father's nature."

I'd watch with bated breath.

"Of course it's a stereotype," he'd retort furiously. "Of course not everyone thinks that. But there are lots who do, and you can't just gloss over it because we don't like to think we're portraying blacks as less sophisticated. It's a reality. A life-and-death reality. To be dealt with."

Where they did mix with Batswana, most white "expats" mixed in businesses and the public sector, with educated urban Batswana. This sector of the population had a more Western outlook and often looked down on the rural villagers. The whites formed opinions accordingly. So in discussions with whites on Batswana beliefs, Dad usually had the last word: partly because he was so hard to argue with, but mostly because not many whites regularly came into contact with the rural, most traditional face of the country.

Jean Kiekopf was one of our few expatriate friends who could tell Dad stories about Botswana that surprised him. As an English teacher with many rural pupils, and as a doctor with several rural practices, Jean and Dad were among a much smaller group exposed to a more traditional, witchcraft-and-ancestor-oriented approach to life.

It was while wearing these hats that Dad and Jean had met—Jean in a state of some panic—soon after we'd arrived from New Zealand, and she had come out from England.

Jean's dog had just had puppies, and she'd gone home during lunch to watch them being born. Returning to her classroom, she explained excitedly to her class of sixteen-year-olds what had kept her. Her students listened in silence. Most looked appalled.

"Did you put ash on your face before you watched?" asked a serious, very traditional boy.

The same boy, Jean later discovered, went all the way to Zimbabwe for his preexam *muti*, because the *sangomas* there were more powerful.

"No, of course not," said Jean. "Why?"

"You will go blind," said the boy somberly.

Momentarily chilled by his earnest, sympathetic face, Jean smiled and continued her lesson. The next morning she awoke, barely able to see through puffy eyes. Her eyes watered, and her swollen eyelids almost obscured her eyeballs. She rang up Dr. Chothia, who had no appointments. "Try Dr. Scott," she was told. "You'll just have to queue." So Jean went and sat in the packed waiting room at Dad's clinic, peering out between slits and silently telling herself that she couldn't possibly be going blind.

"Allergy," pronounced Dad. "I don't think you'll go blind. You'll get over it in a day or two."

Jean took Dad's prescription for the allergy. She didn't go blind. But it did take her a week to see properly again, during which time she couldn't go in to school. Even when she returned, her eyes were still red and sore. The class was unsurprised and unsympathetic. "I told you, Mma Kiekopf," said the serious boy.

Jean, her husband, Klaus, and her son, Luke, had later become good friends, and when we moved to the farm, they were regular visitors. On these weekends at the farm, she often took the opportunity to quiz Dad on medical facts about AIDS, which she was now incorporating into her English lessons.

"Can you get it from kissing?"

"Oral sex?"

"Anal sex?"

"Toilet seats?"

"Touching sores?"

"Sharing razors?"

In one of its late but clever moves, the government had decided that information about HIV and AIDS must be enmeshed in education, and by the end of 1997 this was being taught as part of the syllabus in most subjects.

Jean, who was a gifted and dedicated teacher, approached AIDS education with her usual energy. Determined to be as candid and open as possible, to be able to answer any question, she'd been relentless about becoming well informed. "Thought I knew it all," she told us once, on a visit to the farm. "But it turns out, Keith, I have another question for you."

She had recently devoted a whole lesson to discussing HIV with a class of seventeen-year-old students. Toward the end, she'd opened it up to questions. "Please ask me about anything I haven't covered," she'd said. "Anything that might be worrying you. And if you're too embarrassed to ask here," she'd added, "just slip me a note under my door." One of the boys had raised his hand. "Can you get it from having sex with a goat?"

Some of Jean's students had giggled at the questioner; from a few there'd been curious, expectant silence.

Now, as she told us, Jean paused as everyone laughed.

I said, "*Sis.*" I'd heard about people having sex with goats and donkeys before. And in Zimbabwe, when I said I was originally from New Zealand, boys would sometimes joke that that was where men on lonely farms "shagged sheep." But being reminded of it was always startling.

Jean had said uncertainly, "I don't think so. As far as I know it's a human virus." The boy had raised his hand again. "Can you get it if you have sex with a goat after someone who has HIV has also had sex with the goat?" There'd been more giggles and scorn from his classmates. But still, silence from some.

I said, recovering from my disgust, "That's such a clever question."

"It was," said Jean, "but I have to say I felt a bit out of my depth."

Blushing, Jean had cleared her throat. "I don't think so," she said. "But I'll check and get back to you."

Afterward, she'd questioned some of the Batswana teachers. "Yes, it sometimes happens," they'd informed her, "in the bush at the cattle posts, where there are lots of men on their own."

Now Jean put the question to Dad.

Dad said, "No, I'm pretty confident you wouldn't get it that way. Although I suppose it is technically possible if it happened very quickly."

This led to a discussion about how women are much more likely to catch it through sex than men. Because there's more soft surface area—which might already be damaged through other infections or trauma—and because the virus gets to sit in a moist warm environment, whereas on the retracted penis the virus is quickly exposed to deadly air.

"Which is really not fair, given that it's usually men who don't want to use condoms."

Then we had lunch.

All of this—the gruesome, the curious, and the sometimes shocking—Dad discussed without flinching: matter-of-fact, sardonic, and unemotional as ever. But the worst part of AIDS, the daily reality of his clinics, he rarely mentioned. And about it, we never really asked. We knew enough from his face, which, when he returned from his clinics, was grimmer and more haggard than I'd ever known it.

There was nothing really to discuss, nothing one could say to make it any better. Dad saw at least a hundred patients a day. By the late 1990s, more than half of them had obvious signs of AIDS. He gave them medicines to treat the opportunistic infections. And then he looked them in the eye, told them there was nothing else he could do, and sent them home to die.

Fifty people a day.

26

ELIZABETH

Elizabeth at Molope Farm

I n 1997, two years after Mum had heard about Damien's school-to-be on the radio, she listened to a program that was to define the remainder of our family's years in Botswana.

The interview was with Professor Patrick Bouic, an immunologist conducting a trial with a plant-derived immune supplement on HIV and AIDS. The newly released results from the more than one hundred patients were remarkable. Particularly in the early stage of HIV infection, the supplement appeared to dramatically slow—and in some cases halt—the progression of the disease.

Mum told Dad, and Dad at once phoned Professor Bouic to discuss the results. Immediately afterward, Dad phoned the company producing the supplement to place an order. A few weeks later, he began giving it to his AIDS patients.

Away at school, I followed the story in outline and heard via Mum how excited Dad was about the results from his patients. But not until I returned for the holidays did I really understand what it meant for Dad. He talked about it endlessly. "They start getting hungry again. That's what they all notice first... sometimes it takes just a few weeks. Then they put on weight... I know I've said it before, but I just cannot tell you how bloody nice it is to be able to finally give my patients something...."

Dad had the old sparkle in his eye, the old excited edge in his voice. I was almost as excited by the effects on him as by the effects on his patients, which he repeatedly, elatedly, described. In a few months, this hope had renewed his interest in work in a way that nothing had since he'd decided to be a flying doctor all those years ago when we arrived in Botswana.

For the first time ever, AIDS discussions hijacked the long evening walks and exquisite river paddles. The pristine hours once reserved for happy dreams of extrication from the clinics and ecosystem rehabilitation became a time when Mum and Dad spoke, endlessly, of something that they both believed could change the course of the epidemic in Botswana.

"You see," Dad said, striding out along the dusty path, "even if the government does get around to giving ARVs, you can't give the drugs too early on in the disease process. These sterols and sterolins work best in the early stages. So they're an ideal complementary treatment."

"And of course," continued Mum, "it's an immune booster, rather than directly attacking the virus. So you don't have the risk of resistance if patients don't comply."

Mum and Dad ostensibly talked to us—but really they talked to each other, batting ideas and plans back and forth, building momentum, like a long, elegant rally in a game of tennis.

"And let me tell you," said Dad, "compliance is going to be a hell of a problem. It's bad enough with TB drugs, and they don't make you feel crap like ARVs."

"And sterols and sterolins," said Mum, "are jolly cheap.

Fifty pula at cost. Which is what? The price of a few bags of cornmeal."

"The government could give it to the whole country for next to nothing—"

"Now Dad just needs to get out there and tell other doctors about it."

"There's the inevitable skepticism, of course—"

"But," said Mum, "the results will speak for themselves—"

A giant snort from the river interrupted her.

Sitting on the new wooden deck on the Limpopo, our legs dangling over the edge, we peered through the last of the late dusk light toward the island opposite the channel. In the water beneath the bank, the dark humps of the three now irritated hippos were still just visible.

"Poor chaps want to get out and graze," whispered Mum. "We should leave them in peace. They're a bit stuck here, after all."

Here was one of the last deep pools in the river. The rains had been poor, and the Limpopo had flowed late and stopped early. A year before, rains, water, and dams would have dominated our conversation. This evening, though, they were not even mentioned. Where once the beauty of the farm had been a retreat from the horrors of Dad's work—a microcosm in which there were no hopeless problems—suddenly it was a place from which he was preparing to do battle with the biggest problem in the country.

Mum said, as we packed up our bottles of fruit juice, "Anyway, if anyone can do this, can change things, your father can...."

We set off back home in the near darkness, shining a flashlight on the road for snakes and casting it into the bush, following a rustle, to catch the gleaming, moving eyes of unidentified creatures. All the while, Mum and Dad kept talking, and walking beside them, listening, I felt light-headed with hope and pleasure. When Mum and Dad were like this, rallying against some great challenge, it seemed that no amount of differences between them would ever be enough to push them apart. And I felt no doubt that together, like this, they could change the world.

Thrilled by the response among his patients, Dad visited the company producing the supplement when he next collected his medicines in Johannesburg. He returned home more excited than ever.

The story of Moducare was just the sort of natural medicine triumph Dad and Mum loved. Behind it all was a South African businessman who'd originally commissioned research to assess the effects on cancer of the African potato, *Hypoxis hemerocallidea*, a well-known traditional remedy, when a relative with cancer had experienced a rapid improvement after taking the bulb. The initial laboratory research showed a significant immune-enhancing effect, and further studies narrowed this down to sterols and sterolins, two plant fats that, unlike some of the other compounds in the bulb of the African potato, are nontoxic. Moducare, containing a combination of sterols and sterolins, was created and patented. Importantly, the new supplement did not share the immune-depressing effects of the long-term use of the African potato.

So impressive were the immune-modulating effects that the company made a decision to focus instead on HIV. A clinical trial headed by Professor Bouic was initiated, and several years later, the first results seemed to bear out the hope that the formulation would indeed help HIV-ravaged immune systems.

Dad had spoken excitedly of his anecdotal results, and the company asked him if he'd like to promote Moducare in Botswana. Dad had said yes at once and set about poring over hefty immunology textbooks, educating himself—and anyone else who wanted to listen—about the virus's slow annihilation of the body's defenses. No detail was too much: if he was going to be traveling around the country to present the research to doctors, he wanted to be prepared for any question. He was determined to show that this had real science behind it, that it was not just a flaky hope fueled by desperation for a solution to the insoluble.

I was enthralled. For several days, crouched beside him at the computer, I helped him tinker with his slides, and my head soon swam with pages of bright blobs and arrows representing the com-

ponents and relationships of the immune system. They were fascinating simply as a lens into the body's staggering sophistication;
but when one considered the implications, the colorful pictures we
created were truly gripping.

At the heart lay the crucial CD4 lymphocyte cells, key coor-
dinators of the body's entire immune response. Dad explained
how these cells, targeted by the HI virus, have their DNA
hijacked to enable viral replication, and die in the process—their
inexorable decline paralleling the relentless progression of the
virus and the collapse of the immune system. When the concentration of these key indicators falls to about 20 percent of their
normal blood levels, AIDS generally manifests. But taken before
this threshold, the sterols and sterolins mix appeared to stop or
dramatically slow the decline of CD4 cells, and thus the descent
into full-blown AIDS.

It was utterly compelling stuff. "How come everyone isn't
using it?"

Dad said, "You can't underestimate the resistance of the medical profession to natural solutions."

Mum said, "Everything doctors are taught primes them to
immediately suspect nondrug treatments. Everyone's forgotten
good old Hippocrates. Let food be your medicine and—"

Dad interrupted. "And there is a hell of a lot of bollocks out
there. Mum and I should know—we've tried most of it."

"But this works," I said.

"Well, it does appear to," said Dad. "But it still needs a
double-blind, placebo-controlled trial to be medically kosher.
Unfortunately Prof Bouic's trial was only an open-label trial with
no placebo control. My own philosophy is that if something's
working and isn't toxic and people are dying while you wait, you
shouldn't hang around for indisputable proof."

"Obviously," I said hotly.

Dad smiled. "Robbie, you're a seventeen-year-old vegetarian
who hypnotizes people to augment dental anesthesia. Born during an acupuncture session. And raised on Bach flower remedies,
soya beans, and enough dietary fiber to meet the annual needs of
a small city. The obvious is subjective."

"But I have great hope," said Mum. "Things *are* changing. The fringe is going mainstream. Twenty years ago my book wouldn't have happened."

The book she referred to was not *Living on the Fringe*, which—as the manuscript had just been rejected by the first publisher in South Africa—was anything but happening. "Probably a good thing," Mum had said. "You know I'm sure they wouldn't have been right for it."

Naturally undaunted, she'd been on the verge of trying others when the rejecting publishers had offered her a commission for a different book instead. Mum had said yes at once, and quickly immersed herself in the new project—*Natural Home Pharmacy*, a mainstream, glossy guide to complementary therapies.

"It's such a wonderful challenge," she marveled, at least once a day. "What an opportunity to communicate the benefits of natural medicine! Isn't it amazing how well things always turn out? If I hadn't plugged away at *Living on the Fringe*, this would never have happened.... Perhaps it was never meant to be published anyway... I mean, thinking about it now, who would really want to read about us and our mad life?"

At the dinner table, "the book" and sterols and sterolins vied constantly for airtime.

Dad was technically a coauthor—the thought being that a doctor would give the book more credibility. But really it was Mum's project, and she did all the writing. Dad just occasionally debated some finer point of homeopathy, reflexology, or nutritional therapy and criticized Mum for using too many big words.

Mum said, "Well, you write some then."

Which caused Dad to quickly retreat and say that Mum was the much better writer. "Anyway," said Dad, "all my creative juices are sapped by my articles."

In return for advertising space for Moducare, Dad had agreed to write a medical column in *The Voice* newspaper, a tabloid in Francistown. Initially prepared and eager to inform the district on the big health issues of the day, he had soon been infuriated by the stream of readers' inquiries:

Infertility...

Penis problems...

Bad breath...

Men as well as women can suffer from infertility, Dad wrote again and again.

"Which most Batswana men aren't going to believe anyway."

Do not always blame the woman...

"I wish someone would just ask about AIDS," Dad complained. "It's amazing. The biggest issue in the country, and no one seems interested....thank God for the Elizabeths of this world."

K nowing Elizabeth's story was still no preparation for the experience of meeting her. It was 1998, and Lulu and I had returned to the farm for a few days, eager to witness Mum and Dad's moment of fame.

We were sharing Lulu's room to accommodate the truly weird mix of guests. In my room were John and Beverley Parr, a trendy husband-and-wife team of TV producers from Johannesburg; in Damien's was Elizabeth Kgano, one of the first women in Botswana to publicly admit to being HIV-positive.

Dad had said, "She's not going to feel comfortable staying in the house."

And Elizabeth didn't. She spent most of her time at our staff quarters. She looked deeply awkward at meals, where she hardly spoke. After a while she announced she'd rather join our maids, Dad's nurses, and Shimane and Joseph for dinner around the fire.

Elizabeth had been raised in a village, and had no more than a primary education. She wasn't interested in anything we discussed— except for HIV and AIDS. Enter into the conversation these two words, and Elizabeth was unstoppable, speaking with a cheerful frankness and compulsion that was riveting.

Elizabeth said, "People would stop and say to me, 'Are you the one who has been in the newspaper saying you have HIV?'" She grinned and shook her head in mirth. "They stare at me like I should be ashamed."

Elizabeth tested positive for HIV in 1991. "I *was* ashamed then," she said. "And frightened." Keeping quiet about her own condition, she spent the next few years doing door-to-door campaigns in the villages, talking openly and tirelessly about the problem and encouraging others to do the same. But then the opportunistic infections started to strike. Her weight dropped to seventy pounds. Barely able to get out of bed, and certain she would die, she decided to go public.

Everyone was shocked. Elizabeth lost friends, and received insults from strangers. "But I never looked away when they stared or swore at me," she said matter-of-factly. "Sometimes I think they just wanted to know what someone who has HIV looks like. I think they thought I would look like a monster."

With statements like these, Elizabeth had been shocking not just her neighbors, but radio listeners and newspaper readers across the country. "I have been insulted in every way," she said, "but I don't feel anger anymore. I feel great pity." She paused and sighed dramatically. "I feel sorry for them because they don't understand AIDS is everyone's problem."

Practical, cheerful middle-aged mother of two, Elizabeth let nothing daunt her on her crusade. She hadn't been on television before. But as she sat in our garden, staring intently at the camera, she spoke fiercely and without embarrassment—only encouraged, she said, by the knowledge she was talking to audiences across southern Africa.

"AIDS is everyone's problem!" she said, repeating one of her favorite mantras. She paused, and launched straight into another. "I tell them," she grinned, " 'Intercourse is a short course, AIDS is a long course!' "

Natural Home Pharmacy had just been published, and the film crew was visiting the farm to do a feature on Mum and Dad and the book. One of the angles they liked was Dad's use of a natural treatment for HIV and AIDS. Dad had approached Elizabeth, a Moducare devotee, who had immediately agreed to appear on the program.

"I would be dead without this stuff," she said.

When Elizabeth had gone public, at her sickest, a friend had told her about the supplement. Elizabeth had set up a roadside stall selling single cigarettes to pay for it. Grinning nostalgically, she told us how soon her only problem was not having enough money to buy food for her new appetite. Her weight returned to 150 pounds. She started again to rise at six in the morning to make her bed. "You smile," she said. "But there were so many days when I couldn't make my own bed. Or fetch water, or sweep, or cook. When you get better, you realize it's these little things that matter in life."

Her health renewed, she continued her campaigning with a vengeance and encouraged others to use the product. This was how she'd met Dad, who, as well as writing about halitosis and infertility for *The Voice*, donated Moducare to an AIDS center started by Elizabeth and supported by the newspaper. Elizabeth had also been awarded a small government stipend, which she used to help run the center.

Listening to her speak, it seemed she should have had a whole program to herself. But there were other angles to be covered, and the Parrs soon returned their attention to Mum and Dad.

"Right," said John. "Now we need some farm and family shots."

Keen on the idea of two "natural medicine" authors living in marital bliss in the beautiful bush, he shot some footage of Dad driving up in his car and parking in front of a verdant backdrop of acacia trees. Following instructions, Dad got out of the car, and Mum rushed out across the dirt to meet him, kissing him awkwardly on the cheek as he took her in his arms.

Lulu and I protested that they never did it like that and were brushed aside.

A horse-river combination was next on the program. Mum had never ridden much, and now rode even less after a few bad experiences on Feste. So only Lulu and I saddled up with Dad and headed up the road toward the Limpopo, which had a splendid backdrop of magnificent trees. Riding his majestic, golden Thoroughbred, Squire, Dad looked light-years away from his first days on Quartz, and perfect for TV.

But a few minutes up the road, Dad realized that Squire was lame. "You girls go on," he said. "It's a pity. But you're better riders anyway."

John Parr barely hid his dismay when Lulu and I appeared at

the river without Dad. He asked us to remove our hideous black pudding-bowl riding hats, undo our hair, and gallop past him.

We did.

"Do it again."

After the fifth gallop past the camera, the horses were bucking wildly. We tried to calm them as we waited for the signal for another run. Lulu let out a nervous giggle. "If we fall off, Rob, we might die."

"Not impossible," I muttered. "*Shhh*, girl."

Lulu giggled again. "Say Goodbye, Rob," she whispered.

Say Goodbye was my ominously named Thoroughbred. She was snorting furiously. The prettiest part of the river also happened to hold traumatic memories for her. On her I'd once chased a large troop of baboons who were threatening to savage our two Jack Russells. I'd screamed at the baboons loudly enough to summon Mum and Dad from the other end of the farm, and Say Goodbye had never quite recovered.

Now she lashed out at Beauty, who Lulu was riding because we were worried that skeletal Winnie might provoke viewer outrage. Beauty, who had a generous dose of Feste's character, kicked, bucked, and then reared viciously.

"Shall we ask for our hats back?"

"No, *man,* we can't look like wimps."

"Better than dying. Or being concussed again—"

The distant thunder of hooves silenced us, and quieted the horses.

All eyes and the camera lens focused on the empty road, in the direction of the sound. Moments later, little Quartz tore around a bend in a cloud of dust, Dad standing up in his stirrups and bouncing on top.

Charging towards us, Dad swung his arm in the air. "Yee-hah," he yelled.

He was wearing his pudding-bowl hat, accessorized with a blue sun hat strapped on with Velcro, giving the effect of a flying saucer. His feet dangled well below Quartz's belly, which was filthy with dust, and wet with sweat from the gallop.

"Decided I couldn't miss out on the action," said Dad, grinning, as Quartz skidded to a halt beside us. "Can't let you two hog the camera." He patted Quartz affectionately. "Thank goodness for my trusty steed. What did I always tell you about Boerperds? My kind of horse."

Later Mum and Dad drove down to Johannesburg for a live studio appearance, which Lulu and I watched on satellite TV in Bulawayo. Damien, although not in the preshot film, arrived in time to be in the studio audience. The theme of the week's episode was complementary health, and Mum and Dad were featured beside a crystal healer.

Dad had been on TV once before in New Zealand, talking about biodynamic farming. But sitting there under the bright lights, he looked as if he'd been doing this every day of his life— smiling levelly at the camera, implacably calm. He showed not a trace of his initial irritation at being featured alongside a crystal healer.

Mum, as I'd expected, looked earnest, pale, and tremendously nervous. She grinned unconvincingly.

For days, she'd stayed up late studying her book. Dad had tried to calm her down: "Lin, you wrote the jolly thing. You know what's in it." But Mum would just mutter, "God, how embarrassing if I don't know something in my own book.... You should read it too, Keith. I bet you don't know everything that's in it." Dad had said of course he didn't, but he'd pass all the hard questions to Mum. Which had made Mum panic further and haul out reference books so she could expand upon her own details.

I nevertheless felt confident on their behalf. Dad always said exactly what he thought, and I knew no question would rattle him. And Mum, I knew, would have by now stored enough detail to speak about her book for weeks.

After a discussion about crystals, the beautiful TV presenter turned to Dad and smiled. As a medical doctor, she asked him, what did he think of crystal healing.

And suddenly I was holding my breath. I felt embarrassed in advance for the crystal healer and the presenter. Dad's opinion on crystals would be withering. He paused before answering. Then to my amazement he gave a diplomatic, noncommittal response.

It was one of the only times I'd ever known him not to say exactly what he thought.

Mum looked relieved.

The five-minute film on the Scotts of Molope Farm, condensed from hours of footage, was then shown. There were shots of Mum and Dad in different places around the farm, and of the two of them smiling uncomfortably as they walked beside each other to Dad's car. There were a few minutes of Elizabeth talking. Lulu and I waited expectantly for our moment of glory. Then a shot of Dad pulling up on faithful little Quartz suddenly appeared on the screen. And then it was over. Lulu and I, having gallantly risked our lives, had been edited out altogether. We couldn't believe it.

The presenter turned to Mum. "So, tell us, Linda, I'm fascinated, why did you decide to homeschool your children?"

Now Mum looked like a hare caught in the headlights. I held my breath again. This was her moment: her chance to tell thousands of people about her passionate philosophy of learning. And she was totally unprepared. I could feel her feeling sick. As she started to speak, her voice cracked slightly, as if she might cry.

But Mum had been practicing for years. After making a joke about needing a crystal to calm her nerves, she took no more than a sentence to warm up. Partly, she said, homeschooling was a way to keep the family together when we lived so remotely. Mostly, though, she'd wanted her children to learn in a happy, stress-free environment, to ensure they never lost their interest and enthusiasm for learning. Mum looked like she wanted to say more, but the presenter moved on.

That was the only question Mum was asked.

When Elizabeth's face appeared on the screen, I'd wondered what she was doing—while her voice blared through living rooms across southern Africa—in her tiny ramshackle house, where Mum, Lulu, and I had dropped her back home in the darkness.

There was my lasting memory of Elizabeth: not in our garden, or at the dinner table, or staring at the camera, but standing outside her hut in the warm night, waving cheerily good-bye as we drove off along her dingy, rubbish-scattered street. For a few minutes afterward, Mum, Lulu, and I were silent, staring out into the darkness, our minds reeling from two uninterrupted, uncensored hours of Elizabeth's thoughts.

Then Mum said, "Shit."

Lulu gasped. "Mum!" she admonished.

"Shit!" said Mum. "You know, that woman makes me want to weep with admiration. And weep with shame that I don't do more. And weep with joy that it's possible to do so much, with so little, for so many." She paused, and sighed. "This is a truly Churchillian battle...."

I said, "Don't be so dramatic, Mum." But I was shaken too; with an acute, disconcerting mixture of fascination, hope, and horror.

To begin with, as we'd set off from the farm to take her home, Elizabeth had just repeated all her favorite pithy statements. But as the sun dropped below the horizon, and mile after mile of the darkening bush sped past, she began to elaborate.

"The problem, you know, is that sex is so nice. You understand, Linda?"

"Absolutely," said Mum, as Lulu and I blushed painfully in the backseat.

Elizabeth then proudly reminded us about her daughter, who was part of a "Say NO!" group at her school. "You know," she continued, "once an AIDS educator told me I was going to have to abstain or have safe sex. *Ee!* But did she think I was mad? I told her, 'I love sex. I will never abstain.'" She chuckled. "But, as you know, I have changed my mind about that too."

This fact Elizabeth had shared with the whole country, announcing in a newspaper article that she had trained her mind to resist the sexual urge, and forgotten about sex.

Now she explained why. At first, when she'd gone public, few people, let alone men, had wanted to go near her. She was ostracized in every way. In addition to the blatant insults, there were small hurtful things too. Sometimes when she visited people in their yards, they would look away. Some offered her water in chipped mugs and glasses.

But as she put on weight and once more looked healthy, many people's manners changed. "They thought I did not have AIDS anymore," she said. "Even at the hospital. Sometimes the nurses laughed at me and said I was too fat to have AIDS. I told them I'd had a test, and they laughed and said the test must have been wrong."

Then Elizabeth got a boyfriend. At first, they'd used condoms. But after a while he asked her for unprotected sex. "Skin to skin!" she exclaimed, shaking her head. "Can you believe it?" She turned to the backseat, just to check Lulu and I were looking appropriately shocked. "I told him I have HIV," she said. "I told him, 'The whole of Botswana knows I have HIV.'"

Elizabeth's boyfriend explained he never saw her with another man, so he could trust her. Elizabeth retorted that this was irrelevant. She was still infected. Then her boyfriend said he had special medicine from the *sangoma* to stop him getting HIV. Elizabeth told him *muti* from the *sangoma* doesn't work.

"He didn't believe me," she said, "then he offered me money to have skin-to-skin sex. I told him, 'Intercourse is a short course, AIDS is a long course.' Then I threw him out and told him to go and swim in the HIV sea somewhere else. Then I told him that before he went swimming, he must put on his costume!"

Elizabeth slapped her thigh, and gave an exasperated laugh. "There is this willful ignorance like this everywhere." And then her thoughts on willful ignorance occupied her for at least half an hour. "People are terrified to know they are going to die. Of course they are! And then sometimes they are angry. I had a friend," she said. "*Ee!* This is a terrible story. She discovered she had HIV. She was angry with the man who had given it to her. But she didn't know who he was. She told me, 'I am going to have sex with as many men as possible.' I told her, You can't do that. But she was too angry to listen. Then she sat outside her hut with her legs open and no panties on. Begging men for sex."

Elizabeth said, "This willful ignorance is terrible. This is why I have taught myself to resist sexual desires. Because men do not want to have sex with condoms.... This is why I spend all my time speaking to people about AIDS. So there is hope for our children."

Then she took a deep breath and solemnly repeated the phrase that would ring in my head for days. "AIDS is everyone's problem."

On the few occasions Elizabeth paused, we said things like "That's amazing," or "You're so brave." It was hard to think of anything better than platitudes. And Elizabeth brushed aside compliments.

Her hut was in the outskirts of Phikwe. None of us had been to this part of town, and Elizabeth—in between her endless AIDS chatter—directed us through streets where mangy dogs and the occasional goat wandered languidly in the path of oncoming cars.

"I'm so pleased to be home," she said as we stopped in front of a tiny building that stood on a small patch of swept dust, surrounded by a low wire fence. "But I must get back to my patients in Francistown. They will be missing me."

An AIDS refuge was not enough for Elizabeth. Stretching her small resources to the limits, she'd also set up a support group for terminally ill people in her community—the AIDS patients sent home to die by the overflowing hospitals. Elizabeth and her group took turns visiting these patients, feeding and washing them, and giving advice to their family members on how to care for them, and how to avoid contracting HIV.

Elizabeth shook each of our hands with a warm Botswana clasp.

Mum said, "It's been a privilege having you to stay. You are an inspiration to us all."

Elizabeth just laughed.

Mum said, "You must take a break for yourself sometime. You must look after yourself in order to look after others."

But Elizabeth shook her head and smiled. "No rest," she said. "I have too much work to do. And look at me, I am as strong as a lion. *Tsamaya sentle*."

"*Sala sentle*," we called back. Stay well.

27

DAD

Dad and Beauty

It was the Christmas holidays of 1998. Grandpa Ivor arrived at the farm, yelling.

"I'm losing my identity," he bellowed as he sprang out of the car. "Never thought I'd see the day."

He strode toward us, fending off the three dogs that hurled themselves at his legs. The dogs slobbered briefly and then charged off toward Granny Betty, who was still inching her way out onto the dirt. Grandpa flung his arms despairingly skyward, and then held them out to Lulu, who ran toward him. "Well, if it isn't little Lulu." He grinned delightedly.

Lulu, Mum, and I kissed Grandpa hello. Damien and Dad shook his hand.

Dad said, "Hi, Ivor."

Grandpa said, "Hi, Keith."

Then a smile twitched on Grandpa's face. "Ya bloody stole my identity, Keith. My own son! Can't believe it."

Dad raised his eyebrows, fighting a curious smile. He said nothing, but Grandpa needed no encouragement. As we carried their bags inside, he told us, at high volume, how he'd been stopped at a veterinary post on the way to the farm.

"Told them I was Mr. Scott. And ya know what the little bugger said? He said, 'Ee, you are the father of the doctor!' Can ya believe it? And I said, 'First of all, I am Ivor Scott, and not just the doctor's father. Everyone in Botswana bloody knows who I am.' Dunno what's happening to this country! No respect for their elders anymore."

Dad grinned. "Sorry, Ivor," he said. "But you've had a pretty long reign."

"Whaddaya talking about? I'm just getting started."

Behind Grandpa, Granny Betty winked and smiled. "It's nice to be here," she said.

Grandpa stopped abruptly in the lounge. He dropped his bag and stared at the corner of the room. "Now what the bloody hell is that creation?" He turned to Mum. "Bet ya can't identify that one, Linda."

"It's our Christmas tree," said Lulu.

"Bloody hell," said Grandpa.

Lulu giggled. "It was Damien's idea. Except for the barbed wire. That was mine. Rob helped, but she doesn't approve."

"I just preferred the silver thorn trees," I explained. "But I appreciate Damien's artistic concept."

"Well, I got tired of thorn trees," said Damien. "And I miss welding at school."

Grandpa walked to the tree and peered closely.

The trunk was a meter-tall silver metal pipe mounted on a dinner-plate-size steel disk. The branches were sawn-off metal fencing droppers, which Damien had welded onto the trunk at branchlike angles and sprayed with silver paint. Wound around trunk and branches were several meters of shiny barbed wire—

the equivalent of tinsel. Spray-painted silver stars cut out from flattened tin cans dangled from the branches, and as a concession to Lulu's desire for snow, Damien had spray-painted teased out bits of steel wool, which she had dotted along the branches.

The overall effect was of a stark, hideous beauty.

Grandpa spun around, grinning. "So what's its Latin name, little Lulu? Don't tell me you've forgotten how to speak Latin."

"*Metallum scrapus*," said Lulu, eyeing him gravely as she delivered our carefully planned retort to the inevitable question. "Unique to Molope Farm."

We drove Granny and Grandpa around the farm, showing them the new dams, the pod of hippos, and the most beautiful bird-dense river spots, where cormorants and goliath herons perched on gray rocks, intently studying the mirror water. Granny Betty spent most of her time cuddling the dogs. Grandpa alternately marveled at the scenery and dispensed irrelevant advice.

Then we had Christmas Eve dinner: leek and potato bake, with, in Granny Betty's honor, a special fillet steak of which she ate just a few bites, taking minutes over each mouthful and dropping pieces to the dogs, which Dad frowned at but ignored.

"Who's going to visit the hospital tomorrow?" I asked.

"Plenty of other people doing it," said Grandpa. "Don't ya worry. And it's probably lucky we can't go. Look at your Granny Betty. I think the nurses might put her straight into one of the beds. Might never get you back again, hey, Betty?"

Granny Betty smiled. She looked not at all upset by the prospect.

"Business is booming," said Grandpa. "Can't keep up. Traveling all the time. So Betty has to hold the fort. Look after the cats and dogs. Fend off the burglars. Did I tell you we were burgled?"

Grandpa had, but we listened again as he explained, incredulously, how a few months after the old *muti*-picking witch doctor had died, their house had been broken into when they were shopping in Phikwe. "Nothing for twenty years. Then the old bugger kicks the bucket, and *wham*. Told ya we were protected by witchcraft."

Dad said, "Betty, are you worried when Ivor's away?"

"I actually rather enjoy it," said Granny, "and I have the dogs, and the neighbors across the road. They're very good to me. And of course," she smiled mockingly, "I've always got my crutches to defend myself—"

"Betty's a tough old gal," interrupted Grandpa, "And this is Botswana. They dunno what violence is in this place."

Dad frowned, and I braced myself for a visit-terminating lecture about Grandpa's carelessness. Grandpa, among other things, often forgot to pay their monthly medical aid subscription, and one of Granny's hip operations had almost not happened as a result. Grandpa had got away with it only because he was such a long-standing customer.

But Dad just took another mouthful and chewed impassively.

And Christmas passed with stories of the old days, discussions about the Tuli Block, and not a harsh word between them.

Dad's good humor, these days, seemed impervious to assault.

In crusading-pioneering full throttle, he was inexhaustible and imperturbable, bubbling with an energetic optimism to rival Mum's.

On his free days, he drove around the country giving lectures to private and government hospital doctors about sterols and sterolins. From his long clinic days, he returned still tired, but cheered by his AIDS patients, who continued to respond well to the supplement. He gave the product to his own patients at cost price, but he and Charlie Sheldon had been given agency rights for Moducare, so they received a commission when it was sold in Botswana. To Dad, it offered the perfect opportunity to both help with the epidemic and buy his way out of clinical medicine. And he was convinced it was only a matter of time and persistence before the whole medical establishment caught on.

Meanwhile, back at the farm, in between churning out articles for *The Voice*, Dad flung himself into the problems of the Tuli Block farmers.

Long-standing dissatisfaction with the chairman of the Tuli Block Farmers' Association had at last, in 1998, provoked a vote of no confidence. The chairman, however, flatly refused to stand down. After several months of chaos, a breakaway association—the first of its kind in the history of the Tuli Block—was formed.

Dad was asked to be the chairman of the Limpopo Agricultural Association. But five years after our arrival, he was still not farming anything and he again protested on these grounds. The farmers argued that Dad was the only person who could successfully stand up to the wrath and power of the deserted chairman.

So Dad agreed, reasoning it was an opportunity to help out the change-seeking farmers and "take the Tuli Block into the twentieth century."

Mum said, "I also think your father just can't resist a good fight."

Charlie Sheldon said to Dad, "Don't do it, Keith."

Before moving to Gaborone, Charlie had lived in Ghanzi, an area of freehold land in western Botswana that was also largely dominated by right-wing Afrikaners. "I've seen it before," he said. "Some of these old Boers will make friends with the Englishman. Then one day they'll unite, enemies and all, and fuck him over."

Dad said, "I trust these guys, they're a good bunch. They want change."

The LAA was soon making waves. The old association had done little more than organize a Christmas party and alcohol-fueled *braais* after the monthly meetings, which were always held at the chairman's house. The new one didn't have enough months in the year for all its fund-raising plans, and each meeting was held at a different farm to try and encourage a sense of community.

Lulu, Damien, and I had arrived home for the Christmas holidays, just in time for the LAA's second four-by-four obstacle competition. Held on a gully-riddled stretch of Limpopo riverbank on a nearby farm, the event had even drawn entrants from as far afield as Pretoria in South Africa. Tents and chairs dotted the temporary campsite, and scores of tough, athletic-looking vehicles stood ready for action.

The day was hot and dry, but deep mud from recent rains made for a perfect course.

As truck after truck skidded down and ground up the gullies—cheered by a first gently and then severely intoxicated audience—the slopes and bumps became increasingly slippery. Judges carrying clipboards hurried around the straining, mud-spattered vehicles. A tractor hauled out the chronically stuck. Many of the entrants were drinking as liberally as the crowd, and they became more reckless with the worsening terrain. A truck toppled. People tumbled out amid cheers and yells. Young boys held wild informal races on the dirt roads behind the main course.

Everything felt slightly, exhilaratingly out of control.

Dad looked on, sweating. After the first event, he'd tried to ban drinking. He was told, unequivocally, that no one would come, and he'd reluctantly given in. As doctor in charge, he now strode between the gullies armed with his medical aid kit, examining cuts and scratches. I trailed after him, wanting to be on the scene of any drama and amused by his determined attempts to curtail the drinking.

"I think you've probably had enough beer for the moment," he admonished one red-eyed driver after the next. But no one was listening, and yells and cries accompanied various off-piste excursions down gullies.

When the time came for the blindfolded event, Dad sighed with relief. "At least no one's drunk enough to hurt themselves on this one."

This was a flat course, which the blindfolded driver had to navigate, directed by his codriver. Everyone seemed to manage easily. Dad leaned against a tree, opened a can of Appletizer, and started chatting to some of the onlookers.

Then someone yelled.

A red truck hurtled wildly across the course, ignoring the markers. I recognized it as one that had earlier driven down the wrong gully. The windshield was spattered with mud. The young man driving—his head wrapped in a black blindfold—leaned out the side and peered ahead to take a better look. The navigator laughed and yelled helplessly. Then realizing that leaning out the window didn't help, the driver yelped with excitement and veered back on course.

The crowd screeched with laughter.

Dad put his head in his hands.

But no one was seriously hurt, and the excitement mounted. Between events, some of the serious competitors clambered on fallen tree trunks and up the side of termite mounds, scrutinizing the obstacles from every angle, sizing up the opposition. But most just took the opportunity to crack open another can of beer. Some continued to drink in their cars, raising their cans in toasts out of their windows.

As it was, sometimes drunken bravery was exactly what was needed: outsiders shone, favorites fell by the wayside. It was the Sunbeams boat race all over again. With no Sunbeams.

Mum was part of the catering team. Installed in a little portable hut, she handed out white bread rolls smothered in margarine with a look of stoic sacrifice. "No fiber. Hydrogenated fats. Can't believe I'm doing this. At least there's a sense of community. Maybe," she said uncertainly, "I could even grow to be part of it...."

The previous winners had come from Pretoria, and the day ended jubilantly when a team from Gaborone, the home capital city, brought the champion's title back to Botswana. The riverside party continued late into the night. In the end-of-year newsletter, Mum patriotically hailed the return of the title to Botswana. Dad declared, confidently. "We're going to put the Tuli Block back on the map. And back in Botswana."

From afar, with occasional close-ups in the holidays, I followed Mum and Dad's quests, riveted, hopeful, and full of trepidation.

AIDS, I cared about for what it was: the magnitude of the problem, the tragedy of how it was being dealt with—or wasn't being dealt with—and the immense hope that lay in any part of any solution. The Limpopo Agricultural Association, at least what it did, I cared for hardly at all. I loved what it meant, though: that Mum and Dad had another cause, however small, that they thought worth fighting for, together.

For as long as I could remember, Dad had dreamed out loud of escaping medicine and nurturing a beautiful farm, deep in the bush. Then, he'd always said, he would be content. Mum, beside him, had happily followed every bumpy mile of Dad's little-trodden road to his dream. A thousand times she'd told me that her only intent, and where her idea of contentment lay, was to have a happy family, nurtured according to her philosophy of humanity.

By my final years of school, I suspected both were wrong: that Dad had led Mum to something too easy to ever make him happy; that Mum had followed, determined to create something that would not be nearly enough for her; and that all the while, what they'd really loved was the bumpy road itself: changing countries, building houses, living in cowsheds, laughing at convention, and believing passionately in doing what everyone else said couldn't and shouldn't be done.

And so while Grandpa Ivor feared for his identity, I feared for Mum and Dad's—so long and so inextricably bound to each other's dreams and our family's life together, and suddenly up for renegotiation.

Dearest R,

I hope this finds you happy and not working too hard. Don't forget to sniff your peppermint oil while revising and before tests. I am convinced that this really does help focus the mind and improve your recall. I must warn you, though, do be careful about getting it directly on your nostrils. The other day I discovered how much the neat oil burns, which took my mind off the task at hand altogether. I'd feel terrible if that happened to you during an exam. So just use a few drops on a tissue and inhale deeply.

Otherwise, all is well back here in the Tuli Block. I am being kept busy with my various new book projects. My latest idea is a nutritional cookbook—a series of recipes for different conditions: the heart menu, the diabetes menu, etc. with relevant nutritional info alongside each. I am going to call it *Help Yourself*, and an agent in the UK has put me in touch with two well-known cooks. Dad says that is critical because if I devised the recipes, he reckons the experiential side effects would outweigh the physiological benefits.

No comment!

Meanwhile, the LAA is going from strength to strength, and occupying much of the rest of my time. I'm delighted, of course, to be helping such a positive movement, and I don't resent it at all. But I have to say, Robbie, I occasionally stop and wonder: Is this it? As you know, I've always liked to keep an open mind about my destiny. But I can't help questioning whether "Secretary of the Limpopo Agricultural Association" is really what I'm meant to be doing with my life. Just as you were so clear about your future not lying in netball, I feel sure there must be more for me! What do you think? Anyway, you know me. I don't like to dwell on the negative. And my work does help Dad, who's firing on all cylinders—giving his talks around the country, and doing, what he does best—what we all love about him so much—churning out new ideas, shaking people up, and making things happen.

Lots of love,
Mumsie.

Dearest M and D,

I am working hard, Mum, I'm afraid. But I am, at least, using your peppermint oil. You'd be amused: the other day I was sniffing it before a math test, for which the teacher was late. Getting odd looks (shades of the neurolinguistic programming episode), I ended up explaining to the whole jittery class that I was using it to clear my mind. Then everyone wanted to try it, and the teacher arrived to the sound of deep inhalations and a pungent peppermint classroom. She looked pretty stunned—then less so when I explained it was my doing. Nothing I do surprises them anymore. Anyway, the test was terrible. Afterward, everyone was dejected, and Laura wryly accused me of playing a dirty trick and clearing everyone's minds altogether!

Must go, but quickly, talking of not surprising the school anymore, I did manage it the other day. It was our class's turn to do an assembly play, and I wrote a rhyming, satirical take on the nuns—about their bad habits, and the skeletons in their closets. We really went to town and hired skeleton and nun costumes, and convinced the biology teacher to let us borrow the human skeleton from the lab for a prop. Then Nicola choreographed a dance to "It's raining men, hallelujah..." I knew I was pushing it a bit. But in your honor, Dad, I decided to test how far humor could take me. Well, you would have been proud. Everyone was in hysterics, and the nuns laughed harder than anyone. I think being as unholy and unbaptized as I am, they treat me as a bit of a lost cause, which suits me perfectly.

Mum, do send more updates soon. I have given up on Dad writing but longing to hear what you're both up to. Any news on Moducare? How's the LAA fund-raising?

LOL,

Robbie.

Dearest R,

I have just been churning out another LAA newsletter, and thought I'd update you on some of our triumphs thus far in 1999. Our membership has almost doubled. As we'd hoped, we've now got a much better ratio of black members and we've also got a black committee member (a lovely chap from a farm near Sherwood), which I think is a first in the TB. Another first is a visit from the minister of agriculture, who lavished high praise on our efforts to revive the area as an important agricultural engine. He promised support and said that the Tuli Block will no longer be a forgotten corner of Botswana! (Maybe secretary of the LAA will one day mean something after all.) Dad is also pushing his long-nursed idea that Botswana could be a major world producer of organic, free-range beef.

Membership diversity has also been boosted with the joining of good old Ilona and John Somerset from Phikwe. They're doing great work plotting the steps of all the old explorers in the area. Apparently they've worked out the exact baobab tree beside which Livingstone's party outspanned, and exactly where Baines crossed the Limpopo, which is just downstream from us. Ilona is writing a book on the subject, and Dad and I are hoping she'll give a talk at the next meeting, to enrich the members' historical understanding of this exquisite part of the world.

Talking about educational lectures, I also gave a talk on nutrition to the LAA meeting entitled "Are you digging your grave with your teeth?" It was so funny; me standing there, earnestly lecturing about fiber, phytochemicals and bad fats, with everyone (except faithful Jean v R, who asked lots of questions and has recently admitted to actually enjoying my vegetable concoctions) looking bored—no doubt wishing I'd hurry up so they could tuck into their *boerewors* and chops. Dad could barely keep a straight face. But one has to start somewhere, and I'm nothing if not determined.

Must go as very busy now, preparing for the Orange Harvest Festival—our first birthday celebration and hopefully a big boost to Dad's ambitious fund-raising plans. So glad you'll be here. Don't forget to find something orange to wear.

Lots of love,

Mum.

If Mum and Dad had buckled to local tastes for the four-by-four competitions, they had their revenge at the Orange Harvest Festival, which, surroundings notwithstanding, was a most thoroughly un-Tuli Block affair.

The festivities took place amid the vast orchards of Seleka Ranch, a prosperous farm that once, in the heyday of the Tuli Block, had been owned by Seretse Khama himself. At the festival's epicenter was a huge barn, surrounded by thousands of harvested trees—a dark sea of green, sweeping down to the darker still, tall Limpopo tree line. Eerie as ever in the dusk light, the great river made a perfect backdrop for the barn, which was lit with candles and thickly strung with orange branches. The dense leaves, filling the air with a faint sharp scent, cast soft complicated shadows on the walls, which were covered by a huge mural of oranges that Mum and Lulu had spent the whole day painting.

A bar in the corner served all the favorite beers and brandy, but the drink of the evening was champagne and orange juice served in sugar-frosted glasses. On a hay-bale-surrounded stage, a band played, but none of the favored local Afrikaans *boere* music. The official language of the LAA was English—in Botswana, it had to be that or Setswana—and Mum and Dad were determined that Afrikaans would not creep in, which would alienate the Batswana members. To make sure, they'd organized the band— the Sulphur Junkies from Phikwe, led by Jean Kiekopf.

Named after the belching BCL smelter tower, the Junkies members were: Jean, Klaus, Pius (a Sri Lankan), Jerry (a colored Motswana), and Forti (a Greek). A preagreed song list included the Beatles, the Police, and rock 'n' roll favorites from the Rolling Stones to the Doobie Brothers.

Prophesying that "the ice will not crack easily," Mum had devised a variety of orange-themed games, and as people started to arrive and milled around awkwardly in their orange shoes, orange hats, orange scarves, Mum set to work. Smiling brightly, orange silk baubles bouncing in her hair, she rushed around the barn, beseeching wary drinkers to "join the celebratory spirit of the evening and have fun." But of the Afrikaans members, only Jean van Riet and one other woman took part along with us, various visitors from Phikwe, and the Batswana members.

"Dancing," Mum said. "We need dancing!"

Under her direction, Lulu and I helped clear away the props for the games. Then, downing the rest of her champagne, Mum went to the band and requested that they turn up the volume.

Klaus strummed his guitar. Jean said in her husky voice, "Come on everybody, let's see you on the dance floor now."

I watched with interest, remembering the last time Mum and Dad had danced at a similarly Afrikaner-dominated gathering.

It had been at a wedding across the Limpopo. The river was flowing strongly, and as we'd climbed into the canoe on the way there, Dad's ancient smart shoes had got wet. By the time we left the *kerk*, they'd dried, but the muddy water had accelerated a long-overdue collapse. Following Dad across the lawn to the reception, we watched, shocked, as first white stuffing poured out, and then one sole detached. Lulu, Damien, and I blushed and hurriedly picked up the bits of hard foam. Dad just laughed. "Well, I never was the life and sole of the party," he said, pulling off the wretched shoes. Laughing just as hard, Mum put them in her handbag. Later, when the dancing began, she took off her own shoes so Dad wouldn't feel left out, and they danced, barefoot, to *boere* music and "Macarena," which was one of the few concessions to popular music.

The stares of the onlookers then had been horrified. The stares I watched now, appearing on white faces lining the dance floor, were different. Horrified too, but many here also utterly disapproving.

As the music started, the first people up were the Batswana men, gyrating in an enthusiastic group, with their wives looking on and chatting among themselves. Dad was deep in conversation, so Mum joined the black men, occasionally breaking away to dance wildly arm in arm with one of them. Lulu and I and two female American teachers from Phikwe joined the merry group.

Some of the whites looked away, as if they were embarrassed. Some stared curiously at Dad, who watched Mum with a look of amusement. I looked at the black women to see if they'd noticed the disgusted stares too. But if they had, they weren't bothered, and continued to chat unperturbed. Mum did notice, and smiled defiantly at her disapproving audience.

She came off the dance floor, flushed with pleasure.

Later, as people drank more and relaxed, others got up to dance. But the Afrikaans couples stuck resolutely together, insisting on stiff, long-arm-style dancing, unsuited as it was to the music. And even as people stumbled and giggled drunkenly, the stares provoked by bouts of mixed-race dancing were no less unclear: no amount of alcohol and orange enough to blur black and white in the Tuli Block.

...I know you don't like hearing this, but I do increasingly despair of this place. As you know, we formed the LAA to try and help the farmers who wanted change—to break from the old ways. I thought we were on the side of the goodies, but I'm not so sure anymore. The following was a genuine agenda item: imposing a *maximum* wage on laborers in the Tuli Block, so that they wouldn't hop from farm to farm. In the discussion, the motion was met with resounding approval, as was the associated proposal to draw up a blacklist of workers known for drunkenness—I regret not proposing a blacklist of farmers known for drunkenness and labor abuses. Anyway, I listened to the whole thing feeling sick even to be part of such a group. Dad was of course cooler. He said nothing until everyone had spoken. Then he announced, in a completely deadpan voice, that he agreed with the idea, with one addition. This, he explained, would be that the labor in the Tuli Block must be unionized. He proposed inviting a representative from the governing Botswana trade union to the next meeting. As you can imagine, there were angry mutters and furious faces all round. Then one guy stood up and said something to the effect that, "*Jirre*, we don't want any of this union business here in the Tuli Block!" Dad then asked—with only a hint of glee—whether it had occurred to the speaker that this, the LAA, was effectively a union. The chap was of course silenced, and it came to nothing. But it does say everything....

The dancing at the Orange Harvest Festival was the beginning of the end.

About a year after the organization was formed, Dad stood down as chairman, furious. He refused all requests for him to stay on. Two farmers, sworn enemies when the LAA began, had conspired to sabotage a motion using a loophole in the constitution.

Dad phoned Charlie Sheldon. "I eat my words, Charlie."

Dad stayed on as a member, however, and did not declare publicly why he had stood down, still believing in the principles of the association. Then a few months after he resigned as chairman, the LAA invited local policemen to discuss crime in the area—of which there was very little. But many of the white farmers berated the black policemen, accusing them of racism. Dad stood up, explaining how he'd only ever had good experiences—a stolen pump found in a day, a suspected *tokoloshe* terrorizing his staff promptly investigated. Afterward, ashamed and disgusted by the behavior, he wrote a letter to the police, distancing himself altogether from the racist accusations.

Much later, it was decided to merge the LAA with the old Tuli Block Farmers' Association. But the terms of the merger threw the process into chaos; there was a fight over which name would be kept. Meetings ended in fury. One day, Dad was approached by one of the farmers. "Please," said the young man, in Afrikaans, "won't you negotiate between the two organizations. You are the only one who can bring us together again."

B ut by the middle of 1999, I was so avidly following the increasingly exciting saga of Dad's involvement with AIDS that I quickly lost interest in the resignation story.

The Botswana government was now providing one-off antiretroviral treatment to HIV-positive pregnant women to reduce the risk of transmission to the baby. The women, however, were still reluctant to come forward and be tested, with no long-term treatment available to them. Dad wanted the government to offer them the sterols and sterolins mix, but the minister of health would not do so until it was registered as a treatment for HIV disease. To register the supplement, a phase III double-blind, placebo-controlled trial was required.

Dad at once embarked on the task of arranging a several-hundred-patient trial. The participants would be employees of the Selebi-Phikwe mine; a new laboratory in Gaborone would do the tests; Professor Bouic, who'd done the original work, agreed to draw up the new protocol and oversee the trial. The work involved in the planning was immense. But Dad loved every moment: this was a dream—one that could actually make him happy—coming true.

Dearest Robbie,

We've just returned from a great trip to Gabs for more meetings re the trial. Exhausted as I am, I wanted to write you a quick note—you must be so stressed with your final exams, and I know you'll be cheered up by a little vicarious excitement. After all this time, things are really, finally, happening, it seems.

The meetings went well, and arrangements for the trial continue to fall into place—in Botswana time, of course, but definitely moving forward. Dad is beside himself with excitement, and so am I. If the results from a phase III trial are good, not just Botswana but countries all over Africa— maybe beyond—might start using the stuff. Think what that could do? Sometimes Dad and I want to pinch ourselves just knowing that we're going to help make something happen that we've both believed in so strongly, for so long.

Anyway, having indulged in our big dreams, I must tell you how close it all came to being over altogether, for Dad at least. Setting off for Gabs, just after we'd crossed the Lot-sane, we saw a movement in the grass, and before Dad could brake a huge black mamba shot out in front of us. Unable to see any sign of it behind us, we were obviously worried it had flicked up into the chassis as we drove over it. Dad drove back to the house and gingerly poked around underneath. But he couldn't see anything and we set off again, stopping after about 100 kilometers so that Dad could have a pee. I stayed in the car, watching a lilac-breasted roller in the bushes.

Then out of the corner of my eye I suddenly see this long black thing emerging from the shadow of the car. It's the mamba, would you believe it? Bigger than I thought (well over 2 meters) and now very agitated, understandably, I suppose, after 100 kilometers beneath a hot engine. Anyway, at the same time I see the snake, Dad turns around, zipping up the fly on his shorts. I start waving frantically to him, undulating my arms and trying to mime "snake." He thinks I'm joking, or just being mad old Mum.

He smiles, waves, and starts walking toward the car, laughing. At this point the mamba is still slithering away from him. But with breathtaking timing, a truck roars into view. The snake changes direction, accelerates, and heads straight for Dad. Dad now sees it, and stops smiling. He also freezes, as the snake bears down on him. A second later, the huge black creature slithers straight past his still, sandaled foot, a couple of centimeters away at most. I felt sick, I must say. I really don't know how he did it—remember how scared you were all those years ago with the snake on the loo, and that was only semipoisonous!

Anyway, Dad comes back to the car, white but cheerful. "Wow, Keith!" I say, full of awe, and overwhelmed with relief for him, and relief that it dismounted here, in the bush, and not somewhere in a busy town. Dad just shrugs coolly. "What were you thinking as it came toward you?" I ask, imagining his life flashing before him as he bravely stands his ground in the face of one of Africa's most terrifying snakes. Dad says, "I was thinking about my nuts. How long have I been telling you that snakes love warm, dark places? My shorts would have been a perfect bolthole." Then he continues, in his classic deadpan Dad way, "Reckon life's too good to kick the bucket just yet, Lin. Certainly not with a mamba in my *broeks*!"

So there you go, Robbie.

Lots of love,

Mum

P.S. I can't wait to hear how the talent show goes. Dad and I are both so proud of you for taking on such a big project. What a wonderful, useful thing to be remembered for.

28

LEAVING LIMPOPO

Damien, Robbie, and Lulu

I knelt down in the deserted school hall, shaking.

It was after midnight, and the main lights had been turned off. All but the center of the cavernous space, where I knelt, was in gloom. The stage at one end and the lofty gallery at the other were eerie black holes. Through the dim light, a sorrowful Jesus watched me from a cross high up on the wall. I looked away guiltily, and stared instead at the gallery.

I was kneeling because I couldn't sit any other way in my long evening dress, and I looked up because I couldn't bear to see the chaos around me. My chaos.

I sniffed. It was still just there; the unmistakable smell of marijuana.

Exhaustion and disgrace suddenly overwhelmed me. I started to cry, tears splattering uncontrollably onto the dusty floor. A choked sob echoed around the vast, quiet space, spreading out into the corridors, which the ghosts of nuns were said to haunt. It occurred to me now that if ever they'd had a victim deserving of a good fright, I was she, at this moment, and had I not been so profoundly embarrassed, I might have been scared.

It was my last year of school, a few months before the new millennium, and more than four years since I'd first entered the building to write my entrance exam.

"Money is the root of all evil."

I looked at the floor around the folds of my dress. It was too ironic not to appreciate; I giggled hysterically through my tears.

All around me were dollar notes—overflowing from bright tin cashboxes, stuffed in bulging plastic bags, bundled with rubber bands, or just lying loose on the worn wood. I didn't have the energy to start counting, but there were tens of thousands of Zimbabwean dollars, certainly. Which, then, in 1999—when things in Zimbabwe had only just really begun to fall apart—were still actually worth something.

In the last few months, discontent among Robert Mugabe's "war vets" had provoked riots and marches on the streets of Bulawayo; stones had been thrown—at people, cars, and buildings. The Convent, in the seedier center of town, was close to the action. One test had thrillingly been canceled, as we'd crouched beneath our desks. Once, during an exam in the big basement, we had been locked inside, for fear the protestors would invade the school grounds.

But the shouts of rioters were the only things that had ever reached us. And tonight, because of me, was the first time a militant, uncontrollable crowd had actually made it inside the Convent walls.

The talent show had, until a few hours before, promised to be an unmitigated, unprecedented success. A film premiere, supplemented by a few cake sales, was the usual final year fund-raising strategy.

My class was raising the money to build classrooms at a desperately poor rural primary school that we'd visited several months earlier. Appalled by the raggedly dressed children and dilapidated buildings, we had then resolved to do something grand: to raise more money than any class had ever raised before.

All over Bulawayo, we advertised the Convent Talent Show for Sontala School: "dancing, comedy, a fashion show, pop music, rock music, rap music, hip-hop, and the opportunity to win a variety of valuable prizes from our generous sponsors."

Some of the talent was provided by Convent girls, but several professional performers also donated their time, and groups from other schools auditioned too. The spirit and the diversity were too good to crush, and the program swelled daily; even after the dress rehearsal, acts "too good to miss" were still being squeezed in.

The night was sold out; desperate latecomers willingly paid the full fee just to stand at the back. The nuns, the VIPs of the evening, sat in the front row, and hundreds of parents, students, and outsiders filled the rest of the beautifully decorated hall. Rarely in its history had the school had an event with a large audience drawn from such a colorful mix of Bulawayans.

Clad in elegant evening gowns, my classmates and I ushered people in and then introduced the show, its worthy cause, and the first of the performances. The happy crowd laughed and cheered at all the appropriate moments, and enthusiastic noise rang through the hall. The nuns even smiled tolerantly at the more suggestive pop songs.

But some of the acts took longer than their allotted time.

By interval we were running more than an hour late. During the break, we rushed around selling drinks and food to the starving crowd, as well as hundreds more raffle tickets, "for the excellent cause," we said, stirring up a fever of generosity. The girls manning the doors were sucked in to help. In their absence, as we'd later discover, teenage boys off the street slipped into the hall and mingled with the crowd.

The performances resumed.

A gangster-looking all-boy pop group, one of those I had not seen audition, took the stage. When they finished, the applause—mainly from the riotous, dodgy-looking gatecrashers—was tumultuous. The band, scheduled for only one song, struck up again.

I was watching, from the wings, standing beside Rutendo Maziva, a friend and classmate, who was jointly responsible for organizing the talent show.

"Oh, God! Oh, no," I whispered, as we glanced at each other; first in outrage, then in horror as, moving to the very front of the stage, one of the singers began to gyrate. In time with the music, directly in front of the nuns, he ran his hand up and down his crotch, singing and grinning lewdly. Sickened, Rutendo and I looked on as families with young children stood up and walked out. Gatecrashers rushed forward to take their seats.

"Close the curtains on them," Rutendo instructed the young girl manning the crank.

The tall velvet drapes slithered toward the band. The boys just shifted to the front, dodging the curtains.

I marched on stage, mid-song, and asked them fiercely to leave. They laughed, and kept singing. Desperate, I turned my back to the audience, grabbed one of the boys, and pushed him through the thick red drapes. I pushed another, and the surprised gang, instruments and all, receded shamefaced behind the curtains.

Forcing a smile, I turned back to the appalled crowd. I apologized, joking about the incredible variety and enthusiasm of the evening.

The next act was blissfully professional. The crowd looked calmer, and I started to hope things might be salvaged. I returned backstage, cheered—only to see Laura Hudson, one of my most pragmatic and resourceful friends, slowly thudding her forehead against the wall. "I want to die," she moaned. "They're smoking dope in the gallery... this is so, so, very bad.... What shall we do? This is how we'll be remembered, Robyn..."

A security guard was found to evict the marijuana smokers. But some had hidden in the toilets and reappeared later. Several teenage boy bands were still to come. Egged on by the swelling, insalubrious half of the crowd, they pushed their luck: censored swear words were reinserted into songs, more suggestive movements were made.

By the last act, nearly two hours over schedule, a third of the audience had left. When the curtains closed for the last time, the applause was a dismaying mix of weak claps, from the remaining respectable half of the audience, and drunken cheers, from the now large and misbehaving section.

As the last members of the audience left, twenty shamefaced final-year girls stacked away the chairs and picked up the litter in silence. We were too traumatized to speak. The scraping of chair legs was punctuated only by the occasional despairing giggle, as banished thoughts of the evening resurfaced.

Everyone wanted to go as soon as possible. I was managing the money, however, and as the girls hurriedly departed, they deposited the evening's rich spoils at my feet.

And among these, when the last girl left the hall, I had finally knelt and cried.

"Robyn?"

I jumped, startled in my thoughts about the ghosts of nuns.

Sister Angela, the headmistress, stood in the wide doorway to the hall. I studied my hands as she approached, and sat down gracefully beside me.

"I'm so sorry," I started to babble, "I should've been more careful.... I should've listened to everyone who said it was too ambitious.... I'm so embarrassed—I've disgraced the school...." I tried to stop them, but the tears kept falling. I would have done anything to make amends. If Sister Angela had asked me to get baptized a Catholic right then, I would have agreed.

But all she did was put her arm around my shaking shoulders. Then she said, gently, "Look at all this, Robyn. Look at all this money. No one's ever raised this much money. This is amazing. Think what it can do for those children."

"What about tonight?" I asked miserably.

Sister Angela smiled. "There were some wonderful moments," she said. "And I think you'll find that we'll survive." She squeezed my shoulder. "I'm much more worried about you leaving. You've been a breath of fresh air in this school. You are a credit to your parents."

And that was the final result of one-third of Mum's experiment: me kneeling in a convent, sniffing back tears in the marijuana-scented air, handing bundles of cash to a warmly smiling nun.

The first months of the new millennium brought the heaviest rains in years.

All over the world, people watched images of the catastrophic flooding in Mozambique; hundreds killed and thousands left homeless.

Farther inland, the Limpopo flooded too. Here, there was little humanitarian damage. But the high brown waters ate around dams, swept away ancient trees, and churned with the bloated carcasses of dead cows and goats. After years of moaning for more rain, the Tuli Block farmers were soon lamenting the devastation.

No one escaped. Houses near the riverbank were completely flooded. We were luckier than many, but on Molope Farm, favorite old trees disappeared overnight. The sturdy wooden deck on the Limpopo was torn out of the bank. Where once we'd watched the hippos and the birds, rubbish-filled brown water sped past, drowning out the worried birdsong.

Mum said, "Let's hope it's making a life raft for someone downstream in Mozambique." Dad agreed, pointing out that he could always just build a new, better deck.

The floodwaters worried them for a different reason. Gaborone had become an island—just as, after months of work, Dad had finally arranged a date for a meeting in the capital to discuss a phase III trial of the use of sterols and sterolins for HIV disease. The professor was coming from Cape Town, the doctors from Phikwe, and Dad from the Tuli Block. Government statisticians would be there, as would scientists from the laboratory.

The water made traveling to Gaborone by car impossible. But at the pace things moved in Botswana, Dad feared that to arrange another meeting could take months. We held our breaths, willing the waters to subside. But it rained relentlessly. All roads into the city remained closed.

"Over my dead body," said Dad, "is this not happening. I'm chartering a plane. Don't care what it costs."

The plane collected the relevant people from around the country and flew them to the Gaborone. Everyone, miraculously, was there at the meeting. The consensus was that a large clinical trial should be carried out in Botswana to confirm the results from the South African study. Even with the price of antiretrovirals falling—and the government's intention to provide them—sterols and sterolins, should they be shown conclusively to work, could be used to complement the drugs.

Following the meeting, the protocol was finalized. Mid that year, it was ready for submission, which had to be done through the president's office.

On the way there, Dad and John Penhall, the Phikwe doctor who would run the trial, met Charlie Sheldon, who'd taken the opportunity to arrange a visit to President Mogae himself. Dressed in smart suits and polished shoes, Dad and John were surprised when Charlie greeted them wearing faded jeans, a well-worn homemade potato-print shirt with a "matching tie" of similar vintage, and a battered tweed jacket.

"When are you going to change?" asked Dad.

"I'm not," said Charlie.

Later, chuckling at the memory, Dad described how huge Batswana men in FBI-style dark glasses had eyed them menacingly as they entered the presidential antechamber. Then, suddenly, the faces of the fierce guards had flashed with recognition.

"Ah, Charlie," they said, smiling and slapping him on the back. "Good to see you. Come in. Come through. Welcome."

Charlie, John, and Dad sat with the president and talked about the trial. The president said he was pleased to hear about it and would pass the protocol to the Health Department.

Dad was ecstatic. So was Mum—for Dad, and for the project. And also just generally because she'd found her own "part-time, short-term destiny."

At the same time Dad was in Gaborone, meeting the president,

Mum was in England, starting the first course of a part-time degree—picking up where she'd left off, twenty years before, when my conception had rudely interrupted her.

She'd stumbled upon her new destiny just a few months earlier. She was up in her study, reading about the achievements of old classmates in her college magazine, thinking of things that might have been, had she not ended up in the Tuli Block.

It was the Christmas holidays of 1999, and Lulu, Damien, and I were all at home, sitting with Dad in the lounge downstairs. Mum appeared at the banister, grinning madly as she looked down upon us.

"I've found my new career," she announced.

"Really?" said Dad, looking not in the least surprised.

Mum hurried down the steps, brandishing the magazine. Flushed with excitement, she showed us the article about an old Somervillian who'd started a postgraduate degree program in nutritional medicine at Surrey University in England. The degree was part-time, spanning several years. Not sure what she wanted to do afterward with the qualification, Mum was nevertheless determined to do the degree, and optimistic she could persuade them to accept her. They did, and Mum began a sporadic educational commute between Surrey and the Tuli Block.

In late 1999 Chris Phatswe, an Air Botswana pilot who'd been suspended from flying for failing a medical test, took off from Gaborone's Sir Seretse Khama Airport in one of Air Botswana's three operational airplanes. For more than an hour, with no one else on board, he flew around the airport, threatening to crash the plane into an Air Botswana building—as retribution, he claimed. When the airplane eventually ran out of fuel, he crashed instead into the airline's two other working planes, which stood together on the tarmac. Chris Phatswe was killed, and all three planes were destroyed, effectively suspending the operations of Air Botswana. Later, it was announced that Phatswe had AIDS, and it was widely speculated that AIDS dementia had caused his irrational suicidal behavior.

In 2002 the Botswana government started rolling out the intended countrywide provision of free antiretrovirals to people with AIDS. Botswana, rightly, was widely hailed as a leader in Africa. But it was still too late for many.

Elizabeth, who started to get sick again in 2000, was among them. Mum went to visit her, accompanied by Jenny Dunlop, an old friend of ours who taught Elizabeth's daughter at the local secondary school and who had started the "Say NO!" group.

The teenage girl, who was caring for her once more skeletal and bedridden mother, greeted Mum and Jenny at the door and showed them inside.

Elizabeth smiled and weakly clutched Mum's hand. "I got careless," she said, "about looking after myself. About taking my pills. I worked too hard."

Her daughter tried to feed her. Elizabeth choked and vomited food and blood across herself and the sheets.

Jenny excused herself.

Elizabeth's daughter rushed forward, ignoring the gloves beside the bed. Elizabeth herself had lectured on how caregivers must always use protective gloves. Mum watched, nauseous and dismayed, as the daughter touched her mother's face, wiping away the bloody mixture with her bare hands.

Then they said good-bye.

Elizabeth insisted on staggering to her feet, to say "Goodbye" and "God bless."

. . . God, Robbie, seeing her like that, you know I wondered how Dad had managed to keep sane, seeing people like that, day after day, for so many years. I cannot find words to describe the horror. The despair of that poor girl trying to feed and then clean her mother, forgetting every simple rule. At the time, I couldn't believe it: all that training and knowledge, ignored. And then I thought, What would I do if my mother was covered in blood and vomit? What would you do, Robbie, if it were me? What do you do in an impossibly desperate situation? And we're adults. All over the country it's children doing this. . . .

Not long after, Elizabeth developed AIDS dementia. Ranting and shouting, she dismissed anyone who tried to help her, including, eventually, her own daughter. In the end, she sent everyone away. In early 2001, about fifteen years after contracting the virus, having touched the lives, and probably saved the lives, of thousands, she died mad and totally alone in a room in the AIDS refuge she had started.

Around the same time, about a year after the floods, Dad had still not heard back regarding the outcome of the trial application. Phone calls and faxes to the Health Department went unanswered. Then documents could not be found. Eventually, Dad was told the application had been turned down. No reason was given, no written rejection was provided. The representative said he could offer no further help. In July, a year after submitting the application, Dad and Charlie Sheldon met with the minister to express their frustration. An explanation and documentation were promised. More calls and faxes went unanswered.

The promised explanation never came.

A few months later, Mum phoned me. I was in New Zealand, at university. Her voice as she said hello was soothing and measured—her bad-news voice.

I sat down, feeling weak. "It's one of the horses. Or Dad? What's happened?"

"No, no." Mum laughed. "Nothing like that. But I'm afraid we've decided to leave Botswana. We're going to sell the farm. Please don't be too upset...."

The view from my window was of a sloping green field, dotted with a few muddy sheep; the same lush, safe, soggy world that nearly fifteen years earlier was all Lulu, Damien, and I had ever known. Until Dad had said, "We're going to Botswana."

I felt profoundly homesick, for the first time in my life.

Knowing I'd be back, I'd never minded leaving before. I missed the farm, but always there was the comforting thought of returning—to smell the dusty dry bush, watch the birds glide across the glassy river, see the sun sink over our favorite trees, splendid and golden as ever, and maybe just a little taller. And Mum and Dad, there together, to watch it with, and marvel at the good fortune of living in one of the most beautiful places in the world.

"It's time to move on," said Mum. "There's not enough here for us anymore. We'll only sell it to someone who really loves it too. And just think, it'll be there forever in our hearts and memories...."

...Dad's moving speedily as ever, and has just put his practice on the market. He's getting plenty of interest—the clinics are busier than ever, and only getting more so. But Dad says if they made him millions, he still wouldn't stay. The disgraceful trial debacle has been a real blow for him. Working toward a solution, I think, was what made the horror of his work tolerable for so long. But now it's depressing him more than ever. So many of his patients have AIDS, and it will be so long before everyone who needs drugs has access to them, and then so hard to enforce and monitor. I believe, you know, he's lost faith in Botswana, and more forgiving though I am, I do understand. We're going to move to Cape Town, for the moment. Dad's going to work in emergency medicine, until he can find something else and escape medicine at last.

Goodness knows what life holds for us now, but exciting times, I suppose. I remain optimistic, and on that subject, I am just so glad I had the privilege of helping with the peace pot mission before I left. I will look back forever on that trip, remembering the odd wonderful collection of people and those exquisite places, as a fitting end to wonderful years in a wonderful country....

Every two weeks, for eight years, Mum had crossed the Limpopo to go shopping in South Africa. When she returned, the *bakkie* would be overflowing. Boxes of fruit, sacks of vegetables, and bags of legumes and whole wheat flour fought for space with medicines, fencing wire, bricks, tiles, paint, pump parts, water pipes, horse feed, and generally one or two indigenous saplings— including, once, several fever trees, *Acacia xanthophloea*, which we'd planted in the garden: homage to our old love of Rudyard Kipling and his vision of a "Great grey-green, greasy Limpopo River, all set about with fever trees."

Fewer and less varied loads could provoke hours of searching delays at customs for other people. But everyone knew Mum, and most of the customs officials were patients of Dad's. After updating her on their latest ailments, and thanking her for her standard gift of a newspaper, they'd mostly wave her on with no more than a cursory glance at the form and the *bakkie*. After particularly tedious shopping trips, and if she had an innocuous load, sometimes Mum would amuse herself by testing the familiarity. Over the years she'd successfully entered Botswana as "brick-layer," "tile-grouter," "homeopath," and "Secretary of the Limpopo Agricultural Association."

This time, in 2002, the year we sold the farm, she settled for the standard "housewife." She was returning to the farm from what would be her final trip to England before Botswana was no longer home.

"Mma Scott, what are these?"

The customs official stared curiously at the five yellow plastic pots in the back of the *bakkie*. Bright cloth circles, tied down around the rim in the style of a homemade jam jar, covered the tops of the grapefruit-size vases.

Mum had hoped the vases would go unnoticed, as they had when her flight back from England had arrived in Johannesburg.

A five-hour drive later, standing at the border post to Botswana, she decided the truth was as good as any explanation.

"They're peace vases," she said quickly. "They've been blessed by great spiritual masters from Tibet. I'm going to help bury them in special places around Botswana. Every country in the world is getting some. They're intended to help protect the land and the environment, and discourage war and disease. They just contain herbs and ground-up stones."

The customs official nodded understandingly, took his newspaper, and waved her back through into Botswana.

Rooted in ancient Tibetan tradition, the peace vases Mum carried from England had been created in 1991—she had five of more than six thousand vases destined for worldwide distribution. The pots were to be buried in sacred or important locations in every country, with a particular intent to help war-torn, environmentally devastated, and famine- and disease-ridden places around the world. One of Mum's old Oxford friends, Christine Whaite, was involved in the distribution in England and Ireland—there was a pot for Westminster, and a pot for Stormont Castle in Northern Ireland, handed over by the Dalai Lama himself.

Asked, when she was staying with Christine, to help with the Botswana distribution, Mum had agreed at once, and as soon as she'd brought the pots to Botswana, a peace vase burial party was arranged.

The six-man, two-four-by-four team that embarked on the trip around Botswana consisted of Alec Campbell, a world expert on the Baswara and their rock art; Alec's wife, Judy; Alec's son Niall, an expert on traditional medicine and healing (a white *sangoma*); Robyn Sheldon, the only Buddhist, then training to be a midwife; Christine Sievers (Jonathan Scott's wife), an archaeobotanist then specializing in seed-analysis of Stone Age sites; Nomsa Mbere, a dentist training to be a lawyer, and then girlfriend of Ian Khama. And Mum.

For five days the odd party drove across the country, camping beside and burying the small yellow vases in some of Botswana's most splendid, sacred places. They began in Gaborone, placing the first vase at the top of Kgale Hill, which towers over the capital city. Driving five hours northeast, they buried the next at Nyangabgwe Hill, near Francistown, at a point near the summit where fraught Zimbabwe was clearly visible. Then they traveled two days northwest through Nata and past the great salt pans. Passing around the western panhandle of the Okavango Delta, they headed farther west and buried the third pot in the beautiful Tsodilo Hills, in a sacred rainmaking site. The fourth was laid in the Okwa Valley, traced thousands of years ago by a now-dry ancient river. The fifth pot was to be placed later, but by then Mum would have left Botswana.

> ... Whatever one believes, Robbie, or doesn't believe, these pots, and their intent, are a powerful symbol of what's needed on the planet, and especially on this continent. On a lighter note, and before you accuse me of being too sentimental, what a pity you're not still at the Convent—imagine what a back-to-school story this would have made—your mother, driving around Botswana burying sacred Buddhist pots....

In early 2004, staying up late into the night because of the time zones, Mum phoned Lulu, Damien, and me. Lulu was at Auckland University, starting her psychology and languages degree. Damien was in Australia, in the middle of a psychology and physics degree at Sydney University. I was working in London, having recently finished my first degree in bioinformatics in Auckland. Dad was on a cruise ship near Alaska, in the middle of a three-month stint as ship's doctor.

Mum had to e-mail Dad the news that Grandpa Ivor had died.

None of us could reach Botswana in time for the funeral. Grandpa had arranged with one of his good Indian friends to be cremated Hindu style, and the cremation had to begin before sunset on the day he died.

Henry had been there when Grandpa died, in his sleep, just after one o'clock in the morning, lying on the bed in the old house. Jonathan arrived later in the day, and the two boys went to the funeral parlor to collect the body. Granny Betty, who was then barely able to walk and unable to move from the house, stayed behind, wreathed in cigarette smoke, in the company of her cat, the two fat dogs, the woman who was caring for her, and Ruth, who had moved back home to Selebi to work for Granny and Grandpa.

The funeral parlor was a large warehouse, near a liquor

store in the industrial area in Phikwe. The roof was corrugated iron, and inside, it was sweltering. As they walked past a display room of gaudy coffins, Jonathan and Henry silently gave thanks Grandpa had not died at the height of summer.

Mma Mosikare, the funeral proprietor, reminisced fondly about Grandpa. "I knew him well," she said respectfully. "He used to fly bodies back to Zimbabwe and South Africa."

She pulled Grandpa out of the fridge. He was naked but for a linen cloth wrapped around his thin hips. Jonathan and Henry put on rubber gloves and surgical gowns and washed his face, the top of his body, and his lower legs, blackened by the melanoma that, two years after his diagnosis, had killed him.

Then they chose a coffin, which Mma Mosikare had kindly agreed to lend—given that it was a cremation that would not involve the coffin, and because Grandpa was an old friend.

She offered a choice of any of the coffins on display, from the elaborately gilded and adorned to the simple pine boxes. Limited by Grandpa's height, Henry and Jonathan selected a mahogany-veneered box with a split lid and a white satin lining. They lifted the body into the coffin and closed the lid over the lower half. The upper half wouldn't close, which they realized after a few minutes was due to a raised headrest, operated by a crank mechanism.

The crank, however, was stuck. Mma Mosikare's assistant fetched a hammer and banged away at the mechanism beside Grandpa's face. His head gradually sank, suffering only minor bumps from the hammer. When the body still wouldn't fit, it became clear it was simply too long for the coffin. Henry removed the satin headrest altogether, and Grandpa's head finally sank below the lid.

But Grandpa's mouth was now lolling open. Henry and Jonathan each tried closing it. Each time, it immediately reopened. Knowing he would be displayed on the pyre, they tried again, and still the mouth remained resolutely open.

Later, when I heard the story, I smiled as I imagined Grandpa, determined to shout all the way to his smoky grave in the sky.

But this was not to be. Mma Mosikare spoke to her assistant, who fetched a small tube of Super Glue. "This will fix it," she said matter-of-factly. She handed over the tube, which Henry and Jonathan reluctantly squeezed onto Grandpa's lips, pressing them closed. From alcoholic grape juice to Super Glue—and I thought then that if Grandpa couldn't shout to the end, he would have been pleased to go silenced by Super Glue, for which he had such deep admiration.

The assistant went to fetch the hearse, a Toyota four-by-four. Standing in the parking lot, waiting for the car to reverse, Jonathan and Henry inquired about a nearby hearse with a badly buckled wheel.

"The competition," Mma Mosikare informed them gravely. "Sabotage."

They loaded the coffin, and the hearse drove to the hospital, where the mourners were waiting. From the hospital, the procession of vehicles set off along a bumpy dirt road out of Phikwe, cars and donkey carts stopping respectfully as they passed. The road was the old road between Selebi and Phikwe, which we'd ridden along many times on the way to our riding lessons. The track was badly potholed, and the cars lurched along slowly.

They stopped, in a cleared area, between two big *koppies*. At the center of the clearing stood a large rectangle of stacked mopane logs. Grandpa's body was placed on the pyre, and the cloth removed from his face according to Hindu tradition. Many of the Christian mourners, already awkward or disapproving, looked away uncomfortably.

Standing beside the pyre, Henry gave a brief speech, in which he paid tribute to his father—a man loved by many but "bereft of the ability to receive love"—and praised his strength, in a lifetime of unfulfilled dreams.

Now, as the eldest son, Henry was asked by the Hindu priest to assist in the blessing of Grandpa's spirit. Prayers were recited while slivers of wood were tossed onto a fire beside the pyre. Flowers and rice were sprinkled on the body. The braver mourners placed rice in the eyes and on the lips, and the priest spread ghee with a wooden spatula across the mopane logs and the linen cloth.

A burning torch ignited the mopane wood and ghee in bright

orange flames that quickly enveloped and obscured the body in a furious blaze. The mourners drove away, leaving the grand pyre burning against the last pink and orange light of a splendid, cloudless Botswana sunset.

Two guards remained to watch the body through the night.

The next morning, Henry scooped up the ashes into two earthenware jars.

One half, he sprinkled beneath a baobab on the Phikwe Golf Course. It was the second baobab Henry had suggested; the first, he'd been told, was already standing watch over another old golfer's ashes.

The remaining ashes were to be tossed into the Limpopo by Jonathan on his way back to South Africa. He said good-bye to Granny Betty, who before they parted, and despite never having shown any interest in Hinduism, suddenly announced she wanted to go in the same way as Grandpa. Promising her he would make sure she did, and remembering just in time to take Grandpa's fishing rods, which were the only things he wanted, Jonathan hurriedly climbed into his car and set off for the border.

After nearly a hundred kilometers, far along the road between Selebi and the Tuli Block, Jonathan realized that in his haste to pack the fishing rods and to discuss Granny Betty's cremation, he'd forgotten the ashes. Several hours late, having returned to collect them, he reached Martin's Drift border post. Having passed through the Botswana side of the border, he drove over the Limpopo and parked his car. Then he walked back into the center of the bridge, and poured the gray flakes into the sparkling brown water.

Where they would drift slowly down past Molope Farm, a few molecules perhaps traveling much farther east, and eventually reaching the Limpopo river mouth, where they'd float off into the warm waters of the Indian Ocean.

Where perhaps they'd someday meet with a few particles of the half of Granny Mavis's ashes tossed into the ocean just two months later, when she died, unexpectedly and in perfect health, in her little house in Durban. She, too, had asked for a Hindu funeral, and but for the enclosed furnace, she was cremated in the same way as Grandpa. The other half of her ashes was placed around the statue of a Buddha, where a tree was planted in her memory.

And perhaps, eventually, in the great waters of the Indian Ocean, particles of hers and Grandpa's ashes would meet the ashes of Granny Betty, who died just a month after Granny Mavis.

This time, Dad and Mum managed to make it to the funeral. Henry again gave a speech, and, assisted by Dad, he performed the same rituals that he had just three months earlier performed on Grandpa Ivor.

Then the boys stood back as a flame was placed against the mopane wood.

But now, where Grandpa Ivor had months before blazed so quickly and so splendidly, Granny Betty and her ghee-covered pyre caught alight and burned painfully slowly: slow in death as in life, as if reluctant to meet the skies that had once so tired her.

Some of Granny Betty didn't burn at all. When the boys collected her ashes in the morning, the metal joints from her wrist and two hip replacements were lying in the ashes, perfectly placed, along with several of her bones that had resisted the flames altogether.

At the same spot, in the middle of the bridge over the Limpopo, Jonathan and Henry—driving back together to South Africa—tossed into the water the ashes, the bones, the metal joints, and the earthenware pot.

And so the remains of Grandpa and his two wives—who had each, till their ends, both loved and despaired of him—drift somewhere out there.

Grandpa Ivor had been diagnosed with cancer in 2002, the year we left the farm.

"I'll beat it," he'd said. "Gotta look after Betty. I'm as strong as a bloody ox." But although Granny had long looked ready to die, it was she who hung on determinedly, desperate to outlive him.

As Grandpa had sickened and begun, undeniably, to waste

away, he started to talk more freely about the war, the subject he could never before bear to discuss. On one long evening with Mum and Dad, he spoke about being "tail-end Charlie," the last plane in the formation, telling them how the terror was so great that he'd had to pull his penis out of his suit and pee uncontrollably in the plane as he flew.

On another occasion, he told Jonathan about a period several years into the war, when almost everyone he knew had died. By then, he'd been numbed by death. If the bombers missed their targets, he would turn around and fly back into the face of trained antiaircraft fire, an almost suicidal stunt. Grandpa, by then, simply didn't care, flying—and living—wildly, with a reckless abandon that was thought to be the reason he was famously never promoted. By the end of the war, by which time he was training other pilots, Grandpa Ivor had become affectionately known to all as the Lost Leut.

But if his wild behavior prevented his advancement through the ranks, his bravery did not go unnoticed. In June 1944 he was awarded the Distinguished Flying Cross, an honor he'd always shrugged off. When Jonathan sorted through the old house after Granny Betty's death, he found a letter typed on faded pink paper:

Lieutenant I.A. Scott D.F.C.
c/o O.C., 45 AIR SCHOOL.

Dear Scott,
Following up my signal of event date, I send you my heartiest congratulations, together with those of all Officers and Other Ranks in the South African Air Force, on the award of the Distinguished Flying Cross.
Your courage, determination and devotion to duty are an inspiration to us all and you have set a splendid example to all those now in training to do their part in time to come.
The South African Air Force is proud of you.
Yours sincerely,

                                        MAJOR GENERAL
                        DIRECTOR GENERAL OF AIR FORCE.

All this had a high price, though. After the war, Grandpa wanted nothing to do with the military, refusing even their offer of a free university education, which he would later deeply regret. Instead, he went out on his own and started a business. The business went bankrupt, and the house was seized, leaving Granny Mavis and the three small boys with nothing.

Toward the end, Granny Mavis spoke too, with a mixture of bitterness and affection, of Grandpa's endless war nightmares, which had led, ultimately, to the destruction of their marriage. Tortured by his memories, Grandpa would go on drinking binges for days, leaving his young sons and his wife with no word of when he'd return. When he'd eventually left to try and find some sort of peace in the wilds of Botswana, he was running as much from his demons as from a broken marriage.

None of these revelations and reflections, however, was enough to heal the wounds between Grandpa and Dad. Father and son remained distant to the end, and in Grandpa's final years, after we left Botswana, it was Mum who kept him up-to-date with the family's news:

About her and Dad's sea voyage, in 2003, from Cape Town to England on the RMS *St. Helena*, when Dad had worked as a ship's doctor for the first time.

About Lulu, when she did a chef's course in her gap year at Ballymaloe in Ireland, and smuggled out her live mussels in her apron, tossing them back into the sea; and later, when she started university and decided, as well as psychology, to study French and Spanish. "Seeing she can already speak Latin."

About Damien, who complained that he didn't get to blow up enough things in his degree; who'd phone any of us prepared to listen, regardless of whether we understood, tell us about complex concepts in physics, just as he'd told Ruth about hydraulics and pistons under the ironing board, all those years ago.

And about me, as I battled for six months to get accepted for a master's degree at Cambridge, for which I was not technically eligible. This saga Grandpa followed avidly, loving the struggle, and that it was for a great university, the only education he'd ever felt strongly about, and particularly enjoying the fact the course was geared to entrepreneurial business. "Chip off the old block," he said, delightedly.

Two days before Grandpa died, I learned I'd been accepted into the program. Mum at once phoned the old Selebi house. She spoke to Henry. Henry said, "Ivor's stopped talking, but I'll tell him anyway. You never know, he might just understand."

Forgotten in the flurry of funerals, we learned only long afterward from Henry what had happened when the message was passed on.

Grandpa, who hadn't spoken all day, was lying on the creaky old bed. His eyes were closed. Henry said, "Ivor, Robbie's got into Cambridge."

Grandpa opened his eyes and stared at Henry, briefly but fiercely alert again.

Then, slowly and softly, Grandpa Ivor said what were to be his last words—words that for me told not so much of one event as of the memories of fifteen years of a family in a country that had begun with him, and his two drunken brown fruit moths, fluttering in the last light of the day.

"That's wonderful," he whispered. "Wonderful."

EPILOGUE

Baobab

During the Christmas holidays of 2004, the five of us drove up from Cape Town to visit Molope Farm. The trees were taller, the grass thicker, the rivers and the birds as exquisite as ever. The farm was loved and cared for by its new owners. But in more than just title, it was no longer ours. Lulu and I recoiled at the sight of dead antelope horns displayed on the outside walls of the house. Feeling oddly relieved to depart, we drove back over the border, crossing the Limpopo where earlier that year the ashes had been tossed, pausing to peer into the muddy, sluggish waters, checking for crocodiles. We saw none.

It was the last time we visited the farm and crossed the bridge together, as a family.

In 2005, Mum and Dad separated. When Lulu, Damien, and I had left them, and they had left Botswana, the struggles and purpose that bound them together had gone too. Without these, the strain between two ferociously independent people, finding new wings and new dreams after twenty-five years of marriage in which both, in their different ways, had given up individual freedoms for shared ones, was too great.

I said, "If it's not working, you should separate." Lulu and Damien, though sad too, agreed. I tried to see it as just another great change, a readiness to leap into the unknown, which is so much a part of what I love about my parents, and how I will always remember them together. I succeeded, mostly. But one night, several months later, I awoke, startled by my own tears. I went to my computer and, still half asleep, gently splashing the keyboard, wrote feverishly—as I would never write in the sensible light of day—to Mum and Dad:

> . . . However much I believe in looking forward and changing always, inescapably, so much of us is what we have done, in the good times and the bad. And so much of this is only reachable through the lens of the people we have done it with. There are experiences and parts of me I only remember when I speak with my family, without whom these would otherwise be lost in the overflowing cupboard of memory, from the lack of someone to prompt, understand, or share amusement, and the people you meet in the future, regardless of how much you love them, cannot help with this. I feel sad at the love lost, and the pain this must cause, but I know that romantic love can be found again, with others. What makes me cry is the thought that, through losing each other, you are losing a part of yourselves. So I hope above all else that you might stay friends, or eventually rekindle your friendship, so that one day you can talk and laugh with each other and not forget those parts of you that exist only between you, and through your friendship. And, now selfishly, I hope that sometimes I, and L and D, might

be there too; to remember those yet more subtle pieces in each of us that are reflected only in the presence of our whole family…

Mum and Dad stayed friends.

Mum continued her degree from Cape Town. While studying, she worked part-time, including as a nutritional adviser to a vitamin company, the coauthor of two books on nutrition for children, and a researcher for a Web site featuring nonprofit organizations working in the field of HIV and AIDS in South Africa. In 2007 she graduated with distinction and began her Ph.D., continuing her master's work into the effects of the micronutrient selenium on HIV and AIDS. As part of this, funding was obtained to run an ambitious clinical trial in the prisons in South Africa with the University of Surrey and the Desmond Tutu HIV Centre.

"It might even be groundbreaking, Robbie," Mum told me, smiling.

Dad worked as a ship's doctor, thinking of what to do next. While he was at sea, he had plenty of time to read, and one day came across some of the growing body of research on the medicinal properties of spices. Fascinated, he read more, forming hypotheses about the link between ancient hunter-gatherer diets and the health benefits of spices—which he decided to write a book about, compiling the latest evidence on the wide-ranging disease-preventing properties of culinary spices. In 2006 I helped him finish the book. By this time Dad was back in Cape Town, and had had another related idea. His old inexhaustible self, he was setting up a company to produce and sell a supplement containing a mixture of the most important spices.

"It's the first in the world, Robbie," Dad told me, smiling.

There has still been no phase III trial of the effect of sterols and sterolins on HIV and AIDS. "If I ever make my fortune from spices," said Dad, "I'll set up a trial." Separately, Mum said, "Maybe one day I can do postdoc research on sterols and sterolins."

And I wonder.

At university, I did my master's thesis on the pricing of medicines in developing countries, examining the precedent set by the AIDS drugs, some of which, by 2005, had fallen up to thirtyfold in price. Damien did his honors in solar thermal physics, hoping to one day become a clean energy inventor and entrepreneur. By his final year of university he was working frantically, which, to me at least, he disliked admitting. Once, after lecturing me at length on his latest incomprehensible class on quantum teleportation, he said coolly, "I think, Rob, this is the closest I've ever come to being stressed." Lulu got her university degree in Auckland, taking a year off to teach English in France. Lulu has Mum's brilliant, patient teacher in her. One holiday, when the three of us met in England, we discussed how we'd love in theory to home-school our children. Damien and I both agreed we'd never have the patience, or be willing to make the sacrifice. "Maybe you could do it for us," we suggested, half-jokingly, to Lulu.

In 2007, Mum and I drove up to Botswana from Cape Town.

At the border post, while Mum filled out forms, I looked on in dismay as a young customs official began to dig laboriously through the contents of our packed car.

Watching him, I thought wistfully of the magic doctor's car sticker. Mum's car had only the registration disk, still a Botswana number, on the windscreen. The back of the disk, in a creative attempt to deal with two of the country's biggest causes of death, said: "Buckle Up and Always Use a Condom!" There was a picture of a seat belt strapped across a condom, which looked like: Don't use a condom. "He who tries to kill two birds with one stone," Mum had joked, "bites off more than he can chew."

We were crossing at the Ramatlabama border post, near Gaborone, and far from any of Dad's old clinics. But as the car search dragged on and my forced innocent grin became exhausting, I decided to try anyway.

"I used to live here," I said conversationally. "My father was a doctor."

The official nodded and continued his meticulous excavation of a suitcase.

"But his clinics were farther north. You probably wouldn't know him. Dr. Scott," I added hopefully.

The young man stood up, smiling. "I know Dr. Scott." He closed the trunk of the car and held out his hand, shaking mine warmly, up, down, and up again, in the friendly Botswana way.

Back in Cape Town, Dad did still have his doctor's sticker, but on another car. He'd sold the converted *bakkie* when he and Mum had left Botswana. It had been bought by a funeral company, spray-painted silver, and used as a hearse.

Botswana's HIV infection rate has dropped slightly. But it has far still to fall to meet the country's target for 2016, fifty years after independence, of no new infections. Around 80 percent of those who need drugs now have access to them, the widest reach in Africa. But the rollout has been slower than hoped; there are still problems finding enough skilled staff to conduct the intensive monitoring of patients, and those who develop resistance need new drugs that aren't always available. In 2004, Botswana became the first country in Africa to introduce routine HIV testing. But people can opt out, and still there are those who don't wish to know.

Waved through the border post, Mum and I set off on an epic week's journey around Botswana visiting friends across the country.

Driving as far north as Francistown, we met Seloma Tiro at the Marang Hotel, where he'd once married Neo and reconciled Dad and Grandpa Ivor. Seloma told us sadly that he was now divorced. He'd driven down to meet us from Nata, where he was still living. Northgate filling station had continued to thrive; the half of an island still stood untouched. Over a long lunch beneath the tree canopy, Mum and I discussed our planned AIDS orphan project with Seloma. "That's beautiful," he said after delightedly accepting our request that he become a trustee of the organization. Then he told us, casually, that he was already involved with a trust, which he'd helped found, that provided support to the more than four hundred AIDS orphans of Nata village. It was the first of its kind in Botswana. Seloma shrugged off admiring comments. "It's your family who taught me about giving," he said, waving away our embarrassed protests. In a country of fewer than two million, AIDS is estimated to have orphaned nearly one hundred thousand children.

Back in Phikwe, we met two Peace Corps workers who were starting an AIDS orphan support project. When we learned where the project would be based, Mum and I smiled in wonder. Before being abandoned, the building, which stood beside a small *koppie*, had been a bingo hall. But years before that, it had once, too, been an unsuccessful coffin factory.

Early one morning we drove out to Selebi, passing the old baobab and turning onto the red dust driveway. Now, returning, just as Dad promised I would, I could smell the dust differently—dry and rich, like nothing else, anywhere. For a moment, I wanted to choke with longing on the particles and the memories.

Mum's painted hornbill sign was still nailed to the marula tree. Someone had tried to pull it off, and the bottom, which read "No Through Road," had curled up, barely visible. But the top nails had held fast, and though the sign had faded, it still clearly read "Scotts."

We turned down the road, not sure what to expect.

The cowshed and Grandpa's house were both lived in. But neither of the two Batswana people who greeted us could speak much English, and we discovered little beyond the fact that the new residents had cows. The Aeronca in the shed had long gone to be restored, along with the Piper Colt. The trailers were nowhere to be seen. But the termite mound still towered over the witch doctor's field, though smaller than I remember.

Mum and I stopped at the gate beside Grandpa's house. Smiling at each other and the once mystery tree—identified at last a few years before we left Botswana—we ran our hands down the now unmistakable trunk.

"*Adansonia digitata,*" Mum said thoughtfully. Then she frowned. "You know, I still can't help kicking myself I didn't work it out for so long. I really should have guessed it was a tree that changed its leaf and bark pattern as it matured."

I said, "At least neither of you did. You're equal."

We took pictures, for Dad, Damien, and Lulu.

The mystery tree had become a baobab—our very own baobab that we'd had all along, standing there between the two houses, growing slowly in disguise. It was still only about six meters tall. But in a few hundred years, when all who ever knew it as anything but a baobab are long gone to dust and skies, there will stand one of Africa's greatest trees; gigantic and splendid on the red dirt, reaching up above the bush into the endless blue and starlit heavens.

ACKNOWLEDGMENTS

Knowing so intimately the endless fragmented memories that comprise a childhood, one may risk, by proximity, being blinded to the magic of the stories woven across these years. So it was for me, and I therefore owe, first of all, great debts of gratitude to Patti Waldmeir, who said that here was something to write about, and to Michael Holman, for making the next leap: insisting there was, moreover, a book to fill, and relentlessly encouraging me as I began the daunting process of excavating the memories, and learning, by trial and much mortifying error, how to assemble them into a form fit for the page.

To my family, I owe thanks for so many things, beginning, of course, with their inadvertent gift of this story. For their conscious role, I am above all grateful for the enthusiastic support I received from the moment I declared my intention to commit their characters to the page; testament, if nothing else, to the survival beyond this story of their addictive cocktail of reckless confidence in one another and an astounding ability not to care what the world might think. Pages could not do justice to their and others' many, varied contributions, but I have attempted to provide a more comprehensive acknowledgment on the Web site, www.twentychickens forasaddle.com. For now, suffice it to say that the book could not have been written without the tireless assistance—recollecting, inspiring, critiquing, and fact checking—of Linda, Keith, Lulu, and Damien. My grandparents Joan and Terry McCourt, and Jonathan Scott, Christine Sievers, and Henry Scott also provided invaluable help and guidance.

Many others who helped in this book's creation appear too in its pages and I would like to express my gratitude to Seloma Tiro, Charlie and Robyn Sheldon, Lyn and Melaney Nevill, Nomsa Mbere, Jean van Riet, Jean Kiekopf, the Blair family, Jenny Dunlop, Tiffany McGaw, Laura Hudson, and Nicola Anderson. For steering me away from some of the myriad traps that face an expatriate writing about Botswana, I owe an additional special thanks to Seloma and Nomsa. In this respect, I have also found valuable Denbow and Thebe's *Culture and Customs of Botswana*, with which I cross-checked relevant parts of the text. By its nature, however, a story told through the eyes of a child and a teenager, informed mostly by the experiences of one eccentric family, will inevitably produce a selective portrait of a country. I hope the reader will understand and forgive it as such. To everyone else I write of, I owe thanks too: a story is only as good as its characters and I am fortunate to have grown up surrounded by so many fascinating people, leading lives to rival fiction. It is here appropriate to note, too, that in a few instances where necessary to protect identities, I have used fictional names. Finally, at least among those who shared the Botswana I write of, I would like to thank Ann O'Connell and Karan and Raj Chathley, who, though not mentioned in this text, were so generous to Ivor and Betty, and who made such a great difference to their final years.

Since the conception of this book, many others have given generously of their time and knowledge. For their counsel and support, I am grateful to Christine and Robin Whaite, Sangeeta Puran, Janet Ginnard, Drazen Petkovich, Tulsi Bramley, Lauren Lindsay, Jack Turner, Alan Williams, John Parr, Peter Sievers, Chris Sherwell, Ian Harrison, and the whole Unite and Feinstein clan; for their invaluable critiques of the early text I am indebted to Michela Wrong, Caroline Penley, and Sidney Buckland, as I am, for their encouragement, to Alexander McCall Smith, Peter Godwin, Samantha Weinberg, Judith Todd, and Phillip van Niekerk, and, for their inspiration, to Jacobus Pansegrouw and the remarkable members of the Group of Hope.

To thank all those who have played a part in the publishing of this book is impossible here, but I am, in particular, deeply grateful to Ann Godoff at The Penguin Press, for her brilliant editorial touch and wisdom; Alexandra Pringle at Bloomsbury; Jeremy Boraine at Jonathan Ball; Arabella Pike; David Eldridge; and to all the wonderful people at DGA, agents and friends, who have worked so hard for this book. I am especially indebted to the wise and tireless David Godwin—lion and alchemist of agents—whose enormous levels of determination and creativity only rise when the road becomes bumpy, and who has played such a crucial role in making this book what it is. Lastly, I owe infinite thanks to Mungo Soggot, who believed I could write this book, helped in its writing, and with such good humor survived me as I wrote it.

AFRIKAANS GLOSSARY

bakkie	Pickup truck.
bliksem	To beat up.
boerewors	Spicy sausage with a high fat content.
Boerperd	Breed of small, tough horse.
braai	Barbecue.
broek	Pants.
doek	Woman's headcloth, often worn by maids.
dominee	Preacher or pastor.
donner	To beat up.
duwweltjie	"Devil's thorn," a small, hard thorn with three sharp spines.
ja	Yes.
jirre	Wow (corruption of *Here*, meaning "Lord"; slang).
kaffirs	Black people (slang; derogatory).
kak	Shit.
kakhuisies	Shithouses.
kerk	Church.
kif	Cool, great (slang).
koppie	Small hill, often comprised of large boulders.
kraal	Enclosure used for animals.

lekker	Good, great.
meisie	Girl.
mense	People.
moer	To beat up.
oke	Guy, chap (slang).
perd	Horse.
sjambok	Animal hide whip.
sis	Expression of disgust (slang).
skool	School.
snaakse	Funny, strange, eccentric, queer.
tannie	Woman, often an older woman; also "auntie." Used as a mark of respect.
veldskoen	Tough leather shoe.
voetsek	Go away (rude and emphatic).
weerstandsbeweging	Resistance movement.
windgat	Show-off.
Yissis	Jesus (slang).

SETSWANA GLOSSARY

baðimo	Ancestors.
Batswana	More than one Motswana person.
bogaði	Bride price.
bonna	Penis.
botlhoko	Pain.
ðiphilo	Kidneys.
ðumela	Hello; good day.
ee	Yes.
Ga ke itse	I don't know.
Ke (Re) tsoga sentle?	I (we) am (are) well, how are you?
Keitumetse	Thank you.
kgotla	Traditional village meeting place, forum.
Ko-ko	Announcement of arrival; verbal equivalent of knocking.
leswe	Dirty; also means dirt.
Le tsoga jang?	How are you doing?
maðala	Old man (respectful).
maði	Blood; also means money.
marago	Anus; also means buttocks.
mma	Lady.
mmangaka	Doctor's wife.
molelo	Hot.

monwana	Finger.
Motswana	A citizen of Botswana.
ngaka	Doctor.
ntswa	Dog.
popelo	Womb.
pula	National currency; also means rain.
rra	Gentleman.
Sala sentle	Stay well.
Tsamaya sentle	Good-bye; go well.
Tshaba	Beware; flee